P R A I S E   F O R

*Ars Vitae: The Fate of Inwardness
and the Return of the Ancient Arts of Living*

"Lasch-Quinn has set out in *Ars Vitae* to embody the best of what true philosophical writing has to offer. She writes in a way that makes her readers better thinkers, more reflective and self-aware, and she does so by showing the development of her own thinking—who her influences are, the sources from which she draws her wisdom, and h36ow philosophy informs her understanding of herself, the culture, and the world in which she lives."
—*Los Angeles Review of Books*

"[Lasch-Quinn] is a gifted scholar whose examination of ancient works, their modern scholarly reception, and the appearance of big ideas in popular culture is consistently brilliant. . . . She manages to cover over two thousand years of philosophical development in under four hundred pages, and while those pages are dense in content, they are charmingly readable. The introduction, 'Therapeia,' is worth the price of the book."
—*Front Porch Republic*

"Elisabeth Lasch-Quinn's engaging and learned *Ars Vitae* is an intellectual tour de force that expounds various branches of ancient philosophy, assesses the scholarly debate around them, and critiques much of the modern appropriation of the classical heritage."
—*First Things*

"Elisabeth Lasch-Quinn displays here an amazing familiarity with a vast and technical scholarly literature on ancient philosophy—not only on its relevance to everyday life in present-day America. Her understanding of such sources is juxtaposed with her insight into present-day popular culture—it's all quite astonishing. If ever a book deserved publishing, it is this one."
—Daniel Walker Howe, Pulitzer Prize–winning author of
What Hath God Wrought

"In *Ars Vitae*, Elisabeth Lasch-Quinn provides a new way for us to think about the ways in which modern Americans strive to find meaning in, and strive to realize the potential of, their lives. The book sets into relief the peculiar ways in which Americans grasp at the question of how to live and ultimately calls for a new inwardness in American life. This is a masterwork of a book."

—Susan McWilliams Barndt, author of
The American Road Trip and American Political Thought

"With impressive learning and admirable literary grace, Elisabeth Lasch-Quinn calls on us to take seriously again what Cicero called 'the art of living.' Drawing on a range of classical thinkers and schools, she demonstrates how true inwardness and self-knowledge are the antidotes to shallow consumerism and a narcissistic preoccupation with the self. This is a gem of a book, scholarship at the service of self-understanding and the search for truth."

—Daniel J. Mahoney, author of
The Conservative Foundations of the Liberal Order

"An astute archaeologist of ideas, Elisabeth Lasch-Quinn spies the finest remnants of our classical past lurking within the motley mess of contemporary life. In Ars Vitae, she reminds us, as Faulkner once did, that the past is not dead and that the old Greco-Roman approaches to the art of living still constellate our thoughts and customize our actions, consciously or not."
—David Bosworth, author of *Conscientious Thinking*

"Lasch-Quinn's forward-looking vision, developed through an impressive range of learning, ties wholeness, flourishing, selfhood, and health to goodness, truth, and beauty, which remain attainable through the most basic impulses and features of human life. That she makes her argument through accessible and upbeat engagements with everyday realities like literature, film, architecture, and coffee mugs (for which she has a real fondness) only proves her point."

—*The Christian Century*

"*Ars Vitae* doesn't just stir the imagination—it stirs the scholarly imagination. It makes one think not simply about its subject but also how one might approach any subject. It is thus an example of both innovation and intervention."

—*Christian Scholar's Review*

"Specifically human life is about trying to discover and live the good life. When our politics and culture deny that, such searches reappear in both good and distorted ways, as Elisabeth Lasch-Quinn details in her fine and probing book *Ars Vitae*. One can only agree with her in recommending Plato and Plotinus as transcending the element of immanent rationalist functionalism that threatens to compromise Aristotle's approach to the virtues."

—John Milbank, author of *Theology and Social Theory*

"At a time when we are all too aware of the absence of a web of meaning to guide our life, it helps to draw on the moral resources provided by what Elisabeth Lasch-Quinn calls the 'ancient arts of living.' She takes us on a philosophical journey to give us insights into the predicament we face in our inward life. After reading her beautifully written Ars Vitae, you, too, will want to embark on such a journey."

—Frank Furedi, author of *Why Borders Matter*

"*Ars Vitae* is a remarkable book. . . . The prose feels intensely personal, and even intimate, engaging the reader in the author's search for meaning with an approach that feels consequential without being personally needy."

—*Law and Liberty*

"Elisabeth Lasch-Quinn's *Ars Vitae* is just the kind of reasonable, non-polemical book that our society needs today. Equally adept at diagnosing the problem and offering cogent solutions, Lasch-Quinn balances well the theoretical and the practical, the external and the internal, the philosophical and the theological, the pagan and the Christian, the academic and the popular, the wisdom of the past and the insights of the present. She makes clear that ancient philosophy was as much a system of beliefs as it was a way of life, and she incarnates that message in her book. She surveys and analyzes and synthesizes the ideas of the past, but she never plays with them. Her book deals in serious, life-changing philosophies, and so she is never condescending or frivolous."

—Louis Markos in *Sapientia*

"Lasch-Quinn turns to the ancients to persuade her readers that living, contra postmodernism, can bring us to 'the heights of awe, love and wholeness,' even in the face of great pain and evil. . . . Many of us go through days, weeks, and even years of being beaten down, but suffering, Lasch-Quinn's book tells us, can be transfigured into beauty, even holiness."

—*City Journal*

"In her profoundly insightful and thought-provoking work, Elisabeth Lasch-Quinn . . . notes, 'the problems with contemporary culture stem in part from its inability, even in the event that basic needs are met, to provide adequate resources for the living of everyday life.' . . . Lasch-Quinn's work not only informs but urges the reader to seek a deeper understanding of the current problems we face."

—*Journal of Sociology and Christianity*

"This is what makes *Ars Vitae* such vital reading. It provides both a thorough-going critique of the therapeutic, self-obsessed ethos so dominant today, and a way beyond it, through the potential development of those inner, moral resources on which true selfhood and a moral community rest."

—*spiked*

"*Ars Vitae* is a very deep examination of our time and, like the great preparatory classics, it is also an invitation to examine one's own life and an invitation to philosophy and, more specifically, to the cultivation of an inner life."

—*The Debate from Today*

"The book is not a manual but instead a glimpse into, and an invitation to join, a conversation about what is good and how to live. . . . In the end, those who take up Ars Vitae may find themselves, as I did, most grateful to Lasch-Quinn for giving them grounds for hope."

—*Voegelin View*

ARS
VITAE

ARS VITAE

The Fate of
Inwardness and the
Return of the Ancient
Arts of Living

ELISABETH LASCH-QUINN

UNIVERSITY OF NOTRE DAME PRESS
NOTRE DAME, INDIANA

University of Notre Dame Press
Notre Dame, Indiana 46556
undpress.nd.edu
Library of Congress Control Number: 2020940870

ISBN: 978-0-268-10889- 2 (Hardback)
ISBN: 978-0-268-10890-8 (Paperback)
ISBN: 978-0-268-10892-2 (WebPDF)
ISBN: 978-0-268-10891-5 (Epub)

This book was selected as the 2020 Giles Family Fund Recipient. The University of Notre Dame Press and the author thank the Giles family for their generous support.

GILES FAMILY FUND RECIPIENTS

2019   *The Glory and the Burden: The American Presidency from FDR to Trump*, Robert Schmuhl

2020   *Ars Vitae: The Fate of Inwardness and the Return of the Ancient Arts of Living*, Elisabeth Lasch-Quinn

The Giles Family Fund supports the work and mission of the University of Notre Dame Press to publish books that engage the most enduring questions of our time. Each year the endowment helps underwrite the publication and promotion of a book that sparks intellectual exploration and expands the reach and impact of the university.

To my mother

and my husband

with love

`

CONTENTS

ACKNOWLEDGMENTS

To all who helped sustain the writing of this book, *Ars Vitae* is my expression of gratitude. To me, *ars vitae* means not just *the* art of living but *your* art of living.

Writing about how to live is a delicate matter, and I am grateful to all those who gave me the time, space, and resources to do so. A Fulbright fellowship at the University of Rome III in Italy and a research fellowship from the Religion and Innovation in Human Affairs Program of the Historical Society and John Templeton Foundation were priceless. James Davison Hunter played a pivotal role, with Joseph Davis and Jay Tolson at the Institute for Advanced Studies in Culture at the University of Virginia, which provided enriching discussions of my work in progress and a treasured yearlong nonresidential fellowship. At Syracuse University, the History Department, chaired by Michael Ebner and Norman Kutcher, and the Maxwell School provided research support, with a Pellicone faculty fellowship and funding for images and copyright permissions, and the Campbell Public Affairs Institute provided a research grant. Some paragraphs, used here with permission, originally appeared in "The Mind of the Moralist," in the *New Republic*, August 28, 2006, 27–31, and "The New Old Ways of Self Help," in *Hedgehog Review* 19, no. 1 (Spring 2017).

I am grateful to dear colleagues, doctoral advisees, and other graduate and undergraduate students with whom I have worked most closely. You know who you are. As a modernist, I was fortunate to be able to return to earlier interests with new or renewed study in Italian, Latin, German, French, art history, comparative literature, and the history of Greece and Rome, and seminars with

Michael Stocker (on love and on the philosophy of emotion), Patricia Miller (late antique philosophy and religion), Marcia Robinson (Kierkegaard), Albrecht Diem (medieval monasticism), and Craige Champion and Matthieu Van Der Meer (Latin). Deep gratitude goes to the memory of my uncle, classicist Steele Commager, who inspired my love of ancient words and ideas from a young age, and to Cynthia Farber-Soule, Charles Goldberg, Robby Ramdin, Paul Prescott, and the memories of Joseph Levine and Jean Bethke Elshtain for nurturing it. Talks with Bruce Laurie and Catherine Tumber were formative and writing sessions with Michael Fisher and Yoshina Hurgobin generative.

At the places I was invited to present my work in progress, those attending offered insights and inspiration: Albion Tourgée Seminar in Intellectual History at the University of Rochester; Common Ground Initiative, Grand Valley State University, and Conference on Faith and History, Calvin College, both in Grand Rapids, Michigan; Front Porch Republic Conference, Spring Arbor University, Spring Arbor, Michigan; Maxwell Citizenship Initiative/Moynihan Institute Brownbag series, Confession symposium, and Chronos Undergraduate Conference, all at Syracuse University; "The Human Person" work group (which produced *Figures in a Carpet*) in Rockport, Massachusetts, and at the Woodrow Wilson International Center for Scholars, funded by the Pew Foundation; the Political Theory Colloquium, University of Notre Dame; the American Enterprise Institute; the Religion and Innovation in Human Affairs workshop, Harris Manchester College, University of Oxford, UK; the Universita degli Studi di Napoli in Naples, Italy; the Centro Studi Americani in Rome, Italy; and the Conversazioni in Italia symposium in Florence, Italy. Special thanks go to Robert Westbrook, Gleaves Whitney, John Fea, Wilfred McClay, Patrick Deneen, Arthur Brooks, Donald Yerxa, and all of my Italian hosts.

Paul Arras provided Herculean research assistance. Key conversations with Todd Gitlin, Jean Stinchcombe, Robert Corban, Audie Klotz, and Paul Murphy were vital for the project. Director Steve Wrinn, editor of my dreams, made the University of Notre Dame Press ideal for the book, with unparalleled anonymous reviewers. I am grateful to Raj, Rahul, Sonam, Sunny, and others at Dosa Grill who made it the perfect place for much of the writing of *Ars Vitae*. Ever in memory, my father Christopher Lasch bequeathed lifelong encouragement. My siblings, Robert Lasch, Christopher Lasch, and Catherine Loomis, and their families, offered loving support. My daughters, Isabel and Honoré, provided loving encouragement. My husband, Ray, and my mother, Nell Commager Lasch, gave spirit-saving sustenance in too many forms to mention or even imagine. I wrote this book to an intricate choreography of unheard melodies that surrounded me with a dance of angels.

INTRODUCTION
Therapeia

Philosophia est ars vitae.
—*Cicero*

Philosophy is the art of living. So wrote the ancient Roman philosopher Cicero during one of the most momentous periods in human history. Centuries after Socrates, in a time of civil wars and Caesar's rise and fall, Cicero thought the ancient Greek schools of philosophy essential knowledge for Romans. Centuries after Cicero, in our own tumultuous times, we might also benefit from heeding his call to engage more fully in the task of *ars vitae.*[1]

Many today seek help and insight for how to live in hard times and have trouble finding the deep answers that really help. Everywhere we see signs of great distress. Yet all around us we can also find signs, some hidden and some staring us in the face, of a return to ancient approaches to the art of living. Ancient Greco-Roman philosophy, an influence on learning worldwide in fields from

1

poetry to physics, is nothing if not deep. It presupposes *inwardness*—the cultivation of an inner life—and the centrality of the search for meaning as the paramount human endeavor. Inwardness is the way the self develops the resources necessary for everything from enduring hardship to soaring to the heights of a fulfilled human life. To provide the conditions for anything less not only betrays the goal of human flourishing but risks our very survival. It is no luxury, no matter how much it might masquerade as a mere matter of grace and style. The art of living is how we get along, how we get by, and why.

This book begins to take the soundings of this new revival of interest. It explores modern versions of ancient Gnosticism, Stoicism, Epicureanism, Cynicism, and Platonism in hopes we can begin to recognize where these ideas appear in our current culture and where they might present alternatives. While observers have noted the surfacing of a particular approach, such as Stoicism, the return of a whole group of approaches from antiquity has largely escaped notice and characterization as a recent historical response, at once popular and intellectual, to our current and enduring predicaments. Tracing the contours of this cultural resurgence, this study sees the different schools as organically interrelated and asks whether, taken together, they could point us in important new directions.

The rediscovery and reinterpretation of earlier thought are often, if not always, the source of movements of individual and cultural renewal. In this movement or in any of its individual schools, can we spot a countertradition to today's culture, a sign of latent cultural vibrancy? Or are they merely solidifying a modern way of life that has little use for a form of inwardness stemming from those older traditions? We expect everything to move at the speed of the flickering image. In a time of technology, marketing, and change, a philosophical approach to living might seem inefficient and impractical. But it could turn out to be the very opposite.

A leading statesman and philosopher of the fateful first century BC, Cicero witnessed the fall of his glorious Roman Republic, the dictatorship and assassination of Julius Caesar, and the civil wars that gave rise to the Roman Empire. Cicero served as Roman consul and defender of the republic. Despite its inaccuracy as a stand-in for modern democratic aspirations, its acronym SPQR still comes down to us as a mythical badge of honor and dignity, representing the senate and people of Rome and resonating with hopes for a government and way of life capable of fostering human flourishing. Beyond the politics and wars, violence and corruption, lay foundational ways of approaching being human, whether prescribed by poets or philosophers, slaves or emperors, women or men. Though some less than others, these different approaches still influence not only our actions but our possibilities as human beings.

Ancient philosophers and those influenced by them certainly thought a lot was riding on their ideas about how to live. In one of the most vibrant public conversations in history, with reverberations to this day, Greek and Roman philosophers disagreed vehemently over their approaches to every aspect of living. Added to other such discussions in other cultural traditions, this is a conversation transcending time and place, perhaps the richest human conversation in which a person can take part. It is a conversation about how we should be living our lives, what the options are, and what is implied by the path we take. The conversation is open to us too, should we choose to partake. We have a standing invitation, just by virtue of having been born. Only by knowing the alternatives can we come to an understanding of how we live now—of what has led to this moment—and the choices we have for the future. According to Socrates, who said the unexamined life is not worth living, not to accept the invitation is not to be fully alive. It was an idea he was willing to die to defend. (See fig. I.1.)

The societies of Greece and Rome were not neutral on the question of philosophy. Their leaders, often tutored by philosophers, at times took these thinkers into their closest confidence. Emperor Marcus Aurelius, himself a Stoic, set up chairs in AD 176 in philosophy representing the major schools.[2] At other times, the powers that be banished philosophers from the city or the realm. Of course not only Socrates but many others over the centuries between him and us died in wars of ideas and beliefs. While condemning all such violations of freedom of speech and conscience—the right to dissent without risking life and limb—one must concede that in the past and on into the present, ideas have mattered, both for better and for worse.

Just as Roman ideas and ideals about life harkened back to the intellectual ferment of the Golden Age of Athens, so did those of later periods and peoples, adding layers of interpretations from other traditions throughout the world before reaching us. The Italian Renaissance, the later Early Modern period, the Enlightenment, the Age of Democratic Revolutions, and many other eras were infused by the ancient Greek philosophies and their Roman variants, as informed and interpreted by others across the globe from Asia and the Middle East to Europe, Africa, and the Americas. In the late eighteenth century, the new American republic would have been unheard of without them. Neither in times of trouble nor in times of rest and peace do the ancient Greek and Roman philosophers promise to have all of the answers we are looking for, but they are essential guides in pointing us in the direction of the questions we should be asking ourselves if we are to live the fullest lives possible.

Standing on the brink of the future is terrifying. What comes next? What should we do? We often forget our good fortune to be able to consider the thoughts of those who came before us and also stood on the crest between their present and the unwritten future. As if designed for us today, given our own concerns, the ancient Greco-Roman schools of thought are "eudaemonistic" philosophies.[3] There is no perfect translation into English of *eudaemonia*. Some translate it as *happiness*, but the meaning of our word *happiness* is also famously hard to pin down, like the state of mind that is its namesake. The closest we might come to capturing the meaning of *eudaemonia* today is probably something more like our *well-being*. The point is that these philosophies offer searching analyses of what it takes—and what it means—to live a *good life*.

EPICTETUS'S CUP

The ancient Stoic philosopher Epictetus is one example of an ancient Roman philosopher who had distinct ideas about how to live and whose ideas are having renewed popularity today. Some of his notions might come as a surprise to us. If he were here today, he would have plenty to say to us for when we are faced with personal difficulty. He would advise us to begin with small things. If we break a mug, we should not get upset: "If you are fond of a specific ceramic cup, remind yourself that it is only ceramic cups in general of which you are fond. Then, if it breaks, you will not be disturbed." From there, we should work up to bigger things: "If you kiss your child, or your wife, say that you only kiss things which are human, and thus you will not be disturbed if either of them dies."[4]

Yet it turns out that people *are* attached, even if that struck Epictetus as irrational. Handling loss and other difficulties is not such an easy task as willing oneself, or others, not to be disturbed. Is this sound advice? Or is there other advice that is better? Around anyone who seeks real wisdom in a time of crisis swirls a plenitude of advice. We live in the era of the aphorism and the several-step program promising to fix everything imaginable. Even before we set up a counseling appointment, wander into a bookstore or library, attend a support group, text an online doctor, google a question, or just ask Alexa, advice jumps off the aisles of the local grocery store in the form of a greeting card or coffee mug offering wisdom from all authors great and small. Pithy sayings purport to encapsulate worldviews. Your mug insists it will help you make sense of anything and everything. From bumper stickers and T-shirts to greeting cards, tattoos, and billboards, every formerly blank space blurts out a statement signaling a whole stance toward the world.

Whatever one thinks of the content of Epictetus's suggestion about remaining unemotional even when losing loved ones, we clearly find his guidelines quotable two millennia after he wrote them. So of course there are even mugs blazoned with the words of Epictetus. One of them encapsulates his philosophy: "There is only one way to happiness and that is to cease worrying about things which are beyond the power of our will."[5] It is a nice mug, with a helpful reminder. As he would be the first to say, we still should not get too attached to it. If we do take it seriously—the advice, if not the mug itself—what do we do next? And what do we do when encountering a message at odds with it? If the Socratic philosophies are about *dialogue* and *inquiry*, is there anything wrong with the way they are being adopted as a pared-down kind of self-help? Why is it so much more difficult to find deeper insights than such fragmented thoughts? A single quote taken out of context makes a poor life companion.

This is not to discount the power and meaning of many a mantra. Sayings can be invaluable, as can programs of all kinds. The problem is that our current approach to finding help and pathways to self-help does not seem to be working. The suffering we face resists pat solutions offered by steps and slogans. Further, whether we can or cannot overcome our current distress, we seek meaning in our lives even beyond our suffering.

Examples of this renewed interest abound. For just a taste, long-forgotten names reappear on a daily basis in the *New York Times*, the *Washington Post,* the *Nation*, and many other places. A recent *New York Times* review of Edith Hall's book *Aristotle's Way: How Ancient Wisdom Can Change Your Life* praises Hall for introducing a "rare middle way . . . to pursue happiness," not with a drastic change of life but with a simple program of self-reflectively pursuing one's natural talents and interests.[6] A review in the *Nation* of Massimo Pigliucci's *How to Be a Stoic: Using Ancient Philosophy to Live a Modern Life* ultimately finds the Stoicism he offers unconvincing, judging an emphasis on happiness through philosophical virtue alone difficult to reconcile in a world of pain and deprivation.[7] To agree in all particulars would not honor the spirit of the conversation, or take seriously the most thoughtful contributions, the depth and value of which bode well for true engagement over words and ideas that matter. Works for readers beyond a single scholarly specialization both build on and push the boundaries of today's disciplines, revivifying intellectual practices of inquiry into enduring personal and public questions. Other such works include *Tragedy, the Greeks, and Us* by Simon Critchley and *How to Be an Epicurean: The Ancient Art of Living Well* by Catherine Wilson. Princeton University Press offers new translations of classic ancient works in a series called Ancient Wisdom for Modern Readers, appealing to nonspecialists with "how to" titles, such as *How to Keep Your Cool: An Ancient Guide to Anger Management*, a modern title for the ancient Roman Stoic Seneca's work "On Anger." These offerings individually and collectively signal a new level of interest in ancient wisdom traditions and their relevance in recent and contemporary culture and life.[8]

THIS BOOK BEGINS WITH A LOOK AT THE GLIMMERS OF a new Gnosticism that make visible what is at stake in allowing our modern therapeutic culture, with its elevation of personal desires into a "secular religion of the self," to set the terms for how we make sense of life. Critics deem the advent of an all-pervasive psychologization of life, in which the "inner [is] the new outer" and the self reigns supreme, as "nothing short of a disaster for the human prospect."[9] In shorthand, the current frame of mind can include a posture of knowingness—the idea that some people are better than others because they possess special knowledge—and can support self-obsession and self-seeking with notions of self-divinity. After setting the stage, this book then goes further back in time to pick up the threads of the earlier Greco-Roman schools and movements and forward to our times to see if they currently offer an alternative to late twentieth-century therapeutic culture. If Gnosticism-inflected therapeutic culture dictates how modern Americans currently answer the question of how to live, what alternatives might offer themselves?

At first glance, a good share of the new interest in ways of thinking from antiquity has to do with Stoicism. Scholars and self-help gurus alike declare its relevance for our own times. We can identify it in one of the most well-known mantras: "God grant me the serenity to accept the things I cannot change, the courage to change the things I can, and the wisdom to know the difference."[10] Originated by Reinhold Niebuhr, the phrase has saved the lives of countless people in its incarnation as incantation of Alcoholics Anonymous. As a form of tough love directed inward, it provides armor against excessive self-indulgence as well as suffering. Directed outward, resurgent Stoicism carries an implied critique of the softer side of the aftermath of the sixties and seventies. In the late twentieth-century culture wars, this meant the sensitive man à la Alan Alda, the welfare state or "nanny state" as it is called in the UK, and an ethos of victimization and entitlement. The "L-word," liberalism's epithet, suggested the exhaustion of a way of life that had failed to solve intractable problems such as poverty through government spending, social engineering, and the helping professions.

The evaluation that Stoicism has the most relevance to our own times comes in a vacuum, rather than in the context of a conversation weighing the other possibilities. Instead of just a vacillation between therapeutic softness or Stoicism, right now there are multiple overlapping paradigms. Ancient Greek and later Roman Stoicism emerged in the form of a fuller conversation about how to live. Its earliest proponents were influenced by the other schools and saw themselves as starting a new school or movement as a rival to those already in existence. Systematized schools of thought had certain elements that were essential—as in an attitude or logic of Stoicism. We can now take a modern source and see if it has the essential elements. Lawrence Becker looks at Stoicism this way, to find a usable version of Stoicism for our times.[11] We can also grasp a school as a disposition or sensibility still with us, albeit in changed form.[12] Our reading of the modern sources makes visible these ghosts of edifices and shows them to be so many worlds coexisting in our mental universes.

If we pursue this resurgence of ancient philosophies further, we quickly see that there has also been a resurgence of interest in Epicureanism. In the age of the foodie, we do not need to go far to find the evidence. Stephen Greenblatt's best seller *The Swerve* and Daniel Klein's *Travels with Epicurus* are two self-conscious attempts to apply Epicurean insights to modern life. Even when unaware of the ancient school, many have participated in its continuing relevance, as we can see in the titles of magazines and names of restaurants, as well as the popularity of cookbooks, cooking shows, and nearly anything else having to do with eating, drinking, and consuming. From Julia Child to Anthony Bourdain, leading tastemakers have helped shape our attitude toward the art of living.

Cynicism is also having a resurgence, as we see in works by self-professed Cynics such as Peter Sloterdijk. Together with many other contemporary observers, Jeffrey Goldfarb identifies an ingrained cynicism as a major aspect of our culture and problem of our times. Among others, philosopher Michael Foucault embraced the persona of the cynic, leaving works that allow us to consider recent versions of Cynicism and what is at stake. Finally, we can also discover hints of a new Platonism.

This study takes as its starting point that the problems with contemporary culture stem in part from its inability, even in the event that basic needs are met, to provide adequate resources for the living of everyday life. It is rooted in concern about the ways our society is torn apart into conflicting groups, isolated fiefdoms, or islands of one. It is concerned with a contemporary culture that exacerbates conflicts, which it then lacks the means to smooth over. As long as there are no viable alternatives to our current culture, these differences are potentially tragic. This book holds up these approaches against what is wrong with contemporary culture. Yet these warring factions can be in part understood as the conflict among different ways to approach the art of living. Identifying underlying dispositions might offer potential sources of agreement and even unity, or at least a way to stay in the same conversation.

INWARDNESS

Who are we, but wanderers of the heavens, amid an abundance of other worlds? What role is there for us in the vast emptiness of space? . . . How are we to find purpose in a seemingly purposeless universe?

—*Marcelo Gleiser,*
"Meaning in a Silent Universe"

In times of despair and loss, torment and injury, anger and absence, everything seems meaningless and the universe feels empty.[13] But there are other times. In times of happiness and presence, our lives overflow with meaning. Good times contain their own purpose—to discover, invent, and maintain the wonder and joy of existence. Bad times fold in on themselves, collapsing possibilities. They are a blow to the core of our being, sometimes fatal. They feel impossible to escape, like a maze of endless nothingness.

Gleiser's questions invoke an existential alienation that can afflict anyone at any time. Pain is intrinsic to the experience of being alive for mankind, as for the entire animal kingdom to which we belong. Love, familial bonds, friendship—all things good—arrive with the possibility of pain attached. The smaller ups and downs of everyday life involve quasi-deaths—an estrangement, a separation, a lover storming out, a friendship ending, a job lost—and endless perceived ones, whether past, present, or prospective. The actual death of a loved one can constitute a calamity of such proportions as to be, when not life-threatening, then life-altering. Collective loss—war, famine, violence, natural disaster, even genocide—is, when not insurmountable, unimaginable. It is the bitter irony of our existence that we are beings capable of happiness yet so constituted as to have to expect to encounter its very opposite. Once we discover death, all else comes to us through its prism.

A basic fact of the human condition, Philip Rieff wrote in *The Triumph of the Therapeutic*, is that we are separate beings, with each of us "different from every other in his identity, his incommunicability, his inwardness," along with his very "real needs."[14] Culture serves a crucial function in managing and to some extent relieving this terrible isolation: by conveying a sense of transcendent ideals or beliefs—a sense of the sacred—it delivers us from the loneliness and the anxiety to which the solitary psyche is prone. Our shared life consists of a "great chain of meaning" that allows us to direct our desires toward shared ends by setting up "permissions and restraints," which are internalized as moral conscience.[15] Socialization is the process by which individuals form moral selves, learning to control their urges and steer them toward "fixed wants" that can be properly satisfied and toward the legitimate outlet of cultural activity. Freudian theory articulated the vital role of sublimation, but it disregarded religious belief, thus depriving sublimation of any deeper meaning than personal adjustment. For Rieff, culture provides both meaning—a focus for aspiration—and consolation for the sacrifice and the suffering that are an inevitable part of ordinary experience.

The replacement of a religious basis for culture by a solely therapeutic ideal—the usurpation of the sense of transcendent purpose by the quest for self-fulfillment and emotional catharsis—was the historical development upon which Rieff unflinchingly fixed his gaze. He faulted Freud's successors for trying to install new "therapies of commitment" where religion once stood. This, he insisted, Freud himself never sought to do. Freud remained a skeptical rationalist, but some of his followers abandoned both skepticism and reason. Carl Jung's cult of the creative individual rummaging through unconscious archetypes, D. H. Lawrence's worship of instinct and sex, and Wilhelm Reich's desire for an erotic utopia were all attempts to revive the therapeutic function of religion: the new religiosity of an age of unbounded self-analysis and self-love.[16] Rieff thought the therapeutic—the psychologizing of all aspects of our lives in a way that elevated the self's needs and desires as supreme—eclipsed inwardness and obscured deeper sources of fulfillment and meaning.

AN ANARCHY OF ADVICE

It is understandable that people would turn to comforting nostrums for help. But we need to consult something more elaborate than a single saying on a mug extracted from the context of its larger vision. What if the saying, shorn of that broader view, turns out to be inscrutable right when we need it most? We could end up doing the very opposite of what the words intended and find ourselves tangled up in something worse than where we started.

Prodded by anxiety or mere curiosity, we encounter oceans of advice telling us how to live or what to make of life. It is a free country with a free(ish) market. The self-help industry is no exception. It is basically a free-for-all. Anyone hanging out a shingle can dispense advice, which can mean the publication of self-help books by major publishers and vanity presses, with Amazon enabling authors whose only qualification is the ability to compose words into sentences. Shingles include websites, blogs, advice columns, college classes, and consulting firms. Luck, pluck, and marketing allow self-help Horatio Algers to ply their trade unchallenged. In a world of short attention spans, any kind of follow-up on the effects of the advice is nonexistent.

This is not to suggest we need more studies. Only willed ignorance would suggest as much. Sadly, the evidence is in. Rates of depression, anxiety, addiction, and suicide have reached epidemic proportions. On arguably the most important question we face—how to live—there is little concerted effort to think through the assumptions or results of one plan versus another or to admit that we are in dire straits, not just as persons but as a people.

In this anarchy of advice, we could call for tighter regulations and more professional training. Yet most professionals these days are mainly trained in techniques of what is called service delivery. Between the vast needs they face and the failure of insurance companies to cover extensive counseling or preventive medicine, they tend to be experts in pharmaceuticals or crisis intervention. Even when they are licensed for some form of talk therapy, certification does not automatically ensure wisdom. It does not generally include education in a deep understanding of ways to think about life's meaning, alternative intellectual approaches to living, and the question of which practices are better for us and why. The best counselor, whether parent, pastor, friend, teacher, or therapist, must eventually send someone off to become master of his or her life. Everything hinges on the content of the advice, or the quality of ideas encountered elsewhere about how to live.

In *New York Magazine*'s "Self-Help Issue," Kathryn Schulz argues that, despite the huge number of self-help books out now, all self-help literature comes down to the same thing, what she calls "the master theory of self-help": "It goes like this: Somewhere below or above or beyond the part of you that is struggling with weight loss or procrastination or whatever your particular problem might be, there is another part of you that is immune to that problem and capable of solving it for the rest of you. In other words, this master theory is fundamentally dualist. It posits, at a minimum, two selves: one that needs a kick in the ass and one that is capable of kicking."[17]

This is a helpful observation for moving us beyond such simplistic binaries. Yet for Schulz, given the lack of a clear understanding of the self—something she thinks we cannot reach anyway—self-help has equal standing with any other safe and legal means the individual can use to overcome depression or other emotional challenges: "Try something. Better still, try everything—throw all the options at the occluding wall of the self and see what sticks. Meditation, marathon training, fasting, freewriting, hiking the Pacific Crest Trail, speed dating, volunteering, moving to Auckland, redecorating the living room."[18]

Schulz's entertaining call to action—any action—aside, all activities one might choose to engage in do not share a moral equivalence. A closer look at self-help offerings, along with a full range of other cultural expressions, reveals vital differences in both content and quality. Identifying the nature of the particular framework at hand can get us into more promising territory for those seeking deeper answers. If ideas matter, then in the course of offering advice, self-help literature has a significant role in shaping what we think are the possibilities of our lives, especially if increasingly purveyed in additional forms and genres outside of self-help. We need to admit that it is time we call our popular culture—from movies to internet sites—what it really is: popular education.

It is easy to mock the offerings we do have. We need to find a path to greater self-mastery or self-care by delving deeper into the role and the types of self-help in our lives. Self-sufficiency includes developing the ability to assess and discriminate among worthy and unworthy approaches and to see beneath the surface to their assumptions and aims. We should be wary of relinquishing to someone else the post of tour guide, let alone architect, of our own inner life. Twentieth-century African American theologian Howard Thurman wrote that "anyone who permits another to determine the quality of his inner life gives into the hands of the other the keys to his destiny."[19] We need a firmer foundation in everyday life, a usable philosophy, a kind of self-education in being alive.

What we have now is a fragile culture centered on the self's needs and wants, which sociologist Philip Rieff aptly called therapeutic. In his 1966 classic *The Triumph of the Therapeutic: Uses of Faith after Freud*, he observed modern changes in the deep structures of custom and belief as resulting in a whole new outlook. Rieff's work was one of the first sustained efforts to make sense of the transition from a culture based on faith to a culture based on therapy. In this book and his earlier intellectual biography of Freud, he traced the rise of "psychological man" and the replacement of shared commitments of traditional religious communities with the quest for individual fulfillment, personal freedom, and "impulse release."[20]

In Philip Rieff's view, at the heart of any culture—the very definition of culture—is a particular set of interdictions and permissions, what one can and cannot do. These are not a set of simplistic precepts but a matter of elaborate complexity. An entire framework of understanding surrounds them, even providing possibilities for a letting up of those strictures through what he called acceptable "remissions." In many ways what gives life meaning and satisfaction in a particular cultural system is that it helps address the question so fundamental to the human condition: How and why should we rein in our strongest and most urgent instincts, impulses, and desires? This is where culture steps in, giving meaning and essential supports for our struggles. In Rieff's view, culture gives people a means of "controlling the infinite variety of panic and emptiness to which they are disposed." In the form of books, music, and love, for example, culture "gives back bettered" what it has taken away by restraining impulse and curbing certain emotions, or at least limiting their expression. What infuses the "interdictions" with possibilities for well-being, and gives people the motivation to accept limits on their desires and behaviors, is some kind of transcendent referent, a collective commitment higher than the self that is deemed sacred. In the absence of such a framework of meaning, individuals have the appearance of being free but in fact are awash in anxiety, disconnection, and "dis-ease."[21]

In *After Virtue* (1981), philosopher Alasdair MacIntyre agrees that to pursue the questions humans have about their purposes and existence requires some kind of coherent moral framework that has a sense of the *telos* or goal of a human life as necessarily involving goodness. In his rendering, what we have now amounts instead to little more than a set of fragments we have inherited from various past systems; we lack the basic capacity to communicate about issues of pressing concern because we have no "moral language" or agreed-upon basis for "moral reasoning." In MacIntyre's view, the closest thing we have is "emotivism," our new default setting, which comes down to appealing to "expressions of personal preference" as the "only basis of evaluative judgments." In this framework there is no basis for solving disagreements, as each party is entitled to his or her opinion, as the common phrasing goes. No individual can appeal to a foundation for judgment shared with others. Thus, instead of articulating reasons to attempt to persuade others, the sole recourse becomes manipulation of the feelings of other people. "What is the key to the social content of emotivism?" MacIntyre asks, answering that "it is the fact that emotivism entails the obliteration of any genuine distinction between manipulative and non-manipulative social relations."[22]

Critics of the therapeutic have charted its ascension over the course of the nineteenth and twentieth centuries, when it joined forces with consumerism in heaping attention, new in both degree and kind, on the needs and wants of the individual. Together, these powerful mentalities—it can be hard to tell where one ends and the other leaves off—have pervaded nearly every sphere of life. The emphasis on what seems therapeutic for the individual validates and rewards excessive self-concern—combining both meanings of self-regard and self-interest—and encourages extreme forms of emotional unleashing. Other critics trace the problems into the heart of American society and culture, where they observe a new Gnosticism, a culture of narcissism, or even a crumbling of culture itself.[23]

The stakes are higher than they might appear. In leisure and entertainment personal preferences seem innocuous, and in politics even salutary, where the right of the individual or group to dissent provides the basis of our liberty. But in the absence of appeals to shared principle and basic checks and balances for some forms and degrees of self-assertion, such as aggression and antisocial impulses, emotivism can bring the erosion of those very rights and freedoms. Without solid foundations for our higher principles, appeals to justice, truth, and humanity can give way to assertions of raw power and desire by the few. Techniques of manipulation of feeling provide legendary assistance.

Some historians and social critics have called the therapeutic at heart a resurgence of Gnosticism. Taking hold in the late nineteenth-century spiritual crisis, this sensibility helped provide the cultural underpinnings for industrialization—its mores and social relations. In *American Feminism and the Birth of New Age Spirituality*, Catherine Tumber builds on the work of Warren Susman and Donald Meyer, who connected the new sensibility with these wider historical developments. In a study of the late nineteenth- and early twentieth-century New Thought or "mind cure" movement, the launching pad for late twentieth-century therapeutic movements and New Age spirituality, Tumber wrote that "'mind cure' helped usher in a new 'modal self' compatible with consumer spending, corporate success, and mass culture."[24] This therapeutic self came to maturity in the spiritual crisis precipitated by advanced consumer capitalism, helping to accommodate dissident subcultures to new economic imperatives. Today this ideology of positive psychology saturates much of our culture, mostly without our knowing.

For Rieff, an incoherent moral framework beyond individual wants and needs—any shared sense that something is sacred—means the very requisites for a culture are lacking. Absent a sense of communal purpose that makes our efforts to rein in self-gratification understandable and manageable as guidelines for behavior, cultural chaos ensues. The unmoored self is left with little in life to go on apart from "manipulable" feelings.[25] Paving the way for both political and personal instability, such conditions invite susceptibility to political manipulation and a chronic sense of insult, offense, and disrespect that threatens community and individual happiness.

Rieff's influential critique of the therapeutic was joined, in the decades since *Triumph of the Therapeutic*, by the work of other scholars who often drew on his analysis to help understand both large cultural currents and particular realms of society in which they saw the therapeutic at work. Jonathan Imber's edited volume *Therapeutic Culture: Triumph and Defeat*, which features the work of some of these writers, such as Ellen Herman and James Davison Hunter, suggests that by the 1990s there had arisen a cluster of scholars, if not a school of thought, we might think of as the therapeutic critics.[26] Herman's *Romance of American Psychology* and Hunter's *Death of Character* broke new ground in their analyses of just how far the psychologization of society had gone and at what cost. The focus of these writers is not as much psychotherapeutic practice as a "more widespread cultural system or code of moral understanding."[27] Frank Furedi argued that stoic strains in British culture gave way to a pervasive therapeutic culture by the end of the twentieth century, with a "form of personhood whose defining feature is its vulnerability."[28]

One of these critics, the sociologist James Nolan Jr., whose work focuses on the ways in which the therapeutic approach has influenced the criminal justice system, lays out what he sees as a working definition of the therapeutic:

(1) a pronounced cultural preoccupation with the individual self, (2) a notable concern with the place of emotions in making sense of oneself and one's place in the world, (3) the emergence of a new class of counselors, psychologists, and therapists who have been socially recognized as those most qualified to guide the emotion-laden self through the complexities of modern social life, (4) the reinterpretation of a growing number of behaviors through the pathologically determined heuristic of addiction, disorder, and dysfunction, and (5) the unique cultural salience of the "language of victimhood."[29]

The very features Nolan identifies as components of the therapeutic might be those that the New Stoicism aims to address. In fact, the therapeutic critics sometimes exhibit a bit of the New Stoicism themselves when foregrounding the role of emotion.

My expanded definition of the therapeutic would include a view of the self as top priority and end point; interpersonal relations as instrumental toward that end; the self's pursuit of projects of self-interest; mandated self-expression without structure and inhibition; enlistment of emotion and reason in furtherance of those projects; manipulative relations with others and with the self; an externalist vantage point on the self, as if seeing the self through the eyes of others; the dominance of the health paradigm as the basis for self-assessment; a functionalist physical and psychological model of health (health as the ability to function within an unquestioned social order); pop psychology as explanatory apparatus; a process orientation and programmatic solutions; social engineering; the monopoly of professional expertise over life skills; a seesaw between dependence and independence in place of interdependence; moral nonjudgmentalism; deprivatization of personal life; a rarified level of self-consciousness; and the absence of a transcendent commitment beyond the individual. The resulting therapeutic ethos pervades individuals' lives in an almost invisible fashion, shaping the external living conditions they face and the internal resources they have or do not have to navigate those conditions. It is a way of thinking that exacerbates self-objectification (the view of the self as a problem to be solved or thing to be acted upon), objectification of others (the view of others as instruments in the self's own projects), and a sense of self-alienation (the view that the self lacks a kind of owner's manual—the resources to understand and develop efficacious approaches to outside circumstances). These characteristics of the therapeutic culture, its manner of self-perpetuation, and its ultimate costs can be summed up as a loss of inwardness. The lack of inwardness as a source of personal and collective regeneration deprives individuals of the ability to mount a resistance to these and other debilitating ways of thinking and to the external challenges they face. The therapeutic thus spells a systematic derision of the individual's own ability to become adept at the art of living.

Clinical practitioners and theorists sensitive to such problems have shifted their emphasis from an individual to a relational model or have embraced cognitive behavioral therapy as a corrective.[30] But it is questionable whether these strategies have successfully broken the hold of the worst traits of the therapeutic. The damage has been done in a more diffuse way beyond the purview of therapists themselves. Using the zoom lens of this broader definition of the therapeutic, we can see how not just the so-called helping professions but many other institutions and practices are steeped in the therapeutic, from business to art, music, education, the military, religion, and beyond. The therapeutic constitutes an entire worldview, causing us to interpret our experiences through it.

Though some criticism faults the therapeutic for an excess of emotion, it is not emotion that is the problem. Emotion is not the same thing as *emotivism*, which is the loss of any shared vantage point and basis for judgment beyond individual subjective desires. While emotivism can come in the guise of emotion, it often works in the service of or as a cover for calculated self-interest. We see this in the epidemic of passive aggression, defensiveness, and the practice of reasoning one's way into rather than out of aggrievement. Though it might appear so at times, the therapeutic culture is not necessarily at root overly emotional and merely in need of a correction from rationality. The question is not whether emotion or reason drives us. We use both in all of our pursuits. Whether self-interest is rationally calculated or emotive—greed is a case in point, as it combines both—it is still self-interest. The key question is whether emotion or reason is impressed into service of manipulating everyone and everything around us, even the environment, all of which we hope and expect will sustain us.[31] The overarching problem with the therapeutic is the assumption of self-interested ends. The cruelty of the validation of this particular notion of ends, its inhumanity, is not only that it uses other people and things in selfish pursuits but also that these ends can never release people from the sources of their yearning and the dependence on instrumentalist forms and mechanisms. Modern therapies are a vicious cycle, providing neither deliverance nor salvation, creating unintended consequences in the process.

The ubiquity of the self-help infrastructure itself, from personal pursuit to billion-dollar industry, can give a wide hearing to any approach that strikes the right chord at the right moment. In "The Power of Positive Publishing: How Self-Help Ate America," Boris Kachka quotes William Shinker, the publisher of Gotham Books and editor who discovered *Men Are from Mars, Women Are from Venus*, as saying, "There isn't even a category officially called 'self-help.'"[32]

This is true. There no longer needs to be a separate category. Self-help is imperial metropole, the rest colonized periphery. As Kachka writes, "Twenty years ago, when *Chicken Soup for the Soul* was published, everyone knew where to find it and what it was for. Whatever you thought of self-help—godsend, guilty pleasure, snake oil—the genre was safely contained on one eclectic bookstore shelf. Today, every section of the store (or web page) overflows with instructions, anecdotes, and homilies. History books teach us how to lead, neuroscience how to use our amygdalas, and memoirs how to eat, pray, and love."[33]

Kachka, a journalist and cultural critic who wrote *Hothouse: The Art of Survival and the Survival of Art at America's Most Celebrated Publishing House, Farrar, Straus, and Giroux*, says this in a gem of an essay that weds a pithy history of self-help publishing trends with a critique of a new kind of "high-brow self-help." For Kachka, these latest forms, from social science studies to "the trend of essayistic self-help," often by journalists, might look more serious—and often have better "data"—but merely hawk the usual types of self-help in another guise. He interprets an observation by literary agent Linda Loewenthal, previously editor and VP of Random House's self-help publisher, Harmony Books, and executive director of Three Rivers Press, as meaning "that we are in a new era of mass self-help, wherein the laboratory and the writer work together to teach us how to change ourselves, rather than our world."[34]

Admittedly vague, Loewenthal's own words were "An increasing segment of the market wants to read about the synthesis of different modalities." While the crossover boom certainly signals the seeping of self-help into other fields—whether we see it as intrusion or infusion—this interest in bringing together different disciplinary approaches and modes of self-help suggests that many readers might be looking for something deeper than the usual fare.

Against this still-expanding terrain of the therapeutic culture, it comes as something of a surprise to see a resurgence of interest in schools of philosophical thought from other places and times, including from Greco-Roman antiquity, and what I see as a return of the ancient arts of living. In addition to the more obvious instances such as the self-proclaimed New Stoicism with its annual Stoic Week, subtler influences of those ancient schools of thought appear both in our rarified intellectual culture and in our more boisterous popular culture, if often in debased, selective, or even contested form.

At the same time, there has been a growing movement to connect philosophy with the concerns we face in the course of everyday life. Besides magazines, journals, and degree programs in practical or applied philosophy, institutions such as websites, blogs, e-zines, book clubs, and conversation groups such as the Socrates Café (discussion groups designed with the goal of sharing different philosophical views) have proliferated. *The Point*, founded in 2008, is one such journal, describing itself as a "magazine of the examined life." This movement for the relevance of philosophy has also appeared in treatments of the philosophical ideas in a particular movie, television show, or graphic novel, especially in the action hero genres. Of uneven quality, these efforts sometimes fall prey to the dominant self-oriented culture, and what might seem like a way to make philosophy more public can end by making it more private. In a misunderstanding that what makes it public is simply appealing to more people, many take pains to make philosophy interesting by connecting it to private, personal concerns. I think this is inside out.

While it is true that self-concern is already everywhere in this era of constant social media sharing, ultimately the question is not so much whether to focus on the self but how to do so. Those ways most dominant now avert our attention from the parts of the self in dire need of cultivation and toward externals. Think Facebook. Meanwhile, crucial forms of self-cultivation receive little sustenance and support or even outside validation as something real.

Mark Greif leads off his essay collection *Against Everything* with a brief "Against Exercise" in which he explores the idea of exercise as self-help. He depicts today's gym as a place where people dress and act, with grunts and sweat, in ways once deemed private: "It is atomized space in which one does formerly private things before others' eyes, with the lonely solitude of a body acting as if it were still in private."[35] When people run for exercise outside, it is even worse because it takes the "proselytizing" implied by the runner's activity into a shared public space: "It lays the counting, the pacing, the controlled frenzy, the familiar undergarment-outergarments and skeletal look, on top of the ordinary practice of an outdoor walk."[36] This is a genuine paradox, and "Our practices are turning us inside out" because people are showing to others just that part of them that has become most associated with their selves, now understood as the outer self: "Though the exerciser acts on his self, this self becomes ever more identified with the visible surface."[37]

Attention to this version of the self today often comes at the cost of others. In a *Washington Post* op-ed, Natalia Mehlman Petrzela and Christine B. Whelan argue that the American self-help industry has, more often than not, had an antagonistic relation with social movements. Self-help focuses on the problems of the individual as failures of will, rather than injustices perpetuated by society, and thus encourages "solipsism at the expense of social change." For example, Tony Robbins, a self-help guru, initially called #MeToo a case of women who "choose victimhood," before backpedaling in haste. What happened in the interim was that a video filmed at his "Unleash the Power Within" seminar in San Jose went viral in which he criticized the movement against sexual harassment. Petrzela and Whelan's criticism of the $11 billion self-help industry describes "the self-serving 'me' trumping any regard for the collective 'we.'" They see earlier best sellers like Ralph Waldo Trine's *In Tune with the Infinite* (1897) and Norman Vincent Peale's *The Power of Positive Thinking* (1952), which trumpeted the success available to anyone who willed it, in this light. Cooked in the cauldron of the 1960s, the human potential movement focused on the individual as the way to bring about change through "self-actualization." Petrzela and Whelan concede that people can work on their own problems "in order to combat the injustices that surround us," as they think feminism did in the 1970s and 1980s. Of the self-help books over time spanning secular and religious realms, "The best of these books extolled character and virtue, but too many had an insidious underlying structure" of blaming victims for their problems, not identifying collective problems and potential solutions.[38]

The problem is not the turn inward, but the question of how and why we look within. If the turn inward ultimately aims to serve both the human person and collective purposes, that end differs drastically from the goal of serving individual success and self-promotion. The culprit is not personal achievement by itself but the larger context of elitism and exclusion that goes with a zero-sum culture that has no recourse to a greater good or public interest, a culture of wealth at any cost and fame for any reason. Only if it takes place within a moral framework does personal achievement transform from a purely private matter to a public good.

THE EMBODIMENT CRISIS

The therapeutic culture operates according to a concept of the self it inherited from an earlier era of secular Enlightenment and Scientific Revolution. Its ministrations rest on a shaky foundation. The source of much suffering is not that the therapeutic culture caters only to the emotional side of the self but that it holds the underlying assumption that there is such a thing as a separate physical self, apart from the other faculties that make up the human person.

The idea that an individual is divided between the mind and the body, the Cartesian self, rooted in the seventeenth-century ideas of René Descartes, yields a certain self-concept. This notion of what it means to be a self in turn leads to a certain concept of other people and our relation to them. The triumph of the therapeutic does not represent a countermovement to Enlightenment rationalism, a pendulum swing to emotion, from mind to body. Rather, it is a blend of notions of the rational and emotional self that lacks the intellectual groundwork to bring them into one human being. This tension between mind and body has escalated to an all-out war, exacerbated by modern institutions that thrive on the conflict. Pressures toward irresolution keep the wounds open, and markets, now the dominant purveyors of norms, capitalize on the conflict, selling products on the grounds that the body is out of control and needs products catering to the mind or that the mind is out of control and needs products catering to the body. Advertisements bombard potential consumers with visions of fast food one minute and fad diets the next. The tension between reining in our desires and giving them free rein lies at the heart of modern consumerism.[39] It has escalated to the level of a full-blown embodiment crisis.

In Ilham Dilman's critique in *Love and Human Separateness*, the Cartesian self underscores the idea that the modern individual is inherently isolated from others and thus is the fundamental unit of society. Even prior to its separation from others, the self is separate from itself. The mind looks to the body as a stranger, as an entity it must exert control over to get it to serve the mind's wishes. This view equates the mind with the self. In Descartes's view, the mind and the body are completely separate. From this separation stems separation of the individual self from others. In ensuing interactions with others, the individual cannot know others because our thoughts and feelings are within, thus hidden from others. For Descartes, because we cannot know other people, we do not have any real evidence of their existence. And because they are their minds, and their minds are closed off to us, and their minds are even closed off from their own bodies, the only thing we can verify is our own existence.[40]

The mind/body division underlies the modern embodiment crisis. The body does not do what the mind wants, nor do other bodies. We can see this self-concept at work in modern individualism. It makes everything relative in the world, everything outside the self subjective and fundamentally unreliable, by undermining the notion that any shared understanding can emerge between people. We can only deduce the existence of others by inference, through analogy with our own, as though our separateness were merely a cognitive matter.[41]

This is both an outer and an inner war. The external Hobbesian war of all against all has moved within. Majorities of those polled even report dissatisfaction with their own bodies. The embodiment crisis manifests itself in the frequency with which people turn to everything from elective operations to so-called enhancement or performance drugs, yet such endeavors pale next to the epidemics of eating disorders, addiction, and self-harm. Unscrupulous marketers capitalize on the anxiety we as limited beings can have about our natural flaws and on the incompleteness that is part of the human condition. Ideals for how to think of the self, those missing from moral discussion, reappear in the form of twisted and truncated messages in advertisements. Many people look at themselves from the point of view of a judgmental and even cruel stranger. When they do not, judgmental and even cruel strangers on social media are happy to oblige.

THERAPY VERSUS *THERAPEIA*

To take issue with the assumptions underlying the modern therapeutic culture does not require abandoning the question of what is therapeutic in the sense of healing or restorative. Each society has its own therapeutic culture, and to unveil the detrimental effects of the triumph of the therapeutic suggests the lack of effectiveness or unintended consequences of the particular approach that has come to the fore in recent history. We need a vocabulary to distinguish between desirable and undesirable notions of what is therapeutic, and in Greco-Roman philosophy we can find such a vocabulary.

Ancient notions of what is therapeutic differ greatly from the modern notions of therapy underlying the therapeutic culture. In part that comes from different diagnoses of the source of what ails us as human beings and in part from different prescriptions for cures. But in even larger part the difference stems from this modern medical analogy itself. If medicine means addressing physical symptoms alone, this medical analogy does not fit our larger quest for healing. If medicine extends to our fuller selves, this medical analogy might fit better. The contemporary search for preventive treatments and holistic cures suggests a felt need for something that takes the bigger picture of a person's life into account. Even then, stopping at the search for treatments and cures confines our notions of what is ultimately therapeutic to individual fulfillment. In the writings of the ancient philosophers, we find a completely different interpretation of what is wrong and what would help.

Political philosopher Martha Nussbaum has made a preeminent contribution to recovering ancient notions of philosophy as a better grounding for the therapeutic than those we have to work with today. With an eye to the continuing relevance of their approach, her *Therapy of Desire: Theory and Practice in Hellenistic Ethics* shows in depth and detail how proponents of the Hellenistic philosophies of Stoicism, Epicureanism, and Skepticism applied philosophy to everyday problems. Members of the schools of thought she studies "all conceived of philosophy as a way of addressing the most painful problems of human life."[42]

Nussbaum weighs the differences and similarities among these approaches, showing how they differ over the answers yet share the quest for a practical philosophy of living. Nussbaum insists that we recognize the central place of reason, argument, and logic in their view of practical philosophy as therapy. In the works of the Hellenistic philosophers, philosophy gives us a way to think about the emotions that roil us and a method to keep them in check as a way toward moral virtue and happiness.

In this and her other books, Nussbaum has emphasized Stoics' interest in emotion, and while not always agreeing with their ministrations—especially Stoicism's "advocacy of various types of detachment and freedom from disturbance"—she thinks they were more ambivalent than they might seem at first (9–10). She sees in them, particularly in Seneca, the need not just for practicality but for compassion and pity (3). Nussbaum writes that the analogy between the role of "arts of speech and argument," or *logos*, in addressing problems of thought and emotion, on the one hand, and medicine in addressing disease, on the other, predated these philosophies: "From Homer on, we encounter frequently and prominently, the idea that *logos* is to illnesses of the soul as medical treatment is to illnesses of the body" (49). Before Aristotle, the idea that *logos* heals was not confined to philosophy but included "religious and poetic utterances, philosophical arguments, friendly advice," and other speech (50). Aristotle was the first to offer a full account of "a medical conception of ethical argument," Nussbaum relates. Aristotle traced the analogy to medicine's and philosophy's shared commitment to a practical goal, the idea that ethical arguments about a good life, like medical treatments, must be useful. Ethical truth also has to adhere to a concept of a good life "judged by a reasonable person to be complete and lacking in nothing," which Aristotle interprets as community-minded and not a purely individualistic response to a particular case (62–63). But for Aristotle the limits of the analogy are vital. Unlike medicine, which draws on knowledge and theory to heal the patient, through logic (*logoi*), "clarification and articulation," philosophy involves examining "the *logoi* themselves." Philosophy "requires the sort of argument that sorts things out and clarifies, that leads people to shift their alleged ground by pointing to inconsistencies in their system of beliefs and, in the process, makes evident not only the fact of our commitments, but also their 'why,' that is, how they contribute to one another and to the good life in general" (72–73). Aristotle emphasizes that philosophy does not aim at the individual alone, does not see logic and clarity as merely instrumental, and does not feature medical treatment's "asymmetry of roles" or discourage "alternative views" (73–77).

Nussbaum admires the Hellenistic philosophies for breaking with Aristotle's focus on "balance and health" (within his stated limits) as they plumbed the depths of emotion, accounting more fully for the complexity of emotional experience. Drawn particularly to the Stoics, for their deeper engagement with emotional complexity, Nussbaum ends up acknowledging the limits to both Aristotelian and Stoic morality. Neither allows for the complications of intense passions, without which our lives are incomplete. She finds more room for this in Senecan tragedy and invokes what she calls the "triumph of love" even in the violent and impassioned scene at the end of Seneca's play *Medea* (483).

Nussbaum suggests that philosophical argument and the exercise of moral virtue alone do not grant the vulnerability of great love or fully serve the cultivation of compassion and mercy that she sees as vital. In her view, this is the role narrative can play, grasping other people's life stories "in their mystery, in their character that is neither that of sickness nor that of health." Beyond the illusion of moral perfection and total calm, we need, in her glowing phrase, "to wait with a certain humility before unpredictable things" (481–82).

This is where Plato comes in. When going back further to Plato, on whose ideas all of these philosophies drew, we find a similar search for a practical way of life but a different answer altogether. Plato keeps ever in focus that the art of living—as opposed to the science, technique, or therapy of living—requires that we cultivate not just the self but the soul.

In *Phaedrus*, Plato uses an allegory to visualize the soul: "We will liken the soul to the composite nature of a pair of winged horses and a charioteer." In heaven, Zeus drives a winged chariot, "whose well matched horses obey the rein," but for humans, because their horses are unmatched, "the utmost toil and struggle await the soul." One horse is "a friend of honour joined with temperance and modesty, and a follower of true glory." The other is disobedient and prideful, and causes longing and the divine madness of love. The charioteer must find a way to balance the rational and moral part of nature with the irrational urges and desires. The charioteer needs to draw inspiration from divine reason to get control and guide them toward enlightenment.[43] Plato conjures up a terrifying scene of the violence and chaos of the human experience when that does not happen.

In *Therapeia*, Robert Cushman offers an elaborate and elegant analysis of Plato's approach, the cultivation of an inner life in recognition of the full range of the human experience. While it would take Augustine to flesh out its implications in the doctrine of di-

vine grace, Cushman observes, Plato's notion of inwardness read-
ied the human person for an unparalleled vision of the good as
something beautiful and sublime. Experienced as a unity, wisdom
is goodness. The cultivation of the inner life changes a person irrevocably in a conversion that is profoundly cathartic, offering the
ultimate release of love.[44] Although it is commonplace to associate
catharsis with the genre of tragedy, as Aristotle presented it in his
Poetics, we can see catharsis in another light in Plato's healing arts,
as we shall see in chapter 5.[45] In the place of modern notions of the
therapeutic, Plato would put philosophy, but a philosophy hardly
recognizable today. It is the aim of this book to envision what it
might look like in the modern context.

THE FOURTH SOPHISTIC

We have entered a period of cultural life it might help us to think
of as the Fourth Sophistic. In ancient Greece, the Sophist was a
type of teacher in the fifth and fourth centuries BC who used tools
of philosophy and rhetoric, as well as subjects like music, athletics,
and math—teaching *arête* (excellence or virtue) to the elite. Plato's
dialogue *The Sophist* portrays this figure as a kind of philosophical
mercenary, charging money for instruction and seeking power and
office through the art of persuasion. The term *sophistic* has come
to describe periods during which rhetoric dominated. Critics have
raised alarms about practices in which it mattered less what one
said than how one said it. A fascination with style over substance,
performance over action, and appearance over inner worth elevated those with bombast over those with wisdom. Plato called
Sophism "a shadow play of words." A continuous thread in his
philosophy is a profound concern about the consequences of some
Sophists' approach. To Plato, the Sophist could argue on any side
of any question. In the context of putting forth an argument, all
that mattered was winning, and the display of skill with words.
Deconstruction can be seen this way, as word games standing in
for the hard part of thinking: deciding on what our commitments
really are. Orthodoxy is not the only problem. Total relativism is

as totalizing as orthodoxy. In part a reaction against totalitarianism, relativism sprouted an intellectual conformism of its own. The idea that there is no one self but endless numbers of them, no grand narrative, and no objective truth may be only temporarily and partially limiting as opposed to the forced imposition of a whole worldview as in Nazi Germany or Stalinist Russia, but to abandon all solid ground is equally inaccurate, unrealistic, and unhelpful.

The First Sophistic refers to the times right before Plato. He had nothing but disdain for those who played fast and loose with the truth. In such antics, words lose their connection to reality.[46] Again and again, Plato sought to pinpoint where the Sophists went wrong and to spell out the particulars of a philosophy that could rival their prodigious abilities to make anything seem to be the case—or not. His lifelong engagement with Sophism is one of the most sustained attempts we have to articulate what is at risk when we adopt the radical relativism—even nihilism—of the Sophist and gesture toward the existence of something that cannot be negated with dazzling displays of images and sophisticated wordplay, a reality resistant to denial or "falsifiability" albeit nearly impossible to capture in words. Nearly six centuries after Plato, the Second Sophistic took place in the Roman Empire, beginning in the late first century AD and extending through the third century AD, an era when the power of the Roman Empire brought both relative peace and a renewed interest in classical culture to Greece. As in the First Sophistic, the Sophists of this period traveled widely. They also established schools, some of which lasted into the fourth century even after Roman support for the movement faded.[47]

Some scholars have labeled the period of late antiquity, beginning around the fourth century AD, as a Third Sophistic, though others have argued it would be better understood as a continuation of the Second Sophistic and thus not a distinct period. Either way, the Sophists of late antiquity were a part of social debate, against and perhaps even alongside, church leaders as Christianity grew in influence.[48]

Recent social critics have lamented the decline of a coherent moral framework as collective commitments of families, communities, and nations have given way to atomistic individualism and polarization. Meanwhile, postmodernism as a philosophical movement has questioned everything from large narratives to the very existence of such a thing as the self—each person an infinite congeries of multiple selves. Reality is just a construct, truth does not exist.

In *Age of Fracture*, Daniel Rodgers noted the fragmentation of American thought and culture and traced its intellectual history and contemporary manifestations.[49] When taken together, both those who celebrate and those who criticize the dissolution of the idea of a self define the question as whether we need stable frameworks and sources of meaning. Our current moral landscape appears to be one of anarchy, for those who celebrate it, or chaos, for those who condemn it. Both sides observe a loosening of social ties, mores, and traditions.

Alasdair MacIntyre describes what he calls "the unity of a life," offering a poetic and spiritual defense of the importance of a stable notion of the self. Postmodernists such as Jean-François Lyotard have, instead, celebrated the absence of that very thing, calling into question inherited notions of the self.[50] MacIntyre has turned our attention in part to the medieval theology of Thomas Aquinas in a new Thomism for sources of the coherent moral framework he finds lacking. His mention of the "Benedict option" at the end of *After Virtue* inspired a book by that name by Rod Dreher in which he envisions a turn to a variation on the monastic life as a response to the divisiveness and chaos of contemporary life.[51] Charles Taylor has taken a different tack in exploring the deep sources of spiritual meaning traditionally underpinning the self and arguing for the liberal self the postmodernists disavow.[52]

This discussion grows more important daily. The US has become increasingly polarized as both politics and markets encourage aggressive self-assertion. We drift somewhere between polarization, which presumes some basis of coherence within enclaves, even if those enclaves become increasingly opposed, and total social dissolution. In this crisis of meaning, extremes win out, demagogues arise, and impatience and frustration devolve into the politics of resentment. This is fertile territory for Manicheanism, the us-them mentality that depicts every disagreement or conflict as part of a cosmic drama between good and evil. In place of heroism, we have demonization, even if the now demon-like heroes claim to serve the right side.

Instead of one undifferentiated mass of competing perspectives, a barely discernible pattern does emerge. Begun as separate schools of thought aware of the explicit differences among them— Stoicism, Epicureanism, Cynicism, Platonism, and others—such approaches now persist as general dispositions, whether invisible or explicit. Once distinct, now they are more diffuse, often overlapping, and far flung from the original roots of the tree. Nearly two and a half millennia later, we hover on the outer limits of the thinnest branches, and those branches are trembling beneath us. Juxtaposing the Greco-Roman schools, as others have done before us, and presenting them together, however loosely connected, ventures a tentative proposal for what could come in the wake of postmodernism, which seems to have played itself out.

Just as Plato responded to the First Sophistic, we need a New Platonism to respond to our current crisis. Postmodernism, and radical relativism in all forms, is the sophistry of our age. Postmodernism was not alone in eroding the concept of the self and fixed meanings. Chaos theory and political discourse untethered from any pretense at truth-telling dovetailed with therapeutic notions of endless self-creation. Thanks to the ever more invasive incursions of advertising, public life itself has the trademark juxtapositions and chaos of postmodernism. This includes not only those academic theorists but aggressive CEOs and politicians who show a blatant disregard for truth and reality, fact and reason, and embrace the creed of the Sophist.

SOCRATIC STIRRINGS

After the inauguration of the ancient Greek schools of philosophy, the Socratic view of philosophy as a way of life went on to exert a towering influence on the Western intellectual tradition and beyond. Subsequent forms of inwardness—the inner life—and their fruits in society and politics are difficult to imagine without Athenian ideas and their legacy. When not providing the central motif, Socratic strains provided the background accompaniment for many of these practices. They still do. In *The School of Athens*, Raphael depicted this conversation, with heroes and heroines embodying whole philosophical outlooks. His painting is still riveting to us today. (See fig. I.2.) Yet in the market triumphalism of the late twentieth and early twenty-first centuries the Socratic insistence on examining one's beliefs and behaviors and holding them up against matters of principle is all but lost in the reign of personal preference as sole arbiter of what is best.

We hardly lack for people taking a look at themselves. After all, ours is the era not just of the self but the selfie. What we see now is a gross caricature of the examined life, with the process, technique, and means—the activity of examining—shorn of the whole point of doing so. The examined life, which entailed a notion of a higher end, has capitulated to the overexamined life. With the ubiquity of confession as the dominant mode of conversation and self-styling, the examined life has given way to hyper-self-consciousness and self-referentialism. A main form of self-examination in religious practice, confession meant scrutiny of one's actions, and even thoughts, for how well they accorded with moral imperatives, divine commandments, and transcendent visions. Confession of sin required an inner reckoning with one's god or gods. Now, all of the meticulous detail remains—the *technique* of examining is intact—but the presumed audience is no longer within but outside, and the moral dimension has all but vanished.[53] In this context, it is crucial to hold up our own practices to examination for what view of life they harken to and to find a different vantage point for examining the self.

Every age has its way of engaging, disengaging, or reengaging with ancient thought and culture. Recent history in the West brought active and passive disengagement in the 1960s' call for relevance and suspicion of ancient thinkers as all guilty by association with politics, practices, and peoples whose way of life relied on slavery and was rigidly hierarchical, elitist, and oppressive to women and children and any others not deemed fit to rule. Politicization of the curriculum and intellectual life of the mid- to late twentieth century led to wholesale dismissal of works once thought the foundation of a basic and advanced democratic education for everyone. This came to a head in the controversy over *Black Athena*, which claimed that Greek civilization had African instead of central European origins. While archaeologists, Egyptologists, linguists, and classicists agreed that this thesis lacked basic evidence, it raised hot-button issues about racism and relevance in scholarship on the ancient world.[54]

In the meantime, by the end of the twentieth century, schools no longer offered Latin and Greek, nor did most students encounter ancient texts and artworks as a matter of course. When they did, those artifacts often arrived via political conservatives as a package of prescriptions for character building and uplift, rather than in their rich variety of competing views, thereby only sealing the belief that they were no longer relevant in the context of the larger, politically and socially diverse society.

It is difficult to give classical tropes, myths, works, and intellectual traditions the slip entirely. They are prominent, even omnipresent, in the mix of influences on intellectual and artistic movements in subsequent periods, including times of ferment such as revolutions, on which twentieth-century social movements drew, even when their debt was not explicitly acknowledged. There is much allure in the dramatic events of antiquity in their own right, thanks to the people, places, and events of mythic proportions, in part because of that very influence and in part because they have been the source of so much mythologizing—whether by glorification or demonization. Even at the nadir, when classical study seemed to be on the way out, popular culture kept alive distant memories of heroism and accomplishment, however tinged with irony or criticism. Thankfully, fields like moral and political philosophy also sustained and rekindled interest in the interim.[55]

Signs of a broader movement have included the flowering of the field of classical reception studies, the interdisciplinary study of encounters with ancient ideas and literature in Greek and Latin and portraits and interpretations of antiquity in different times and places.[56] In some ways, this book is a study of the reception of ancient philosophy in the modern and contemporary US. Before this new wave of interest, studies of classical culture in American history mainly focused on early America, especially the founders of the new republic. More recently, works such as William Cook and James Tatum's *African-American Writers and the Classical Tradition*, Caroline Winterer's *The Mirror of Antiquity: American Women and the Classical Tradition*, and Patrice Rankine's *Ulysses in Black*, to name just a few, have helped draw attention to later periods and to the engagement of nondominant groups with classical ideas. Art exhibits and new books have drawn many new viewers and readers to the works of Romare Bearden, an African American artist, writer, and social worker greatly influenced by classical themes, and to black American classicists.[57] Prominent intellectual and early civil rights leader W. E. B. Du Bois studied both Greek and Latin in high school and read widely in the classics as he studied philosophy at Fisk University and later at Harvard before turning to sociology, politics, and history, and his pioneering role in founding the NAACP.[58] The vibrant field of Classica Africana, initiated in 1996 as a subfield of the Classical Society, brings renewed attention to the longtime engagement with the classical tradition shown by black thinkers such as Bearden and Du Bois as well as Phyllis Wheatley, Ralph Ellison, Toni Morrison, and many others.[59]

THE NEW CLASSICISM

Observers see a new "Millennial Cynicism" among the so-called millennial generation, those born in the 1980s and 1990s and coming of age in the two decades of the new millennium.[60] But the cynical mood of our times, and the developments that led up to it, can hardly be pinned on them.[61] If anything, what I see instead arising in the early twenty-first century is a broader interest beyond any one generation in ideas, the intellectual life, and the philosophies that find expression all around us, in everything we do, in art and architecture, fiction and film, self-help and spiritual life. Rather than a millennial cynicism, what we see is a resurgent New

Classicism, after recent movements in architecture and other fields, a kind of new-millennium popular classicism, referring to the period rather than to any one generation.

One place we see the resurgence of classical themes and motifs is in public and residential architecture. For example, architecture is seeing a resurgence of interest in classical style in the form of a movement dubbed "the New Classic Architecture." The photo-sharing website Flickr includes a group called "Neohistorism–New Classic Architecture," where members post photos of new architecture that incorporates classical elements.[62] This style dovetails with efforts for the revitalization of cities and sustainability, with the movement's interest in human scale and the integrity of a work of architecture as an integrated whole. Some key works are the Schermerhorn Symphony Center in Nashville, opened in 2006, as discussed on the blog devoted to the New Classicism, *Classical Addiction* (and its predecessor, *The New Classicism*). The movement has an Instagram account (newclassicalarchitecture), a Twitter feed (@NewClassicism), and a Pinterest board (new classicism).[63]

An article in *Architectural Digest* refers to a "classical groundswell." Architects Cynthia Filkoff and Armand Di Biase designed a pool house for a client who asked them to study eighteenth-century Scottish neoclassical architect Robert Adam. Filkoff calls the pool house, which looks like a temple, "Arcadian." It sits on a 120-acre estate in Millbrook, New York. Architect Peter Pennoyer built a house named Drumlin Hall drawing on Venetian Renaissance architect Andrea Palladio, Robert Adam, and British-American neoclassical architect and designer of the US Capitol Benjamin Henry Latrobe. It sits nestled into the rolling hills or drumlins in Dutchess County, New York. Kevin Clark, trained at the University of Notre Dame, which pioneered in the New Classicism, also drew on Palladio in designing Serenity, north of Savannah, Georgia. Gil Schayer III, author of *A Place to Call Home* (2017), was president and then chairman of the Institute of Classical Architecture and Art. The *Architectural Digest* calls him a "contemporary classicist" who "looks for inspiration to architects, well versed in the classical idioms, who advances gracious living." According to Schafer, "Architecture is about delighting the soul."[64]

The Institute of Classical Architecture and Art awards national Arthur Ross Awards. Robert A. M. Stern, former dean of Yale University's School of Architecture, asserts that the institute "advances classicism in a vigorous way." He leads a nearly three-hundred-person architectural firm, RAMSA (Robert A. M. Stern Architects, LLP).[65] The Institute's president Peter Lyden praises as a sign of wider interest in the return of classical architecture a recent documentary film about director James Ivory featuring classical sites in his films, such as Versailles (*Jefferson in Paris*) and Florence, Italy (*A Room with a View*). The institute hosts a summer studio and sponsors travel programs that allow people to see famous sites and buildings.[66]

Inspired by artists of the Italian Renaissance, the German artist Yadegar Asisi creates large panoramic scenes with 360-degree views. He displayed his view of Rome, which measured 27 meters high and 107 meters long, in Dresden in 2012. Viewers stand on a tower in the middle so they can be immersed in the ancient cityscape. Architect Daniel Libeskind tapped him to draw a panorama of his plan for the 9/11 Ground Zero site in New York City, the plan that ended up being selected. Andreas Scholl, director of Berlin's antiquities collection, explains the popularity of Asisi's vast panoramas: "It seems Asisi's artistically and archaeologically-underpinned reconstruction of an ancient cityscape fills a large audience with enthusiasm for panoramic scenes and classical antiquity even today."[67]

While many with an interest in antiquity are little known or forced to operate on the margins of the corporatization of the modern university, both inside and outside it we can witness a plethora of stirrings of renewed interest in classicism ranging across whole disciplines, occupations, and realms of study and practice. This shift dovetails with efforts to return to representation and figurative art, with its focus on the human being, experience, and the question of what it means to be human. In painting, Patricia Watwood points to an avant-garde movement of Contemporary Classicism. Her 2013 exhibit *Venus Apocalypse*, at Dacia Gallery, displayed her own works in this vein.[68] A spring 2018 exhibition at King's College London displayed works since the 1930s that reverberated with classicism. That exhibition, *The Classical Now*, was connected to a larger project called Modern Classicisms, a project of the Department of Classics, that crossed disciplines and transcended the usual academic/public divide. The event included a competition calling for entries on the question "What does the classical mean to you?"[69]

An interest in classicism has manifested itself in education, from classical curricula to character education. Some efforts accompanied a resurgent post-1960s conservatism, but to dismiss all such efforts to reintegrate classical elements into the curriculum as reactionary does not capture this moment. Across the board, there are numerous attempts under way in communities and educational settings earnestly interested in the classical past. In the push for social relevance, careers, and credentialing, late twentieth- and early twenty-first-century college and university administrators often abandoned the ideal of a liberal education, departing from a longstanding tradition of education for well-rounded, community-minded citizens, not just career-minded, technical specialists.

It is crucial to recall that the same past that has provided cultural riches to support movements against tyrannical regimes and in favor of freedom and self-government has been used for the opposite. In another whole area of inquiry, historical scholarship exposes the specific ways Nazis, for instance, misappropriated the classical past for their own pernicious ends.[70] Turning to the contemporary scene, the website Pharos: Doing Justice to the Classics likewise confronts real-time distortions of Spartan and even Athenian symbols and traditions—and much else from antiquity—by hate groups.[71] Named after the ancient Greek word for "lighthouse," the vital service provided by Pharos has received attention in other important works on malign misappropriation of classical sources to promote social oppression and on elitist blinders on perception and understanding.[72] These and less extreme misuses and misunderstandings offer more reasons to take notice of a resurgence of interest and to weigh these schools carefully, untangling their different strands, weighing their implications, and vigilantly observing their presence and absence.

British classicist Mary Beard, author of the best-selling *SPQR*, has made a noted impact with her scholarship and public engagement, fomenting the new interest in all things ancient. In "The Cult of Mary Beard," journalist Charlotte Higgins, an award-winning contributor to this movement in her own books, including *It's All Greek to Me: From Homer to the Hippocratic Oath, How Ancient Greece Has Shaped Our World* (2010), presents a scintillating profile. Higgins provides a taste of the range of Beard's activities, which have reached millions of viewers and readers, from the TV documentary *Pompeii* to her blog, *A Don's Life*. Beard's eclectic work has ranged from a regular classics column in the *Times Literary Supplement* to *Women and Power: A Manifesto* (also a best seller), *Confronting the Classics*, and other publications, documentaries, and television appearances.[73] Higgins writes about Beard:

> Out and about, she is regularly flagged down by fans, often, but not always, young women. (One admirer, Megan Beech, published a poem called *When I Grow Up I Want to Be Mary Beard*—a phrase that now adorns T-shirts worn by her fans. Characteristically, Beard befriended Beech after they connected on social media, and Beech is now studying for a PhD at Newnham.) Caterina Turroni, a television producer who has worked with Beard since the Pompeii documentary, recalled filming with her in Tiberius's villa on Capri in 2013, when a party of English schoolgirls spotted the cameras. "You could hear them saying, 'What if it's her?' 'Do you think it's really her?' and then they saw her and they went insane—it was like they'd seen a boyband."[74]

A review of Beard's book *Pompeii: The Life of a Roman Town* captures her ability to bring the past to life: "Mary Beard, like Mary Shelley, revitalises old corpses. Readers will want to visit, or revisit Pompeii, with their own senses freshly shaken and stirred." It also situates public interest in her work as part of a larger resurgence of interest in antiquity: "With the decline of grammar schools in Britain, Classics seemed to be heading for a fall. Recently however, both in the UK and USA, the subject has achieved something of a renaissance. Popular culture, ironically, provides the impetus: Latin is the working language at Hogwarts; Gladiator and Troy are two of the most testosterone-fuelled films of recent years; Lindsey Davis and Steven Saylor translate sassy, hard-bitten detective fiction to the weird world of Rome."[75]

Intense interest has arisen not only in female classicists but in female classicist philosophers. Hypatia (AD 355–415) is one of the earliest-known female mathematicians and astronomers and has received attention across genres, from children's books to feminist art. A Neoplatonist, she was well known in her day as a lecturer and writer in Alexandria. Much controversy surrounds her death at the hands of a faction of Christians.[76] A 2009 film, *Agora*, characterized Hypatia as a guardian of classical knowledge against the religious turmoil of the times.[77] A major early work of three-dimensional feminist art helped draw attention to figures like Hypatia and encouraged explorations of the role of women the artist thought missing from the history of thought and culture, extending back to antiquity. Judy Chicago's *The Dinner Party* commemorates 1,038 names of women in history, and Hypatia is one of a select thirty-nine to receive a place setting. (See fig. I.3.) For Hypatia's place setting, Chicago used red, green, and orange, drawing on Coptic motifs for the rows of hearts and interwoven bands bordering the tablecloth and the mirroring leaf pattern on the plate. Chicago explains that the butterfly-like form on the plate evokes flight, representing Hypatia's efforts to "break free from the constraints imposed upon so many women of her time." In the depiction of Hypatia's face, she peers through an embroidered "H," but her mouth is covered, referring to the violence employed to silence her voice. The construction of the artwork—the setting of the table—drew on a team of craftspeople skilled in everything from embroidery to ceramics, evoking women's traditional roles in both form and content.[78] Laying the table for a dinner of invited luminaries across the generations is encouragement for just the kind of conversation we might imagine at Plato's *Symposium* and have in our heads and with others about the art of living.

This is a book about taking back philosophy. Joining other such attempts, it proposes a way to do so, sifting through the ruins of long-forgotten and recent history alike, for any shards helpful in piecing together the coherence of a moral framework that allows us ways to move forward toward the life we want and need.

The schools of thought from ancient Greco-Roman philosophy offer a typology—an assortment of approaches—with perennial applicability. Are you a Stoic? Do you treasure self-control as the best path to a good life? Are you an Epicurean who values pleasure above all? Have you given up on the hypocrisy and materialism of social life in the manner of a Cynic? Do you seek to climb the ladder of love and dwell in a realm where truth is beauty and beauty truth? Plato did.

One need not accept the argument that these schools of thought are universal in order to sense that abandoning them altogether risks, at the very least, losing sight of an important historical source of self-understanding, since these approaches have exerted enduring influence on Western culture and beyond. Even if not the only choices, out of the complications of life there emerges a common set of categories of options to most real choices or decisions that have a strong pull on our thoughts and emotions: act, refrain from acting; forbid, permit; resist, give in. This begins from our existence as animals—embodied beings with urges and instincts, hormones and drives. We are nothing if not creatures of desire. At the same time, the pursuit of desire or impulse imperils our existence in a world of others. As social beings, born into families and reliant on communities, continuous unleashing is not an option. Even in solitude it would play itself out quickly. Limits are needed, and self-restraint is a vital element in basic survival. In the heyday of Hellenic philosophy, these behavioral options had advocates who worked out their implications in minute detail.

Religions center on this classic set of basic choices—which desires to indulge, which to resist, and why. Without religious community, religious thinking is harder to live by. Religious oppression has often been cruel, hostile to freedom, and violent. Yet without some foundation for moral thinking it is unclear why anyone should ever be inhibited from doing anything. The emotional-moral economy is what guides behavior and makes community and society possible. It also reminds us of our capacity for a self-transcendent vision. In Rieff's description of a culture as the complex of restraints and permissions, once in motion, it does not run on its own but requires constant cultivation. The inner life is where it is cultivated and sustained, the place where the individual encounters the requirements and gifts of social existence, as well as the call of freedom and the will of individual existence, and negotiates between them.

There are, and should be, playful dimensions to even the most serious pursuits. A popular pastime today is taking personality tests. In some ways, we can think of these ancient schools of thought as a bit like different personality types. Like astrology, another popular pastime today as in antiquity, intense interest in our own personality and others' is not unrelated to inquisitive searching for reasons for what we do, remedies for what ails us, and ways to navigate our lives. It is also an interest in and curiosity about other people's inwardness and how to deepen our own. This book is as an extension of these everyday activities. Rather than stand apart from other pursuits that might seem a matter of superstition or overly esoteric, we can be interested in insights gathered from all sources we encounter. After all, it is not the science but the art of living we are after here. For those who get to the end of a personality test or a horoscope craving to know more about the sign or category in which they or others fall, the following chapters seek to convey some of the intricacy of this particular typology of approaches.

Quoting Samuel Taylor Coleridge's famous observation that "every person is either a Platonist or an Aristotelian," Arthur Herman even provides a personality quiz claiming to tell you which personality you have. His quiz asks whether you own a dog or cat, pay your bills online or not, use a to-do list, prefer baseball or basketball or football, wanted to be a rock star or movie star when you were growing up, and more. The answers run something like this: "If your answer was a dog, you're an Aristotelian. Aristotle believed human beings were naturally social animals; so are dogs. . . . If your answer was a cat, you score one as a Platonist. The relationship between cats and their owners, as we all know, is spiritual and intuitive." Herman's dichotomous thinking simplifies the difference between Aristotelianism and Platonism as similar to that between science and religion, or practicality and idealism. But these characterizations do not hold. To cast the Platonist as hopelessly idealist and as "tender-hearted and altruistic" versus "tough-minded, logical, and skeptical" Aristotelians simplifies Herman's own work.[79] The differences between thinkers are important, but their roots run deeper into the intricacies of each approach. Plato was obviously interested in science, and Einstein and other scientists drew deeply on Plato. Philosopher Lloyd Gerson, a renowned scholar of Platonism and Neoplatonism, actually sees Aristotle as a Platonist.[80] For manageability, and because the architects of our public philosophy have focused so much more on Aristotelian thought in recent years, we will focus here on Plato and Neoplatonism as our final school of thought.

Rebecca Goldstein's *Plato at the Googleplex: Why Philosophy Won't Go Away* also tries to take philosophy beyond the academic journal, conference, seminar, and lecture room. Like Herman's work, it makes claims of echoing the voice of its protagonist. Her best-selling book has Plato confronting life today. Using the dialogue form herself, Goldstein offers serious reflections and helps convey the continuing resonance of what Plato had to say, even if her attempts to speak for Plato fall short.

Looking at what these philosophers themselves said and accompanying our close readings with some of the most sensitive later interpretations—scholarly, artistic, popular—we can decide for ourselves what we think of their views and what we think they would make of our quandaries. This will allow us to see important differences between and among Gnosticism, Stoicism, Epicureanism, Cynicism, and Platonism.

Running deeper than personality types, the schools of thought in this book constitute a set of overarching dispositions or basic approaches to the art of living, whether consciously chosen or not. These five common sensibilities present a typology for us to consider, an analytical tool for helping us make sense of our own and others' perspective. If we can see these approaches at work, as moving parts of a historic and ongoing conversation, we can perhaps understand each other better, before citing irreconcilable differences and ending communication. We might too identify missing alternatives to our own way of thinking. Even if we neglect their riches or are unaware of their influence, these schools of thought remain part of our shared cultural resources. The ancient philosophical schools of course do not explain the social divisions and differences among us. But ideas become very real in our interaction with them and their entry into history.

To attempt to construct pure replicas of the ancient schools today would not be possible because those schools had great diversity of opinion within them, let alone among them, in antiquity as in modernity, and even specialized scholars admit to the limits of what can be known definitively. The intervening centuries brought patterns of translation, interpretation, and dissemination—texts lost, texts found, texts corrupted, texts missing, many no doubt forever. There are more gaps in the record of literary history or intellectual transmission than areas filled in. Present culture is the result of accretions of readings, misreadings, and nonreadings of the ancient texts. This study's emphasis is on the resonance of those ideas in recent cultural history and contemporary life. The precise genealogy of ideas resembles our uncovering of buried ruins. Even now there is also the possibility of discovery of a central text at any given moment of our lives.

AS TERRIBLE AS OUR TIMES ARE IN MANY RESPECTS—WITH instability in the world, domestic as well as international terrorism, the degradation of political discourse, and destructive influences on our very self-concept—these are exciting times. We can piece the evidence together, like so many modern relics, of intellectual ferment and interest in the life of the mind. The cruelty, crimes, and catastrophes of our times make it urgent and imperative, as it always has been, that those still here make the most of the gift of life, community, and our cultural riches, including our democratic polity. We cannot afford to let vital reflection on the human condition be hijacked by the therapeutic consumer culture, or by specialists and gatekeepers who claim to have privileged knowledge. Sorting through the ruins is all we can ever do. We need to tap our cultural resources to outline an alternative kind of outward-facing inwardness that can raise a challenge to the inward-facing outwardness that masquerades as inwardness in our time.

In these times we face many gripping dramas. As long as we look in the direction of attention-grabbing trivia, in the celebrity and consumer culture, we are distracted from the archaeological finds that transform what we know about the past and open new doors to a more enriching present and future. The Villa dei Papiri is a symbol of all of this, a place for ideas. Buried by the AD 79 eruption of Vesuvius, the villa was first uncovered in the eighteenth century, and excavators discovered the only surviving library from Greco-Roman antiquity. Further excavations in the 1990s and early 2000s have added to the archaeological understanding of the villa itself, which served as an unintended time capsule of so much ancient knowledge.[81] When the volcano erupted, besides taking people's lives, the heat and gas charred the library's scrolls that had recorded their ideas. In attempts to open the scrolls since then, the papyrus often fell apart when opened or the ink faded afterward, ruling out further openings. Today, a team led by University of Kentucky computer scientist Brent Seales is at work trying to read the scrolls with new high-energy x-ray and machine-learning techniques. It is exciting to know we are always just one fragile papyrus sheet away from a discovery of a lost text and the sound of a voice from another time, whether in poetry or philosophy, that could prove invaluable in our lives, filling us with the gratitude of connectedness.[82]

When we revisit or discover new ideas from the past, they can be as enlivening as these kinds of physical discoveries. Through intellectual history and contemplation, we embark on similar digs, but in a way anyone can afford. The location is within, where we too can discover what one novelist calls "Beautiful Ruins."[83]

Within each of us, as in our culture at large, lie the remains of earlier ideas and sensibilities from long-forgotten epochs. They affect us, often unconsciously, the decisions we make, and the way we approach the world today. *Are* you a Stoic or an Epicurean, a Cynic or a Platonist? The answer is fascinating and important.

ONE

THE NEW
GNOSTICISM

We are stardust . . .
—*Crosby, Stills, Nash & Young*
(written by Joni Mitchell)

Dan Brown's 2003 novel *The Da Vinci Code*, translated into over
forty languages and with estimated sales of eighty million copies,
along with the 2006 movie version directed by Ron Howard, with
worldwide box office earnings of nearly $800 million, opens with
a murder.[1] (See fig. 1.1.) The setting is the famous Louvre Museum
in Paris, and the body is that of the museum's distinguished curator, Jacques Saunière. Called in by the police to help make sense
of the murder scene is an American professor named Robert Langdon (played by Tom Hanks in the film), in town for a visiting
speaking engagement, for this is not just any murder scene.

As the curator lay dying after being fatally wounded by a killer
who then fled the museum, Saunière used every last ounce of his

vital energy to prepare a set of clues that would not be apparent to just anyone, so were perfectly suited to a mystery thriller. With the only ink at his disposal—that of his own blood and of a special curator's pen visible only with a black light—he wrote numbers, words, and symbols on his own body and on the floor around him. At one point, chief investigator Fache turns to Professor Langdon and asks, "To your eye, beyond the numbers, what about this message is most strange?"

"*Most strange?* [thought Langdon] . . . What about the scenario *wasn't* strange?"

"Perhaps this will clarify." Fache backed away from the body and raised the black light again, letting the beam spread out in a wider angle. "And now?"

To Langdon's amazement, a rudimentary circle glowed around the curator's body. Saunière had apparently lain down and swung the pen around himself in several long arcs, essentially inscribing himself inside a circle.

In a flash, the meaning became clear.

"*The Vitruvian Man*," Langdon gasped. Saunière had created a life-sized replica of Leonardo da Vinci's most famous sketch.[2]

Though a fifteenth-century pen-and-ink rendering of the human body according to the proportions spelled out by the architect Marcus Vitruvius Pollio in the first century BC, Leonardo's iconic work has become a ubiquitous symbol of the modern self. (See fig. 1.2.)

A GNOSTIC MICHELANGELO

The Da Vinci Code reverberates with echoes of Gnosticism, a movement rooted in the first century AD yet still given a hearing in subsequent eras including our own. Considering it in this light helps us understand the cultural currents explored in this book. Twentieth-century thinkers have described a parallel between ancient Gnosticism and various movements in modern times. Hans

Jonas begins the preface of his foundational history of Gnosticism, *The Gnostic Religion* (1958), with an evocative image: "Out of the mist of the beginning of our era there looms a pageant of mythical figures whose vast, superhuman contours might people the walls and ceiling of another Sistine Chapel." In the next paragraph he adds the equally prevocative statement about the history of Gnosticism: "The tale has found no Michelangelo to retell it, no Dante and no Milton."[3] It seems almost as though Dan Brown set out to remedy that by suggesting that the tale does have its Michelangelo: Leonardo Da Vinci.

No matter what the truth (and that is part of the point—the truth hardly matters), this fictional series undoubtedly has many people believing Leonardo was a prescient postmodernist, proto-feminist Neo-Gnostic. For Brown, the work of art even more emblematic is the small painting hanging on the wall nearby, the *Mona Lisa*, whose enigmatic half smile and mysterious gaze are there in his story for a purpose. She seems to look upon the scene as if surveying with bemusement the unfolding of human history itself. (See fig. 1.3.)

In Brown's rendering, this history is replete with conspiracy designed to stifle the human spirit. *The Da Vinci Code* goes on to follow a trail of symbols, codes, and clues to a whole web of historical entanglements between secret societies and the Roman Catholic Church, cast as villain. Langdon's partner in crime solving, Sophie Neveu (played by Audrey Tautou in the film), granddaughter of the curator, is a cryptologist intentionally roped into the quest by her grandfather's deathbed signals. Besides the main mystery (who killed her grandfather), a new mystery begins to unfold, which is nothing less than the search for the Holy Grail. Its true meaning, the hidden treasure sought throughout the story, turns out to be the divine feminine principle, intentionally suppressed by the institutionalized church since antiquity so it could cement its power and male hierarchy. A third mystery, more personal but hardly less disturbing, is introduced when Sophie Neveu reveals that she has been estranged from her grandfather for a decade because she accidentally caught him in the act of . . . we do not know yet. All we know is that it was some unmentionable act performed in a group setting. Its meaning and import remain a mystery for most of the book and movie, and thus must for most of this chapter.

What is there not to like about a book and a movie—a whole *phenomenon*—that is equal parts crossword puzzle, numbers game, murder mystery, tourist attraction, museum visit, artifact collecting? It *is* fun.[4] While the whole *Da Vinci Code* sensation might seem innocuous, falling somewhere on the seriousness spectrum between harmless mind-twister and inane make-believe, critics have not seen it this way. Ranging from scholarly refutations to protests organized for the day of the book's publication and the film's debut, objections centered on its way of playing fast and loose with history and religious belief.[5] Passionate positions for and against *The Da Vinci Code* arose in the context of the larger culture wars of the late twentieth century (and continuing) charted so presciently by sociologist James Davison Hunter.[6] The phenomenon can also be understood as part of what we might see as a new kind of romance with antiquity, with a peculiar postmodern cast, which has a noticeable—and noteworthy—presence in American life in our era. Finally, the *Da Vinci Code* phenomenon helps foreground an element it shares with the therapeutic culture, a kind of new Gnosticism.

GNOSTIC ATMOSPHERICS

For a contemporary Gnostic mood we need look no further than a leading popular culture relic of the last year of the last millennium. At the opening of the 1999 movie *The Matrix* we find protagonist Neo (played by Keanu Reeves) leading a meaningless life. Caught between a dreary work life and a nonexistent personal life, he has a cave dweller's existence, spending most of his time alone in his apartment, at home but clearly not *at home*. He is lost. His head is not in the clouds of yore but in his computer. As if expected, and certainly predestined, the phone rings with a call that has all of the undertones of a *Mission: Impossible* assignment but none of its clarity of purpose.

As it turns out, the task is to ask. Rather than find answers, fulfill a mission, or attain a goal, the point is as much to figure out what the question is as to find an answer. After many twists and turns, in equal parts mysterious and mystifying, Neo's charge turns out to be to wake up and ask himself who he really is. Beyond himself, the world around him is revealed as nothing more than an elaborate illusion. Everything is a hall of mirrors constructed by an imperialist corporation run by machines to exploit human beings, harnessing their biokinetic electricity to its own ends. A select set of humans, escaping the enclosed pods in which humans are kept alive and stimulated with virtual images archived from a human history now lost, gain the knowledge that reveals the new state of things. Reality exists for humans no longer. Solely survivors have access to the inside knowledge about the human condition.

Besides Neo, characters include Morpheus (Laurence Fishburne), head of the resistance, and Trinity (Carrie-Anne Moss), another rebel who originally takes Neo to Morpheus. Morpheus holds out a blue pill in his left hand and a red pill in his right, offering Neo a choice: "This is your last chance. After this, there is no turning back. You take the blue pill—the story ends, you wake up in your bed and believe whatever you want to believe. You take the red pill—you stay in Wonderland, and I show you how deep the rabbit hole goes. Remember: all I'm offering is the truth. Nothing more."[7] In this reference to Lewis Carroll's *Alice in Wonderland*, the Matrix is the weird, wacky, world-as-illusion Wonderland Alice encounters when she falls down the rabbit hole.[8] While Alice eats and drinks things that make her big or small, Neo can reject reality by taking the blue pill and returning to the cocoon of the artificial world, or he can stay and fight. He takes the red pill.

The setting is dismal and bleak. Black and gray dominate the filmscape. It is the future, alternatively postindustrial and terrifyingly post-postindustrial. In the postindustrial tableaux, people are shown as hapless drones. Oblivious that this is all an illusion, they trudge city sidewalks en masse, like the soulless specters in Edvard Munch's *Evening on Karl Johan Street* (1892) or George Tooker's

Subway (1950). In the post-postindustrial, they float like fetuses in liquid solitary-confinement cells, just so many bodies being fatted for harvest agribusiness-style. There is no middle ground. Resisters are in the know but on the run. With no physical place to call home, they see the world of other humans is an illusion but have no basis for any kind of real daily existence in the high-tech totality of the Matrix. They inhabit a hostile and alien world that is rapidly dissolving their very beings into thin air.

These themes of bleakness, alienation, and suffocation are now ubiquitous in popular culture, not just thanks to movies like *The Matrix*. Our imaginative world, from its alternate reality games to its fixation on worst-case scenarios, reflects an embodiment crisis that has been exacerbated by ingenious new technologies and their seductions. In movies, this translates into an apocalypse that is forever just about to arrive—when it has not already. The apocalyptic genre is no longer a genre but a way of life. Doom, destruction, and desolation have become hook, line, and sinker in whole seas of artistic expression from novels and movies to graphic novels and video games. The end-of-our-world genre yields new genres, breaks out of old ones, remakes old and new ones alike, and ends by forcing us to question genre itself.

Futurist themes and landscapes, whether utopian or dystopian, are so prevalent that it is difficult to separate out the thread of Gnosticism. Bleakness is a tip-off. Yet we must look for further clues, since not all apocalyptic scenarios are Gnostic. In Gnosticism, from ancient to postmodern, the world is sheer illusion, the evil product of a false divinity. To a sense of meaninglessness and alienation already in full bloom in earlier forms of modernism, we must add not merely suspicion and distrust of the physical world as perceived by the senses but its complete dismissal.

Gnostic atmospherics are not just moods of movies. American life is awash in Gnosticism. For example, the New Gnosticism finds expression in a flood of blogs, e-zines, and websites. Just a few titles give a taste of the offerings: Gnosis—Quetzalcoatl Cultural Institute; Gnostic Teachings: The Art, Philosophy, Science, and Religion of Consciousness; *The Gnostic Path to Oneness: How to Know Yourself and Use Your Mind to Access Parallel Realities*; The

Gnosis Archive; *Key to Heaven: Christian Gnosticism*; the Gnostic Center of Long Beach; Denver School of Gnosis; *The Negative Psychologist*; The Exploration of Consciousness Research Institute (EOC Institute): How to Reach Gnosis; Greater Church of Lucifer (GCOL): Light Bearers; and Free Will Astrology.[9]

ANCIENT GNOSTICISM

While not one of the ancient Greco-Roman schools, Gnosticism is included here because of its role in the therapeutic culture so prominent in our time. As one of the most available sensibilities today, it provides the context in which the older schools are re-emerging. When it comes to the ancient movement, almost everything about Gnosticism is still being debated, from the timing of its emergence and its influences to the question of whether there really was such a thing. Some scholars settle on the idea of Gnosticisms plural, others see Gnostic elements in many religions, and still others think it should be seen as a religion in its own right.[10] In this book, we are not concerned with the accuracy of the scholarly portrayals of the historical phenomenon of Gnosticism, but with Gnosticism as a cultural sensibility right up to our own day.[11]

The term comes from the Ancient Greek word γνῶσις, *gnōsis*, meaning "knowledge," and γνωστικός, *gnostikos*, meaning "having knowledge." The term generally applies to a religious belief system emerging in the first and second centuries AD. Gnostics held that the material world was created by an evil god, the demiurge, who was inferior to the ultimate divine force, and that an elite group of human beings emanated from this divine force and possessed a divine spark within them that would allow them to be saved upon their attaining *gnosis*, a special esoteric spiritual knowledge. The discovery of the Nag Hammadi Library in Egypt in 1945, which included forty-eight Gnostic treatises, spurred enormous excitement and renewed interest in Gnosticism in the late twentieth century, as long-term projects of reconstruction and translation slowly brought the documents to publication and dissemination. One of the most important, popular, and best-known Gnostics was Valentinus, who lived from about 100 to about 160 AD, founded a movement in Rome known as the Valentinians, and wrote prolifically, though only fragments remain.[12]

One of the Valentinians' major texts, *The Gospel of Truth*, gives a helpful introduction to at least one strand of Gnosticism in the form of an overview and a sensory portrait of its cosmogony.[13] It starts with an image of a terror so all-encompassing that it was like an invisible "fog," a diffuse fear that arose in the absence of knowledge "of the Father." Amid this condition of mass ignorance and inattention, an entity called Error reigned by assuming the figure of beauty, a mere "substitute for truth." Into all this came Jesus Christ, who enlightened a select few—"the perfect," Gnostics called them—"those who were in darkness because of forgetfulness." Error persecuted and crucified Jesus: "He was nailed to a tree, and he became fruit of the knowledge of the Father. The fruit of the tree, however, did not bring destruction when it was eaten, but rather it caused those who ate of it to come into being. They were joyful in this discovery, and he found them within himself and they found him within themselves" (37). The Father, "illimitable" and "inconceivable" in his perfection, has "the All" within him. He "kept within himself their perfection, which he had not given to all" (37). Their means of returning to the Father is knowledge or *gnosis*.

There is a "living book," according to *The Gospel of Truth*, that people were forbidden to read on pain of death. Those who are "inscribed in the book of the living" are those whose knowledge contrasts with the ignorance of the masses and reunites them with the Father. He calls only the names of those with access to this special knowledge, not those who have no name or voice. At first, those who are called live as in a nightmare, in a world that is nothing but an illusion. But their knowledge awakens them and permits them to fulfill their need for "what would make them perfect": a return to the Father. The knowledge they seek and need is about themselves, "where they come from and where they are going" (38–39).

In *The Gospel of Truth*, a great, unbridgeable chasm separates those capable and incapable of *gnosis*. The document cites a

"Parable of Broken Jars," which explains that some jars are full and perfect, while others are defective. It does not matter when defective jars fall and break. The perfect have been fated to be so. Among them, "those who have not yet come to be" might do so still (41) if they have roots in the Father in the first place. Only those who come from the Father can reunite with him. Forgetfulness has cast them into a deficient state, lacking in grace, and knowledge is their key to salvation.

Restoration, or repentance, returns the perfect to unity and completion. Once restored, these select humans reach a state called "fullness." Fullness is a condition in stark contrast with their initial state of deficiency, which turns out to have been unreal. Discovering the truth is the only path to this fullness, and to an ultimate paradise, a place of rest as well as repleteness (44–45). "Those who possess something of this immeasurable majesty from above" do not end up in the underworld, nor "is death with them" (47).[14]

The *Gospel of Truth* helps us identify a set of traits that appear in many other Gnostic documents as well: suspicion of the physical world, the senses, the body, and the ordinary, based on a sense of reality as illusory; celebration of God as a divine cosmic force beyond the universe; designation of a select few as divine, apart from the majority of people, who are "broken vessels"; belief in *gnosis*, a secret knowledge known only to the few, as the sole way they can reunite with "the Father"; and a sense of individuals' fates as predestined for better or worse. In shorthand, our list might read: reality as illusion; a divine cosmic force as the ultimate God; divinity of the elite; knowledge as the elite's sole salvation; and fatedness.

THE "GNOSTIC SPIRIT"

In his twentieth-century study of Gnosticism, Jonas spelled out how his approach parted ways with extant scholarship. He appreciated new works that had proliferated in the waves of the discoveries. They added immensely to the "wealth of historical detail" and identified different streams coming from separate traditions, especially through the careful work of philology and genealogy. These were at root efforts of exact historical reconstruction. He described his own approach as something different from such studies: "To these I neither presumed nor intended to add. My aim, somewhat different from that of the preceding and still continuing research, but complementary to it, was a philosophic one: to understand the spirit speaking through these voices and in its light to restore an intelligible unity to the baffling multiplicity of its expressions." He sought to explore not just the traditionally informed history of the movement but the "Gnostic spirit" from a philosophical perspective as "one of the more radical answers" to the question of what it means to be human, thus contributing to "human understanding in general."[15] This study proceeds in that same spirit.

Jonas traced the broad contours of the studies of Gnostics, beginning with the early church fathers, who attacked it as a Christian heresy. These early heresiologists put forth a "Platonic thesis," faulting Gnosticism for its pagan roots and interpreting it as stemming from Hellenistic philosophy. The last of these was Epiphanius of Salamis in the fourth century AD. Something similar was taken up by nineteenth-century Protestant theologians (mostly German), who continued the Hellenic interpretation of Gnosticism as Greek and rational, with Adolf von Harnack's famous portrayal of Gnosticism as "the acute Hellenization of Christianity."[16] Yet early in the nineteenth century another interpretation arose, which instead cast Gnosticism as "Orientalist" and irrational.[17] As scholarship progressed, inspired by new discoveries, both classical scholars and "Orientalist" scholars contributed to a broader interdisciplinary inquiry into late antiquity, identifying particular "national" traditions and separating out Hellenism into heterogeneous influences. As a counterweight to the "Greek-philosophical-rationalist" view of Gnosticism, scholars included mythological material from Coptic and Mandaean texts. The overall portrait, as the approach turned into "genealogy," became "syncretistic," including now Judaism. Because of this identification of different "pedigrees," the subject became not just Gnosticism but "the whole civilization in which it arose," a culture of "syncretism."[18]

MODERN GNOSTICISM

Late nineteenth- and early to mid-twentieth-century discoveries of long-buried original sources rekindled interest in Gnosticism. Translation of the original sources and dissemination through their publication, as well as academic scholarship, fanned the flames. A small set of writers we might see as conduits of Gnosticism to modern readers actually included virulent critics of Gnosticism. They hoped to point out the links between the ancient movement and the modern setting because they saw its reemergence as pernicious.

A major twentieth-century thinker, Eric Voegelin, saw Gnosticism as lying at the heart of modern life, the essence of modernity. In his introduction to a 2004 reissue of Voegelin's 1968 book *Science, Politics, and Gnosticism,* Ellis Sandoz summarizes Voegelin's view that Gnosticism inflected "such modern phenomena as positivism, revolutionary activism, fascism, communism, national socialism, and the rest of the 'isms.'"[19] For Voegelin, modern Gnosticism constituted an overarching mode of thinking that influenced everything about how we live.[20]

Voegelin thought the modern Gnostic made a claim to science that actually ended up negating science as he understood it. True science involves the exercise of *ratio* (reason) through questioning, analysis, and "perception of the order of being."[21] Such a view of science (and he largely meant political science here) presumed "givenness" (40)—a preexisting world that humans did not create. Political science was not just about proving the "validity of positions" but about exploring the "truth of existence" (15). People should engage in it not only to decide whether an opinion is right or wrong in the sense of true or false but also to figure out whether opinions are "symptoms of spiritual disorder" or not. Rational analysis involves not only observation but persuasion, as it is the role of reason to help us, an essential way to replace existing opinions with others. Gnosticism is, rather, knowledge that rules major questions to be out of bounds for investigation. It poses as a form of knowledge yet lacks ties to reality or to our spiritual state and strivings. Rational analysis thus involves big-picture concerns, such as a view of what is necessary, not just expedient. Through rational analysis, an individual can decide not to be part of the larger spiritual disorder of the age (xi). *Ratio* is a vital way we order our lives: Voegelin writes that "analysis is concerned with the therapy of order" (15).

In Gnosticism, on the other hand, "*Doxa* [δόξα] takes the place of philosophy." It recasts science as knowledge. This form of knowledge is severed from the search for truth or meaning. Claiming to be science, Gnosticism instead reifies what Voegelin sees as nonscience. *Doxa* seeks to make a logical and airtight theory but can do so only by disallowing questions that might contradict whatever system currently passes for knowledge. While the practice of philosophy in antiquity did not prohibit "analytical inquiry" (14), modern movements such as positivism, socialism, and fascism rely on suppressing certain kinds of questions. In this view, Gnosticism amounts to the very opposite of rational analysis and constitutes an "anti-philosophy," not another philosophical position (x).

For Voegelin, philosophers and nonphilosophers have a lot in common (x). Political science is the practice of *politike episteme*, which "deals with questions that concern everyone and that everyone asks" (16). Yet its method still amounts to "scientific analysis." In this concept of science, the prerequisite for analysis is a mode of "perception of the order of being," including "its origin in transcendent being" (16). Out of this sense that there is something larger than human existence—out of spiritual longing—philosophy originally arose: "For only then can current opinions about right order be examined as to their agreement with the order of being" (14).[22]

Invoking a vision of a transcendent order, a universe not made by man, Voegelin turns on its head what is now a commonplace (after the Cartesian division of the self into mind and body): that clinging to a notion of transcendence rules out rational inquiry.

Religious faith since the Enlightenment seems to be the apotheosis of the irrational—the very definition of what it means *not* to be rational. To engage in rational analysis means being willing and able to subject all propositions to questioning. Religious believers can always solve disagreements, end discussions, and win debates, or so goes the dominant narrative, but only with an appeal to faith that is out of bounds in a secularized culture. Believers supposedly do not need to support their views; they simply believe them to be right.[23]

It is difficult to turn such things around. Instead, Voegelin sees this modern version of rationality as a way of disallowing further inquiry. When there is no transcendent order, there is no way to explore a particular proposition about the world. This is because there is only the human world and nothing beyond it. Another way to think of this quandary is that without ideals there is no way to weigh whether one opinion is better than another. Religion can be more rational than atheism because the latter lacks a transcendent basis for reasoning. We must have some sense of the good for rationality to work, or it devolves into the chaos of competing perspectives. Lacking a transcendent referent, today's ersatz science does not allow us to hold up a proposition for questioning. Thus it is not an actual science. Faith and philosophy are based on experience of the world as something in existence before our own lives enter it. Any real inquiry stems from "the loving openness of the soul to its transcendent ground of order" (16).

To Voegelin, Gnosticism does the opposite. It casts the world as simultaneously evil and yet as a place for immanent, historical realizing of change. It rejects the given world yet wants to remake it. In so doing, Voegelin argues, it participates in the "murder of God." Christian ideals of perfection are cast as something possible only after death, while Gnostics see them as attained historically (66). Modern mass movements share this Gnostic "activist mysticism." For instance, in the case of Marx and Comte, their speculative systems include both a *telos* and a way to bring it about (68). God is unmasked as an illusory projection of human beings, and the world as something that can be re-created through human will. Gnostic movements seek to usher in a "world-immanent order of being, the perfection of which lies in the realm of human action." This "immanentization" is utopian thinking that has at its core an elevation of man to the status of a god (75).

Inherent in philosophy, on the other hand, is an understanding that humans are limited—and precisely not gods. Looking closely at these terms, Voegelin says, "If we translate them back into the Greek, into *philosophia* and *gnosis*, we then have before us the program of advancing from philosophy to gnosis" (31). Plato's dialogue *Phaedrus* draws this distinction: only God can be considered *sophos*, and a person, because finite, can only be *philosophos*, a *lover* of wisdom. Voegelin writes: "In the *Phaedrus* Plato has Socrates describe the characteristics of the true thinker. When Phaedrus asks what one should call such a man, Socrates, following Heraclitus, replies that the term *sophos*, one who knows, would be excessive: this attribute may be applied to God alone; but one might well call him *philosophos*" (31). This is a crucial distinction: "'Actual knowledge' is reserved to God; finite man can only be the 'lover of knowledge,' not himself the one who knows." Seeing history as unfolding according to scientific law, Hegel wants to replace "love of knowledge" with "actual knowledge." Those who do this, according to Voegelin, are "not advancing philosophy, but abandoning it to become a gnostic" (31).[24]

Voegelin's view of Gnosticism rests on portraits drawn by scholars such as Jonas, which lead him to view it as far more than a Christian heresy—rather a movement that predated the birth of Christ and continued through the Middle Ages, Renaissance, and Reformation. He identifies six main characteristics of Gnostic movements: dissatisfaction with the present situation; a view of the world itself as evil; salvation as actually possible; the need to change the "order of being" in real historical time; man's ability to make these changes; and special knowledge or *gnosis*, a "formula for self and world salvation." The Gnostic as prophet provides this formula (65).

In modern mass movements, Voegelin thinks we can see "the Gnostic attitude" expressed through "a rich and multiform symbolism" (65). These "complexes of symbols" include "modifications of the Christian idea of perfection" (65), shorn of its location after death and resituated as attainable in life on earth through a doctrine of progress toward "the goal of a perfect, rational existence in a cosmopolitan society" (67).[25] Voegelin's modern Gnostic, believing in fantasies of engineering perfection, attempts to make the *world* perfect.

To Voegelin, modern mass movements share a Gnostic belief in the possibility of constructing manmade utopias to replace a world that is fatally flawed. The notion of "immanentization" captures the sense that perfection is a possibility in the real world. What troubles him is the failure by human actors to acknowledge their limits in remaking a world they did not construct. Since it is not possible to make the "program to change the world" appear, essential aspects of reality must be disregarded. For instance, Thomas More can imagine the abolition of private property in his utopia only by setting aside human *superbia*, the lust for possessions, and Hegel can picture the fulfillment of the current phase of *logos*, Reason, in history, in a manmade epoch of consciousness, only by setting aside the mysterious nature of history, "the mystery of a history that wends its way into the future without our knowing its end" and our inability as humans to see all of history: "History as a whole is essentially not an object of cognition; the meaning of the whole is not discernible" (79). What Hobbes leaves out of the picture is the *summum bonum*, suggesting instead that fear of the *summum malum*, death, is the natural state and that merely the threat of death can restrict the drive for power. Only a sovereign can keep order, as there is "no orientation of human action through love of God, but only motivation through the world-immanent power drive" (78).[26] In order to work, Hobbes's "strange construct" relies on setting aside traditional notions of the *summum bonum*, the highest good, as a possible source of human motivation.

Hobbes is well aware that "human action can be considered rational only if it is oriented beyond all intermediate stages of ends and means to a last end, this same *summum bonum*" and that "the *summum bonum* was the primary condition of rational ethics in the classical as well as the scholastic thinkers." For Voegelin, there are dire consequences of suppressing the notion of a highest good:

If there is no *summum bonum*, however, there is no point of orientation that can endow human action with rationality. Action, then, can only be represented as motivated by passions, above all, by the passion of aggression, the overcoming of one's fellow man. That "natural" state of society must be understood as the war of all against all, if men do not in free love orient their actions to the highest good. The only way out of the warfare of this passion-conditioned state of nature is to submit to a passion stronger than all others, which will subdue their aggressiveness and drive to dominate and induce them to live in peaceful order. For Hobbes, this passion is the fear of the *summum malum*, the fear of death at the hands of another, to which each man is exposed in his natural state. If men are not moved to live with one another in peace through common love of the divine, highest good, then the fear of the *summum malum* of death must force them to live in an orderly society. (77)

To achieve this, Hobbes placed at the center of the human the *libido dominandi*, which is "the revolt of man against his nature and God" (78). All that remains is a contest of raw power.[27]

These all-encompassing systems, in which a major aspect of reality is ignored, are to Voegelin emblematic of "the strange, abnormal spiritual condition of Gnostic thinkers" (76). Since adherents must bracket major factors, whether bad or good, like *superbia* or the *summum bonum*, for change on such a scale to seem possible, the explanation for their projects must lie in the domain of psychology, beyond logic and sense. To Voegelin, the modern Gnostic yearns to rule the world. Knowing the enactment of this program is impossible, the Gnostic persists in pursuing "a fantasy satisfaction" (106).

The impulse for the thinker to construct an image and for masses of followers to believe it must come from profound uncertainty. Voegelin attributes this condition to widespread Christianization without the institutional support most needed for the challenges of faith. He cites Thomas Aquinas's articulation of the notion of faith as defined in the Epistle to the Hebrews as the "substance of things hoped for and the proof of things unseen" (82). Given the nebulousness of spiritual matters, this precarious spiritual position made those "who were not strong enough for the heroic adventure of faith" turn to Gnostic beliefs. Many, if not most, fall "from uncertain truth into certain untruth" as a result of "the absence of a secure hold on reality" and the imposing spiritual demands of the human condition (83). Absent institutions that shore up "strength of the soul," insecurity can create instability, which opens the door to disenchantment and distrust. As a result, many fall prey to large-scale projects to reduce the complexity of the world and seek to remake it altogether.

GNOSTIC APOLOGETICS

While Voegelin and other modern critics of the Gnostic spirit viewed it as a danger, others have seen it as potentially liberating. Another of the small set of writers we might see as conduits of Gnosticism to modern readers is the scholar Elaine Pagels, whose *Gnostic Gospels* introduced a wide readership to Gnosticism and served as a kind of Gnostic apologetics. In her best-selling work, she offered a new, more favorable reading of Gnostic sources that struck a chord in post-1960s America. *The Da Vinci Code* later reverberated with the sense of mystery Pagels brought to her account of the Gnostic gospels.

Pagels begins her accessibly written study by recounting the story of the latest unearthing of Gnostic sources to date, fully capturing the excitement of the find itself and conveying the real story of the gospels as the enthralling real-life mystery thriller that it was. The body of *The Gnostic Gospels* goes on to present an interpretation not only of what Pagels sees in the Gnostic sources themselves, but also of how they diverged from orthodox Christian beliefs of their own time.[28] She argues that early Christian leaders separated out a few key tenets to pass on from a great diversity of beliefs as a power play—a kind of land grab for what would count as Christian belief. In her view, their process of selection in the decision about which beliefs to enshrine as scripture mainly involved the politics of inclusion and exclusion and the construction and maintenance of church hierarchy.

Writing at the time of the women's liberation movement, one of her main points addresses the place of women in Gnosticism, which undoubtedly explains some of its cachet in its particular moment.[29] While orthodox Christians described God in masculine terms and restricted authority to men, Gnostics often did so in both masculine and feminine terms and allowed for women's participation in worship and service in important roles. The orthodox take literally the condemnation of Christ and his crucifixion, a mainstay of Christianity, as a historical event and Christ's suffering to be literal, physical, "bodily." Gnostics instead differentiate between Christ's human nature, which suffers, and his divine nature, which remains untouched by suffering.[30] The orthodox view upholds Christian martyrdom while the Gnostic view calls it into question. The orthodox see Jesus as a physical person. The Gnostics see Jesus as "a spiritual being" (101).[31] The Gnostics "dismissed" physical life as a distraction from spiritual life, even an illusion, while at the heart of orthodox Christianity lies a belief that physical life and "one's religious development" are conjoined (101). The Gnostic text *The Testimony of Truth*, for instance, questions physical rituals such as baptism in favor of "the baptism of truth," which requires "renunciation of [the] world" (111).

Pagels thinks there was a common religious perspective running across the different Gnostic groups centering on their interpretation of evil: not sin but ignorance caused human suffering. She draws a parallel between Gnosticism and modern psychotherapy: both place a premium on knowledge, particularly self-knowledge or insight, positing that knowledge alone can fulfill the individual. Further, both equate knowledge with self-knowledge and teach that this self-knowledge must come entirely from within: "The psyche bears *within itself* the potential for liberation or destruction" (126). To achieve self-knowledge is a lone struggle because people prefer to remain asleep, in unconsciousness or oblivion. Wisdom alone will liberate them, as it keeps them from giving in to any desire and going off course, "like a ship which the wind tosses to and fro," as Silvanus put it in his *Teachings* (127).

Pagels even goes so far as to liken Jesus's role to that of the psychotherapist. Jesus offers only temporary counsel until the individual outgrows discipleship, finds his or her inner light, and becomes akin to Jesus: "Whoever achieves *gnosis* becomes 'no longer a Christian but a Christ,' according to the *Gospel of Philip*" (133). *Gnosis* is knowledge of God within. This is directly contrary to the orthodox view of worshipping God as other. It is instead an attempt to "realize that potential" of infinite, divine power within the individual (135).

In a vital distinction between Christianity and Gnosticism, Pagels points out that the orthodox view holds that the physical world is real and matters. Christ is seen "not as one who leads souls out of this world into enlightenment, but as 'fullness of God' come down into human experience—into *bodily* experience—to sacralize it" (146). Orthodox rituals involve "biological existence" and human relationships: "the sharing of food, in the eucharist; sexuality, in marriage; childbirth, in baptism; sickness, in anointment; and death, in funerals" (147). The conflicts between the Gnostic and orthodox versions of Christianity came down to a difference "between a solitary path of self-discovery and the institutional framework that gave to the great majority of people religious sanction and ethical direction for their daily lives" (149).

Though her treatment of Gnosticism is a sympathetic one, Pagels states her aims—not to take a position for Gnosticism or orthodox Christianity, but as a historian only "to discover how Christianity originated" (151). Many of the Gnostics' ideas—against martyrdom, against the clergy and hierarchy as necessary for spiritual fulfillment, in favor of women's religious authority, and in favor of a personal path to self-knowledge—clearly fit the expressive liberationist ethos of the 1960s and '70s. In its context of the counterculture, social movements, the human potential movement, and New Age spirituality, Pagels's portrait resembles Philip Rieff's—as well as Voegelin's—except that her assessment is positive and theirs negative.[32]

More recently, still other observers actually endorse Gnosticism or consider themselves Gnostic in more ebullient terms. They take the resurgence of Gnostic themes in the opposite direction, self-consciously drawing on Gnostic beliefs as relevant to our everyday lives today.

Some critics have shown how New Age religion has certain similarities to Gnosticism,[33] but April DeConick takes a novel tack of reversing this, to show what she sees as New Age elements already apparent in ancient Gnosticism.[34] She sees "uncanny parallels" between what she calls "the ancient and modern New Age worlds." To her, these movements constitute one long, continuous movement (17). She nods to recent work that has revised earlier scholarship on Gnosticism, portraying it as an alternate form of Christianity rather than, as in the view of its early enemies, simply a Christian heresy. While some revisionists wish to dispense with the term *Gnosticism* altogether, on the grounds that it was never a unified religion, DeConick finds the term necessary, not to evoke visions of a separate religion per se, but to acknowledge "a form of spirituality" (10). To get rid of the designation would obscure what she encourages readers to see as a vital movement.

DeConick lays out what she sees as the five main characteristics of Gnosticism: a personal religious experience of a transcendent God (leading to *gnosis* or special knowledge); rituals to prompt this experience; a notion of the divine spark, or *pneuma*, within human beings; a countercultural interpretation; and an open-ended, all-embracing disposition of the Gnostic as "seeker." She identifies the "transgressive nature of Gnostic spirituality as its distinctive feature" (13).

Turning to today, DeConick sees Gnostic tendencies in all of our religious practices, not just New Age movements. This would seem to place her in the camp of critics who see Gnosticism as involving modernity in its entirety or at least modern religion broadly.[35] Like some therapeutic critics, and like Pagels, she locates a Gnostic strain in the therapeutic. In DeConick's view, the ancient Gnostics are the forerunners of the modern movements: the

Gnostics "established religious ideas and practices of liberation and therapy" by "virtually conquering the traditional gods and empowering themselves as immortal" (14).

To DeConick, this is all good. Gnosticism is "a powerful transgressive and experiential spirituality that has eroded conventional religions today just as it did in the past" (17). A belief that human beings are part divine—and immortal—is the ultimate self-esteem builder.

So while some scholars argue that certain modern movements can be best understood as Gnostic, DeConick reads from the present backward, turning this around to argue that the ancient Gnostic movement can be best understood as the nascent New Age movement. *Gnosis* results from "direct experiential knowledge of a transcendent God": "In these ecstatic moments, the Gnostics felt immersed in the overwhelming presence of transcendence, believing that they had been reunited with the very ground of being. The experience was utterly transforming, as therapy that restored them to spiritual and psychological wholeness" (11). Although Gnosticism has gone from the margins to the center, she thinks that the transformative and therapeutic experience described by ancient Gnosticism is the same in contemporary religion that "offer[s] us spiritual well-being, psychological restoration, and an emotional attachment to a God of love": "Its therapeutic understanding of religion has become our own" (17).

DeConick does not deny the precise characteristics that disturb Gnosticism's staunchest opponents, both ancient and modern. In fact, she often celebrates the very traits they most despise. Seeing in ancient history the foreshadowing of a modern vanguard, she writes that before ancient Gnosticism emerged,

There was nothing like the extreme Gnostic orientation that empowered the individual person and subverted religion's traditional purpose of serving the gods. Before Gnostic spirituality surfaced, the religions in the Mediterranean basin conceived the human being and God to be vastly different, in terms of both substance and power. The metaphysical orientation of these traditional religions understood the human being as a mortal creature made by a powerful God for the sole purpose of obediently serving God and his appointed King as slaves and vassals.

To the contrary, Gnostic spirituality spotlighted the perspective that human beings are more than mortal creatures fashioned by God to do his bidding. The human being is perceived to be bigger and more powerful than the conventional gods, substantially connected to a divine source that transcends creation. (13)

What was once heresy—casting humans as divine and even higher than gods—becomes not only acceptable but mainstream through New Age Gnosticism.

Whether critics or advocates, these authors claim the complete contemporary cultural terrain for Gnosticism. This blurs vital distinctions, giving too much credit to the cogency and allure of Gnosticism and no credit at all to opponents and whole countertraditions of resistance. DeConick sees the essence of Gnosticism as countercultural and transgressive, but that raises a key question: How oppositional can it be if it is now *all* of culture? It may have become hegemonic, but then by her own logic of paying attention to dissenting movements, we should look for the alternatives to Gnosticism today. For those alarmed by the resurgence of Gnosticism in recent times, our prospects would be hopeless if *all* were lost to Gnosticism.

In DeConick's portrait of an "uncanny similarity" (18) between ancient Gnostic and modern spiritual movements, *uncanny* is the word, in the sense of "out there." Actress Shirley MacLaine gives an account in her 1983 book *Out on a Limb* and in her autobiographical mini-series of the same name (1987) of a spiritual crisis and subsequent awakening that strike DeConick as representative. In her seeking phase, MacLaine was reading everything "metaphysical" she could find, now that she had become belatedly interested in finding the "purpose" of life (341). In the midst of this, New Age artist David Manning took MacLaine to a like-minded bookstore. Gazing at the myriad books, she asked him what she should read. He answered, "'Well, you could read some of the more esoteric books on this wall, or you could just read Plato, Pythagoras, Ralph Waldo Emerson, Walt Whitman, Voltaire. They all wrote on the subject'" (342). DeConick concludes that "Shirley links into a spiritual conversation that has survived since antiquity, that goes back to the Gnostic New Age" (343).

MacLaine's particular quest does have perhaps greater affinity with ancient Gnosticism than with any other ancient movement. Yet that is not because Gnosticism inaugurated all such quests but because it offered a particular set of answers that now appeal to MacLaine, DeConick, and others. As Manning indicated, such spiritual seeking of course predated Gnosticism and continued in many different intellectual traditions.

From the first-century Gnostics to Shirley MacLaine and other New Age figures, "transgression" is what defines Gnosticism, according to DeConick. Both ancient and modern manifestations are "aggressively countercultural and highly critical of conventionally organized religion" (343). Further, they share a "quest for wholeness" or "holism" (344), "transpersonal spiritual integration" attained through "some kind of sacred psychological therapy" (344). DeConick sees Gnosticism as therapy.

DeConick grasps the problem of linking movements separated so drastically in time. While dying out as formal institutionalized religions because of religious persecution, Gnosticism persisted in the works of its critics. Since the ideas were preserved by those hostile to Gnosticism, she engagingly calls these fragments "Trojan horses" of dissenting ideas that kindred spirits could revive later (347). She sees other sources as "Gnostic artifacts," including the Gospel of John and the letters of Paul (347).

Rather than through a traceable, continuous institutional history, Gnosticism persisted because of episodic revivals of Gnostic thought. DeConick posits four "Gnostic renaissances": first the medieval movements of the Paulicians, Bogomils, and Cathars as well as debates among Islamic philosophers (347–48); then the fifteenth-century revival, prodded by the Renaissance scholar Marsilio Ficino's translations of Greek classical literature; then the nineteenth-century recovery of Gnostic texts; and finally the late twentieth-century recovery, beginning in the 1960s (349–50).

In discussing Ficino's efforts of cultural retrieval, DeConick fails to differentiate Platonists from Gnostics. In fact, her wide net seems to catch almost everything up in Gnosticism, including Renaissance humanism—everything she sees as sharing "skeptical, spiritual-but-not religious sensibilities" (350). Gnosticism serves as a catchall category for anything modern or protomodern. In DeConick's own view, we can identify a recognizable and characteristic Gnostic dualism. The "God of damnation," in her view, is replaced in Gnosticism with "the God of love" (350). She favors replacing talk of sin and damnation with liberation and acceptance—moving away from guilt (based on moral conscience) to self-esteem.[36] Gnosticism moves away from institutions, traditions, and disciplines of religious practice to a spirituality of personal liberation and therapy. She concludes that "the demand is for therapy, for religion that is useful. To be successful, religion today must promote personal well-being, health, and spiritual wholeness" (350). Spirituality of this sort often accompanies a whole slate of other propositions: "It must be attuned to a raising of consciousness, to global awareness, to life that is linked with the transpersonal or transcendent" (350). Though DeConick melds them, the transpersonal and transcendence are not interchangeable.

DeConick offers a moral inquiry into both past and present, an attempt to account for a worldview—with parallels across large time spans—that is shared even when not evidently historically continuous.[37] What should give us pause, however, is that it fails to distinguish among different points of view, sensibilities, and theological perspectives, rendering all serious spiritual seeking as Gnostic.

Gnosticism is just one view in a larger intellectual tradition. To accept Gnosticism as the mental framework that is most valid or most encouraging of the human spirit begs the question of legitimate differences of opinion about the best way to live. DeConick's account simplifies the choices into good and bad, liberating or oppressive, institutional or individual. This positive portrait fails to address the content of the critiques of Gnosticism. As just one example, DeConick does not explain how the Manicheanism of Gnostics fits the New Age quest for "holism." It is unclear how Gnostic dualism and the New Age quest for holism can be reconciled.

Literary critic Harold Bloom, who sometimes called himself a Gnostic, argued that religion in the US had become primarily Gnostic: "Though it mostly calls itself by the name of one Protestantism or another, this American Religion is post-Protestant, indeed post-Christian. It has three principal characteristics. What is best and oldest in each of us is already part of God and so is no part of the Creation. Spiritual freedom depends on being alone with God and so demands a preference for solitude over society. Finally, God loves each of us on a personal and individual basis." While Bloom presents a sympathetic interpretation of this individualist religion, he adds a dissonant coda: "There is immense spiritual strength in these marks of the American Religion, but they combine pragmatically to remove social compassion from the national soul."[38]

Bloom points to the dualism of Gnosticism as its essential trait. Gnosticism shares some characteristics with other religious traditions, such as Jewish mystical practices of the Kabbalah. Scholarly debate about where one set of practices left off and another began in the early years of the first millennium is lively and complex, complicated by the difficulty of pinning down the religious history of a period for which we have limited sources.[39] Bloom writes that despite ancient cross-fertilization, Gnostic beliefs ran directly against the grain of basic tenets of Judaism:

> Gnosticism was always anti-Jewish, even when it arose among Jews or Jewish Christians, for its radical dualism of an alien God set against an evil universe is a total contradiction of the central Jewish tradition, in which a transcendent God allows Himself to be known by His people as an immediate presence, when He chooses, and in which His creation is good except as it has been marred or altered by man's disobedience or wickedness. Confronted by the Gnostic vision of a world evilly made by hostile demons, the talmudic rabbis rejected this religion of the alien God with a moral passion surpassing the parallel denunciations made by Plotinus.

Bloom succinctly sums up the dualism of Gnosticism, after Hans Jonas: "'Dualistic' here means that reality is polarized into: God against the creation, spirit against matter, good against evil, soul against the body."[40]

KNOWLEDGE THERAPY

Returning to *The Da Vinci Code,* a third mystery alluded to throughout the story involves Sophie Neveu's having caught her grandfather in some horrific act. Throughout the book there are references to the event's traumatic effect on Sophie as a young woman. At the end, all has been revealed about the other mysteries: the Priory of Scion, an ancient society, guards the secret of Jesus's marriage to Mary Magdalen; a whole family lineage derives from Jesus and Mary; their descendants required protection from publicity because the Catholic Church's conspiracy against them would not stop short of murder. Sophie had caught her grandfather in naked violation of the norms of modern society but adhering to the ancient ritual of a secret society whose only sin was celebrating fertility by worshipping in the nude. But for the purposes of this chapter, the third mystery does not end at his ritual. The real mystery of the book and movie is attuned to the familiar register of the therapeutic. Ultimately the puzzle involves a traumatic event in Sophie's past. When the circumstances have come forth, no more explanation is needed. She experiences an immediate therapeutic recovery from that special knowledge and a reunion with a grandmother and brother she thought she had lost forever. As in a staged talk show reunion, the mystery at the heart of *The Da Vinci Code* is solved. Sophie needs in the end this therapeutic unveiling: truth equals knowledge that makes you feel better.

Picking up on this therapeutic role of the story, a website called Good Therapy Australia includes an article that even advocates an approach to therapy based on *The Da Vinci Code.* Asking, "What is good therapy?" the author suggests that the answer needs to fit these particular times. Today's approach must address various contemporary longings: for the transcendent; for a synthesis of different methods "that cross the boundaries that separate"; and for intimate relationship skills. The author assumes that the immense popularity of the novel and film must lie not only in its success as a thriller but also in its capacity to speak to this deeper hunger. The times cause people to seek "greater balance where the sacred feminine is restored to its rightful place" in this "patriarchal and materialistic culture" and "time of gender upheaval, isolation and an excessive individualism that alienates." The author describes the rising numbers of those seeking counseling not as people with serious mental health problems but as what another calls the "worried well." For these seekers, counselors are drawing on more than the usual "models" for new approaches that "are like a path to tread or a way of life."[41]

The article speaks to fellow counselors, without irony suggesting as a proper organizing principle for their work none other than the Holy Grail. Therapists themselves need to embark on an inner journey in order to guide their clients, "paying attention to the inner path of the healer, as much as to the outer skills of 'therapy'": "Training in therapy can offer a modern day path of initiation, a modern Holy Grail that can reveal the sacred feminine and provide training for inner development to meet the challenge of our times." The author's "truly holistic" practice draws on "the Process Oriented approach" of Arnold Mindell, who in turn is influenced by Jungian psychology, ancient Eastern Taoism, and Western modern physics: "He says 'I have yet to meet a guru or wise, enlightened, educated, shamanistic, mediumistic person who is as intelligent as the process which unfolds in the channels of our own perception.'"[42] The author quotes Ken Wilber, author of *Up from Eden*, as saying that "history is the unfolding of human consciousness," going in the direction not of "a final judgement" but rather an "ultimate wholeness": "This view has no more 'hidden metaphysics'—no more 'unprovable assumptions' than has the standard scientific theory of evolution since both rest on the same type of 'unseeable' postulates."[43] For a vision of the direction in which this unfolding consciousness is taking us, the author cites the "new civilization characterized by an harmonious integration and cooperation pervaded by the spirit of synthesis" of founder of Psychosynthesis Roberto Assagioli.[44] The author sees *The Da Vinci Code* as part of this larger movement.

Drawing a parallel to *The Da Vinci Code*, the author envisions this process as elevating "the qualities of the sacred feminine," a transition "from reductionist, competitive, linear, rational thinking that quantifies, specializes and compartmentalizes to greater synthesis, co-operation, interdependence, and relational understanding that facilitates wisdom, patience, and compassion." Granting that this change has not yet made a great difference, the author says, "I see the popularity of the Da Vinci Code as evidence that slowly a change is occurring." Observing a "polarisation" between this new synthetic approach of holism and fundamentalism, with its "hardening of beliefs, boundaries and of control," the author cites Hugh Mackay's statement that in this context "counsellors are beginning to look like the unsung hero's [*sic*] of a society struggling to come to terms with 'the Age of Discontinuity.'"[45]

The author refers to Austrian reformer Rudolph Steiner's view that the medieval legend of the knight Parzifal (Parsifal), as told by Wolfram von Eschenbach in his thirteenth-century epic, is "a metaphor of the inner search for self-knowledge and its relationship to the world of today": "It is a metaphor for a modern-day esoteric path, or path of inner development, for those who seek a new spirituality that reinstates the sacred feminine in its rightful place next to the sacred masculine." After a grand quest, Parsifal finds the Grail Castle, where the Grail King lies in his sickbed. Parsifal gets distracted by women bringing him food and drink and fails to ask the king "the right question." After a second seven-year quest, and all that he encountered and learned, he finds the castle again. Prepared this time, Parsifal manages "to ask the right question." It is telling that the answer is to ask, "What ails thee?"[46] This question is the crux of the therapeutic culture. Medicalization has overtaken the art of living and nearly eclipsed all other approaches.

In this case, what would make a Gnostic movie therapeutic? In the case of a movie like *The Da Vinci Code*, it might be the self-esteem-boosting message of female divinity, or the let-your-hair-down rejection of centuries-long Catholic strictures unveiled as a conspiracy against self-expression. But what about movies like *The Matrix*, whose dark corridors seem to lead to nowhere good? Here the link between New Age therapeutic religion and Gnosticism might be the key.

COSMIC CONSPIRACIES

An author called Red Pill Junkie (after the red pill in *The Matrix*, which wakes one up to the illusions masking grim reality) sees *The Matrix* as explicitly Gnostic. Possibly it shows the Gnostic therapeutic at work—how it actually works as it plays itself out. This author admits to being influenced by the writings of 1960s countercultural figure Carlos Castañeda, who left his position teaching anthropology at UCLA to pursue psychedelic consciousness expansion. Upon viewing *The Matrix*, the author was hit by the similarities between the movie and Castañeda's *Teachings of Don Juan*. Don Juan was a "Yaqui *brujo* [a sorcerer] who was in possession of a magical tradition harking back thousands of years." He introduced Carlos to consciousness-expanding "power plants" like peyote. The author says, "It was all so obvious! Neo was Carlos, Morpheus was Don Juan, and the red pill symbolized the power plants the *brujos* used to enter a '*state of non-ordinary reality*' and help them train their will to accomplish one of the greatest feats in the magical tradition, known in the Castañedian lore as 'Stopping the world.'"[47]

Affinity with Castañeda and *The Matrix* led to the author's pseudonym: "So now you know why I chose the silly moniker." The author notes that besides Castañeda, other influences on the directors of the film, Lana and Lilly Wachowski, included William Gibson's Cyberpunk, Japanese anime, and especially the science fiction of Philip K. Dick. The author offers a theory about why Dick's works reached "cult-like status" only after his death: "His writing was just *too* weird and *too* contrarian for an American public who still dreamed of colonizing space and building a better tomorrow, thanks to the blessings of science." Dick was both very ancient and ultramodern, the author continues. Like the ancient Gnostics, Dick believed "that this world, what we humans recognize as reality, is nothing but an *illusion* [emphasis in the original]; an illusion put before our eyes to imprison us by powerful entities, which seek to keep us trapped and deceived for their own selfish benefit." Red Pill Junkie describes a trend of "Gnostic cinema" in the 1990s as a category including not only *The Matrix* but *Dark City*, *The Truman Show*, and *The Thirteenth Floor*.[48]

Like DeConick, Red Pill Junkie celebrates a Gnostic "zeitgeist" that is not as confined to the views of the Gnostics as historical figures but instead connotes "a universal concept, that is continuously recycled and presented anew" in each new era. The author sums up the central tenet that is "repeated over and over again":

Wake up!
The world is not what it seems to be!
You're trapped and you don't even know it!

The author draws parallels among the movies to highlight the shared zeitgeist, providing pithy summaries of their Gnostic themes. For instance, *The Truman Show* portrays "the story of a seemingly ordinary man living a seemingly unassuming life, who is actually a prisoner inside a world-size tv set peopled by actors who are in the know, including his wife and parents." The author concludes, "Might we humans fare better if we learned our existence was the decision of *bored* [emphasis in original] multidimensional entities?"[49] The dim view of the world of *The Matrix* and the conspiracy mentality of *The Da Vinci Code* are clearly not confined to the screen.

The Gnostic attitude is, in the simplest terms, the feeling that some people are better than others because of special knowledge they alone possess. Since we do not know everything, to think this way is to play the role of gods. The word *hubris* (*hybris*; ὕβρις) evokes Greek tragedy and the overweening pride that comes before a fall, as in Sophocles's 429 BC play *Oedipus Rex* (*Oedipus Tyrannus*), but its meaning, usage, and importance extended far beyond this one context.[50] In our times, that hubris takes the form of knowingness, a kind of know-it-all attitude infusing the excesses of Information Age boosterism and of technocracy, rule by technologically expert elites. The premium on specialized information erodes traditional sources of wisdom by displacing the common, conventional, and historical bases of truth claims that allow everyone to be part of the conversation about our collective fate. Some of the privileged, from CEOs to celebrities at the top of economic, social, and political hierarchies, but also hate groups of all kinds share the belief that only their worldview is the correct one. Without agreement on standards of truth, such as logic and evidence, and with technologies that spread memes at the speed of light, conspiracy theories become what passes for knowledge. This is not knowledge but *gnosis*.

Gnosticism is an expression not of unity but of division. We can see this in the notions of a cosmic drama between good and evil, a divine spark in some people and not others, and *gnosis* as knowledge that comes to an elite few. In science fiction and film this makes for a thrilling adventure. In real life, it is cause for concern.

WAKE UP!

In Plato's allegory of the cave, human beings en masse sit in darkness in chains in a cave, watching the movement of what they think are real objects in the world but are actually merely shadows cast on the cave wall. Those who are dragged or later venture outside the cave are struck with illumination as they encounter the real world. In Gnostic lore, human beings similarly trudge through a world of illusion, and those few who wake up to that reality are struck with illumination. In both cases, human beings wake up. The difference lies in what they wake up to. Plato's cave dwellers wake up to an unparalleled vision as they grasp the beauty and goodness of the real world and their knowledge of it as a unity.[51] The Gnostic humans wake up to an unparalleled vision as they grasp the evil of the real world and their special knowledge that will save them. They wake up to a better existence not rooted in the real world, which proves to be nothing but an illusion. The difference between awakening to the real world in a state of Platonic wonder and awakening to an unreal world in a state of Gnostic knowingness could not be more stark. The first roots spiritual goodness in the physical world, the second abandons rootedness altogether.

New Agers preach 1960s authenticity as if they were born yesterday. Calls to "wake up" have the repetition featured in *Groundhog Day*.[52] In this movie, a cynical and snobbish weatherman, Phil Connors (Bill Murray), finds himself stuck in a time loop after being assigned to cover the annual first appearance of the groundhog Punxsutawney Phil in the small town in Pennsylvania that the animal is named after. At first, he embraces the chance to replay the prior day so that he can have another occasion to woo news producer Rita (Andie McDowell). He botches his second chance, too, and his third, and on it goes until he realizes he must be stuck in an endless loop, for each time his alarm clock rings he finds he must wake up and live the same day over and over forever. Spoiler alert: he wakes up in the end. While the ubiquity of the "Wake Up!" call in our New Age even puts *Groundhog Day* on some lists of Gnostic movies, this iconic movie has the protagonist wake up to embrace ordinary life through contrition and redemption and thus dovetails with traditional world religions from Buddhism to Christianity and Judaism, as critics and viewers have noted.[53]

It is no wonder our times are so ripe for conspiracies, claims of special knowledge, and the hubris of elite insiders. The prospect of technology as the new deliverer of the ultimate therapies we need brings all of these themes to a terrifying culmination in movements that unironically argue for the human mind merging with computers, robotic replacements of people in the workplace, and artificial intelligence outliving planetary disaster. Those wealthy enough—and Gnostic enough—to do so are supposedly busy building underground mansions that will allow them to survive a nuclear holocaust.[54]

Transhumanists take modern therapies to a new level in envisioning the ways to enlist science and technology not only to heal the sick and infirm but to augment the healthy human body and mind. In their dreams, innovations in robotics, genetic engineering, pharmaceuticals, and computing promise a new era of living beyond natural human limits. This means everything from bionic limbs and performance-enhancing drugs to "powered clothing," or exoskeletons that can propel the body, and memory chips embedded in the brain.[55] The website of the nonprofit think-tank Humanity Plus (aka Humanity+), originally called the World Transhumanist Association, cofounded by Nick Bostrom, touts well-being enhancement as a new frontier, declaring that "we want people to be better than well."[56]

Posthumanists, by some definitions, take the transhumanist project of physical enhancement to its logical extreme in imagining that machines with artificial intelligence may eventually replace humanity. Assuming the inevitability of human extinction, some advocates push for investment in technologies they even conceive of as superior replacements for humans (though some posthumanists call this antihumanist and admit to worries about the risks of misuse of the new technologies).[57] Both posthumanism and transhumanism share an underlying assumption of the inefficiency of the human body in the face of the benefits of future technology and exuberance about technology's potential to transform life for the better.

Inventor and writer Raymond Kurzweil has helped popularize the notion of the "singularity," which forecasts that technological intelligence will merge with and surpass human intelligence by the middle of the twenty-first century. For Kurzweil, who has worked at Google since 2012, domination of the universe by artificial intelligence is a desirable and natural stage of human civilization.[58] Kurzweil and billionaire venture capitalist Peter Thiel support the cryogenic storing of human bodies, including their own, in facilities such as the Alcor Life Extension Foundation in Arizona, so that they can later benefit from advancing technology when they are thawed.[59] Posthumanism takes the Gnostic vision of waking up elsewhere quite literally.

Fittingly, in this technological dystopia, a figure central in Gnostic lore, Sophia, has reappeared as a real-life robot. In Gnosticism, everything from the feminine part of the soul to the bride of Christ, and light emanated from God but now fallen, she has helped create the evil material world.[60] In our world, Sophia, developed by Hanson Robotics in Hong Kong, is a robot who can feign a range of human emotions. The company's founder David Hanson explains that, at the "intersection of humanity and technology," Sophia shows "that technology can enhance humanity, help us actualize to higher states of being."[61]

The ultimate irony of New Age Gnosticism lies in its enthusiasts' claims to health and holism. Another figure—Sophia was also the Greek goddess of wisdom—appropriated by the movement is Gaia (alternatively spelled "Ge"—hence, "geology"). (See fig. 1.4.) Often portrayed in art coming out of the earth as part of it, holding out her infant to place in the hands of Athena for adoption, Gaia is the mother goddess of Earth. According to Greek mythology, she was the first goddess to be born after the primeval void emerged (Chaos). Her many children include the mountains, Uranus (the sky), and Pontus (the sea), as well as various monsters and races of gods.[62] Literally no one could less serve the self-avowed dualism at the heart of Gnosticism. Plato, in his *Timaeus*, presents the *anima mundi*, or World Soul, the idea that the entire universe is one living creature containing all other living creatures. This concept, linked to the myth of Gaia, informs the environmental scientists and others who entertain the "Gaia hypothesis." The idea that all organic and inorganic matter is connected, that human life and society are intrinsically connected to the life of the earth and the physical universe, has inspired efforts for sustainability and stewardship of the land and ecosystem.[63] Whether one agrees or not, one must concede that this is holism and not dualism. In a work that fuses the environmental and feminist movements alike, Rosemary Radford Reuther envisions the goddess as consistent with Christian spirituality.[64] Gaia is clearly not Gnostic. To suggest as much reflects a gross misunderstanding and underestimation of her mythical, spiritual, and poetic importance as consummate earth mother. Symbols of female wisdom and creativity, Sophia and Gaia evoke the beauty and power of women's intellectual and bodily selves, as well as those of men, born of women.

GNOSTIC ARCHITECTURE

The grim spaces of the Gnostic imaginary are even mirrored in real-world architectural constructions. Eric Owen Moss calls his own buildings works of "Gnostic architecture." A close look at one of them, the Samitaur building in Los Angeles (really three coming together as a complex over the space of a city block), allows us to envision the New Gnosticism three-dimensionally. Overall, Gnostic architecture does not seem much different from postmodernism. It forsakes tradition, history, and custom and proclaims a radical break from the past. It shares with postmodernism a propensity for pastiches, randomness, asymmetry, borderline chaos. It is not complete chaos because it must still use time-tested techniques and structures and meet needs of use according to current customs (or market use): stairs, party rooms, place to park. Some elements are striking because they are reminiscent of values that mattered in the past, such as grandeur. But they live off capital from the past, having nothing to refer to now. Moss touts the Samitaur as "progenitor of a new and renewed urban conception," "as much an attitude toward city planning" as anything.[65] In a spread of full-page color photographs, the building appears alienating and even scary. The sizes and spaces are vast—all out of proportion to a single individual, as though built for a herd of dinosaurs. Reminiscent of the facelessness of modern fascist and post-riot US architecture, which sought to discourage group gatherings and keep people separated in their own worlds, its message is: you are alone.

Moss's building is Gnostic in the sense of hewing to a different cosmology, one that requires a specialized expertise to understand. It looks impersonal, cold, prison-like, industrial, shabby, disjunctive, and instantly dated with shades of an abandoned factory. It shrieks of atheist secularism, the absence of God. At times grandeur and the spirit break through, as in the juxtaposition of beams, glass, and ceiling, partly because of the sky, the beauty of the natural materials themselves, and the accidental suggestions of other styles of enduring aesthetic appeal—California style and Arts and Crafts, for example. It has blank windows, dark doorways to nowhere, stripped-down hallways, and uninviting entryways. Its subject is nothing.

Those vistas make it almost worthy of attention but reveal the imploding of our spiritual imagination as it seems the only divinity being celebrated is humans' own industry—a monument of the hubris of the industrial age. In that sense it is true to the times, as though dedicated to showing what we can do, with no sense of human limits or acknowledgment that we are not gods. It is almost eclipsed by the sky because there is no way to get around the beauty of the cosmos when our eye is directed to it. The triumph of the industrial age is the redirected sight, from such wonders to TV and computer screens, ersatz windows. Big indoor expanses look like airport terminals—nondescript, warehouse style. Sometimes an element catches the eye, but as you follow it further it ends in disappointment, as the message always seems to be: Ha! Fooled you—you thought this would end somewhere different.

The Gnostic aesthetic appears to be in love with none other than itself—and not even the being imagining it but the creativity deracinated from an embodied being and a particular lived context. All such particulars are wiped away, as though in an attempt to wipe the slate clean—of memory, of accumulated experience, of the warmth of life, of the hot mess of teeming humanity.

Buildings stand rigid as so many ruins of a civilization that never came into existence yet is somehow already past. This is the postindustrial sublime, with many elements once considered inner, private, and behind the scenes, purely instrumental or service-oriented, now made prominent—from steel grates to girders, screws and bolts, steel support beams, flanges, light fixtures, wires. An apt symbol of the see-all, bare-all age, it is a building turned inside out.

As a composition it falls short, as it randomly acquiesces to older forms, such as square or rectangular windows, while pushing boundaries with the rest, so the areas of departure look like wounds. Some elements even suggest violence—like chandeliers that look like clusters of gigantic bullets or small missiles.

The architect Moss expressly calls his style Gnostic architecture. His book by that name presents a combination of informal sketches and drawings, from pages torn from a retro hotel memo pad for recording telephone messages to full-page photographs of the final product. It is difficult to make out precisely what Moss means by *Gnostic*. He presents the book in the style of a celebrity's notebooks as memoir, ostensibly putting forth and defending an architectural approach without feeling any real responsibility to defend it with logic or argumentation or even illustration. It is equal parts genius notebook and coffee-table book, self-advertisement and scrapbook. Its stream of consciousness reads almost like parody. Strewn through its pages is a kind of intellectual pastiche, making the whole a collage of illustration and text. He begins by quoting Percy Bysshe Shelley's *Ozymandias*, the Greek name (Ὀσυμανδύας) for the Egyptian pharaoh Ramesses II. In that famous poem, the ruins of a once colossal statue crumble—"Two vast and trunkless legs of stone / Stand in the desert. Near them, on the sand, / Half sunk, a shattered visage lies"—symbol of the inevitable twilight of even the greatest civilizations and human constructions. The poem imagines Ozymandias, "king of kings," commanding to a passerby, "Look on my works, ye mighty, and despair!"[66]

The book actually ends up revealing limits to Moss's Gnosticism. In a discussion of Akira Kurosawa's *Rashomon*, a movie that tells a series of events from the vantage point of several different narrators, Moss points out that Kurosawa did not necessarily rule impossible a narrative that gets closer to the truth. Moss even questions the knowingness pose of much new architectural work while failing to explain the difference between his own efforts and those he criticizes. He says he wants to go beyond the "'techno' cheerleading" and "self-confidence turned to arrogance" of modernism and faults "the avant-garde" for its vanity.[67] Yet his distance from Gnosticism and its hubris does not win out. Particular schools of thought, from the New Urbanism to Deconstructionism and Neominimalism, do not appeal to him because they "miss the point that there are always useful contradicting points" (1.3). Instead, he prefers Gnosticism, for which he goes on to give his own gloss: "Gnostic architecture is autobiographical. The thesis originates in my efforts over a number of years to provide an explanation for the world in which I (strangely) find myself. The intention is to avoid any dependence on questions of technique or technology. I am not concerned with accounting for building as a consequence of site circumstances. The process of developing the Gnostic argument requires stripping away every kind of empirical dependency that has been previously used to explain why buildings are what buildings are" (1.3). He tries to capture a "balanced imbalance," an "intellectual dialectic," a tension or contradiction that is then resolved with something "not answerable to empirical logic," more in the realm of lyric. Architecture should not "ratify a consensus view of what's real" but "should rearrange the consensus" (1.4).

"To move forward architecturally I have to erase something that was previously present," Moss writes. For instance, in approaching building in an existing location, the Plaza Vieja in Havana, Cuba, "I couldn't come reverentially to the Plaza Vieja and say 'I love Spanish colonial architecture'" (1.6). His projects attempt a deliberate intervention in history, modeled on psychology, looking both backward and forward. So in Havana, he writes, "I had to be prepared to contest the old plaza but still acknowledge that it is part of a continuum—be conscious of each era's belief systems and their incompleteness. We can't master it all—neither the arrogance of empirical progress nor the cynicism of retrogressive reverence will succeed. So Havana became the Plaza Vieja Nueva" (1.6). The irony of coming in from outside and renaming a place as a critique of arrogance seems to escape him. As of 2020, the Plaza shows the results of the decades-long revitalization of the city led by Havana's historian Eusebio Leal as a project of historical restoration and not Gnostic architecture, a route not taken. It still goes by Plaza Vieja.[68]

VITRUVIAN WOMAN

The Da Vinci Code purports to take the side of a cosmic feminine against the ostensible entrenched masculine culture of the last two millennia. It turns an awful, buried family secret, which traumatized a young girl and haunted her for all of her years as an adolescent and young adult, into a beautiful, understandable, normalized event. With its revelations, it claims to overthrow a noxious cultural regime that suppressed women and to elevate knowledge of the reality of religious belief as a deliberate fabrication, the result of a centuries-long conspiracy by the Roman Catholic Church. In doing so, it associates (one could say saddles) women with all sorts of things, including bizarre rites and rituals, if not orgiastic, then at least voyeuristic, all in the name of health and the beauty and wonder of the feminine. But these are strange grounds for the value of women. Gnosticism is known for its radical dualism, which pits mind against body. In its attempt to grab hold of an elusive, receding embodiment, it falls into a disordered relation of thought and feeling. In his *Confessions*, Augustine speaks of his wayward early years, including a flirtation with Manicheanism, a religion founded by Mani in Iran, which, though not identical to Gnosticism, shares its radical dualism. Gnosticism proudly parades the dualism mistakenly attributed to Platonism. Yet rather than see Gnosticism as dualistic, April DeConick, Dan Brown, and others cast it as fully embodied (or holistic) by association with the feminine.

So the real mystery of the *Da Vinci Code* is solved. The book exemplifies the contemporary therapeutic culture, reifying its rites and rights to celebrate with its own self-chosen rituals. The real Holy Grail found at the end of the book is the release of the individual from all strictures, judgments, and traditions. Ever new and improved, invented tradition offers freedom through personal choice. The content of the choice no longer matters, only our freedom to choose. The real Holy Grail is whatever is therapeutic. All desires earn its stamp of approval. It suggests that all that matters is that people find what is therapeutic to them. Not only do the ends justify the means, but the means justify the ends. The means is to be freed. The problem is that it is unclear what for. Therapy with no notion of what life the individual is undergoing therapy to return to amounts to therapy for therapy's sake.

Catherine Tumber identifies Gnostic elements prevalent among late nineteenth- and early twentieth-century spiritual reformers who pioneered the New Thought movement, a precursor to the mid- and late twentieth-century therapeutic movements, including the post-1960s human potential and New Age movements. To the New Thought spiritualists, "Jesus Christ's ministry was not based on redemptive love and forgiveness but on healing," to be achieved through imparting "divine knowledge to humanity," which in turn went so far as to plant in some people a seed of divinity.[69]

Yet Tumber argues that "to reduce New Thought to psychology, depriving it of its radical theological force," underestimates the way it "helped to upgrade 'Desire' to a metaphysical principle, or how it helped to recast the cosmological perspective from which one made sense of desire in context with other human deeds, principles, and emotions": New Thought "seeks nothing less than extreme detachment from the self and the world."[70] More than just a new self-concept compatible with modernity, it provided a complete worldview, with "a theology that regarded the material world as radically evil, the creation of a malevolent demiurge who intruded himself between man and the disembodied spirituality that they [Gnostics] maintained was the real God": "Salvation lay, therefore, in acquiring knowledge (gnosis) of the divine spark within—the fragment of uncreated spirit violently broken off from the divine estate—and learning how to master its mysterious forces. The ancient Gnostics held that this privilege was reserved for a special few given access to esoteric texts that preserved the secret wisdom of the ages. . . . The Gnostic's singular preoccupation is with the self and the cultivation of 'special powers' that enable one to execute a cosmic exit at will."[71] Tumber's pithy description beautifully encapsulates the Gnostic personality. To a list of its basic traits—elitism, detachment, self-divinity—we must add her emphasis on their belief in the possibility of "a cosmic exit." This is crucial in making sense of a variety of movements arising in the late twentieth and early twenty-first centuries such as posthumanism.

Talk of end times, cosmic exits, and salvation for the few is hardly new. It might be tempting to explain the current Gnostic obsession with the apocalyptic as a familiar refrain. It is. Yet scholars have noted that the apocalyptic was (and is) a Christian trope, infused by a belief in history as fulfilling spiritual purposes. The apocalyptic was distinctly Christian, not Gnostic. In a *New Re-*

public article on the brink of the third millennium, Anthony Grafton surveyed new scholarship on apocalyptic belief. Older scholarship, he surmised, lumped all apocalyptic thought into one big tradition. In reviewing recent works, he praised them for their identification of different strands but found them wanting in another way: they seemed to lack historical empathy. He suggests instead that we ask why people are so drawn to such visions. He locates the reason in our overarching interest in time, drawing a difference between a lively, engaged drama and a disengaged, rationalistic view that lacks the warmth of human passion.[72]

The therapeutic quest for cures, whether personal or political, closes off the real conversation, which has room to flourish only when we admit there are no cures to life other than living. The conversation is about how to live and must always be open-ended by definition as long as we are alive. Only when we die do we no longer need to think about it. It goes on through life because each minute brings demands and possibilities we cannot predict by virtue of being human. All "posthuman" approaches and others that deny our limits lack intellectual humility and miss the point of the *unfolding* of life. All the evidence is never in. Therapeutic regimens replace our seeking of meaning with a quest for the quelling of anxieties, doubts, and all else that gives momentum to our seeking and makes it urgent. Social engineering can result from the hubris of those who think they know the answers to our greatest life questions because their next step is to try to make everyone else agree. Those who have not conformed are forced or coerced, often via a detour through the therapeutic. And meanwhile those basking in the warm glow of their special knowledge prepare their path to survival—with room enough for themselves alone.

The debate over *The Da Vinci Code* is a microcosm of the larger culture wars, which devolve all too easily into showdowns between atheism and religion that do not serve us well. In these battles, criticism of the therapeutic seems to imply right-wing criticism of the welfare state. A whole host of attitudes and dispositions have hardened into an ossified dichotomy between a version of society that normalizes aggression and an anything-goes version that is often characterized by a heightened sense of victimization.

The party of aggression invokes a pseudomasculine claim to small government, adopts the mantle of Stoicism, and preaches self-reliance. The anything-goes party projects a pseudofeminine claim to social welfare, veers toward Gnosticism, and preaches compassion. Yet they share certain assumptions. For both sides, social and political life has become a contest for power and control within a survivalist, health paradigm. No one side has a monopoly on the therapeutic, nor does either genuinely adhere to even its own presumptive values. Fact and principle are the first to topple in the race to the top, as the Right accepts welfare for big business and exploits a sense of victimization for demagogues and billionaires, and the Left accepts neoliberalist policies and multinational corporations in the guise of globalization and cosmopolitanism. There is a cost to leaving the discussion to the two sides in their extreme, drastic, and reductionist versions, and we see this being played out all too painfully on the national and even world stage. There are deeper questions of human existence that should not be politicized like this and large concerns about the *meaning* of life that *inform* politics but should not be reduced by it.

In the United States, the rise of movements of spirituality centered on the notion of the divine feminine coincided with second-wave feminism, as the influence of the women's movement reached into religious structures in the 1970s, critiquing their patriarchal frameworks. Drawing from traditional religions and New Age spiritualism alike, divine feminine spirituality has since seen various articulations and imaginings. In general, it imagines God either as simultaneously male and female or as dominantly feminine. In some cases, this movement of spirituality leads to a reassessment and elevation of historical religious women; in others, a rediscovery of ancient goddess religions.[73]

But modern adherents paper over any dualist tendencies. They elevate the feminine divine principle as a celebration rather than a renunciation of embodiment. In a Gnostic feminism, Western patriarchy is revealed as a hoax perpetrated by a massive church hierarchy, and its practices as a rejection of the body, represented in this way of thinking by the feminine spiritual principle. But a return to a philosophy that is, in its very constitution, antireality makes for a strained defense of embodiment. Rather than elevating women to equal standing with men, it lowers the importance of both and of ordinary life in general, paving the way for a trans-human and posthuman future. Modern Gnosticism ostensibly defends embodiment yet ends up undermining it by casting reality as nothing but an illusion.

An interest in what constitutes a good life presupposes an interest in ethics and in the common life of the community. Contempt for the real world and a desire to be free of it by acquiring privileged knowledge are the linchpin of the Gnostic view. From its vantage point, Gnostic dualism spells freedom because the cord between the spiritual and physical can be severed. The more the material world fades away, the farther out one gets in a Gnostic cosmos. Once the individual's spiritual life is deracinated in this way, there is no common basis for contemplating what a good life is, let alone trying to live one. Gnosticism gives no means to judge one way of life as better or worse than another. An inner journey without a viable and trusted outer world transforms the outer world into a purely interior phenomenon, where we harbor the illusion that reality exists. Only those privy to special knowledge can know anything about it.

Ultimately, Gnosticism is about giving up on life as it is. In its exploration of the idea that modern culture has persistent Gnostic tendencies, this chapter suggests the need of a real-life referent for explorations of the question of how to live. A Gnostic sensibility undercuts our yearnings for the good life in ways sometimes difficult to discern because it masquerades as our champion. It is also often mixed with other more benign approaches. Here, this chapter shows the need for a valuing of embodiment and for real-life referents for spiritual life. Later, chapter 5 will argue for the need for transcendent ideals for real, embodied life.

Gnosticism contributes to the embodiment crisis of our times. Finding a way to live within our bodies and inhabit our world is a much different goal from that of the Gnostics, who explicitly give up on it. Yet navigating this world is the primary human project. Successful navigation relies on a basic faith and trust in this world's existence—no matter how great the all-too-real evils of this world.

A sense of reality requires a belief in its goodness, or at least its capacity for goodness.

Discounting the real world contributes little to countering the instability of our times. Presenting a virtual world as real does us no favors. It exacerbates feelings of this world as illusory in a dangerous way and adds to the isolation of the individual. The logical end of the current trajectory is multiple fiefdoms of one, each with its own version of reality to suit each sovereign's wants and needs. As a kind of collective psychosis, Gnosticism offers no viable way forward and no way to live in the meantime. Fantasies of personal perfection through endless rounds of elective surgery, cryogenics, and other transhumanist, hubristic acts eclipse modest pursuits at once more realistic and more idealistic, deeply rooted in our animal beings and our spiritual traditions.

Fantasy for the sake of fantasy, fiction that knows its own fictive nature and does not mistake itself for reality, plays a major role in our moral imagination. But to perpetuate no-way-out-but-another-world-altogether scenarios—to peddle the idea that real life is an illusion, particularly in an era of the very real phenomenon of the virtual world of the internet, has at times disastrous real-world consequences.

We are living on borrowed time. Reinvigorating an earlier conversation can allow us to recover the other "more radical answers of man to his predicament," as Voegelin called them, which have historically given Gnosticism a run for its money. We currently have a plentitude of dark answers to the art of living—which amount to an abundance of nonanswers. We need real answers, no matter how ever-changing, debated, and provisional. Always, tentative attempts surpass no answers at all.

The Gnostic is so entwined with the therapeutic culture that the two often seem to be one and the same. Thus critiques of the therapeutic culture often include its Gnostic tendencies as one of the reasons it steers us wrong. While Gnostic entertainments can be engrossing, and caricatures and satirical treatments of the therapeutic sensibility can be serious or hilarious, it is easy to downplay how crucial it is that we understand how much hangs in the balance. Perhaps the stakes of the age of therapy are more visible if we begin to call it the Triumph of the New Gnostic Therapeutic. But the therapeutic culture is more varied than this—other sensibilities also offer themselves in the larger therapeutic culture. They might look like alternatives to the new Gnosticism yet might have more in common as they are all part of the therapeutic or risk being hijacked by it.

FIFTY SHADES OF PINK

We might be surprised to find Gnostic themes not just in dark black and white and shades of grimmest gray but in bright pink. The easily recognizable hue of the cult of the princess is splashed across bookstore shelves, toy aisles, bedroom walls, and beyond: bubble gum meets Pepto-Bismol in an altogether new shade we might dub princess pink. It is doubtful whether swathing ourselves head to toe and floor to ceiling in princess pink can transform a cultural landscape made dismal by the ugliest "50 shades of grey."[74] With friends of the feminine like Dan Brown, who needs enemies?[75] Why do we have to tell our little girls they are princesses to make them feel happy, fulfilled, or valued? If we are relying on the likes of *The Da Vinci Code* and other Gnostic fantasies for a kind of New Age therapy, we are in deep trouble. Only in a cultural landscape in which the real world, with all it has to offer, complete with its shortfalls and limits and struggles, no longer matters would anything like that be remotely necessary. Otherwise, the infinite, endless, and uncategorizable allure of sheer human existence, once our basic needs are met, always, as ever, will more than suffice.

THE NEW
STOICISM

The manifestation of the wind of thought is not
knowledge; it is the ability to tell right from wrong,
beautiful from ugly.

—Hannah Arendt

SPQR. Few sets of initials have had, even in times and places far
removed from ancient Rome, such resonance. They still do.[1] In the
2001 movie *Gladiator*, we encounter those four famous letters tat-
tooed on the muscular bicep of the protagonist hero, Maximus,
played by Russell Crowe. (See fig. 2.1.) Then, before too long, in
one brief scene we find him removing that same tattoo—himself.

In earlier camera shots, with the ink acronym as focal point, we
see the SPQR on his arm go from proud symbol to seething wound.
Originally branded with the tattoo as a soldier in the Roman le-
gion, Maximus had advanced to the position of Roman general,
seen leading his men to glory at the start of the movie. He had

proven himself so worthy that a dying emperor Marcus Aurelius (Richard Harris), who loved him as a son, had just beseeched him to be his successor. But circumstances have changed. The assassination of Marcus by his own son, Commodus (Joaquin Phoenix), put that lesser man in the position of emperor, and Maximus refused to continue to serve under the new corrupt regime. Plagued by festering jealousy toward Maximus, always Marcus's favorite, Commodus ordered Maximus to be hunted down and executed. Maximus managed to escape this fate but was wounded and captured, and he now finds himself in the ranks of enslaved men to be trained as a gladiator.

In the initial training exercises, a dejected and dispirited Maximus refuses to play along. When an experienced gladiator strikes Maximus with a sword, he just stands there, refusing to fight back. He absorbs the pain and eventually falls to his knees from the strength of the blows.

Afterward, the camera finds him sitting in a dark corner, where just a fire and candle flames flicker in the background. At first it is a peaceful sight, with Maximus now at rest on a kind of window seat, with the crumbling stone around the window behind him evoking timeless ruins, and ceramic bowls stacked neatly at his feet. A closer view shows him preoccupied with the tattoo on his arm, now dripping with the dark burgundy of his own blood. Juba (Djimon Hounsou), an African fellow gladiator in the process of befriending him, emerges from the shadows, with the gentle query, "Why don't you fight? We all have to fight." Panning back to Maximus, the camera shows him cutting his own flesh with a sharp object to remove his tattoo. His face twitches with an almost imperceptible flinch. A closeup shows that only the Q and the R are still visible next to the bloody wound. He looks at the other man as though awakened from a trance. Juba moves closer, squinting his eyes to look at the gash. Maximus applies more pressure, the flesh ripples slightly, and blood oozes red and black. Juba asks, "Is it the sign of your gods?" Marcus exhales a silent hiccup of a laugh as brief as the frisson of pain. The other man continues, "Will that not anger them?" Maximus gives the slightest of nods and goes back to work on his flesh. A sudden spirt of bright red blood gushes forth onto a white background, but it turns out to be the hairy back of an ox—just a filmmaker's trickery of juxtaposition, a surprise start to a new scene.

The ox belongs to a general ordered confusion, a raucous procession to the arena of animals, audience, and gladiators. Through buildings, branches of trees, and banners of shredded cloth glows a red light, as though everything is infused by blood. The slave owner and trainer Proximo (Oliver Reed, who sadly died during the filming of the movie) speaks to the gladiators before sending them out, possibly to their deaths: "Some of you are thinking you won't fight, some that you can't fight. . . . Ultimately we're all dead men. Sadly we cannot choose how, but we can decide how to meet that end in order that we are remembered as men." Maximus decides to fight. Side by side with Juba, he proves his own proficiency as gladiator and comrade. As Maximus rises to glory as a gladiator, the plot continues.

SPQR is an abbreviation for *Senātus Populusque Rōmānus* (the Roman Senate and People). It has also come to be a kind of shorthand for Stoicism.

A CHANGE IN MOOD

In a 1991 article in *Harper's Magazine* entitled "Victims, All?" journalist and social critic David Rieff marveled that a country as rich as the modern, industrialized, consumer-driven US could exhibit signs of what might seem to outsiders as complete emotional crisis: "Imagine a country in which millions of apparently successful people nonetheless have come to believe fervently that they are really lost souls—a country where countless adults allude matter-of-factly to their 'inner children,' who, they say, lie wounded and in desperate need of relief within the wreckage of their grown-up selves. Imagine the celebrities and opinion-makers among these people talking nightly on TV and weekly in the magazines not about their triumphs but about their victimization, not about their power and fame but about their addictions and childhood persecutions."[2]

Rieff did not discount all-too-real cases of abuse and suffering but instead pointed to an overall mood in the culture he found deeply troubling. As suggested in the Introduction of this book, this has become a kind of therapeutic paradox. We can see that this mood he describes, although it concerns individual therapy and well-being, can become a limiting approach that does not seem to help people with the very problems it claims to address. Rather, it can suspend them in a state of insecurity and excessive self-concern.

David Rieff questioned statistics bandied about by self-help gurus who have everything to gain from inflating them. Dr. Charles Whitfield, author of the recovery movement classic *Healing the Child Within: Discovery and Recovery for Adult Children of Dysfunctional Families* (1987), claimed that only about 5 to 20 percent of Americans manage to come from healthy homes. Rieff noted that groups taking the twelve-step approach pioneered by Alcoholics Anonymous had proliferated to include every imaginable source of distress, from grave concerns like incest and drug abuse all the way to chronic lateness and "taking too much interest in some activity" such as sex or work. This had reached the point where "any conduct that can be engaged in enthusiastically, never mind compulsively—from stamp collecting to the missionary position—would be one around which a recovery group could presumably be organized."[3]

In faulting Americans for falling prey to the ministrations of self-help gurus and pop psychology, David Rieff pointed to the embrace of victimization as a counterproductive tendency within the late twentieth-century therapeutic culture. The general feeling of helplessness troubled him but even more the particular form that helplessness took: an inability or unwillingness to deal with *emotion*. This emotional incompetence and a kind of dependency that resulted from it became a self-fulfilling prophecy for those who lacked both the confidence and the conviction that simply coping on their own was an option. As an antidote, in Rieff's view, we might turn to a renewal of a more Stoic approach to the challenges of everyday life.

David Rieff has not stood alone in prescribing Stoicism for what ails Americans. A kind of Greek chorus has arisen in numerous genres and forms, sounding a common call for a return to a more Stoic approach to life. At first listen, one can easily dismiss this New Stoicism as merely the latest of the evanescent and eminently replaceable fads in the self-help culture. But when we add to the list of lightweight titles, venues, and expressions the work of scholars in disciplines like philosophy, history, and classics, as well as novelists, filmmakers, and journalists, it is worth taking a second glance. What should we make of the salience of Stoicism—such an ancient school of philosophical thought—in the recent and contemporary West?

To what extent does this new form of Stoicism represent a departure from or a genuine alternative to the therapeutic? On the surface it might seem counterintuitive that Stoicism would come forth as a viable option right now. In everyday language, we use the word *stoic* to describe strength in the face of adversity and the overcoming of emotion. While the therapeutic culture as well as the triumph of a consumerist ethos and entertainment culture would seem to be its very opposites, in the last couple of decades the shelves of self-help sections of bookstores and libraries, to say nothing of Amazon listings, have seen a noticeable presence of works suggesting a revival of interest in this particular way of approaching the enduring question of how to live. Here are some examples of the plethora of books that have appeared: *Don't Worry, Be Stoic: Ancient Wisdom for Troubled Times*, by Peter J. Vernezze; *The Stoic Art of Living: Inner Resilience and Outer Results*, by Tom Morris; *Everything Has Two Handles: The Stoic's Guide to the Art of Living*, by Ronald Pies; and *Stoic Serenity: A Practical Course on Finding Inner Peace*, by Keith Seddon.[4] To get a sense of the contours of the movement, let us now look briefly at the movement as a whole, then turn to linger on two recent direct calls for a New Stoicism and some artifacts of today's movement.

Today's revival of Stoicism seems at first glance to be little more than a coinciding of a few novels and movies, nothing more than a small presence of the theme in popular culture. But the further one looks, the larger this presence looms. Tom Wolfe's best-selling 1998 novel *A Man in Full*, with its prolonged exploration of the theme, undoubtedly increased interest in and awareness of Stoicism.[5] One of the book's main characters, Conrad Hensley, in prison with nothing to read except Epictetus, becomes a Stoic himself. *A Man in Full* received hundreds of reviews in every outlet imaginable and immediately upon publication even spurred the purchase of hundreds of copies of an expensive version of Epictetus's *Discourses*.[6] *Gladiator* grossed $187,705,427 and won five Academy Awards, including for best picture and best actor (Russell Crowe), and received notice in numerous articles, many of them concerning its Stoic themes.[7] The adulation of John McCain, upon his death on August 25, 2018, offered a brief cease-fire in the political skirmishes rending the nation. People of all political persuasions and walks of life joined together to mourn as a fallen hero a man whose endurance during over five years as a prisoner of war earned him the designation of modern-day Stoic in the eyes of millions.[8]

British journalist Jules Evans has remarked perceptively on the role of Stoicism in American politics in the early aughts. Policy director at the Center for the History of Emotions at the University of London, and an organizer of the popular London Philosophy Club, he ran an article on his website entitled "The Re-birth of Stoicism" in 2012.[9] The article highlighted several prominent Stoic-related ventures, including Stoic Week, an international event launched that same year at the UK's Exeter University and held regularly since.[10] Evans's website, philosophyforlife.org, follows various trends in philosophy and popular culture, with an eye toward classical influences and "the revival of philosophy as a practical way of life."[11] Evans and other scholars, such as psychotherapist Donald Robertson, have also traced the link between Stoicism and cognitive behavioral therapy—perhaps the dominant form of talk therapy in use today—pioneered by Albert Ellis.[12]

In his engaging book *Philosophy for Life and Other Dangerous Situations*, published in 2012, Evans profiles several schools of thought. For his chapters on Stoicism, he interviewed several people who consider themselves significantly influenced by Stoicism, such as Major Thomas Jarrett, who teaches "Stoic warrior resilience." There is a visible presence of Stoics online, to which Evans steers readers of his website and book. The virtual world of Stoics today includes an email list, a Facebook group, and websites such as The Stoic Registry (for a time called New Stoa), Modern Stoicism, The Stoic Place, The Stoic Life, and The Stoic Library.[13] The Stoic Registry, "the Online Stoic Community," as it calls itself, has maintained a registry of people who identify themselves as Stoics since May 8, 1996, by 2020 listing 3,176 members from all over the world. Its website offers a free newsletter as well as a "College of Stoic Philosophers" with online courses and certificates upon graduation.[14] While these offerings can be of mixed quality and degrees of comprehensiveness, many operate on a serious intellectual plane. They join a number of scholars who not only study Stoicism as a historical phenomenon but promote it as a school of philosophical thought they think is still relevant today.

ANCIENT STOICISM

In broad brushstrokes for our use here, we will draw on overviews provided by prominent scholars in the field to recall some of the key questions the Stoics found compelling, then delve a bit deeper into the implications of their larger philosophical views for individual behavior, especially regarding emotion. Stoicism emerged as an intellectual force in Greek philosophical thought in the fourth and third centuries BC, named after the *stoa poikilê* or porch adorned with murals where like-minded Hellenistic philosophers used to congregate in the agora in Athens. The philosophers of the Old Stoa, from whom no complete works survive, only fragments and references in later works, included the first three heads of the school and their students: the "founder," Zeno of Citium in Cyprus (344–262 BC); Cleanthes (d. 232 BC); and Chrysippus (d. ca. 206 BC). Founded around 300 BC, the school continued until the start of the first century BC. Although Athens declined as a center of philosophy at that point, Greek Stoics remained influential, including in Rome, which became the new center of Stoicism in the mid- to late first century BC, the time of Marcus Cato, Cato the Younger (95–46 BC), and Cicero (106–43 BC).[15]

The main period of Roman Stoicism came in the first and second centuries AD. Seneca, philosopher and tragic playwright of late antiquity, lived from around 4 BC to AD 65. Born in Corduba (what is now Córdoba or Cordova, Spain) and educated in Rome, he has come down to us as one of the most important of the ancient Stoic thinkers. In this he is joined by Epictetus (ca. AD 55–135), the ex-slave who became a leading Stoic philosopher of the early second century, author of the *Discourses* and, stemming from them, the *Encheiridion*, a manual or handbook for Stoic living. Completing the triumvirate is Marcus Aurelius (AD 121–80), emperor of Rome from AD 161 to 180 and author of the *Meditations*, his diary, also called *To Himself.* While only fragments remain from the Hellenistic Stoic philosophers, entire original works by these later Imperial Stoics have survived.

While these names are perhaps those most familiar to modern ears, ancient Greek and Roman Stoicism stretched well beyond the writings of this handful of philosophers. And in their work alone, as we might guess, a great deal of variation arose in the interpretation of even what are considered key Stoic tenets. Here, we can only refer briefly to some of those complexities, pointing to some central themes and debates to keep in mind, to suggest how they might help us begin to think about the New Stoicism.

In *The Cambridge Companion to the Stoics*, David Sedley lays out the basic contours of the founding and development of this school of thought in ancient Greece. Influenced by, although dissenting significantly from, existing schools, currents, and methods such as Platonism, Aristotelianism, and Cynicism, the first Stoics coalesced around Zeno and were, in fact, originally called Zenonians. Born at Citium in Cyprus, a Hellenized Phoenician city, Zeno moved to Athens at age twenty-two to study with the philosophers practicing there in the living tradition of Socrates, and he remained there until his death. Not necessarily systematic in his philosophical thinking, Zeno developed what Sedley calls "a distinctive Cynical orientation." He was a powerful intellectual influence and source of inspiration in the emergence of Stoicism, which went on to take its place as "the dominant school of the Hellenistic Age." The Stoics' "ethical system," in Sedley's astonishingly efficient wording, was "characterized by its intellectualist identification of goodness with wisdom and the consequent elimination of non-moral 'goods' as indifferent."[16]

In summarizing some of the major intellectual influences on Zeno, as far as they can be determined, Sedley raises a fascinating difference of opinion. Like other Stoics, Zeno was influenced not just by their philosophical abstractions but by the actual early Cynics, who were known for rebelling against social norms and conventions. The Cynics believed, in the tradition of Socrates, in "the moral indifference of such conventional values as reputation and wealth." Zeno's teachers included Polemo, then head of the Academy, and the philosopher Stilpo. While Palemo allowed room for physical as well as intellectual goods, Stilpo argued that nothing having to do with the physical realm could be considered good or bad. Zeno's thought drew from both sides of this debate. As Sedley tells us,

> In this synthesis of his teachers' contrasting positions, we can already glimpse the makings of the most distinctive Stoic thesis of all. For according to Zeno and his successors, bodily and external advantages such as health and wealth are not goods—Stilpo was right about that—but they are, on the other hand, natural objects of pursuit. We should, therefore, in normal circumstances, seek to obtain them, not caring about them as if their possession would make our lives any better, but on the ground that by preferring them we are developing our skills at "living in agreement with nature," the natural "end" whose attainment amounts to perfect rationality, happiness, and a good life.[17]

Zeno's position differed from that of fellow first-generation Stoic Aristo of Chios, whose Socratic-Cynic leanings led him to argue against Zeno on a key point. Zeno held that bodily and external advantages can be ranked by order of preference, even though he accepted their status as morally "indifferent." Aristo, along with many Stoics after him, maintained that these physical factors could not be preferable, one over the other, because they had no ethical standing.[18] Since physical states were neither morally bad nor good, there was no basis for judging one better than the other.

Christopher Gill, in his overview of Roman Imperial Stoic thought in the same volume, defends this later period against a widespread assumption that it was less original and creative, characterized by a narrower focus on ethics and "practical moralizing" based on centuries-old teachings and by an unfocused eclecticism. In fact, Gill sees Stoicism as a serious intellectual force in the first and second centuries AD in Imperial Rome. It was then the dominant movement in philosophy, and a major foundation stone of the ensuing movements of Neoplatonism and early Christian thought. He emphasizes the degree to which Stoicism played a vital role in the cultural milieu of Roman elites, who drew on it when thinking about moral decisions and behavior in the political arena. For example, Musonius Rufus (ca. AD 30–100) was a major Stoic teacher, as was his student Epictetus, whose advice to Roman elites Gill calls a "'tough' version of Stoicism." Gill suggests that this view, which "de-emphasizes the role of selecting 'preferable' advantages in ethical life and which favors the austere Cynic ideal rather than the practice of virtue within more conventional lifestyles," harkens back more to Aristo than to Zeno or Chrysippus, the third head of the school.[19] This crucial difference between Zenonian and "tough" Aristo-style Stoicism is an essential nuance in the traditions of both Stoicism and Cynicism itself.

Stoicism was indebted to Socratic and Cynic influences for its commitment to *nature* over the *conventions* of the Greek *polis*. According to Brad Inwood, the concepts of nature and reason lay at the heart of Stoicism, and "its most important conviction was that they converge."[20] But this was not the modern dichotomy of nature versus culture or body versus mind with which we are familiar now. Nature is "rational, explicable, and purposive," and the happiness of the rational human being is to "live according to nature," in Diogenes Laertius's phrase.[21] Stoic philosophy had a tripartite structure, falling under the rubrics of logic, physics, and ethics yet resting on the connections among them. In logic, both rhetoric and dialectic were means toward truth, knowledge, and the eradication of error and falsehood. The sense "impression" was fundamentally important and held to be reliable by the early Stoics, unlike the (then skeptical) Academy.[22] In physics, which included religion, the universe was thought to be "a living being made and governed by a rational god," as in Plato's *Timaeus*, with the difference being that the Stoics thought the divine was both "immanent and material."[23]

The precise meaning and interrelation of these tenets were matters of contestation among Stoics and targets for outright opposition from outside their ranks. Yet generally the school is understood as having tendencies toward naturalism, moralism, materialism, and rationalism. Their thought was also teleological. For Stoics, humans' purpose and that of the cosmos coincided. In ethics, Stoics shared the Socratic tradition's commitment to *eudaemonia* as the goal of human life—a form of human flourishing they deemed the fulfillment of human nature. Since all nature is rational, and the ultimate form of reason is virtue, only attainment of virtue through living according to reason will truly fulfill an individual's life.[24]

Upon this philosophical basis, Stoics constructed a theory and method of decision-making designed to allow for a life lived according to the dictates of reason. Problem-solving rested on a fundamental dichotomy they saw in the value of things, not simply between the moral categories of good and bad, but within each of these categories. Only those things that had to do directly with virtue could fall in the category of the good. The rest, assumed by the average person to be good, were thus mere "advantages." Likewise, the only truly bad things were so because they lacked virtue, so matters such as ill-health or lack of wealth were only "disadvantages," not something bad. Stoics cast advantages and disadvantages as things that could be only "preferred" or "dispreferred" but that were at root "indifferents." Since even when a person possessed great advantages, he or she could put them to immoral uses, "only virtue was truly useful." Decision-making thus became a search for the underlying truth or knowledge of the situation and had to be rooted in nature. Determining which things were good, bad, or indifferent became the task of reason. Action that was virtuous was thus one and the same as action that led to happiness, or human flourishing. "Right action"—also called "appropriate"—was that which afterward "admits of a rational justification."[25]

EMOTION AS JUDGMENT

How would these views translate into guidelines for behavior? In his rich and complex study *Emotion and Peace of Mind: From Stoic Agitation to Christian Temptation* (2000), Richard Sorabji describes the application of Stoic insights about the self in decision-making, which centered on a particular view of emotion. He writes, "It was the Stoic Chrysippus (ca. 280–206 BC) who developed the standard Stoic view on what emotion is. . . . In Chrysippus' view, all emotion consists of two judgments. There is the judgment that there is good or bad (benefit or harm) at hand, and the judgment that it is appropriate to react in ways which he specifies precisely."[26] If we accept a view of emotions as judgments, we realize that we are able to give or withhold assent, and this allows us to have more control of both the more troubling types of emotions and the extremes of even desirable ones. While not all Stoics were in agreement, Sorabji argues that "those who, like the Stoic Chrysippus, wanted to eradicate emotion hoped to eradicate not only the strong ones, but very nearly all."[27] Sorabji prefers the word *emotions* rather than *passions* for the Greek word *pathē* because in contemporary usage passion is considered very strong emotion, while the Stoics were concerned with all levels of intensity.[28] They identified four main emotions under which other emotions could be grouped (given in Greek, then Latin): "distress (*lupē, aegritudo*), pleasure (*hēdonē, laetitia*), fear (*phobos, metus*), and appetite (*epithumia, libido, appetitus, cupiditas*)."[29]

In their theory and practice of emotional control, Stoics put faith above all in the will: "Emotion involves an oscillation between two impulses . . . the emotional impulse and one's better judgment."[30] This meant that emotion was, in fact, "voluntary." In Stoic therapy, Sorabji writes, "The voluntariness is based on the idea that one is free to question appearances and withhold assent from them. If you do not bother to do so, that is your own fault."[31] Stoics sometimes did identify good or positive emotions, *eupatheiai* (Sorabji notes that there were very few and that those were thought to be attainable only by the sage, not the layman). Yet Stoics mainly sought "freedom from emotion," or *apatheia*. This contrasted with Aristotle's aim of spurning extremes and reaching balance by finding the mean, or *metriopatheia*. In Sorabji's view, Stoics aimed "not to suppress emotion . . . but to dispel it through understanding the real situation."[32]

Sorabji thus shows how the Stoics' "theory of indifferents," introduced above, promises to lead us to a state of tranquility if we manage truly to regard everything as an "indifferent," something we can do nothing about. The only thing we *can* influence is the quality of our own character. The preferred and dispreferred indifferents—life and health, for instance, which do have value and on many occasions are to be selected—are still indifferents in a moral sense. Other ones include "pleasure, beauty, strength, well-functioning sense organs, wealth, reputation and their opposites, low repute, and ignoble birth."[33] None of these ultimately matters.

When we turn to one of the most famous ancient Stoic texts, we can see the classic Stoic moves we have been examining. These are the elements most influential in the use of Stoicism as a spiritual discipline. In his renowned *Meditations*, Marcus Aurelius, who was emperor of Rome from AD 161 to 180, rehearses the theory of indifferents in his discussion of paring life down to the essentials. (See fig. 2.2.) In what might be seen as a doctrine of simplicity, he counsels, "Occupy thyself with few things, do not many things."[34] He was presumably addressing himself with this second-person styling, since these writings constituted his own diary, thought to be for his use only, jotted down during his planning for and leading of military campaigns.[35] He was to accomplish this renunciation by following the Stoic approach of figuring out which things he should categorize as indifferents: "Wherefore forget not on every occasion to ask thyself, *Is this one of the unnecessary things?*" These even included thoughts, which could trigger action so sometimes qualified as indifferents as well: "But we must retrench not only actions but thoughts which are unnecessary, for then neither will superfluous actions follow" (4.24; pp. 81, 83).

WHAT TO CARE ABOUT

The Stoics' theory of indifferents was closely tied to their view of emotion as judgment (though they disagreed on how much and in what manner emotion came down to judgment). This rendering of emotion appears prominently in the *Meditations*. We should cultivate the skill of separating ourselves from the outside world not only to ask what is necessary or unnecessary but to determine what we can and cannot control. We can accomplish this by holding fast to two certainties: "One, that objective things do not lay hold of the soul, but stand quiescent without; while disturbances are but the outcome of that opinion which is within us. A second, that all this visible world changes in a moment, and will be no more." In his shorthand, "The Universe—mutation: Life—opinion" (4.3, p. 71).[36] Once we grasp the importance of our own judgments in shaping how we view our predicaments and how we decide to act, we can shake free of what troubles us. "Efface the opinion, I am harmed, and at once the feeling of being harmed disappears; efface the feeling, and the harm disappears at once," he repeats (4.7, p. 73).

While we can identify this Stoic approach to indifferents and to emotion in his writing, Marcus Aurelius's text reveals much more about the larger view of the world in which his Stoic strictures and advice made sense to him. Four themes that pervade the *Meditations* are the insignificance of the human being vis-à-vis the vastness of the universe and the brevity of life; the omnipresence of suffering and loss; closely connected to it, the importance of the social realm; and, finally, the existence of a transcendent realm. As he lays out the logic and reason behind his Stoic approach, both suggesting our ability to grasp the broad contours of how the world works and granting the limits of that ability, this fuller worldview emerges.

In the foundational texts of ancient Stoicism, these two classic Stoic moves, when taken together—the theory of indifferents and the view of emotion as opinion or judgment—yield a way to decide what in human life matters. Put another way, by bracketing so much as unworthy of care or preference, they suggest what we *should* care about, and why.

The *Meditations* are not free from the kinds of assertions we saw in Gill's "tough" Stoicism. As we have seen in the Introduction, Epictetus callously dismisses grief as illogical when he draws a parallel between breaking a favorite cup and losing a wife or child.[37] A major influence on Marcus Aurelius, Epictetus makes a direct link between having an emotional reaction and judging something (or someone). Likewise, Marcus asserts that even people can be indifferents. They too might deserve an emotional response of detachment: "So far as any stand in the way of those acts which concern us closely, then man becomes for me as much one of things indifferent as the sun, as the wind, as a wild-beast" (5.20, p. 119). In some cases, he suggests, this detachment is necessary because the immorality of many people makes them difficult to abide (2.1, p. 27). In other cases, it is part of a strategy to guard against desire and loss, so detachment is needed for the exact opposite reason: instead of being unable to tolerate the presence of other people, one might be unable to tolerate their absence. Marcus sees it as desirable behavior "to remain ever the same, in the throes of pain, on the loss of a child, during a lingering illness," turning only to "Reason" in all cases (1.8, p. 7).[38]

A passage on prayer reveals this same ideal of detachment. Marcus has practical suggestions for transforming the content of what one asks of the gods by looking at the problem from a different angle: "One man prays: *How may I lie with that woman!* Thou: *How may I not lust to lie with her!* Another: *How may I be quit of that man!* Thou: *How may I not wish to be quit of him!* Another: *How may I not lose my little child!* Thou: *How may I not dread to lose him!"* (9.40, p. 255). Instead of devoting our thoughts, then, to the acts that are motivated by strong feeling, we need to address the feelings themselves. If we can tame those feelings, even eradicate them, then we will not have to endure the emotion of having them disappointed or the consequences of acting upon them.

A MATHEMATICAL FORMULA
FOR FEELINGS

Stoic discipline has a totalizing aspect to it, at least to modern ears, in urging us to guard against emotion in general. But the implications of this formulation are important to consider. What it seems to come down to is a formula, even, by which the eradication of feelings adds up to a way to eradicate the deleterious *effects* of feelings. This circularity suggests that it is not feeling, pure and simple, but certain feelings or emotional states that raise the greatest concern. So a more fine-tuned formula derives from a calculus of emotions, whereby we can ascertain the stakes of feeling a particular way. For instance, if an individual can overcome a feeling of strong desire—and this may be the crux of the entire system[39]—he or she may manage to prevent the agonies of grief and sorrow that are usually attendant upon loss.

While Marcus Aurelius, much like Epictetus, is known for his precepts and guidelines for behavior, his *Meditations* take the reader well beyond any such codification. When taken in full, his advice and observations range from factual, logical, and eminently practical to profoundly introspective, philosophical, and even poetic. All of life is his subject. As such, his musings lend themselves to broad ruminations about the nature of man's existence. His observations about how we should live are so intricately intertwined with the nature of the universe, and man's place within it, that it is sometimes difficult to discern their precise relation. At the very least we can say it is a logical one, suggesting that because the universe is this way, and humans are that way, it makes sense for us to approach life in the manner he suggests.

A theme that recurs with particular frequency in the *Meditations* is the fleeting character of the life of a single human being. Book 1 lays out the traits of the people Marcus thought exerted the most influence over the formation of his own outlook, as well as elements of good fortune he received from the gods. Then the brevity of life makes an almost immediate appearance. "Thou art an old man," he tells himself. His advancing age means that "now, if ever before, shouldest thou realize of what Universe thou art a part" (2.4, p. 29). He tells himself he should likewise realize "that a limit has been set to thy time" (2.4, p. 29).[40]

From these admonitions to make the most of life, accept impending death, and try to glimpse the bigger picture, since it goes by so fast, the text goes on, through the particular imagery and emphatic references to the quick passage of time, to reveal the fundamental importance of Marcus's conception of time to questions about the use to which he should put his life. Although Marcus is engaged in nothing if not a life of action, his paramount concern is his inner life.

Time comes up throughout the *Meditations*. For instance, we read later in book 2, "How quickly all things vanish away" (2.12, p. 35); in book 4, "how short-lived are all mortal things, and how paltry" (4.48, p. 95); in book 10, "Thou hast but a short time to live" (10.15, p. 275). Such lines appear again and again and can be extracted this way, as implied pieces of advice. Yet it is crucial to note that each one is inseparably entwined with reflections about philosophical matters of great concern to Marcus, from the smallness of human concerns in the larger cosmic scheme of things to reputation, memory, change, and the nature of time itself.

All of these themes are introduced early on in the passage following "How quickly all things vanish away," which continues, "in the universe their actual bodies, and the remembrance of them in Eternity, and of what character are all objects of sense, and particularly those that entice us with pleasure or terrify us with pain or are acclaimed by vanity—how worthless and despicable and unclear and ephemeral and dead!" (2.12, p. 35). This early quote lays out many of the concerns to follow—the ever-changing nature of the physical world and, with it, those things contingent on human faculties, such as memory and feeling. Vanity is cast not only as a moral shortcoming or character flaw but as something "unclean." "Remembrance," or rather the lack thereof, is summoned to answer the question of whether Marcus should be preoccupied with fame: "But will that paltry thing, Fame, pluck thee aside? Look at the swift approach of complete forgetfulness" (4.3, p. 69).

Marcus Aurelius looks at human life as if through a wide-angle lens—the widest imaginable, with eternity ever in mind. In doing so, he distinguishes between two kinds of time: one for the individual and one for the cosmos. This diminishes the duration of a human life almost to the vanishing point: "Of the life of man the duration is but a point, its substance streaming away, its perception dim, the fabric of the entire body prone to decay, and the soul a vortex, and fortune incalculable, and fame uncertain. In a word all the things of the body are as a river, and the things of the soul as a dream and a vapor; and life is a warfare and a pilgrim's sojourn, and fame after death is only forgetfulness" (2.17, p. 41).

A life occurs in what we might visualize as a point from which two arrows (rays, in geometry) shoot out, one extending backward in time and one forward—both without end: "Ever beside us is this infinity of the past and yawning abyss of the future, wherein all things are disappearing" (5.23, p. 121). Marcus sets human time against "universal Time, of which a brief, nay an almost momentary, span has been allotted thee" (5.24, p. 121). Mutability figures prominently in his picture, yet so does continuation. (Note that "the infinity of the past" is "ever beside us.") In these dual infinities of universal time, change is endless, even more noticeably because nothing ever vanishes entirely. This is because every present material body has a fleeting existence in its current form but is reconstituted into something else. Turning to his own body and soul, he reflects on the persistence of everything: "I am made up of the Causal and the Material, and neither of these disappears into nothing, just as neither did it come into existence out of nothing. So shall my every part by change be told off to form some part of the universe, and that again be changed into another part of it, and so on to infinity. It was by such process of change that I too came into being and my parents, and so backwards into a second infinity" (5.13, pp. 113–15).

This rendering of past and future time as dwarfing the period of one human's existence highlights a particular notion of the present as momentary. Marcus celebrates the ability of "Reason" to guide us toward only those opinions in "harmony with Nature" and toward "due deliberation and fellowship with mankind and fealty to the Gods." He tells himself to value only what matters in light of this broader horizon: "Jettison everything else, then, and lay hold of these things only, few as they are; remember withal that it is only this present, a moment of time, that a man lives: all the rest either has been lived or may never be" (3.10, p. 59). Against the backdrop of the time before and after us, both infinite, our lives are brief almost to the degree of impossibility.[41]

This is the foundation for a different conception of time itself, according to which the usual measurements of duration have no relevance. It does not matter whether we live for three thousand or thirty thousand years because we have only our current life; were we to die we would lose only this life anyway, not the past and the future. Those are not ours to begin with. From this vantage point, lives are leveled: "The longest life, then, and the shortest amount but to the same. For the present time is of equal duration for all" (2.14, p. 39).

According to the logic of cyclical time, a tenet of many ancient philosophies and religions worldwide, "All things from time everlasting have been cast in the same mold and repeated cycle after cycle, and so it makes no difference whether a man see the same things recur through a hundred years or two hundred or through eternity." Someone who dies sooner than another person loses nothing more than someone living longer: "For it is but the present that a man can be deprived of, if, as is the fact, it is this alone that he has" (2.14, p. 39).

Even further, the notion that everything derives from a single entity, the "ruling Reason of the universe," means that if we are able to observe the present, we can by extension see what has existed and will exist throughout time. This means that, in effect, the present is the eternal (6.36, p. 151). It is smaller than imaginable and yet infinite: "He, who sees what now is, hath seen all that ever hath been from times everlasting, and that shall be to eternity; for all things are of one lineage and one likeness" (6.37, p. 151).

The brevity of life is often coupled, in the imagery Marcus uses, with the smallness of man in relation to the universe. The temporal shades into the spatial and back. Just as the life of an individual was likened to a point, the two thoughts involved here—that our life is fleeting and that the space we take up is minute—are often conjoined, as in his observation that "within a little thou shalt be non-existent, and nowhere, like Hadrianus and Augustus" (4.3, p. 69; 8.5, p. 201). In the passage from book 4 already cited ("But will that paltry thing, Fame, pluck thee aside?"), he argues against caring about fame on the grounds of this smallness: "For the whole earth is but a point and how tiny a corner of it is this the place of our sojourning!" (4.3, p. 71).

Marcus even proceeds to describe the individual person in spatial terms: "From now therefore bethink thee of the retreat into this little plot that is thyself" (4.3, p. 71). When speaking of the inner life, the image is a whole plot, for it is larger than the "point" one life takes up in relation to eternal time, where the vantage point is from without, not from within the individual observing. What makes up the individual also suggests physical size or measurement: "Keep in memory the universal substance of which thou art a tiny part" (5.24, p. 121). And so the world itself appears this way. Marcus's imagery reduces it physically, as it does the individual: "Asia, Europe, corners of the universe: the whole ocean a drop in the universe: Athos but a little clod therein: all the present a point in Eternity—everything on a tiny scale, so easily changed, so quickly vanished" (6.36, p. 149). From the individual to the vast mountain of Athos, all is a plot or a clod at its most substantial, or even a "tiny" part or a "drop," but often so small as to be imperceptible, when it has any presence at all. If we zoom out, the earth is infinitesimally small, just like a human being.

How can time both matter and not matter? Is this radical reduction of the size and scope and duration of one human life at all comforting? What might be the ramifications of viewing time in this way for how we are to live our lives? Marcus places a premium on the present, and at the same time defines the present as no different from the rest of time, and thus a window onto the eternal. These observations could lead to very different possible conclusions. If we keep in mind that our lives are of fleeting duration and emphasize our smallness in relation to the vastness of the universe, we might conclude that it does not matter so much what we do. Fleeting in temporal terms, life might matter little in the larger scheme of things.

The *Meditations* surely works this way in regard to reputation. Marcus comes back repeatedly to the subject of fame, a topic bound to occur to him frequently as emperor of Rome (for example, 6.16, p. 138). While Stoics are associated with equanimity and calm, in fact certain topics plague Marcus deeply. Reminding himself of how quickly time passes and that change is the only constant, he eventually seems to arrive at a consistent way of dispatching with the subject. He tells himself that glory—and memory itself—are ultimately insignificant because memory is so fleeting. Time's march gives comfort. But both the repetition and the vehemence of his case, as well as the extremity of its terms, suggest otherwise. The constant vertiginous sweep of the pendulum from the fleeting and microscopic to the all-enduring and cosmic suggests that these two poles are the only choices.

Whether Marcus has come to any peace on the subject of fame, his words sound a lament about the facts of things. And in any case, what kind of comfort is this? If time and space are so vast, does that not reduce the importance of our actions? Why behave well? If we are so insignificant, why is it so important that we dwell, in Stoic fashion, on virtue, right action, and good character? It is painful enough to exist in a moment so fleeting, but to have to refrain from giving oneself fully to the pull of emotion seems to add yet another layer of agony.

Our answer might be, quite simply, that it is not so important, it is not at all required to behave well. Given our own transience and the smallness of our concerns, it is unimportant what we do. But the reverse could be true. Things might not be so fleeting or insignificant as Marcus allows: perhaps what we do *is* important. Either conclusion would point to a major contradiction in his thinking.

Still another possibility is that both parts of his equation are true—life is fleeting *and* we should act virtuously—but they stand apart, independent of the other. There is no given consequence of the fact of brevity and smallness for how we act. There might be separate reasons for acting virtuously, even in the face of these realities, but not *because* of them. There could simply be no connection.

However, Marcus's presentation of these realities suggests the closest of ties. *Meditations* lays out the philosophical grounding for a particular way to approach and evaluate day-to-day living. If human memory is so temporary, reputation and fame do not hold up as reasons for virtuous action and character development. To discover sound reasons, we must take seriously the Stoic belief that living according to nature is the right, good, and proper thing to do.

Living according to nature, a truism of our own day, now means something very different. The phrase varies in meaning over time, depending on its historical context, on how we define nature. In Marcus's text, in the Greco-Roman philosophical tradition, divine reason has pride of place. Coming in as a close second is something more earthly, and more surprising: man's social inclinations. Ultimately, nature is connected, as is reason, with transcendence.

Skipping ahead centuries, we can find helpful interpretations in the reception of ancient ideas by others. The rendering of Stoic themes in the work of Nicolas Poussin, according to art historian Paul Barolsky, gives us a visual representation of precisely this notion of brevity and smallness that is so strong a motif in Marcus's *Meditations*. Painting in the period of the French Baroque, Poussin is known as a leading example of a new seventeenth-century classicism, with both form and content that draw deeply on design elements and themes from antiquity. Writing in 1998, Barolsky judged Poussin's portrayal of "Ovidian subjects" a neglected aspect of the influence of Stoicism in Poussin's work. Though Ovid is not a Stoic himself, his "portrayal of nature in *Metamor-*

phoses, of its ever changing forms, intersects, however, the Stoic doctrine, which dwells on the flow of all created things, the understanding that, as a thing comes to be, it is swept away in return." While other artists also saw the Stoic resonances of *Metamorphoses*, a Latin narrative poem in fifteen books written by Ovid in AD 8, Barolsky believes Poussin was the poem's "deepest reader."[42] Poussin's reading thus helps illuminate subtleties of the original Stoic texts.

THE REALM OF FLORA

Barolsky sees Poussin's *Realm of Flora* as an exploration of the precise Stoic themes we have been examining. The painting depicts an outdoor scene, with gradations of gray and reddish brown in soft, dark tones for the earthy setting. (See fig. 2.3.) The rich terracotta color of the ground on which the figures are sprawled blends into the outcropping that flanks the entire left side of the composition, in which there is no clear demarcation between the manmade (the ruins) and the natural (the hillside). Jumping out from the earthen tones of this background, tones extending even to the full, dense clouds, and the hair and drapery adorning most of the figures, is the clarity of the blues—in the drapery of two figures, the sky (and some of the flowers)—and the white of the highlighted edge of one drapery and shine of a jar. The flush of one of the figures stands out, and the white coat of one of the dogs, but much of the skin, including that of all the babies, is more of a light terracotta that helps give an overall impression of blending with the background rather than marking a contrast. The difference between the figures suffering and the other figures is not visually stark but rather strangely continuous with the activities of the others, who gaze lovingly or, especially in the case of the cherubs, are given over to self-entertainment.

An arbor cradles the figures horizontally, and a number of vertical lines—of swords, poles, and the waterfall—lead the eye upward. Sprinkled among the figures, birds and blooms, mostly ivory and periwinkle, speak in their symbolized terms of the myths narrated by Ovid, in which after their deaths these characters—Narcissus, Clytie, Hyacinthus, Adonica, and Crocus—become flowers. With the cycle of death and renewal as the setting, Poussin refers to Ovid's telling of "stories of vehement passions stoically absorbed into the greater flux of nature."[43] This absorption takes place with Apollo's chariot in commanding position as a reminder of the fleeting nature of time, by means of the Stoic emphasis on the evanescence of all things human: "In his vernal encyclopedia, Poussin presents an Ovidian image of nature in which the human being is a fleeting presence. Nowhere is this Stoic sense of mankind's smallness more graphically rendered than in Marcus Aurelius's *Meditations*. No matter that this work was composed after *Metamorphoses*, for it typifies the Stoic tradition that Poussin inherited and brought to bear in his reading of Ovid. Poussin's sentiments are those of Aurelius as he collects Ovid's tales of metamorphosis in which human beings take their modest place in the cosmos."[44]

In these sweeping renderings of the universe, from Poussin's back to Ovid's and forward to Marcus's, the divine is part of nature, and nature is part of the divine. All suffering and enjoyment are subsumed in both. This is why we behave virtuously, because virtuous behavior has divine sanction. According to divine reason, it is morally and spiritually best.

A NEW STOICISM

In a 2001 article entitled "The Rebirth of Stoicism," William O. Stephens asked why the Stoics' "ancient creed is enjoying a renaissance today, in, of all things, popular culture." In his view it is "because the Stoic way of thinking is as relevant, indeed, as urgently *practical*, today in twenty-first century America as it was 1,900 years ago in the Roman Empire." Much of his short article centers on Epictetus (AD 55–135), who he thinks is of major importance in this latest revival, including in both *A Man in Full* and *Gladiator*. Stephens gives a pithy summary of what he sees as the overarching theme in operation: "Epictetus' Stoic philosophy, which influenced the likes of Roman emperor Marcus Aurelius, is basically that the goal of life is to live in harmony with nature. That means to live the good life, we must both live in accord with our human nature—as essentially rational, reflective and thoughtful beings—and conform our actions to the actual conditions of the natural world." Stephens sees Epictetus's "passion for freedom" as lying at the heart of his work: his philosophy offers "a kind of psychological freedom from physical circumstances that only disciplined adherence to Stoicism makes possible." The path to this freedom is the exercise of reason to control those things we can control in order to live virtuous lives, with the assumption that we *can* control "our attitudes, emotional responses and mental outlook," because they are voluntary. On the other hand, we should not "worry about, fear or get upset" about things we cannot control. "In this respect," Stevens writes, "Stoicism is a kind of coping strategy."[45]

Stephens sees Stoicism as an alternative to the current American "glorification of power, possessions, fame and money." Our freedom of decision-making means that if we wish to we can choose "morally offensive endeavors." Bad behavior is an option: "We are free to compete *against* others for wealth, power and status. We are free to vie *against* others and try to coerce, manipulate and exploit them in a desire to win material possessions and enhance our reputations." A reason for not doing so, however, can be found in the superiority of the Stoic's pursuit of "honorable intention," "rational judgment," "peace of mind," and "virtue and social harmony"—which do not rely on chance in the same way as a "life of conspicuous consumption and consumerism."[46]

Even earlier, another call for the New Stoicism came in the form of an academic study by just that title. In *A New Stoicism*, published in 1998, philosopher Lawrence Becker begins with a chapter entitled "Conceit," which presents in a mere six paragraphs an overview of what has happened to Stoicism since antiquity. It is worth capturing some of his style and language. The first five paragraphs blaze through that history—a story, in his telling, of how Stoicism sustained one assault after another, a thriller-in-miniature. So "pillaged by theology and effaced by evangelical and imperial

Christianity," by the Middle Ages, Stoicism was in "shards." Renaissance Neo-Stoicism brought renewed attention to this school of thought but "bore only a strong family resemblance" to ancient Stoicism; modern science questioned its metaphysics; Romanticism was "contemptuous of Stoic moral training"; and late nineteenth- and twentieth-century philosophy decimated it through "a blizzard of fads that undermined commitments to reason and nature." With shades of *The Da Vinci Code*, *The Matrix*, and *The Gospel of Truth*, the final paragraph of chapter 1 reads: "It is a complete disaster. Only a few are escaped to tell you."[47] In all of these, the survival of an embattled coterie requires elaborate heroics.

Throughout this sort of intellectual history in miniature qua adventure tale, Becker employs the first-person plural *we*, a pronoun rarely encountered in contemporary scholarship, at least in quite this fashion. He writes: "The term Stoic came to be applied merely to people who use our remedies"; after the "brief effusion of interest in our historical roots" in the Italian Renaissance, "wider interest in our views soon dwindled"; in the scientific revolution, we had to abandon "our doctrine that the universe should be understood as a purposive, rational being"; over time "we lost contact with theology"; and, finally, "our obliteration" occurred in the wake of modern secular philosophy.[48]

Becker's use of the first person is particularly striking in a work of modern academic philosophy that features a twenty-five-page appendix entitled "A Calculus for Normative Logic" and a seven-page scholarly bibliography. Becker is an unapologetic advocate. This view of Stoicism as a minority position of a few die-hard soldiers—"actual or otherwise," as Becker puts it—is the starting point from which he elaborates, through complex argumentation, a detailed program for a twenty-first-century Stoicism. Working from the assumption that he is writing for an audience that is "skeptical" at best, he provides a substantial commentary at the end of each chapter, furthering the argument by anticipating objections.

Becker aims to show how the essential elements of Stoic doctrine still have as much coherence as in the works of the early philosophers. He grants that ancient Stoicism does need updating, conceding that some developments must be reckoned with. Above all, he suggests the ancient Stoics' now "discredited form of naturalistic ethics" is the main stumbling block for us. Otherwise, a New Stoicism can and should still be, in Becker's view, "eudaimonistic, in identifying the good life or happiness with flourishing," and "intellectualistic, in identifying virtue with rationality." It can even remain "naturalistic." To attain this latter designation, Stoicism would require a major emendation. The ancient Stoics believed in a cosmic *telos* in the sense "that the natural world is a purposive system with an end or goal that practical reason directs us to follow." In Becker's view, modern science rules out such a belief. Instead, we can hold to the centrality of nature in Stoic ethics—"its insistence that facts about the natural world" should be part of "the substance of practical deliberation."[49]

Becker thinks the revised Stoic orientation offers an alternative to the central problem plaguing most ethical philosophy today—its assumption that ethics is independent of science and logic rather than intrinsically connected, even subordinate to them. While he does not think natural science points to ultimate answers about a cosmic teleology that suggests a coinciding of the individual and universal goals, he does see a role for empirical observation and "explanatory theories" that are directly involved in ethical decision-making. Rather than beginning with abstract principles about human beings or ethics, Stoicism involves "the particulars—about how particular people in their particular circumstances ought to live." It is based not on the idea of an essential human nature but on "fully situated individuals."[50]

Creatures of particular settings, human beings have goals by virtue of being agents: they do things and, even further, are engaged in "projects." To Becker, "Projects are constitutive facts about agents: to be an agent is to be purpose or goal-oriented—that is, motivated (at least dispositionally) to act toward some end(s). The motive force is internal . . . typically experienced as coming from within—as pressing or pushing one to act." In addition, "Rational deliberative power (rational agency) is a defining feature of mature human consciousness." In Stoic practice, the point of acting according to reason, weighing all of the facts and other kinds of knowledge available, is to make decisions that adhere to the pursuit of virtue. If humans are rational animals by nature, they fulfill their nature when they act rationally, and if they act rationally when they act virtuously, virtuous action constitutes the ultimate good, "the perfection of agency." Thus the question becomes, in Stoic discipline, how best to employ rational capacity in the choices facing the individual throughout his or her life. Science and nature become part of the "particular and intricate deliberate field" in which an individual acts.[51]

THE NEW GLADIATORS

How well does Stoicism equip one to act in the field? Often touted by the New Stoics as the ultimate Stoic film, *Gladiator* is indeed a modern epic in many ways steeped in Stoicism. The New Stoicism often lauds the film as an example of Stoicism in action. Overall, the plot, characterization, themes, and many individual scenes clearly evoke a Stoic approach to life. It is an epic of our day because it speaks to our own desires, searches, and journeys. In the persona of the protagonist, Maximus, we encounter a hero in the mold of the Stoic warrior. This is signaled from the start, when the dying emperor Marcus Aurelius, the real Stoic warrior-philosopher and author of *Meditations*, strongly prefers Maximus over his own son, Commodus, for his successor. As Stoic hero-designate, Maximus goes on to exhibit behavior that contemporary viewers would automatically associate with Stoicism, with its common connotations of emotional restraint and strength in the face of adversity. In fact, the epic is one long series of events in which Maximus gets tested by some of the most extreme calamities: the loss of many of his men in battle; the death (by patricide) of Marcus, his mentor and father figure; his own close call with death by (intended) execution and in combat; the murder of his wife and son; his enslavement and forced combat with fellow gladiators (sometimes to the death); and the list goes on. He rises to the occasion and proves himself a man of extraordinary courage and valor.

On the many occasions when he faces a situation that might ordinarily provoke an extreme emotion, Maximus maintains an impassive demeanor—at least on the outside.

As we have seen, once enslaved and undergoing preparation for gladiatorial combat, Maximus is pictured stripping away his own skin and flesh from a bloody wound on his bicep as he removes a tattoo that would reveal his identity as a Roman soldier. Not only does he fail to flinch during this act of self-mutilation, but he nonchalantly carries on a conversation with a fellow gladiator. In scenes marked by escalating threats to his own person as well as heartbreaking loss, he noticeably fails to display the ordinary human emotions we might predict for such situations, such as fear and rage. While the film as a whole is cast as a tale of revenge, Maximus forgoes many opportunities to kill the vicious tyrant Commodus, who has become ruler of Rome, even when Commodus openly taunts and belittles him in that most public setting of the Colosseum. Maximus takes the slave trader qua gladiator manager Proximo's advice—to keep the crowd on your side—well beyond the public entertainment of the staged combat, into the realm of politics and the quest to redeem Rome (which stands for democracy in this film, as just one of the legions of historical inaccuracies it proudly parades).

By the time he takes action to kill Commodus, Maximus does have the crowd completely on his side. Yet by then the entire coup, which had the support of the Roman army, has failed. Behind the scenes, Commodus has delivered the fatal stab wound to Maximus and ordered a guard to cover it up, so that he can partake in a staged man-to-man struggle in the Colosseum. This way Commodus can demonstrate his superiority and win the love and admiration he so desperately seeks. Maximus walks gingerly out into the arena and fights valiantly despite his wound. He overcomes physical pain to the remarkable degree that he even manages to kill Commodus. He summons all of his dying energy and makes the final thrust.

This is the climax awaited by the viewers, who vicariously get a small taste of what emotional restraint might feel like by virtue of this prolongation of gratification. They can finally witness an evil tyrant punished and his actions halted. Tellingly, even now Maximus's reactions are muted. The release of pent-up anger at all of the suffering inflicted on him, his loved ones, and his compatriots is subtly delivered by means of an attenuated scene picturing the fatal stabbing of Commodus. The long, glistening point of the blade moves slowly toward Commodus's neck, leaving time for viewers to wonder whether Maximus will follow through this time or again display his extraordinary powers of restraint, even mercy. It is this slowing down of time, during which we hear only a gentle gurgling—the ghastly sound of the blood bubbling out of Commodus's mouth—that stands in for Maximus's emotions. Visual and aural imagery speaks eloquently of the implied rage and desire for vengeance. That desire satisfied, Maximus gives in to his own fatal wound and slowly sheds his mortal coil. Now in a dreamlike state, he floats and then, in the afterlife, walks to his wife and son, who lovingly greet him in the idyllic fields of his farm. Just as he and his friend and fellow gladiator had imagined, he does manage to return home after all.

What are we to think about this depiction of Maximus as a man who must find a way to exist despite the trials and tribulations of life, immensely magnified in this way for ultimate effect? Clearly, the movie aims to portray him as Stoic. Indeed, he most certainly practices the basic tenets of Stoic discipline at numerous points in his life. However, let us turn briefly to the kind of "tough Stoicism" some of our contemporary authors associate with Aristo and Epictetus, which is surely the kind to which the film means to allude, and only then return to the question of Maximus's Stoicism.

The self-discipline of tough Stoicism aimed beyond simple restraint of emotion to its eradication; the goal was to retrain oneself entirely vis-à-vis emotion. Epictetus's *Encheiridion*, cited directly in much of the New Stoicism, is by definition a simplified version of Stoic ethics in the form of a manual of moral rules. Embodying what we have glimpsed in our earlier overview, the manual begins by setting a mood of detachment from the ordinary attachments and concerns of everyday life. This preamble bears extensive quoting for our immersion in the psychological state of the discipline required in Stoic decision-making:

> Some things are under our control, while others are not under our control. Under our control are conception, choice, desire, aversion, and, in a word, everything that is our own doing; not under our control are our body, our property, reputation, office, and, in a word, everything that is not our own doing. Furthermore, the things under our control are by nature free, unhindered, and unimpeded; while the things not under our control are weak, servile, subject to hindrance, and not our own. Remember, therefore, that if what is naturally slavish you think to be free, and what is not your own to be your own, you will be hampered, will grieve, will be in turmoil, and will blame both gods and men; while if you think only what is your own to be your own, and what is not your own to be, as it really is, not your own, then no one will ever be able to exert compulsion upon you, no one will hinder you, you will blame no one, will find fault with no one, will do absolutely nothing against your will, you will have no personal enemy, no one will harm you, for neither is there any harm that can touch you.[52]

Once immersed, we can approach decision-making with the requisite understanding and resolve:

> Make it, therefore, your study at the very outset to say to every harsh external impression, "You are an external impression and not at all what you appear to be." After that examine it and test it by these rules which you have, the first and most important of which is this: Whether the impression has to do with the things which are under our control, or with those which are not under our control; and, if it has to do with some one of the things not under our control, have ready to hand the answer, "It is nothing to me."[53]

As foreshadowed in the Introduction in the case of Epictetus's cup, this internal practice of self-discipline has ramifications for how we handle feelings of all kinds, including those that arise from sorrow and loss.[54] Grief, like other emotions, is all in the head: "It is not the things themselves that disturb men, but their judgements about these things. For example, death is nothing dreadful, or else Socrates too would have thought so, but the judgement that death is dreadful, this is the dreadful thing. When, therefore, we are hindered, or disturbed, or grieved, let us never blame anyone but ourselves, that means, our own judgements."[55] The call to disregard death, taken out of context by an emergent tough Stoicism, risks misinterpretation as an incitement not to noble forbearance but to violence.

THE GENTLE STOIC

It is easy to dismiss such advice from Epictetus as excessively harsh and even simplistic, but even those other kinds of Stoic writings that explore the human predicament with depth and complexity explicitly counsel us to erect barriers against feeling. To see this we might turn briefly to one of the philosopher Seneca's three letters of consolation, *Ad Polybium De Consolatione*, translated into English by John W. Basore. Famous for his tragic dramas as well as his Stoic philosophy, Seneca wrote this text in the tradition of the literary genre of consolation, from exile under the reign of the Emperor Claudius sometime in the decade of the 40s AD. He addressed this letter to Polybius, a freeman who became wealthy and had an official post under Claudius (not to be confused with the historian Polybius of the second century BC). The extant fragment of the letter consists of eighteen chapters, with each chapter presenting one or two reasons why Polybius should not grieve at the loss of his brother. A listing of just a few of the dozens of reasons gives a sense of the kind of discipline a Stoic could recommend regarding grief.

1. All things perish. "Whatever has a beginning has also an end. . . . This universe, which contains all the works of gods

and men, will one day be scattered and plunged into the ancient chaos and darkness."

2. Everyone must die. It is vanity for anyone to think he will be the exception to Nature's law. It should be a comfort to realize that nature treats all people the same.

3. Grief does not accomplish anything.

4. We can't change Fate; tears do not change it.

5. No one gets pleasure from your tears, neither you, your brother, or any of the people around you.

6. You should be an example to your other brothers and bear Fortune bravely. Pretend to be happy. Try to cast out bad feelings, but if not, hide them.

7. You can't live a private life that will allow you to mourn secretly because you have a public role: "They watch your eyes!"

8. It is "vulgar," "base," and "womanish" to show excessive sorrow.

9. You have a public trust, a debt, a moral responsibility, to be a consistent self.

10. Your "claims to be a sage and scholar" oblige you to do certain things. "You may not weep beyond measure." You cannot sleep late or travel abroad.[56]

There are still others. It is not certain whether Maximus would have managed as well to refrain from anger if Commodus had proceeded down such a list after describing, as he did, how Maximus's son and wife had suffered while being tortured to death.

In fact, Maximus's love and devotion to his wife and son have a palpable presence throughout *Gladiator*. Far from eradicating emotion, Maximus is deeply motivated by it. His greatest show of emotion comes after he finds the bodies of his wife and son, who have been hanged and burned. In a scene that conveys deep passion through its understated pathos and brevity, Maximus lies in a loving embrace of the two mounds of dirt where he has now buried the bodies of those most dear to him in the world. With his spent body fitting naturally the curves of the earth, we are reminded of another kind of ultimate experience, the passionate union possible between two people that makes loss so grievous. In this case, the deaths threaten Maximus's will to live.

If *Gladiator* does not completely carry out its Stoic imperative, neither does it entirely fit the themes of the modern therapeutic described by Philip Rieff and others. Not only does Maximus actually feel something beneath his Stoic-seeming exterior, he experiences the full depth and range of his emotions. Even further, he evidently feels a profound connection to something above, beyond, and outside of himself. While this transcendent is sloppily cast, with complete anachronism, as a Rome that symbolizes modern democratic hopes, it does nevertheless refer to something beyond self-interest and the pursuit of the goals of the self alone, untethered by the bonds of deep affection.

Yet *Gladiator* also potentially violates Stoic directives by centering itself on the themes of violence and vengeance. Early on in the saga Maximus betrays his desire and plan to get revenge. In the scene in which he kills Commodus, time slows down, as if making it possible for Maximus to choose another course of action. It seems almost as though it is Stoicism, the Stoic choice, that hangs in the balance. It feels like a test of ancient Stoic principle, a referendum in which it fails, ousted by the modern therapeutic, a lesser-known version of the therapeutic that centers on violence. This suggests possibilities for how Stoicism, when appropriated in certain contexts, might actually support the opposite of restraint. The tough brand of Stoicism, which sees everything but virtue as indifferent and seeks to minimize the importance of death, could support violence. This also shows us the stakes of the therapeutic. The New Stoicism, rather than an alternative to the therapeutic, could support an even more extreme form of the therapeutic. As a result, this film that comes so highly recommended by adherents of the New Stoicism may actually be decidedly un-Stoic in its sensibility.

So what are we to make of this movement to bring Stoicism back? At times it only *appears* to be a departure from the age of therapy à la Tom Wolfe's caricature in his essay "The Me Decade."[57] While any return of reticence and reserve seems a welcome development, disciplining oneself *in this particular way* and *for this particular reason* might err toward what social critics have found wrong with recent American culture. What is so alarming about the therapeutic culture is not its focus on emotion in itself but rather its focus on the individual at the exclusion of his or her deep need for connection with others and the loss of a sense of sacred transcendence as a basis for that connection. Stoicism, at least of the tough and codified variety, involves a systematic interior reeducation program geared toward the vanquishing of emotion. The program risks encouraging the individual to pursue his or her own goals at all costs.[58]

TECHNE

University of London philosopher John Sellars, founding member of the Stoicism Today project, which started Stoic Week, offers a sustained exploration of how Stoic philosophy might look in practice. He emphasizes that Stoicism in particular, more than any other school, cannot be understood without realizing how irrevocably it weds theory and practice. Sellars writes that Epictetus's *Handbook* was most likely geared toward advanced students as the second major part of their philosophical education. The first part would have focused on studying philosophy more abstractly and theoretically. The *Handbook* in this context was a distillation of that work into guidelines (possibly by his student Arrian, who, it is thought, wrote them down). These precepts were then to be practiced by living a certain kind of philosophically informed life. The *Handbook* was and is a helpful guide to have at hand while living according to Stoic doctrines.[59]

Sellars considers ancient Stoicism the epitome of a particular view of philosophy, one in which philosophy is tightly connected to the way we live our lives. Of all of the ancient schools, Stoicism is to Sellars the school of thought most in the Socratic-Platonic vein. It ran against approaches, like that of Aristotle, which figured philosophy as mainly about rational argument. Sellars uses the term *techne* (τέχνη), the Greek term for art or craft, to describe the form of philosophy we find in Stoic teachings. He supports this argument by showing that the three areas of Stoic inquiry—physics, logic, and ethics—were not separate areas of inquiry, as they are today. We can see their connections in Stoicism's devotion to the art of living.

Other scholars have observed what appears to be the underlying structure of Epictetus's *Handbook*. Sellars quotes the "key" to this structure, which he finds in the *Handbook*'s opening section, the first part of the preamble quoted above. These themes, "conception, choice, desire, aversion"—or "opinion, pursuit, desire, or aversion," in the slightly different wording of another translation—make up the parts of life we can control through our own actions, as opposed to those "not our own actions."[60] The literal translation is "up to us," which Sellars gives as equivalent to "in our control."[61] This translation would support Sellars's view even further because it suggests a spiritual dimension beneath the tenets of advice. Sellars draws a parallel between these three themes and the tripartite nature of Stoic philosophy in the *Discourses* of Epictetus, eloquently arguing that each element in the quote from the *Handbook* lines up with one of those mentioned in the quote from *Discourses*.[62] The "three types of exercise" in the *Handbook* and the "three types of philosophical discourse" show a direct "correlation": "opinion with Logic; impulse with Ethics; desire and aversion with Physics" (135–36). By demonstrating this correlation, Sellars suggests that these Stoic texts evince the two stages of philosophy: λόγος (*logos*), or philosophical discourse, and άσκησης (*askesis*), or philosophical exercises, representing two discrete activities.

Sellars guides the reader through the *Handbook*, showing that each of the three parts suggests how we might put into practice the Stoic teaching in each realm. The first, spanning sections 2 to 29, concerns "physical exercises" dedicated to controlling one's desires and aversions "in accordance with nature" (136–37)—meaning here "the order of universal nature, the cosmos" (137n35). The second, spanning sections 30 to 41, concerns "ethical exercises" dedicated to controlling one's impulses in accordance with what is "appropriate"—"to one's own nature, to one's place in society, or the particular situation in which one may find oneself" (140). Sellars points out that it is helpful to think of *appropriate* in this context as translated by Cicero into Latin as *officium*: "It is defined as an action that is in accordance with one's nature and has been understood as 'function,' 'proper function,' 'task,' or 'duty.' It is applied to infants, animals, even plants, so it clearly cannot be understood as 'duty' in any narrow sense" (140n49).[63] The third part of the text, sections 42 through 45, concerns "one's judgment" and "one's assents," to be exercised not according to impressions but according to "what is true, what is false, and what is doubtful" (142). Sellars suggests that the remainder of the *Handbook*, where this structure might seem to break down, actually involves the "philosophical life," which reminds students "why they began to study philosophy in the first place": these three areas are not just theories but the areas in which the theories are to be put into practice by those seeking to live philosophically.

PRACTICE

Sellars follows a long tradition in pointing to two strains in philosophy, one that is not intended to have practical application, centering on logical argument and theory, and one tied to everyday life. He argues that Stoicism is the main school of thought among all the others to pursue the latter, in seeking to put in practice the idea of philosophy as the art of living. But he does this by showing that Stoics focused on the person and the life of the philosopher, suggesting that the most important manifestation or expression of philosophy is in how we live. This is ostensibly the test of the school of thought itself and of the person seeking to live according to it. The individual embodies a particular view in his or her person and actions.

Though at one level this view is intuitive, it raises potential problems. One is the problem of hypocrisy. When an adherent of a school is found not to live according to its tenets, it might seem to invalidate or cast doubt on particular tenets or the school of thought altogether.[64] Or else those tenets can still ring true, even when they are not sound.

Another problem has to do with the limits of supposed realism. In today's culture, other values, precisely such as realism, as well as efficiency, cause many to dismiss principled philosophical views on the grounds that they are too unrealistic, impractical, and unreachable. Few can live such unimpeachable lives. Thus the whole view in question must be flawed and rest on an incorrect assessment of human beings' capacities. The view can also be dismissed on functional, consequentialist grounds: it does not work. So there is a problem intrinsic to the concept of a practical philosophy. Saddling a philosophy with the need for practical application can risk an instrumentalism about logic and truth claims. Only those that can be applied and get desirable results seem valid or trustworthy.

An answer to this problem, according to Sellars, can be found in distinctions between types of practices or techniques, or arts and crafts. Sellars describes the stochastic (unpredictable) arts, like medicine, as those that, even when practiced with excellence, cannot always succeed and get the results desired. In the practice of medicine, because of outside factors, the patient can die even after the best medical care. Whether a philosophy is or is not getting practical results is hard to show because results are not always a scientific matter. Sellars distinguishes Socrates's philosophy as different from this and instead calls it "transformational." The transformational arts, when practiced properly, are always successful because the change comes from within, in the state of one's soul. Judging a philosophical view by its results does not have to be incompatible with the search for truth. To Sellars, they go together: "The idea that philosophy is concerned with one's way of life should not be assumed to imply that practical concerns outweigh a commitment to truth. Instead it combines a commitment to the truth with the claim that that commitment is not merely theoretical but will also have real-world consequences" (x). Sellars goes on: "A contrast is sometimes drawn between analytic philosophy committed to 'truth and knowledge' and populist forms of philosophy serving up 'moral or spiritual improvement' or 'chicken soup for the soul'" (ix). The references here are to Scott Soames and Simon Blackburn (ixn9).[65] The idea that philosophy has practical consequences for personal life seems to go against the idea of a pursuit of knowledge and truth as embodied in "the famous Socratic thesis that virtue is knowledge." But even if one might not agree that virtue is knowledge in and of itself, one can still hold "to the view that a philosophical pursuit of truth and knowledge will have an impact upon and express itself in one's way of life" (x).

As Sellars clarifies in the 2009 preface to his book, which was first published in 2003, he is arguing against the view of those who interpret Epictetus, or Socrates before him, as holding an "intellectualist conception of virtue," who take these two philosophers as saying that "knowledge (of, say, virtue) is on its own enough to impact on a person's life" (x). This intellectualist conception is the idea that "knowledge should be sufficient on its own" (x–xi), that "philosophical knowledge should be identified with mastery of philosophical doctrines" by themselves (xi). Sellars does not understand this concept of philosophy to be the one operating in the teachings of either Socrates or the Stoics.

Sellars's argument rests on the idea that the Stoics (following Socrates) had an idea of "philosophy as an art or craft." This means that the *content* of philosophical knowledge is not just abstract doctrine but has to do with everyday life. One can still have an "intellectualist concept of virtue," but the content of that concept is crucial. It includes *both* theory and practice: "Philosophical knowledge will require both mastery of philosophical doctrines *and* a subsequent period of training or exercise designed to digest those doctrines." Philosophy is thus like other arts and crafts, in the eyes of the Stoics. So just because philosophy is practical, it is no less a search for truth. It is just not truth as separate from life. The dichotomy between truth and knowledge, on the one hand, and how to live, on the other, does not fit Stoic teachings.

Sellars describes the two concepts of philosophy as one in which "knowledge (ἐπιστήμη) is conceived as rational explanation or intellectual analysis (λόγος)" versus "the kind of knowledge found in an art or craft (τέχνη)" (171), and as "theoretical knowledge" versus "practical wisdom." This is an Aristotelian distinction "between ἐπιστήμη [episteme] and φρόνησις [phronesis]," or between "rational understanding of the world" versus "how one should act." Sellars's point is that these two fall under the aegis of one view of "knowledge as technical knowledge," which entails "training or exercise ἄσκησις [askēsis]" resulting in action, and also including "knowledge as rational understanding primarily expressed in words; as λόγος" (171).

Sellars insists it is this understanding of philosophy as an art or craft (τέχνη) that best explains Stoicism, which consisted of two stages—the mastery of philosophical doctrine and then practical training. He cites Sorabji as cautioning against too "automatic" a connection, as in "the creation of a theory in abstract followed by the application of theory."[66] Instead, these two elements *are* philosophical knowledge. Both are "constitutive of philosophy as conceived as a τέχνη which is at once both theoretical and practical" (170n12). It is a case not of theory *versus* practice, knowledge *versus* application, but of knowledge as in a craft's knowledge of both theory and practice. The idea of knowledge as craft-type knowledge is Sellars's central point—that the Stoics' knowledge was intrinsic to their practice. Theory and practice are not separate but complementary, "both necessary components of a technical conception of philosophy" (xi).

What stands out is the formulation from Epictetus that Stoicism involves focusing only on those things in our control, not those out of our control. The Stoics might have been emphasizing that some things are in our control, assuming fate as the default, while we assume freedom as the default and might need the reminder that some things are not. Was Stoics' emphasis on what was actionable, our moral responsibility, whereas ours is on what is controllable?[67] The ancient Stoics emphasized the forging of character in meeting challenges and advised against being caught up with those things that had no bearing on our moral character. So the former is part of a process of deciding what is good and virtuous, the latter of deciding what we can control.

It is unclear how important action is for Sellars. It certainly was for Socrates. In Sellars's discussion of the Stoics' indebtedness to Socrates and their desire to harken back to Socrates's notion of "deeds not words," Sellars may be reflecting modern terms in thinking of it as a case of how a philosopher lives—as a more important reflection of philosophical thinking than the teachings or writings themselves, the difference between a modern notion of lifestyle and an ancient art of living. Socrates and the Stoics could be placing the emphasis on the need to act, the desirability of taking action, as a person's philosophy becomes clear through those actions, as in Aristotle's notion of the *telos*, or purpose, of life. Sellars does say, "Philosophy is something primarily expressed in one's way of life" (54).[68] *Eudaemonia* might be anemic without a concept of *telos*.

The problem is that this approaches the argument for a utilitarian form of pragmatism, which tests ideas for their use value. If some ideas are true but cannot be enacted, they then risk being cast aside as useless. We must caution against too automatic or mechanical a relation between theory and practice. The idea that the most usable theories have the most value puts the onus on the question of how we define what is useful—what we need. This should not be assumed, though; it is something we must argue. When it is assumed, the rest becomes a matter of technique or process, as if the only things that are debatable are *how* to live, as in technique of living—*how-to*—versus how we could, would, should live, what it means to be fully alive, and how it is possible to be fully alive. In the modern version of accepting the things we can and cannot control, something vital gets lost in translation. Stoicism was in antiquity more a system for figuring out *what was good and what was not* by determining whether it was relevant to one's moral character, and thereby worth acting upon. Now the decision is about what can and cannot be controlled, or what is relevant to our psychological comfort or sense of power. Then it was about what was or was not good. Morality is missing from the modern therapeutic version of Stoicism. We have the outward appearance of Stoicism without the moral component. The point is just to feel better, whereas for ancient Stoics the question was how virtuous one was. Inheritors of the general goal of the eudaemonist philosophies but not the details, inhabitants of therapeutic culture come up against the difficulty of feeling better when only thinking about feeling better.

Sellars identifies ἀρετή as the raison d'être of Stoicism, translated as virtue or excellence of the soul. The ethical theory of the Stoics rested on the concept of οἰκείωσις, variously translated as orientation or appropriation (57n10). This idea rests on the notion that self-preservation guides both animals and humans, who gravitate toward what supports their "own internal nature" and guard anything that would damage it. For a rational being, this means preservation of one's "constitution *qua* rational being" (Sellars, 58) beyond the mere pursuit of "one's primary impulses such as food or health or wealth," which lead only to self-preservation "*qua* animal" (58). "The famous Stoic claim that only virtue or excellence (*arête* in Greek) is good and that all else are "indifferents" must be understood within this framework (58). The reason why some things are our concerns and some are not is that some do have a role in the pursuit of excellence and self-fulfillment of humans' rational nature and some are irrelevant and may involve our animal nature.

That this can at times sound like a cold and unfeeling doctrine is apparent in the toughest instructions of Epictetus. To have concern only with one's own moral excellence can sound solipsistic as it can still be concern only about oneself. Shorn of the aspiration to virtue or excellence, it sounds like mere selfishness—concern for the self to the exclusion of others.

EMOTION THERAPY

It might appear that Stoicism would be an antitherapy movement today. Yet it is in many ways compatible with modern therapeutic culture. Some of the modern interpretations suggest that Stoicism is currently being viewed through a therapeutic lens. Even Richard Sorabji, who in his prolific writings presents fine-grained scholarly analyses of the ideas of very different philosophers and philosophical traditions, points to the continuing relevance of Stoic insights about the self for personal use. In *Emotion and Peace of Mind*, Sorabji paints a more general portrait of what he would like us to keep in mind when characterizing the school of thought as a whole and when using Stoic insights about the self and emotion as a kind of self-therapy—which is precisely what he suggests we do.[69]

Massimo Pigliucci, a philosopher at City College of New York, grew up in Rome, Italy, where he encountered Stoicism as part of his education. He shows one contemporary interpretation of what it means to be a Stoic in his *New York Times* op-ed "How to Be a Stoic." Rather than the stereotype of "keeping a stiff upper lip and suppressing my emotions," this means engaging in a set of spiritual practices. He notes the popularity of Stoicism as seen in the thousands who participate in "Stoic Week" in the UK. He decided to "become a Stoic" by practicing Stoicism for a year. To him, this meant a ten-minute morning meditation on the day's upcoming demands and what virtues they would require. It involved exercises such as "Hierocles' circle" (illustrating connection from family to community to the entire living world with a series of expanding concentric circles), *premeditatio malorum* (imagining and thus anticipating life's inevitable setbacks), and repeating a Stoic saying several times. It entailed practicing "mindfulness" throughout the day and ending the day by writing in his journal about how well he handled himself. It meant "Pretty much every decision I make has a moral dimension," as it did for the Stoics, since they held that one's moral character is paramount. Pigliucci grants that those Stoic practices and principles were originally tied to their wider outlook, including particular metaphysical, scientific, and epistemological views he does not adhere to, such as a belief in *Logos*, divine reason—the rational principle as "the manifestation of a divine creative mind." As a guide to everyday behavior, Stoicism entails applying the concept of identifying which things in life hold any importance for our attention and energies, according to whether they affect our moral character and are in our control or not. Even given elements that he "cannot subscribe to as a modern secular philosopher and scientist," he is interested in "exploring just how much one can recover of the original Stoic spirit." He ultimately sees it as "simply another path some people can try out in order to develop a more or less coherent view of the world, of who they are, and of how they fit in the broader scheme of things."[70] The modern version seems to eclipse the ancient, as being a Stoic replaces living Stoically, and on donning a self-chosen identity versus taking action.

Edmund Kern, a professor of history at Lawrence University, sees the Harry Potter cultural phenomenon, based on the books by J. K. Rowling, as signaling a Stoic response both to the position of children in general and to the insecurities of the post-9/11 world. In an article published the week of the opening of a new Harry Potter movie and before the fifth book's publication, Kern argues that the popularity of the series comes in part from their Stoic themes: "Focusing on the books themselves shows that Rowling develops an essentially Stoic moral philosophy through the ethical dilemmas in which she places Harry and his friends—dilemmas requiring them to think in complex ways about right and wrong. Her version of Stoicism is admittedly an updated one, but nonetheless one whose chief virtue is old-fashioned constancy. Harry's resolution in the face of adversity is the result of conscious choice and attention to what is and is not within his control. Harry worries about who he is, but realizes that what he does matters most. And, I believe, so do the children reading the books."[71]

Kern thinks that Rowling "has measured the sensibilities of today's kids," providing a formula that draws adults as well as children. Kern sees Stoicism as having a special appeal today. Originally, he planned only to suggest why readers might gravitate to Harry Potter's Stoicism. Yet, writing a couple of months after the 9/11 attacks, he concludes by conjecturing that many people actually "have found solace" in the Stoic themes of Harry Potter. The series manages to "tap into a philosophy that offers comfort to readers—both children and adults—as they try to work their ways through the uncertainty of the world." This notion of the books as a salve seems to point to the therapeutic function of literature. There is a tension between the content of the philosophy and assumptions about its use or function that highlights the possibility that the main differences between ancient and modern versions are ideas about what is therapeutic and should be. It is a confusing article. On the one hand, children like the message of meeting adversity with strength and courage, and on the other the "chief motives" of the Harry Potter characters are "empathy, compassion, and tolerance." These are not quite the virtues the Stoics emphasized—"courage, equanimity, self-control, and wisdom," as Pigliucci puts it. What explains this disjuncture is the therapeutic overlay onto the Stoic views: the Harry Potter series is most useful, perhaps, in exploring the tensions between these sensibilities.[72] The Stoics suggested a self-discipline that could also provide comfort but was based on their notions about the world, not aimed to provide comfort by altering the way they viewed the world.

In *Stoic Warriors*, ethical philosopher Nancy Sherman, professor at Georgetown University, examines the Stoic philosophy that imbues the modern military ethos. When she taught ethics at the US Naval Academy, she found that Epictetus resonated for her students. While she acknowledges the ways Stoicism does help with many of the challenges facing members of the military, she points to the costs of the particular version of Stoicism operating in the American military today. Returning to the ancient texts, she argues that the Stoics grappled with the very questions that need to be faced today and had more nuanced answers than today's stereotypes about Stoicism allow. Fears that a Stoic attitude, stripped of these nuances, can obscure questions of right and wrong emerge in Sherman's treatment. She advocates a chastened "gentle" form of Stoicism to guard against such possible misunderstandings and misuses.[73]

Richard Sorabji invited James Stockdale to the University of London in 1993 to speak about his own Stoicism, and the talk is reprinted in the middle of Stockdale's book, *Thoughts of a Philosophical Fighter Pilot*. Stockdale read Epictetus and concluded, "For the Stoic, the state of his *inner* self . . . is all that is important [italics in original]."[74] Stockdale was a US Air Force fighter pilot who, like John McCain, was shot down over Hanoi, Vietnam, and was tortured in captivity. Stockdale's ability to endure that torture is central to his understanding of Stoicism, as it has applied to his life. In McCain's version, which, through his multiple bids for the presidency, has blended into his public persona, he learned his Stoicism as much from his parents as from Epictetus.[75] Even after McCain's funeral, the press described his then-106-year-old mother as "stoic," and while the description did not directly evoke ancient Stoicism with a capital S, it indirectly continued the public perception of the family's Stoicism.[76]

Stoicism has also become a popular self-help philosophy for CEOs. Scores of books for businesspeople now tout the usefulness of Stoicism. One of the most influential is *The Obstacle Is the Way*, by Ryan Holiday. Holiday extracts a paragraph he thinks is the most essential part of Marcus's *Meditations*: "Our actions may be impeded . . . but there can be no impeding our intentions or dispositions. Because we can accommodate and adapt. The mind adapts and converts to its own purposes the obstacle to our acting. The impediment to action advances action. What stands in the way becomes the way."[77] He interprets the main message of Stoicism as one of overcoming any and all challenges and makes this his mantra: "In Marcus' works is the secret to an art known as *turning obstacles upside down* [italics in original] . . . making certain that what impedes us can empower us."[78] Holiday offers an interpretation of society as divided into those who are "paralyzed" and "dissatisfied" by all of the problems in their own lives and in the world and those who transform "those very obstacles . . . into launching pads for themselves."[79] He lumps together all successful people, including John D. Rockefeller, Demosthenes, Abraham Lincoln, Steve Jobs, James Stockdale, Laura Ingalls Wilder, and Barack Obama, because they all share one thing: the ability to turn the obstacles they faced into motivation.[80] Though he says all of Marcus's wisdom is contained in that single paragraph and that his own book is not full of "gushing, hazy optimism" or "folksy sayings or cute but utterly ineffectual proverbs," that does not prevent him from going on for another couple hundred pages with . . . exactly that. Each chapter of *The Obstacle Is the Way* begins with a motivational quote, profiles a different famous person, and interprets his or her life story in light of Holiday's formula for success: taking control, keeping going, not quitting, and working hard. He has published numerous other books—such as *Trust Me, I'm Lying: Confessions of a Media Manipulator*, *Growth Hacker Marketing*, and *Ego Is the Enemy*—which have sold millions of copies. Even the NFL finds inspiration in Stoicism via Ryan Holiday these days.[81]

Other people rarely figure into the plan Holiday lays out, nor does he worry about the consequences of the actions people might take if they followed his philosophy, which is not much different from Nike's advertising slogan "Just do it." One suspects tough Stoicism comes in handy as a rationale for cutthroat business practices (such as the firings dramatized on *The Apprentice*). After all, business is the battlefield the CEOs have in mind. As their salaries soar in the era of downsizing, automation, capital flight, and AI, a Stoicism retrofitted for both quelling a guilty conscience and continuing such practices serves the bottom line. Holiday admires Theodore Roosevelt for his embodiment of "the strenuous life": "To Roosevelt, life was like an arena and he was a gladiator."[82] Holiday's diagnosis is that people today need to be tougher. The way to do it is to reevaluate our individual behavior, since we cannot hope to make any difference in the world. The problem, he says to the reader, is: "You're going soft. You're not aggressive enough." He calls for a reconsideration of certain traits: "For some reason, these days we tend to downplay the importance of aggression, of taking risks, of barreling forward." In the end, the problem plaguing modern Americans is "thinking negatively."[83] Predictably, the Serenity Prayer fits his model of caring only for what is in our control. At the end of the book, he leaves the reader with a call to action, as if all actions were equally good: the goal is "to see things *philosophically* and *act* accordingly [italics in original]."[84] Deceptively shrouded in soft therapy-speak, this tough Stoicism risks sweeping up with it all the other more valiant attempts to find a Stoicism for our times.

In today's climate, it is too easy to imagine what goes wrong when we do not have a gentler Stoicism of the kind Sherman suggests. It is possible that part of what we are seeing in modern politics, economics, and social life is a kind of misplaced Stoicism. Firings and plant closures, exclusion of immigrants, and tough-on-crime stances all become a new therapy for those frustrated with complexity and leniency. The irony of Stoic emotional therapy is that Stoicism is associated with being unemotional, with the aim of discouraging irrational thoughts. Early Stoic philosophy acknowledged the power of emotion and advocated control of the emotions through thought and technique, and even through their eradication. Only gross misinterpretation can equate Stoicism with heartlessness. Making a modern therapy of hardness and self-interest can all too easily go awry to funnel emotion into aggression or even violence.

Another approach has arisen that offers a potential alternative to the therapeutic mode. The practical philosophy movement has opened a window onto something that could provide a truly different mentality. As long as our contemporary culture is governed by a therapeutic mentality, it risks being subsumed by the dominant culture. Yet there is a memory of something else, or an instinct. This keeps us stuck in a back-and-forth motion between poles at the extremes of the same orbit. These pendulum swings harken back to elemental categories and have the potential to foster disastrous conflict. Unrestrained, a pendulum swing unhinged becomes a wrecking ball. We often remedy what we see as the problems of one disposition with a drastic swing to another. Put in the most crass and simplified terms, the struggle often emerges as a primordial conflict between the masculine and feminine, with the feminine in this case connoting the therapeutic. The feminine is connected, in this vision, with feeling, and the masculine with thought and reason. So the correction to an overly feminized therapeutic government—the term *nanny state* says it all— and ideals of love and care is a hard and tough application of supposed masculine practicality. Brexit may be a case in point.

When the alternatives are pared down in this way, the only result is division and disaster. Human social life is not so simple, and human nature resists such gross categorization. The knee-jerk resort to hypermasculinity as a solution simplifies problems and current conditions needing addressing. It lends itself to political reaction and social exclusion, hierarchy and domination. Fierceness replaces compassion as defenders of a return to masculinity marshal a whole history of martial values, wrongly singled out and wrested from honor-based cultures. An ideology of toughness lends itself to attacks on social groups—whether women or children, blacks or Latinx immigrants or refugees, Jews or Muslims, and the list goes on—on a categorical basis.

Identifying the handful of dispositions undergirding our different approaches to life can aid in the all-important task of separating a disposition from an entire social group. When a social group is seen as the repository of an undesirable approach, set of traits, or ideology, that group might experience greater inclusion at times but is at risk when the pendulum swings in the opposite direction. It is probably inevitable that societies will go through times of greater expansion and contraction, since actual resources or perceptions about available resources play a role. To ensure that such times do not lead to ostracism, exclusion, expulsion, or other forms of oppression—sometimes milder, sometimes much worse—we must be able to identify strains of thought underlying our different approaches to social problems and the need to coexist in a world of others by definition not identical to ourselves. The upsurge of right-wing reaction, racism, and sexism makes this task urgent.

TO BE MOVED WITHIN

It is crucial not to fall into a mode of simplistic dismissal of all Stoicism as being the tough variety, for we do not even need to wander far from such moral guidelines as presented by the Stoics to find, in their own works, hints of the limits of the logical mode of thinking so carefully laid out for us.[85] Near the very end of Seneca's *Consolation* cited above, for just one small example, there is a moment that offers something quite different from what he has been recommending all along:

> Nature requires from us some sorrow, while more than this is the result of vanity. But never will I demand of you that you should not grieve at all. And I well know that some men are to be found whose wisdom is harsh rather than brave, who deny that the wise man will ever grieve. But these, it seems to me, can never have fallen upon this sort of mishap; if they had, Fortune would have knocked their proud philosophy out of them, and, even against their will, have forced them to admit the truth. Reason will have accomplished enough if only she removes

from grief whatever is excessive and superfluous; it is not for anyone to hope or to desire that she should suffer us to feel no sorrow at all. Rather let her maintain a mean which will copy neither indifference nor madness, and will keep us in the state that is the mark of an affectionate, and not an unbalanced, mind. Let your tears flow, but let them also cease, let deepest sighs be drawn from your breast, but let them also find an end.[86]

Does this recognition of the reality of emotion even in a text arguing for the need to overcome emotion suggest the limits of Neo-Stoicism as a compelling alternative to therapeutic and other ills of our own age? In *The Corporeal Imagination: Signifying the Holy in Late Ancient Christianity* (2009), Patricia Cox Miller suggests that ideas like those of third-century Neo-Platonist Plotinus and others rather than Marcus Aurelius be reconsidered for our times: "When Plotinus directs the eye of the soul inward, the vision that emerges is starkly different from the internalized self-watchers of Marcus Aurelius."[87]

As even the Stoic Seneca seems to acknowledge here, no matter how hard we might try to reason our way beyond it, we are truly creatures of emotion. Granted, we have reason, the opposable thumb, and an unusual ability to adapt; we are not beholden to any one environment. But we also possess a prodigious capacity for feeling. We have in our inner lives a vast, intricate palette at our disposal when we choose to use it. Any list of our capacities—any description of our very makeup—would be woefully incomplete if it did not feature prominently the truly remarkable ability we have to experience the world not only through sense perception—sight, smell, sound, taste, and touch—but through profound alterations, sensitivities, responses, and resonances in our internal feeling-state. Within this inner world, at any given time we may be going through affective states of remarkable variety, complexity, and depth. There is no telling which ones, in what order or combination, and at what intensity. And we may or may not be doing so in response to our immediate surroundings. Our psychological state—because of our capacity for abstract thought in the form of memory, imagination, and anticipation—may be more influenced by something elsewhere entirely; it represents a unique combination of our immediate and less-than-immediate lives, our multitudinous pasts, coexisting presents, and infinite futures. Further, our emotional capacity is not merely a *response* to concrete given realities and rational or irrational thoughts about other realities, real or imagined: it is part and parcel of this very ability to move us in and out of our most immediate surroundings and imagine alternative realities. Our emotions are, in many ways, our very ticket to the experience of transcendence and immanence alike. They are the starting point of abstract thought.

The capacity to be moved *within* lies at the core of who we are. The Stoics knew this more than most. That is not to say emotion is what makes us stand apart from other animals, for no one who has spent time with a canine companion need ever question whether other species have the capacity to feel. Rather, it is emotion, in large part, that makes us who we *are*, both individually and collectively, not in distinction from anyone else but in ourselves. Our ability to feel sets the limits and opens the possibilities of what we can do and think. As a portrait artist sketches the outline of a figure to be painted, our experiences, capabilities, and enactments of emotion give rise to the particular character of what we become— filling in the portrait that is our completed life. Emotion is thus implicated in nearly everything we do.

Once we begin considering the powerful role of emotion in our lives, it becomes everywhere apparent as a factor in everything from historical events to the way a particular society is structured and arranged. In modern thought in the West, Sigmund Freud, another twentieth-century Stoic, notably emphasized the force of emotion as motivation and explanation for human behavior. In *Civilization and Its Discontents*, he lucidly drew out the broader implications for humans of the interconnections of emotional, intellectual, and psychological states, targeting the nexus between our instincts and drives, on the one hand, and the imperatives of living socially, on the other, as the locus of concern.[88] For it is at this crossroads, where two very different courses intersect, that battles of tragic potential break out again and again in each of us, as well as in whole societies. The battles can be triumphs, or they can decimate us, or still more often, they can rage or simmer over the course of a lifetime of irresolution. But whatever their length or scope, it is the precise nature of the battles fought that defines us. Our self-definition is in the details.

FIGURE I.1. Socrates. Marble bust and base, Roman origin, first century AD. Musée du Louvre, Paris. Photo: Daniel Lebée/Carine Déambrosis. © RMN-Grand Palais/Art Resource, NY.

FIGURE I.2. Raphael (Raffaello Sanzio) (1483–1520), *The School of Athens*, ca. 1510–12. Stanza della Segnatura, Apostolic Palace, Vatican City. One of the murals Raphael painted for Pope Julius II. In the center background, Plato (resembling Leonardo da Vinci) discourses with Aristotle. Right: Euclid (resembling Bramante) explains a geometrical problem. Photo Credit: Erich Lessing/ Art Resource, NY.

FIGURE I.3. Judy Chicago (b. 1939), Detail—*The Dinner Party*, Hypatia place setting, 1979. Mixed media. Brooklyn Museum. Photo: © Donald Woodman. Photo Credit: Photo courtesy of Judy Chicago/Art Resource, NY. © 2019 Judy Chicago/Artists Rights Society (ARS), NY.

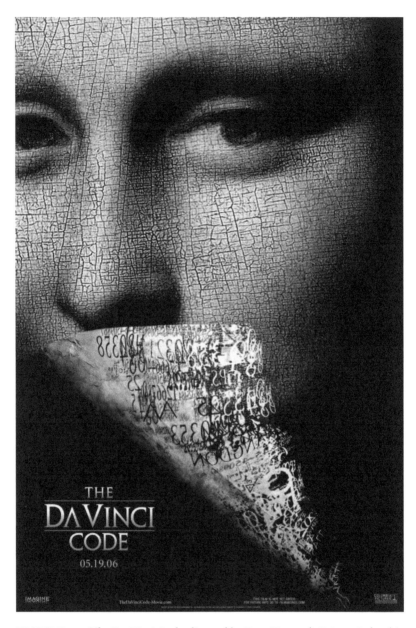

FIGURE 1.1. *The Da Vinci Code*, directed by Ron Howard. © 2006 Columbia Pictures Industries, Inc. All Rights Reserved. Courtesy of Columbia Pictures.

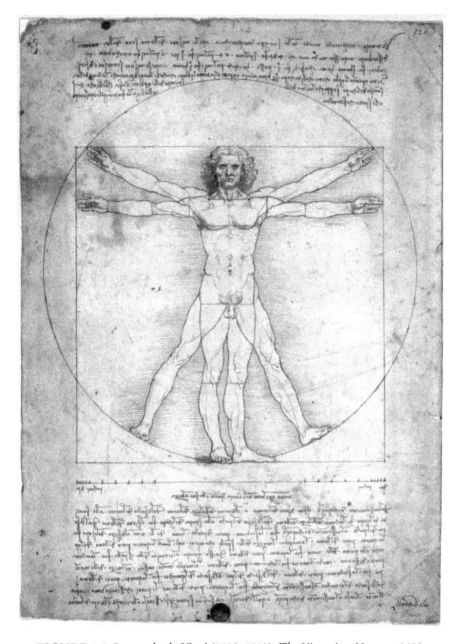

FIGURE 1.2. Leonardo da Vinci (1452–1519), *The Vitruvian Man*, ca. 1490.
Proportions of the human body according to Vitruvius. Pen and brown ink,
brush and some brown wash over metalpoint on paper, 13 9/16 x 9 5/8 in. Gal-
lerie dell'Accademia, Venice. Photo Credit: Scala/Art Resource, NY.

FIGURE 1.3. Leonardo da Vinci (1452–1519), *Mona Lisa*, ca. 1503–17. Musée du Louvre, Paris. Oil on wood, 77 x 53 cm. Photo: René-Gabriel Ojéda. © RMN-Grand Palais/Art Resource, NY.

FIGURE 1.4. Gaia (the primordial Earth goddess). Marble bust. Hellenistic, third-second century BC. From Zarko (Phayttos), Thessaly, Greece. Archaeological Museum, Istanbul. © Vanni Archive/Art Resource, NY.

FIGURE 2.1. *Gladiator*, directed by Ridley Scott. © 2000 DreamWorks LLC and Universal Studios. All Rights Reserved. Courtesy of NBCUniversal (worldwide, outside U.S.) and Paramount Pictures Corp. (U.S.).

FIGURE 2.2. Marcus Aurelius (r. AD 161–80) with a cuirass. Marble bust, h. 62 cm., ca. AD 170. Musée du Louvre, Paris. Photo: Hervé Lewandowski. © RMN-Grand Palais/Art Resource, NY.

FIGURE 2.3. Nicolas Poussin (1594–1665), *The Empire of Flora (Flora's Realm)*, 1631. Old Masters Picture Gallery (Gemäldegalerie Alte Meister), Dresden. Three gods—Flora, Apollo, and Pan; Ajax killing himself, Adonis and Hyacinth both wounded: spring and flowers issue from death. Oil on canvas, 131 x 181 cm. Photo Credit: bpk Bildagentur/Gemäldegalerie Alte Meister/ Elke Estel/Hans-Peter Klut/Art Resource, NY.

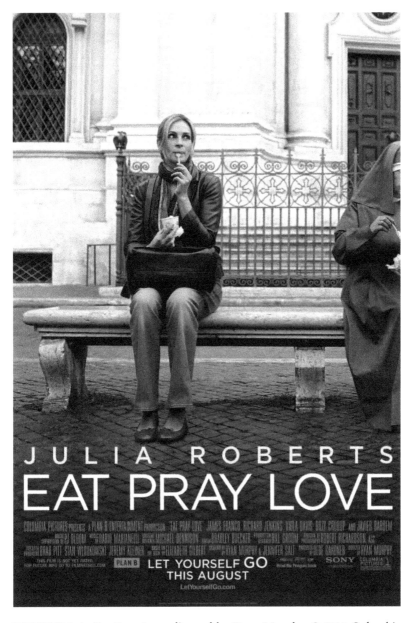

FIGURE 3.1. *Eat Pray Love*, directed by Ryan Murphy. © 2010 Columbia Pictures Industries, Inc. All Rights Reserved. Courtesy of Columbia Pictures.

FIGURE 3.2. Epicurus (Epikouros). Marble bust, second century AD, Roman copy of a Greek original (first half of the third century BC). Metropolitan Museum of Art, New York. Rogers Fund, 1911. Open Access, Creative Commons Zero (CC0) license.

FIGURE 3.3. Lucretius, *De rerum natura*, first century BC. Manuscript frontispiece by Girolamo di Matteo de Tauris for Pope Sixtus IV, 1483. Vatican Library, Vatican City.

FIGURE 3.4. Sandro Botticelli (1444–1510), *Primavera*, ca. 1481. Uffizi Gallery, Florence. Tempera on wood, 203 x 314 cm. Photo Credit: Scala/Art Resource, NY.

FIGURE 3.5. *The Lunchbox*, directed by Ritesh Batra, 2013. Artwork from "The Lunchbox" appears courtesy of Sony Pictures Classics Inc.

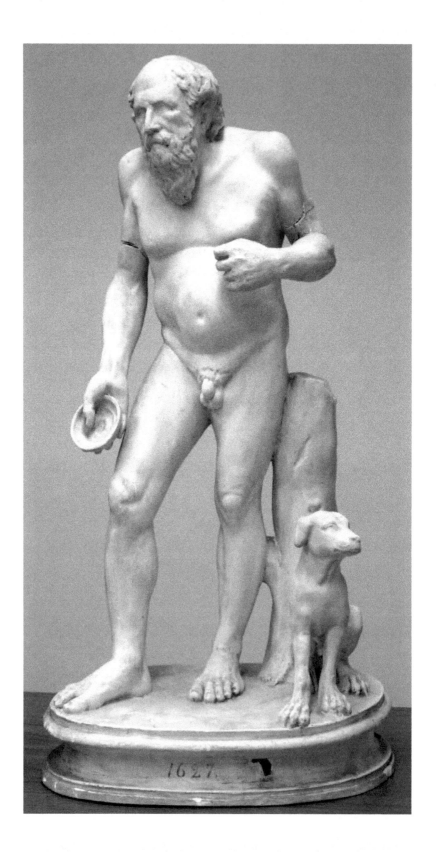

FIGURE 4.1. (*left*) Diogenes. Plaster cast, ca. 1890–1900, of a Roman copy (second century AD) of a Greek original (third or second century BC). Cornell University cast collection, Ithaca, NY. Photographer: Danielle Mericle. © (photo) Cornell University Library, Annetta Alexandridis, and Verity Platt.

FIGURE 4.2. (*below*) Jean-Léon Gérôme (France, 1824–1904), *Diogenes*, 1860. Oil on canvas, 74.5 x 101 cm. Image courtesy of the Walters Art Museum, Baltimore.

FIGURE 4.3. Crates and Hipparchia, wall painting, ca. first century AD. From the garden of the Villa Farnesina, Museo delle Terme, Rome. Photo: The Picture Art Collection/Alamy Stock Photo.

FIGURE 4.4. John William Waterhouse (England, 1849–1917), *Diogenes*, 1882. Oil on canvas, 208.3 x 134.6 cm. Purchased 1886. Art Gallery of New South Wales, Sydney. Photo: AGNSW.

FIGURE 5.1. Plato. Marble bust, date unknown (Hellenistic) (the inscription "Xenon" at base is possibly modern). Sala delle Muse, Museo Pio Clementino, Vatican Museums, Vatican State. Photo credit: Scala/ Art Resource, NY.

FIGURE 5.2. Plotinus (?). White marble bust, date unknown. Museo, Ostia, Italy. Photo credit: Album/ Art Resource, NY.

FIGURE 5.3. Philippe de Champaigne (Flanders, 1602–74), *Saint Augustine*, ca. 1645. Oil on canvas, 78.74 x 62.23 cm. Gift of the Ahmanson Foundation, Los Angeles County Museum of Art, Los Angeles. Painting in Public Domain. Image courtesy of www.lacma.org.

FIGURE 5.4. (*above*) *Hidden Figures*, directed by Theodore Melfi. © 2017 Twentieth Century Fox. All rights reserved.

Figure 5.5. (*opposite*) Romare Bearden (1911–88), *Martin Luther King, Jr.— Mountain Top*, 1968. Screenprint, 76 x 49.8 cm. Smithsonian National Portrait Gallery, Washington, D.C. © 2019 Romare Bearden Foundation/Licensed by VAGA at Artists Rights Society (ARS), NY.

FIGURE 5.6. *Serenade, after Plato's Symposium*, by Leonard Bernstein. © 1954 by Amberson Holdings LLC. Copyright renewed by Leonard Bernstein Music Publishing. International copyright secured. Reprinted by permission. All rights reserved.

FIGURE E.1. *Once*, directed and written by John Carney, 2007. Courtesy of Lions Gate Films Inc. and Samson Films.

THREE

THE NEW EPICUREANISM

Bon appetit!
—*Julia Child*

"I'm in love," declares Julia Roberts's character, Liz, in a famous scene in the 2010 movie *Eat Pray Love*. Based on the memoir of the same name written by Elizabeth Gilbert, the movie chronicles the personal transformation of a young woman who flees her stifling life of marital, social, and work commitments in New York and embarks on a year of travel.[1] (See fig. 3.1.) Once in Italy, she awakens to new feelings and experiences. In this scene we find her dining with her new friend from Sweden, Sofi (Tuva Novotny), at a real restaurant in Naples known worldwide for its pizza, L'Antica Pizzeria da Michele. Between mouthfuls of soft dough dripping with cheese and tomato sauce, Liz continues, "I'm having a relationship with my pizza." At the same time, she takes stock of the body language of Sofi, and adds, "You look like you're breaking up with your pizza. What's the matter?" With a look of regret, Sofi replies, "I can't." Liz asks, "What do you mean you can't? This is Pizza Margherita in Napoli. It is imperative to eat and enjoy that pizza."

A heart-to-heart exchange follows, increasing the intimacy of their friendship. Sofi confesses that she has been gaining weight in Italy and points to her stomach, asking what the word is for the extra inches. "A muffin top," Liz retorts. "I have one too." Sofi glances at the pizza, saying, "I unbuttoned my jeans like five minutes ago just looking at this." Liz replies by asking whether any man who has ever seen her without clothes has ever left the room, and when Sofi admitted no one has, Liz delivers a minisoliloquy:

> Because he doesn't care. He's in a room with a naked girl. He's won the lottery. I'm so tired of saying no and waking up in the morning and recalling every single thing I ate the day before. Counting every calorie I consumed so I know exactly how much self-loathing to take into the shower. I'm going for it. I have no interest in being obese; I'm just through with the guilt. So this is what I'm going to do, I'm going to finish this pizza and then we're going to go watch the soccer game and tomorrow we're going to go on a little date and buy ourselves some bigger jeans.

The follow-up scene shows them trying to shoe-horn their way into jeans from every position, including splayed out flat on the dressing room floor. Intermittently, the camera flashes back to the soccer game, with the competition and cheers of the crowd a backdrop to their own physical exertions as they try to squeeze into a smaller size. The scene ends with them purchasing their new larger jeans, poised to go on to enjoy Italy to the fullest.

EXPERIENCING EXPERIENCE

Working in what might appear to be a modern Epicurean mode, *Eat Pray Love* is a widely known self-help-type crossover, a production that became virtually a genre unto itself. Taking the form of a kind of personal travelogue, this wildly popular movie alluded to in Kachka's comment in the Introduction, was based on Gilbert's equally sensational 2006 memoir.[2] The book was reissued in 2016 in a tenth-anniversary paperback, along with a volume of readers' stories about their responses to the original book called *Eat Pray Love Made Me Do It*.[3] The whole phenomenon offers a perfect glimpse into current-day Epicureanism and some of the contradictions of contemporary culture.

Perhaps some of *Eat Pray Love*'s appeal was that it rode the wave of a resurgence of Epicureanism, in developments often quite different from one another, including the gourmet revolution that began in the late twentieth century, the massive expansion of the leisure and entertainment industry, the celebrity culture boom, and consumerism more broadly. We can see explicit and implicit Epicurean themes in movements such as slow food, clean eating, and buying local, as well as in aesthetically focused pursuits such as architecture, urban redesign, gardening, and the simple life movement. As is the case with other schools of thought, movements drawing on some form of Epicureanism diverge widely, embracing everything from hedonism to asceticism, often departing unrecognizably from the school's origins.

Some of the more explicit references to a new Epicureanism include the rise of the foodie culture, film and television minigenres such as the vineyard or wine movie (*Sideways*) or the chef or cooking show or movie (for instance, *Julie and Julia*, about Julia Child, or *The Great British Baking Show*), and a larger group of movies involving food, well-being, and settings long deemed Epicurean paradises like Italy, France, and India (*Eat Pray Love, Under the Tuscan Sun, The Lunchbox*). Magazines, e-zines, and websites like *Epicurious* (English), *Epicuro* (Italian), *Epicure* (French), *Epikur* (German), *Epicurean Travel*, and epicure.com, as well as innumerable blogs, present modern visions of Epicurean life in vivid detail. The new Epicurean sensibility at times seems to offer welcome relief from dominant behaviors and cultural patterns. In *Eat Pray Love*, as in another cultural phenomenon, *Mamma Mia!*, audiences clearly reveled in its visions of women and bodily pleasures that offer an alternative to those in so many advertisements, women's magazines, and another self-help genre, the literature of fad diets. Yet in other ways *Eat Pray Love* blends smoothly into mainstream marketing messages, as we see in the rise of "the experience economy."[4]

Current-day Epicureanism turns to experience as the goal of life, giving rise to a sort of "bucket list" culture. The best-selling travel book series *1,000 Places to See before You Die*, not to mention hundreds of similar listicles on the internet, demonstrates how ubiquitous this culture has become. Travelers are so willing to risk their lives for the experience of a lifetime that they have spawned a whole industry around extreme tourism, while stories of tourists dying while posing precariously for a selfie are now commonplace.[5]

In "The Concept of Experience (The Meaning of Life, Part I)," one of the essays in his 2016 book *Against Everything*, Mark Greif, a cofounding editor of the journal *n + 1* and author of *The Age of the Crisis of Man*, identifies a widespread sense today of missing out—a chronic feeling that one is misusing and wasting time—all of which he traces to a certain "*concept of experience* that gives us the feeling we are really living, but makes us unsatisfied with whatever life we obtain."[6] While it is happiness that people pursue, Greif argues, it is such an evanescent, ambiguous, "vague bliss" that instead they become "lifelong collectors" of experiences. Since they cannot live in the most intense moments of feeling and because they wish above all to know what "it *feels like* while doing them," they attempt to stretch out the pleasure by amassing as many of these experiences as possible and having mementos at the ready to revisit during the in-between times. The peaks overshadow the plateaus, and from this cult of experience emanates "a myth of the happier race of people who live on the peaks."[7]

Quantity matters. Not only do we collect multiple experiences, but "we really wish to be multiple." "Televisually," Greif explains, we are constantly fed images of other people living many other kinds of lives, images that promise happiness but leave us feeling disappointed and empty. Besides sex and intoxication, a dominant "technique" for accumulating experiences is travel: "What did you do last year? 'Well, I took a trip to Washington'—or London, or Katmandu. . . . The water cooler conversation in which job holders have the best relief from work revolves around the places they're going or have been."[8]

To equate the "cult of experience" with unlimited self-indulgence would be to ignore crucial tensions, and perhaps even a paradox at the heart of Epicureanism. Indeed, if we pursue Epicureanism seriously, we quickly find that originally it was not equated with indulgence. As classical Epicureanism taught, anyone wishing to live a life filled with enjoyment must know when to refrain from as well as when to surrender to the call of pleasure—a point some modern versions miss. It seems no coincidence that so many Epicurean memoirs and movies spell out a precise time frame for the newly energized and unfettered life. The more difficult question is not how to enjoy a vacation but what to do upon returning to one's day-to-day existence. This is where we need more penetrating explorations of the question of how to live.

ANCIENT EPICUREANISM

The philosopher Epicurus, who was born a few years after Plato died, lived from 342/1 to 271/270 BC. (See fig. 3.2.) Epicurus developed a school of thought aimed at ethics yet joined to its particular understanding of physics, just as we saw with Stoicism. Dedicated to happiness as the aim of human life, he saw that happiness as coming solely from pleasure. Epicurus placed the highest value on a stable (*katastematic*) form of pleasure (*hedone*). This state entailed an absence of both physical pain, *aponia*, and disturbance in the soul, *ataraxia*.[9] Epicureanism became one of the longest-lasting schools, beginning in Epicurus's circle in Mytilene, from which he had to flee, and Lampsacus, then in Athens. Epicurus was the leader, or "hegemon," of a school in Athens called the "Garden" (κῆπος). Founded around 307–4 BC, it was still active centuries later in the Roman Empire. Marcus Aurelius devoted one of the imperial chairs of philosophy he founded in the 170s AD to Epicureanism.

The three areas of Epicurus's system are the canonic, or core, principles; physics, the science of nature; and ethics, everyday choices and the goal of human life. In one scholar's elegant and succinct summary, "The fully materialistic Epicurean science of nature (*physiologia*) is, so to speak, the heart of Epicurus' philosophy. Physiology is based on two eternal and unlimited principles, from which everything originates: atoms and void."[10] A main concept in Epicureanism is the notion of a "swerve" (*clinamen* in Latin), a term later used by Lucretius, who drew closely on the teachings of Epicurus to refer to spontaneous and predictable motions of atoms. The concept came from the physics of the early atomists, upon whom Epicurus drew in turn.

As in the case of the other schools, most early writings have been lost. Thanks to a variety of attempts at preservation or retrieval, events still going on today, there is a growing body of primary sources. Epicurus's major work was considered a masterpiece on the science of nature, *On Nature* (*Peri physeos* / Περὶ Φύσεως), in thirty-seven books. Fragments of that work, those from the excavations from the Villa dei Papiri in Herculaneum in Italy, are all that remain. Fortunately Epicurus's work was widely read and discussed at the time and in the Roman period, so much is known about his ideas. Extant works by Epicurus include those presented in Diogenes Laertius's *Lives of Eminent Philosophers*, a Vatican Library manuscript (containing eighty-one maxims, some overlapping with other works that we have) called the *Vatican Sayings*, and the Herculaneum fragments. Works by other Epicurean philosophers also exist, including those by Philodemus, also excavated in Herculaneum. The famous poem *On Nature* (*De rerum natura*), by Lucretius, exists in its entirety. There is also a stone inscription by Diogenes of Oinoanda (now a part of southwest Turkey). Ongoing excavations and translations continue to reveal new fragments in our own century.

With most of Epicurus's prolific writings lost, Diogenes Laertius's treatment of Epicurus is one of the main sources available on the thought of Epicurus himself. Fortunately, Diogenes preserved three letters that contain Epicurus's system in microcosm as well as his *Sovran Maxims*, widely read in Roman times, intended as a guide to Epicurean thought and practice. The *Maxims*, assembled by either himself or one of his students, were also widely known in his own times and were afterward thought to capture the heart of his philosophy. The three letters to Herodotus, Pythocles, and Menoeceus covered physics, natural science, and ethics, respectively—the three pillars of his school of thought. Taken together, these ancient sources provide a window onto a whole way of thinking about everything from the heavens to the conduct of daily life.

In his letter to Herodotus, Epicurus begins by pointing to the contents he is setting forth in his letter as "the epitome of the whole system" of his philosophy, a convenient summary for those unable to read more in his extensive oeuvre or for advanced students in need of a simplifying outline for review. He calls it a "manual of the doctrines as a whole."[11] This guide is still convenient, even ideal, for our purposes at a remove of over two millennia.

Epicurus advocates memorization of the guiding principles and a brief outline of his philosophical system as important even for scholars at a high level because of the essential role of simplicity in true understanding. This simplifying of complexity will allow one to place the plethora of detail in a larger framework and to grasp "the entirety of things" (10.36–37, p. 567): "For a comprehensive view is often required, the details but seldom" (10.35, p. 567). Epicurus emphasizes to Herodotus the importance of clarity about the meanings of terms as well as the use of the senses and "our actual feelings" as the basis for differentiating sound conclusions from what is still unsupported or "obscure" (10.38, p. 569).

After these preliminaries, which are vital elements in his approach, Epicurus lays out his primary findings. In common with the pre-Socratic "atomist" philosophers, notably Leucippus and Democritus, he holds several key beliefs about the physical world: nothing in the world is either created out of nothing or destroyed beyond a trace (10.39, p. 569);[12] the world is composed of only bodies and space, or the "void" (10.40, p. 569); all bodies are composed of minute particles too small for the eye to see, or "atoms" (along with *void*, a term already used by the atomists); atoms are "indivisible and unchangeable" (10.41, p. 571) and move constantly and "inconceivably fast"—"quick as the speed of thought," in his beautiful phrasing—only slowing down or veering off course if met with resistance in the form of a collision with other atoms (10.43–44, p. 573; 10.46, p. 577; 10.61, p. 593).

Epicurus thought that whatever is unknown and unavailable to the senses we must use reason to understand. He guides us through the reasoning behind his description of the physical world, making his reasons as transparent as his conclusions. It is important to have a taste of the logic behind the observations, as they too tell us about his philosophical system and are intrinsic to his ideas about how to live.

Too small to be seen, atoms must behave in the way Epicurus describes because of what we can say about them or do know. From our senses, we know that bodies exist. We also know they move. Thus, in between there must be space (the void) to allow for that movement (10.40, p. 569).

Atoms must exist and must be eternal and infinite, because we know that "nothing comes into being out of what is non-existent." If it did, anything at all could be created. However, we know things require their "proper germs" to become their particular selves. All things must instead come from something else already in existence. Atoms do not disappear after those things come to an end, because by that logic nothing would exist: if atoms could be "destroyed and become non-existent, everything would have perished, that into which the things were dissolved being non-existent" (10.39, p. 569). If they cannot be reduced to nonexistence, this means atoms must be "indivisible and unchangeable" and of a "strong," "solid," and physical nature: "It follows that the first beginnings must be indivisible, corporeal entities" (10.41, p. 571).

Both atoms and the void are infinite according to Epicurus's intriguing logic. Something finite has its outermost limits, "an extremity." We can get at its extremity only "by comparison with something else." But there is nothing large enough to compare to aggregated atoms and the void. Thus they must be without limit (10.41–42, p. 571). This is confirmed by holding the atoms up against the void. If a limited number of atoms entered an unlimited void, atoms would not remain in existence forming bodies all around us. Instead, the atoms "would have been dispersed in their course through the infinite void" (10.42, p. 571). On the other hand, if an unlimited number of atoms entered a limited void, the atoms could not move, so no motion would swirl around us and, in any case, they could not fit. In a finite void, "the infinity of bodies would not have anywhere to be" (10.42, p. 573). Both bodies and space must thus be infinite.

Just as we lack a comparandum for atoms and the void, when we go the other direction, reason suggests that atoms must be the smallest building blocks of things. Their finitude comes on the small side, where at a certain point they are no longer divisible. In a given body, the number of atoms is finite, and the atoms themselves are finite in size, even though they are unimaginably miniscule: we must "reject as impossible subdivision *ad infinitum* into smaller and smaller parts, lest we make all things too weak and, in our conceptions and aggregates, be driven to pulverize the things that exist, *i.e.* the atoms, and annihilate them; but in dealing with finite things we must also reject as impossible the progression *ad infinitum* by less and less increments" (10.56, p. 587). This image of tiny atoms fading away infinitely inward is enchanting. Perhaps we might imagine atoms looking at themselves in a tiny set of opposing mirrors infinitely. Yet Epicurus guards against thinking this is the case. An individual body is cleanly delimited, and its boundaries make it and the atoms of which it is composed necessarily finite.

Epicurus continues with other observations and the reasoning behind them. The atoms differ in shape, or we would not see such a wide variety of bodies. Yet he does not think the varieties of forms are infinite, just the number of atoms and bodies (10.42, p. 573). Since the number of atoms is infinite, he does think that there is "nothing to hinder [there being] an infinity of worlds" (10.45, p. 575).

Some of Epicurus's ideas fit fairly closely our own. Others sound far-fetched yet might still have a certain appeal to the imagination and even a kind of poetic truth. He speaks of the existence of "images" or "idols," which are outlines of three-dimensional bodies in their same shape yet microscopically thin. These images, which are made of atoms, constantly move, as do individual atoms: "Particles are continually streaming off from the surface of bodies," yet those bodies do not appear smaller because "other particles take their place" (10.48, p. 577). To Epicurus, atoms play a major role in our experience, stimulating all of our senses. He explains hearing as the result of atoms leaving the body making the noise and extending to our ears yet without becoming separate from the original body (10.52, p. 583). It is the same with smell. Particles from the object stimulate the nose, "some exciting it confusedly and strangely, others quietly and agreeably" (10.53, p. 583).

In Epicurus's words, atoms become not only a focal point of interest and basis for scientific explanations but sometimes seem to take on a life of their own. In his descriptions of their behavior and qualities, atoms even seem endearing. Atoms do not share the qualities of the bodies to which they belong, instead possessing independence, uniqueness, and a noble endurance: "For every quality changes, but the atoms do not change, since, when the composite bodies are dissolved, there must needs be a permanent something, solid and indissoluble, left behind, which makes change possible: not changes into or from the non-existent, but often through differences of arrangement, and sometimes through additions and subtractions of the atoms. Hence these somethings capable of being diversely arranged must be indestructible, exempt from change, but possessed each of its own distinctive mass and configuration. This must remain" (10.54, p. 585).

Qualities of the bodies made up of atoms are "accidents," traits that the whole does not possess permanently, since the atoms must go on in new arrangements to form other bodies with the passage of time. In this loving rendering, much rides on their shoulders, but atoms are up to the task. Put this way, we might even feel a certain gratitude for everything they achieve. It should perhaps come as no surprise that the soul, too, is made of tiny particles, even the part of us that causes sensation. In Epicurus's view, the soul is "a corporeal thing" composed of atoms "dispersed all over the frame, most nearly resembling wind with an admixture of heat" and one more substance (10.63, p. 593). This nebulous "third part" has even smaller particles and is more closely entwined with the frame, as demonstrated by the "ease with which the mind moves," by thoughts and feelings, "and by all those things the loss of which causes death" (10.63, p. 595).

Epicurus goes on with this fine-grained description of the relation between the "frame," or the body, and the soul. The soul lies within a body and has sensation because it is housed there. It thus requires embodiment to exist. The body has sensation because the soul imparts it, yet the body also has something else that gives a "quality of sentience" (10.64, p. 595). While the body does share something with the soul, it does not possess the same qualities of it. This explains how body and soul are related and why death occurs: "So long as the soul is in the body, it never loses sentience through the removal of some other part." This happens only when all of the atoms that make up the soul depart. Once that happens, both body and soul no longer live. As long as "the containing sheath" has some life left, so will the soul, but when the body "no longer has sensation," "the whole frame is broken up, the soul is scattered and has no longer the same powers as before, nor the same motions; hence it does not possess sentience either" (10.65, pp. 595–97). In sum, the soul cannot outlive the body.

All things are not created by a divine entity in this schema. Yet this is not because no god exists but because such a being "enjoys bliss along with immortality." The world, on the other hand, is full of "troubles and anxieties and feelings of anger and partiality," and all these "do not accord with bliss, but always imply weakness and fear and dependence upon one's neighbors" (10.77, p. 607). The gods would not have created such troubles. This is no foundation for disbelief, however. It would cause "the worst disturbance in our minds" if we were to give up on "all the majesty which attaches to such notions as bliss and immortality." The "inconsistency" between the divine, with this majesty and undisturbed bliss, and the disturbances of reality would be too much for us to bear. If we see "phenomena invariably recurring," which presumably might turn our minds to the divine, we must explain this by the arrangements of the atoms at the formation of the world (10.77, p. 607).

Epicurus continually returns to the subject of feeling and sensation as the sole adequate basis for our knowledge. As his letter to Herodotus comes to a close, he explains why this is vital to understand. To him, knowledge and feeling are completely intertwined.[13] He goes so far as to say that "happiness depends on" accurate scientific knowledge—"knowledge of celestial and atmospheric phenomena" (10.78, p. 607). It relies on "knowing what the heavenly bodies really are" (10.78, p. 607). If we do not have this knowledge, we will be plagued by fear. The reason we need to attend to the senses, feelings, and facts based on our direct observations is to banish those fears.

Epicurus is not neutral on the notion of whether the gods exist. He explains that our misconceptions about the gods are dangerous: "The greatest anxiety of the human mind arises through the belief that the heavenly bodies are blessed and indestructible, and that at the same time they have volitions [sic] and actions and causality inconsistent with this belief." Fear of "some everlasting evil," irrational belief in myths, and a dread of death lead to terror. To achieve "mental tranquility means being released from all these troubles" and remembering "the highest and most important truths" (10.81, p. 611). We need to listen to our thoughts and feelings, evidence and facts. We must study nature. Learning about the world around us enables our "accounting for celestial phenomena and for all other things which from time to time befall us and cause the utmost alarm to the rest of mankind" (10.82, p. 611).

The point of scientific inquiry is thus a plan for dispelling anxiety and dread. The end point of knowledge is a certain state of mind. We need to know "the true story of nature" because it is the only thing that can give us peace of mind (10.85, p. 615). We need facts and reason so that we can lead an "untroubled existence"

(10.87, p. 615).[14] The science of nature offers a kind of balm for the mind.

WHERE THE GODS ARE

In his letter to Pythocles, Epicurus illustrates in vivid imagery how this works. He begins by saying that he is happy to fulfill Pythocles's request for "a clear and concise statement respecting celestial phenomena," since Pythocles is having trouble remembering the basic points in the longer works (10.84, p. 613). Epicurus reminds Pythocles of the overarching goal of studying the heavens: "In the first place, remember that, like everything else, knowledge of celestial phenomena, whether taken along with other things or in isolation, has no other end in view than peace of mind and firm conviction" (10.85, p. 615). The study of celestial matters does not lend itself to the clarity that can be reached in the other branches of Epicurean inquiry—physics or ethics—so there needs to be an openness to entertaining numerous possible explanations for events that can occur.

Here Epicurus reiterates the importance of facts and sensory observation and emphasizes the need to forsake myth. As he says in the letter to Herodotus, he tells Pythocles that as a prerequisite for scientific speculation it is crucial to abandon the idea of divine intervention as a cause for celestial events. Epicurus is certain, however, of both the nature of a world and the infinite number of worlds in existence. The definition of a world is fascinating and evocative: "A world is a circumscribed portion of the universe, which contains stars and earth and all other visible things, cut off from the infinite, and terminating in an exterior which may either revolve or be at rest, and be round or triangular or of any other shape whatever" (10.88, p. 617). In the *intermundia*, or the "spaces between worlds," a new world can emerge (10.89, p. 617).

Our world is thus not the only one that exists. Worlds are not only multiple but without number: "Moreover, there is an infinite number of worlds, some like this world, others unlike it. For the atoms being infinite in number, as has just been proved, are borne ever further in their course. For the atoms out of which a world might arise, or by which a world might be formed, have not all been expended on one world or a finite number of worlds, whether like or unlike this one. Hence there will be nothing to hinder an infinity of worlds" (10.45, p. 575). These infinite worlds even come in different shapes and sizes (10.73–74, p. 603).

Besides conveying the precepts of Epicureanism for us, these phrasings convey the poetry of the logic the ancient philosophers had to use. Epicurus reasoned by means of such devices as analogy, inference, and any other technique available to figure out what it took millennia to figure out with the help of modern tools and methods. Though he was building on earlier speculation by the atomists, he was connecting ideas and observations in a manner that offered a whole new way to look at the world.

Epicurus's reasoning for abandoning the idea that the gods have anything to do with celestial occurrences can be found here too. The divine is the epitome of peacefulness. Calling on divine beings to explain tumultuous human events does them an injustice: "The divine nature must not on any account be adduced to explain" what goes on in our world, "but must be kept free from the task and in perfect bliss" (10.97, p. 625). It is disrespectful to implicate the gods in our turmoil.

Epicurus goes on to offer possible arguments against what he calls the "servile artifices of the astronomers" (10.93, p. 623). In place of such simplistic schemes, he offers replete explanations, laying out multiple possible causes of a variety of natural occurrences, which include the movement of the sun, moon, and stars; the different lengths of days and nights; and the formation of clouds, rain, thunder, lightning, whirlwinds, earthquakes, hail, snow, dew, frost, ice, rainbows, halos seen around the moon, and "falling stars" (10.92–116, pp. 621–43). For example, "Lightnings [sic] too happen in a variety of ways. For when the clouds rub against each other and collide, that collocation of atoms which is the cause of fire generates lightning; or it may be due to the flashing forth from the clouds, by reason of winds, of particles capable of producing this brightness" (10.101, p. 629). The passage continues with several more theories regarding the causes of lightning.

For navigating human experience in the world, the portrait Epicurus draws of the "wise man" is someone who does have and express emotions but does not allow emotion to eclipse reason (10.117, p. 643). He is someone who is always happy and would be so "even on the rack" (10.118, p. 645). He will vent emotion by groaning and the like, but he will not fall in love, engage in sexual indulgence, make "fine speeches," or participate in politics. He will not be a tyrant, Cynic, or beggar. He will sue and care for his property and future (10.118–20, pp. 645–47).

Epicurus's third letter, this one to Menoeceus, is perhaps the most well known, but his ethics are better understood when placed in the context of his views here on physics and natural science, as he sees all three areas as interconnected. He begins by associating health and happiness with wisdom. Wisdom is the "health of the soul" for both old and young (10.122, p. 649). He goes on to convey the "elements of right life"—or how one should live an Epicurean life. The right life entailed a certain attitude toward the gods, death, emotion, pleasure, and virtue.

Epicurus laid out guidelines, beginning with the right posture toward the gods, which starts with belief in their existence but is tempered by a recognition of their nature and what is and is not in their purview: "First believe that God is a living being immortal and blessed," and because of this, do not believe anything that is "foreign to his immortality or that agrees not with his blessedness" (10.122, p. 649). This means not following "the multitude" in its "truly impious" and "false assumptions" (10.124, p. 651).

Death is no more than the "privation of sentience" and thus should not be determined good or evil: "Death is nothing to us" (10.124, p. 651). We must accept our mortality and stop believing in an afterlife and yearning for immortality. The wise man does not fear death but accepts the simple fact of our existence stripped down to bare bones: "When we are, death is not come, and when death is come, we are not" (10.126, p. 653; 10.125, p. 651). If we accept this, we will lay the foundation for a happy life: "The sum and end of a blessed life" is "health of body and tranquility of mind" (10.128, p. 653).

Epicurus writes that "the end of all our actions" is "to be free from pain and fear." The way to live is to lay to rest "the tempest of the soul" (10.128, p. 655). The ultimate goal is pleasure. Pleasure is "the alpha and omega of a blessed life," "our first and kindred good" (10.129, p. 655).

The Epicureans' praise of pleasure is not a recipe for extreme pursuits of pleasure, however. This is not a principled objection as much as a calculation. Quantity matters, as extreme pursuits can sometimes result in unpleasurable events. As a rule, we should forgo potential pleasures if disturbances would result. Pain should even be borne if a "greater pleasure" will ensue. The way to know if an opportunity before us is a pleasure to which we should submit is feeling, which is "the rule by which to judge every good thing" (10.129, p. 655).

From the beginning, detractors misconstrued Epicureanism as unlimited license or philosophical permission to pursue pleasure to any degree and of all kinds. Yet Epicurus clarifies that a pursuit of pleasure is not the same as licentiousness. He advocates "plain fare" in eating, for example (10.131, p. 657), and offers a clear definition of pleasure as he sees it: "By pleasure we mean the absence of pain in the body and of trouble in the soul. It is not an unbroken succession of drinking-bouts and of revelry, not sexual love, not the enjoyment of the fish and other delicacies of a luxurious table, which produce a pleasant life; it is sober reasoning, searching out the grounds of every choice and avoidance, and banishing those beliefs through which the greatest tumults take possession of the soul" (10.131, p. 657).

A TASTE FOR VIRTUE

Instead of being a blueprint for unbridled passion, ancient Epicureanism has virtue at its core. The highest good in the Epicurean view is not even philosophy but the virtue of "prudence" (10.132, p. 657). Prudence gives rise to all the other virtues, such as honor and justice, and pleasure comes from living a virtuous life (10.132, p. 657). This happens because what causes the most pain is *within*. People wracked by fear and anxiety are never at peace, so a pleasurable life is impossible for them. According to a kind of pleasure calculus, reining in pleasure in the short term leads to more pleasure in the long run.

Epicurus argues that having a low bar for pleasure means that desires will be easily met (10.131, p. 657; 10.133, p. 659). Limiting what it takes to make us happy inoculates us against potential twists of fate. He does not believe in destiny but instead thinks everything happens by either chance, agency, or necessity (10.133, p. 659). By abandoning a belief in fate and a preoccupation with death and the afterlife, we invite peace. The effect of living according to Epicurean principles is that you will "live as a god among men" (10.135, p. 659). The gods live lives of unperturbed peace and pleasure, and so should we.

Laertius continues summing up the ideas of Epicurus by exploring the precise link between virtue and pleasure. Epicurus sees pleasure as the ultimate goal of human life. To support this idea, he points to what he sees as a basic fact, that from birth human beings seek pleasure and avoid pain, according to nature and not reason. We act morally because of this natural pursuit of pleasure: "And we choose the virtues too on account of pleasure and not for their own sake, as we take medicine for the sake of health. So too in the twentieth book of his *Epilecta* says Diogenes, who also calls education (ἀγωγή) recreation (διαγωγή)" (10.138, p. 663).

To "set the seal" on his life of Epicurus, Laertius delineates the forty items of advice that constitute the *Sovran Maxims*. For the reader of the *Maxims*, the end of the reading will constitute "the beginning of happiness" (10.138–39, p. 663). The *Maxims* cover a lot of ground, presenting a set of interlocking themes: the need for a life of quiet and security; the quietude of the gods; the undesirability of anxiety about death; pleasure, defined as freedom from pain, as the ultimate end; the need for limits on pleasure for the sake of greater pleasure; the need to endure some pain, also for the sake of greater pleasure; the need to study the natural world; the need to trust in the senses; and the need for justice (10.139–54, pp. 663–67).

To understand the precise way some of these themes interlock gets us more deeply into vital aspects of Epicurus's philosophy and puts together the pieces we identified in the letters. In the very first maxim, we encounter a vision of the gods and of the very nature of their divinity, as having to do with their peace and calm. The behavior of the gods is the reason why people should also overcome negative feelings like sorrow and anxiety. The paradigmatic feeling for the human being is the fear of death. This is where the study of science comes in. If we base our judgments solely on the senses, we observe that life, and thus feeling, ends at death. Accepting death as the end is vital: "But the mind, grasping in thought what the end and limit of the flesh is, and banishing the terrors of futurity, procures a complete and perfect life, and has no longer any need of unlimited time" (10.145, p. 669). According to Epicurus, this realization of our mortality should calm our fears. The Epicurean gods were connected to science, as science would enable humans to live a more godlike existence.

As we have seen, all roads for Epicurus lead to pleasure. He defines pleasure as "the removal of all pain." But pleasure is not purely bodily; it also occurs in the mind. This means "to live a pleasant life" entails not just material well-being but "living wisely and well and justly" (10.140, p. 665). The goal is a quiet and self-sufficient life free of the convulsions of terror and worry. Fear comes from myths and superstition, which only an understanding of "the nature of the whole universe" can dispel (10.143, p. 667). The faculty of reason allows for the vanquishing of fears resulting from not understanding the cataclysms in nature and mistaking them for the result of the anger of the gods and their conflicts.

The *Sovran Maxims* reveal a recognition of the problem of moral relativism. It is not in justice itself but rather in the fear of punishment that evil resides. If someone inflicted a wrong, he or she will be haunted for life (10.151, p. 675). There is no such thing as "absolute" justice, in fact, only local agreements against doing harm (10.150, p. 675). Justice is "expedient in mutual intercourse" and "varies under different circumstances." As soon as it does not serve "mutual intercourse," it is no longer just (10.151–53, pp. 575–77). Without faith in the senses, there would be no basis of moral judgment, as it is the senses that allow us to differentiate right and wrong. The senses accomplish this by providing an assessment of whether an action coincides with nature (10.147–48, pp. 671–73). Impossible to separate from bodily feelings, the soul is the ultimate sentient faculty.

As we shall see, some treat the Epicurean mentality as secular, even atheistic. However, it is crucial to understand that the reason for using the senses to observe causes and effects in nature to dispel fear and superstition lies in the logic of Epicurean belief. If the gods are divine, blissful, and immortal, they must not be concerning themselves with turmoil such as that wrought by climatic disturbances.

We should emulate the gods' irenic temperaments and realize there are explanations we can find through natural science (10.77, p. 607).[15] Epicurus criticizes traditional religious beliefs, not on the grounds that the gods do not exist or do not care about us, but on the grounds that their nature makes them models for us. It is impious to think anything about the gods other than "God is a living being immortal and blessed." No belief about God is valid unless it "may uphold both his blessedness and his immortality" (10.123–24, pp. 649–51). Those who live according to the gods' temperament, which centers on the good, will receive "the greatest blessings," while the "wicked" will receive "the greatest evils" (10.124, p. 651). The gods will "reject as alien whatever is not of their kind" (10.124, p. 651). The very first maxim makes clear what that is: "A blessed and eternal being has no trouble himself and brings no trouble upon any other being; hence he is exempt from movements of anger and partiality, for every such movement implies weakness" (10.139, p. 663). Reason is a divine faculty.

The opening of Lucretius's poem also makes this focus on the gods clear from the start.[16] He invokes Venus, Aeneadum genetrix, mother of Aeneas and the Roman people. In an illuminated frontispiece of the poem from 1483 this is made clear in the layout of the print and illustrations. (See fig. 3.3.) An offset vertical rectangle, held on each side by a plump cherub, frames the line, in all capital letters, "[A]EN EA DVM GENI TRIX HOMI NVM DIVVM QVE VOLVP TAS [spacing in the original]": "Mother of

Aeneas and his race, darling of men and gods, nurturing Venus." The imagery celebrates Venus as sowing the seeds of spring, inspiring "all creatures . . . greedily to beget their generations after their kind" (1.1–20, p. 3). In a hymn to Venus as the premier muse, Lucretius describes Mars, god of war, as still and restful, gazing lovingly into Venus's eyes. He "casts himself upon your lap wholly vanquished by the ever-living wound of love" (1.30–40, p. 5). The poet condemns superstition, worrying that his elevation of philosophy and his rejection of conventional views of the gods will seem impious. The real impiety, he believes, is acting on superstition to do "evil deeds," such as the sacrifice of a young woman by "a father's hand" to try to earn the gods' favor in war (1.80–101, pp. 9–11).

The poem is a hymn to pleasure and the natural world, without a doubt. But the gods are a constant presence, even if it is for the purpose of elucidating Epicurus's view of their detachment from the human world. Lucretius declares his desire to hew closely to the words of Epicurus, his idol, and addresses him, "O glory of the Grecian race" (3.1–5, p. 189): "For as soon as your reasoning begins to proclaim the nature of things revealed by your divine mind, away flee the mind's terrors, the walls of the world open out, I see action going on throughout the whole void: before me appear the gods in their majesty, and their peaceful abodes, which no winds ever shake nor clouds besprinkle with rain, which no snow congealed by the bitter front mars with its white fall, but the air ever cloudless encompasses them and laughs with its light spread wide abroad" (3.10–20, pp. 189–91).[17]

Lucretius does describe the swerve, though Epicurus's remaining writings available to us today do not (2.216–93, pp. 113–19).[18] If the atoms followed their usual course, they "would fall downwards like raindrops through the profound void" and nature would be empty. But instead the atoms "swerve a little from their course" (2.216–24, p. 113). This swerve is "will wrested from the fates by which we proceed whither pleasure leads us" (2.255–60, p. 115). It means, not that everything is random, but that intelligence, reason, decision, and passion play some role in determining the direction of things rather than just luck and fate or the constant intervention of the gods (2.225–62, pp. 113–45). The swerve establishes the possibility of free will.

This notion of humans' role in their own fate at the same time that the gods mean everything to them comes forth in spatial terms in the description of where the gods are. Lucretius questions the idea that the gods live in the world: "Another thing it is impossible that you should believe is that any holy abode of the gods exists in any part of the world" (5.146–48, p. 389). For one thing, there is not just one world. There are multiple, indeed infinite worlds, complete with life (2.1048–66, pp. 177–79). As we have seen, the Epicureans taught that the gods live in the spaces between worlds (μετακόσμια, *intermundia*), and Lucretius states this (5.146–55, pp. 389–91).

THE SWERVE INTO THE NOW

A major event in contemporary Epicurean thought was the 2011 publication of *The Swerve: How the World Became Modern*, by Stephen Greenblatt. The book recounts the fortunes of Epicureanism over the ages by relating the story of a Renaissance book-hunting humanist named Poggio Bracciolini. In a monastery in 1417, Bracciolini discovered Lucretius's long-lost work *On the Nature of Things*, which we have been discussing. This discovery, according to Greenblatt, changed the course of history.[19]

Greenblatt relates this story as a tale of adventure, filling in the context of several historical periods along the way, from medieval monasteries to Renaissance humanist circles and the intrigues of the papal court. An unlikely adventurer, Poggio, as Greenblatt calls him, had exquisite handwriting and skill with Latin and worked as a scriptor and then apostolic secretary to several popes. *The Swerve* is a paean to books and booklovers as well as to Epicureans and Epicureanism. Its style and suspense show how a set of words can have a gripping history and how one person's idea can end up being pivotal in the lives of other people, societies, and intellectual and artistic movements.

In Greenblatt's telling, the story of the poem's discovery possesses high drama and mystery, like other quests. Actually, it puts one in mind of *The Da Vinci Code*. In fact, one of the blurbs on the back cover of *The Swerve* calls it "an intellectually invigorating, nonfiction version of a Dan Brown-like mystery-in-the-archives thriller."[20] What evokes *The Da Vinci Code* is not merely the excitement of the story but also the way the author sees small details of daily life as connected to sweeping changes in history. Greenblatt connects Poggio's aim for a tangible worldly achievement with the largest frameworks in which we understand our lives. In Dan Brown's novel, this is a literal quest for the Holy Grail (later revealed to be the divine feminine, as we saw in chapter 1), while in Greenblatt's nonfiction work it is something more figurative, more of a modern attitude toward living.

Greenblatt also tells the story of the rediscovery of Lucretius's poem as the ultimate treasure hunt. It is not a case of just any missing work from classical antiquity turning up again after a millennium. It is *the* book, the one that allowed history to turn out the way it did. In Greenblatt's telling, this book opened hearts and minds to the light of reason and learning in a way not possible in the hundreds of years it was lost. The poem becomes another modern Holy Grail.

Greenblatt sees it this way because to him Lucretius expresses a whole new worldview—the one Greenblatt sees as our own. He interprets *De rerum natura* accordingly. The poem weds its physics (all things break down into tiny irreducible particles) with its ethics (pleasure should be the goal of life). Though the poet composed these lines and this vision well before the tools of modern science, he thought everything was made up of minute particles. Infinite in number, these particles were always in motion, enabled by the voids in between them, which made room for movement. What kept the particles from streaming in straight lines into the void and vanishing was "the swerve." Because particles moved in completely random ways, unguided, they collided into each other and departed from any orderly pattern, plan, or path. This was Lucretius's idea of how everything came about.

Greenblatt identifies "the swerve" as a trope that helps explain the Renaissance and modernity, which he sees as its direct offshoot. Renaissance humanism is, in his hands, an Epicurean movement. It planted the seeds of our own times, and the rediscovery of Lucretius's poem in turn planted the seeds of the Renaissance. Before the Renaissance's swerve, the world was on a much different course. What modernity swerved away from was dogmatic thought and orthodoxy of all kinds, both religious and pagan. *On the Nature of Things* dispelled that darkness.

Greenblatt thinks that Epicureanism brought nothing less than a radical revision of ideas about the world. This school of thought had a kinship with skepticism and atheism, to him, and was antagonistic to most traditional religion. It is a materialist theory, by which he means a theory that leaves God or the gods out of any involvement in human affairs. While not dispensing with the gods altogether, Epicureans thought they had better things to do. Thus there was no notion of God as creator, no such thing as predestination, and no persistence of the soul after death. Events occurred only by chance or by human will.

The Swerve gives the impression that to be modern is to be Epicurean. Ultimately, it is an interpretation that casts Epicureanism as the dominant or sole view today. In doing so, it is very much an interpretation. To make the argument, Greenblatt sometimes demonstrates convincingly the appeal of Epicurean ideas to a particular thinker, as when he discusses Giordano Bruno, the Italian philosopher and mathematician, or Michel de Montaigne, the French philosopher and statesman. Usually he only gestures to later figures, such as Machiavelli or Thomas Jefferson, who once declared, "I am an Epicurean."[21] On the shoulders of such figures too much rests. There were others who resisted Epicureanism, and some who outright suppressed or punished its adherents. Greenblatt lumps all who disagreed with Epicureanism together as antimodernist villains, out to crush the human spirit. Any holdouts were destined to be overcome in time, as we are supposed to know by virtue of our standpoint looking back.

Greenblatt's story is all the more absorbing for the tensions it displays between and within individuals influenced by Epicurean and non-Epicurean ideas. Yet his story rests on the assumption that those conflicts eventually dissipated in the clarity of modern thinking. This premise fails to appreciate the endurance of other views capable of being held by reasonable people. It is questionable whether Epicureanism really fits the beliefs of many of the Renaissance figures in humanist circles. Greenblatt holds Epicureanism as the voice of resistance and radicalism for being at odds with Christianity, but at other times he seems to appreciate those who could hold both the ancient philosophies and Christianity in mind as compatible, such as Raphael, as displayed in his *School of Athens.*

The Epicurean notions that most disturbed Christians included the thought that the soul dies with the body, that nothing is predestined, and that the world is not the creation of God. Epicureans are too often associated with atheists, but wrongly so. They did believe in the gods, just not in the idea that the world was their creation or that man was the center of the universe, unique and special.

Greenblatt interprets Poggio Bracciolini's writings as representing a wide range of outlooks. He wrote in many genres. His works included a book of jokes from his time at "the lie factory," which was what he called the workplace he shared with fellow scriptors at the Vatican. Greenblatt argues that his book is a collection of some of the most cynical jokes imaginable (141–50). Yet he does not consider Poggio as having a dark vision. In a parallel, just as the Renaissance rescued his society, Greenblatt's Poggio was saved from that cynical setting by his love of book hunting (183). The universe struck him as a wonderful place (237). At one point, he visits the baths at Baden and praises them for being "Epicurean." Greenblatt finds this suggestive of Poggio's Epicurean tendencies, even if they are not proven. There is no evidence that the poem resonated for him, except as one of the coveted (and potentially lucrative) relics of antiquity.

Another blurb writer calls *The Swerve* itself "an epicurean delight."[22] It is truly a stunning achievement and a pleasure to read. But the notion of Poggio Bracciolini as the "midwife to modernity" is overdrawn—not because he lacks importance but because the assumption of an Epicurean modernity hardly does justice to competing views of modernity. Modern life does have strong Epicurean leanings. Yet it is questionable whether Renaissance humanism is the dominant spirit of modernity and postmodernity and, in any case, whether the muse of humanism was predominantly Epicurean. Rather than all of modernity, the rediscovered poem might be a midwife to a modern Epicureanism, one approach among many, for Poggio Bracciolini's efforts surely helped keep that one school of thought in full view.

In casting all of Christianity as villain and Lucretius as lone hero, Greenblatt minimizes the tensions between Epicureanism and other schools of thought. Here Catholicism, as reduced to the Inquisition, wages war on freedom of all kinds, which cannot account for the far richer complexities of intellectual history then and now. Scholars have largely dismissed this kind of reductionist rendering of the Dark Ages as a caricature of the Middle Ages. We can see part of the problem in the way Botticelli's painting *Primavera* figures into Greenblatt's discussion. (See fig. 3.4.) The painting pops out from the inside cover of the paperback of *The Swerve* and figures into the story in several places. But if we consider Botticelli's work further, we find that it was Neoplatonism more than Epicureanism that exerted so much influence over the painting and provides clues to its meaning. A more careful look illuminates crucial dimensions of Epicureanism.

PRIMAVERA

Botticelli's *Primavera* depicts several figures standing or dancing in a dark woods. On the trees are small clusters of tiny white flowers and large orange fruits, and on the forest floor lie hundreds of flowers and other plants of all different kinds. In the middle stands a Madonna-like figure, serene and at one with nature. To our left, we see three female figures with flowing hair and wisps of dresses hinting at their curves underneath. They are suspended in a circle mid-tiptoe, their fingers entwined in an exquisite echo of their own choreography. Further to the left is a young man draped in a kind of tunic, with a dagger in a scabbard. On the right side of the painting stands a woman covered in flowers—on the cloth of her dress, in garlands around her neck, in her hair, and in a bouquet in the folds of her gown, which overflows with blossoms. The gown is intricate, with pink and red and gold petals and darker leaves, echoing the scene's colors overall. A younger woman almost trips onto her with hands open as if she is falling, lifted by a male figure flying in the trees. A cherub hovers over all of them, with a tiny bow and arrow.

The pale gold of the people in the painting contrasts with the dark tree trunks and foliage around them and with the blue-gray figure coming out of the trees. His cheeks puff out and produce a stream of air. A silver-gray sky shines between the trees. The figure at the center, set off by an arch in the foliage, wears a light dress and reddish robe, in harmony with the colors throughout, which include shades of gold, reds, rust, whites, gray, and darker contrasting shades. The overall mood is a sacred one, ordered, sweet, and harmonious. There is a formality and even timelessness to the composition. It invites us into a moment of goodness. The only element of concern is the bluish, ashen figure in the trees. His body looks smooth and sculpted and his robe billows softly behind him, in graceful arcs. His look is serious, and his touch appears to be a gentle one but might not be. The young woman he is carrying looks back at him intently, her gold hair falls lightly around her face, and out of her mouth seem to come flowers— strange, perhaps, yet of less concern. We almost hear the music accompanying this scene of purity and serenity. It captures the beauty of the physical world and spirit that infuses it. Inspired by a natural yet spiritual force, these figures celebrate and worship nature and worship *in* nature, surrounded by the bounty of the earthly world.

Once we learn more about Botticelli and his period, it becomes clear how important the symbolism of the painting is for explaining certain of its central features. Botticelli worked and lived in close communication with artists, poets, philosophers, and other kindred spirits in the period of the Italian Renaissance known as the Quattrocento. As one of the artists enjoying the patronage of the famous Florentine Medici family, Botticelli was influenced by the circle of Italian humanists that surrounded and included leaders and supporters of the arts such as Cosimo, Piero, and Lorenzo de' Medici. Inheritor of the library of Niccolo Niccoli, Cosimo fell in love with books himself and opened the Library of San Marco to the residents of Florence. He also gave a country villa to Marsilio Ficino, a scholar engaged in studying and translating Plato and Plotinus, in order to establish an academy of Platonic studies. While Cosimo's son Piero died young, he was a crucial supporter of painters such as Fra Filippo Lippi, Botticelli's master. In turn, his son Lorenzo il Magnifico, illustrious statesman and de facto ruler of Florence from 1469 to 1492, a classically trained poet and writer himself, was a proponent of what came to be known as Italian humanism. He was educated alongside and greatly influenced by his close friend, the poet Angelo Poliziano, who studied under Ficino. Ficino's work fused classical and religious elements, as communicated visually by Domenico Ghirlandaio in *Angel Appearing to Zacharias*, a depiction from 1486–90 of Ficino in the midst of this social milieu.[23]

While some argue for Epicurean elements, Neoplatonism was the dominant intellectual influence on Botticelli's depiction. Art historian Liana Cheney presents the different layers of symbolism in the *Primavera*, helping us see what is actually going on in the picture. Also known as the *Allegory of Spring*, the painting depicts Zephyr, the west wind, representing winter, bringing to the earth a pregnant nymph, Chloris, who in turn brings the message of spring's arrival, as she becomes Flora, goddess of flowers.[24] Venus, goddess of love and beauty, presides over the scene, with her son, Cupid, above her aiming arrows of erotic love. The Three Graces together represent such gifts as excellence and plenty, while Mercury, looking into the distance, is both messenger of the gods and patron of the merchants. Politically, *Primavera* represents the thriving of Florence under Lorenzo, with the golden oranges associated with the Medici family's bounty and protection (49). A festival brought back from ancient Rome, Floralia was a springtime feast. In the seasonal imagery, Zephyr (February) impregnates Chloris (March), who matures into Flora (April), with Venus (May) presiding, accompanied by the graces (June-July-August), and by Mercury (September) (127). Poetically, the painting may refer to Angelo Poliziano's *Stanze*, which honors Lorenzo's brother, Giuliano Medici (Mercury), and his bride, Simonetta Vespucci (Flora) (44, 127–28).[25]

Philosophically, the *Primavera* has further layers of meaning. The painting's political, civic, and seasonal elements help it to embody the Neoplatonic ideas at its foundation. As Cheney shows, Neoplatonism, the form of Platonism in Plotinus's works, as inflected by other intellectual currents by this period, centers on the One. From the One came everything, starting with *Nous* (Mind or Intelligence), Psyche (both World-Soul and individual soul), and Matter. Humans are a mixture of spirit and matter, so they have access to the natural world through sensation and insight into the ideal "intelligible" world through rationality. Beauty comes from the One, so if humans are to have access to beauty they must "try to reach the spiritual world by relying on the soul, an intellect which can recognize beauties as emanations of the splendor of the One" (30).

Marsilio Ficino drew on Plato's and Plotinus's ideas and combined them with Christian theology rooted in the ideas of Augustine.[26] Cheney describes how, under Ficino's influence, Renaissance Neoplatonism placed humankind at the center of the universe and emphasized the "inner ascent of the soul towards god (Plotinus' One)" (30). This ascent takes place through contemplation. Ficino shared with the medieval Thomists a belief in the immortality of the soul, to be attained through this practice of spiritual contemplation.[27] This allows for "the enjoyment of God" and "the dignity of man," based on the notion of free will to choose this spiritual access to the divine and immortality. There is one way to get there, according to Ficino: "The soul must make a leap of spiritual love" (31). This leap is captured in the concept of "'Platonic love' or spiritual love for one another, or the love of the soul for God" (32). Love lies at the heart of Ficino's philosophy. Cheney quotes Ficino:

Everything is in God
God Loves himself

Therefore
Everything loves God.
(32)

Cheney concludes that, for the Medici humanists, strongly influenced by Ficino, "The motive of the whole universe is love" (32).

Ficino's aesthetics center on the fulfillment of spiritual love. The Good (God) gives off light that forms images in each of the four spheres in the universe: "In the Angelic Mind are ideas, in the Rational Soul or World-Soul are Concepts, in Nature are Seeds, in Body or Matter are Shapes" (33). Love begins as spiritual love and can become sensual or erotic love in the encounter with the physical world. The human being has the free will to choose the corporeal or intelligible sphere: "Art, through the spirit of love, moves the soul to a new feeling, a transcending appreciation of beauty" (33–34).

Renaissance Neoplatonism evoked the ancient idea of the "Twin Venuses"—the Heavenly and the Earthly (Aphrodite Urania and Aphrodite Pandemos). Platonists had arrived at two worlds: the Angelic (or intelligible world, Plato's world of forms) and the World-Soul, reason, action, and begetting nature. The Neoplatonists added a third, the World-Body, or nature itself. Ficino "adds a fourth world, the Corporeal matter formed by inorganic substance" (34–35). The Twin Venuses figure prominently in Ficino's Renaissance Neoplatonism, the Venus of the Angelic Mind (Venus Celeste or Venus Genetrix) and the Venus of the World-Soul (Venus Volgare or Venus Humanitas). When originating in the Angelic Mind, love is *amor divinus* (divine love). When originating in the World-Soul, it is *amor vulgaris* (human love). This is the basis for the difference between spiritual and physical love. The former is attainable through contemplation, "the highest faculty of man," the latter through "perceptions, sensations and desires" (35):[28] "Through the Heavenly-Venus, love is stimulated to know the beauty of God, as this Venus has the love of God and gives it to the Earthly-Venus who in turn procreates the same beauty in other bodies so that they may also share the love of God. Love exchanges beauty for beauty; love is a desire to perceive beauty, hence beauty is the good or God" (36). Human love can become divine love when the spiritual interacts with the physical (36).

The Medici were deeply immersed in Ficino's Neoplatonic emphasis on this Platonic conception of love as inextricably tied to beauty and art. Ficino's version of Renaissance humanism centered on "immortality of the soul, 'dignity of man,' and 'universal man'" as terms that helped bridge the human and the divine (37).[29]

All of these terms set the stage for Cheney's reading of the philosophical meaning of Botticelli's *Primavera*: "The *Primavera* is an allegory of Venus' reign, an ideal world in which nature and instinct (Zephyr-Chloris-Flora) are guided and controlled by Venus through her daemons [spirits between God and humans]: love, beauty and felicity (Three Graces), and reason (Mercury)" (128). To convey the centrality of Venus, Cheney has us imagine the canvas divided into two sections. On our right is "culture (Zephyr, Chloris, and Flora)," or *Humanitas*. On our left is "civilization (graces, Mercury)," or Venus (128). Cheney explains: "Natural forms and basic instincts may be reflected in life through ability to desire, to create and to procreate—Zephyr pursues Chloris, Chloris becomes impregnated by Zephyr, and Flora is the result of this union. Intellectual or super-natural forms are illustrated in the *Venus-Humanitas*, the three graces and Mercury—intelligence, love and reason respectively" (128–29).

The Neoplatonic vision addresses the apparent clash in human life between the call of the physical and the spiritual. It does not see reason and emotion as polarized. The role of Venus shows the importance of love in both and the centrality of emotion in each. The intellect pertains to the realm of the divine yet infuses the physical when humans practice contemplation, transforming the physical side of life and lending it a spiritual aspect. The mind/body split keeps us on the surface level of understanding, missing the spiritual nature of love and beauty underlying contemporary aesthetics. By connecting love and beauty with the good, the Neoplatonic aesthetic has a prominent role for *virtu*. *Virtu* is not just a matter of self-deprivation, or even of self-development, though it does have everything to do with self-discipline. *Virtu* is ultimately the doorway to self-formation. Without it, one is not yet individualized (37).[30] *Virtu* allows close bonds of affection and even access to a kind of civic ecstasy (37–38). Far beyond the notion of calculable rewards for hard work or good behavior, the dividends of self-discipline are immeasurable.

The use of Botticelli's *Primavera* in the cover design of *The Swerve* is a shorthand for an Epicurean Renaissance. Greenblatt's interpretation of the discovery of *On the Nature of Things* as launching the modern world rests on his assumption that we are all Epicureans now. *The Swerve* is a tale of the triumph of secular and scientific modernity over the benighted past of religious belief and the supposed imprisonment of the human spirit. Yet one need only read his take on the *Primavera* to see his oversight regarding the Renaissance Neoplatonism that infuses that work. It is impossible to understand the painting, like so many other great works of the Renaissance, without realizing that their creators, admirers, and even critics more often than not assumed a spiritual context for the form and content of artistic productions in all genres.

Just as the opening of Lucretius's poem is a hymn to Venus, not the unbridled sensuousness of spring, the painting resists characterization as an embrace of the season of rebirth alone, shorn of God. To see in it a source for modern liberationism neglects the significance of the Neoplatonist movement to the Renaissance and discounts the role of religious elements in Epicureanism itself. To read Botticelli as representing erotic desire unleashed reduces the multilayered concept of love in Neoplatonism to only one of its aspects, Eros. Instead, as Cheney's luminous reading establishes, *Primavera* offers the viewer "a tapestry of Neoplatonic images" (125), a testament to the "classical aesthetic" of the Medici circle (1).

EXPERIENCE THERAPY

A key to Greenblatt's celebration of Epicureanism lies in his prologue. He describes how his mother had such a fear of death that she brought it up continually, subjecting Greenblatt to constant anxiety as he grew up. It is no mystery why he might be drawn to a philosophy that dramatically contradicts any notion of deferred happiness. In the process, his book shows the way in which the new Epicureanism weds the therapeutic with the contemporary cult of experience.

Intellectual historian Martin Jay considers the quest for experience central to modern and postmodern understandings of the self. In *Songs of Experience*, he dons the mantle of a guide, beckoning us through a dense philosophical thicket so that he can point out scenes of interest in the occasional clearing. His mission is to follow the theme of experience over a vast swath of time—especially the past two or three centuries, with a nod toward ancient times and the early modern period.[31]

Drawing his title from William Blake's illuminated poems from 1789 and 1794, *Songs of Innocence and of Experience: Shewing the Two Contrary States of the Human Soul,* Jay alternates between the metaphor of journey and that of musical variations on a theme. In a study centered less on experience than on "the 'songs' that have been sung about it" (1), Jay holds that the sheer prevalence and changeability of the word means that "we must speak of 'songs' in the plural" rather than misguidedly adhere to one "metanarrative of this idea's history" (2). Jay wishes to avoid "a totalized account, which assumes a unified point of departure," and to relieve us of "seeking to rescue or legislate a single acceptation of the word" so that "we will be free to uncover and explore its multiple, often contradictory meanings" (3).

Jay traces the vicissitudes of experience as term and concept over time. Beginning with the ancient Greeks, emphasizing later readings more than their views themselves, Jay brings us up through humanism, the scientific revolution, British empiricism, pragmatism, and twentieth-century Marxism, to postmodernism. The study presents a series of roughly chronologically ordered synopses of the ideas of roughly thirty luminaries, from Aristotle to Foucault.

In Montaigne, Jay sees both the Renaissance's general "fascination with experience" and a unique approach foreshadowing modern concerns. Questioning deductive reasoning, Montaigne sets his sights on "living the good life" (26), not the search for absolute truth. In his essay "Of Experience" written in 1587–88, Montaigne rejected both strict adherence to inherited dogma and overreliance on the senses as a guide or basis for knowledge, arguing for the role of both feeling and intellect in judgment and the connection between bodily and mental pleasure. Jay praises Montaigne's "remarkable serenity and balance, his capacity to live with uncertainty and doubt and find solace in a world of contradictions and ambiguities" (27). Instead, he was "cheerfully resigned to what life as he knew it might provide" (28). Jay's Montaigne celebrated "integrated, balanced, holistic, but always open-ended and provisional experience" (30).

The telling word here is *holistic*, one invoked frequently in *Songs of Experience*. In the brief etymological discussion that opens the book, Jay touches upon the ancient sources of the English word *experience*. The Greek *empeiria*, also the origin of "empirical," implied "raw, unreflected sensation or unmediated observation" apart from "reason, theory or speculation." It also suggested particularity rather than universality. The Latin, *experientia*, had to do with experiment or trial, including the sense of encountering danger and "having survived risks and learned something from the encounter" (10). Much more prominent in the rest of Jay's study, however, is the German distinction between two very different concepts of experience, *Erlebnis*, which he most often uses to mean "the intensities of immediate prereflective experience," and *Erfahrung,* or the "narrative coherence of a meaningful journey over time" (264). *Erlebnis*, or "lived experience," involves "commonplace, untheorized practices," sometimes even a primitive unity prior to the subject/object differentiation. *Erfahrung*—with its root in *Fahrt* or journey—implies "a more temporally elongated notion of experience based on a learning process, an integration of discrete moments of experience into a narrative whole or an adventure" (11). Jay's treatment helps us to identify and separate out strands of these distinctly different ways of thinking about experience. For him, the tension existing between them strikes at the heart of what it means to be modern.

This dual meaning of experience helps Jay explain why twentieth-century critics can speak of a crisis, decline, or disappearance of experience at the same time that we see a cult of experi-

ence: the two-sided nature of the term "enables both the lamentation ... that 'experience' (in one of the senses of *Erfahrung*) is no
longer possible and the apparently contradictory claim that we
now live in an 'experience society' (*Erlebnisgesellschaft*)" (12).

In Jay's analysis, this dichotomy in the concept of experience
stands in at times for the mind/body dualism itself. The degree to
which an author embraces (or doubts) reason versus the senses
seems to Jay to illuminate his or her view of experience—thus his
discussion of the "quest for certainty" of Bacon and Descartes and
the "materialist realism" of Locke and skepticism of Hume in the
early part of the book (31, 56).

The eighteenth century ushered in what Jay calls the "modalization" of experience, or a move away from more "holistic" notions.
After various movements cast doubt on old certainties (he is vague
about the weight of different causes but mentions the "seculariz-
ing, anti-clerical, 'pagan' Enlightenment's multifaceted assault on
religion" in one context) (82), experience gained new authority,
but in new, specialized terms: the "characteristic differentiation
process of modernization" resulted in "the development of rela-
tively autonomous discourses about cognitive, religious, and aesthetic experience" (402). Jay places in this context Kant's "break
with sensationalist empiricism" in his belief in an active role for
human understanding, Friedrich Schleiermacher's elevation of the
intuitive and emotional in subjective religious experience or pious
practice over "intellectual assent" and faith (92), the trend toward
the subjective in aesthetic experience from Kant to Dewey, and the
increasing importance placed on "lived experience" as a basis for
political and historical knowledge. Ultimately, diverse thinkers
and traditions are loosely bound by the ribbon of diversity itself—
subjective versus universal, different versus conformist, prereflective versus judgmental.

EAT PRAY LOVE EPICUREANISM

In the *Eat Pray Love* sensation, the premise of the story, explored
here most explicitly through the film treatment, is one woman's

growing concern that what passes for successful adult life in the early twenty-first century is not all it is cracked up to be (the same premise, really, as Greif's and Jay's searches for prereflective experience). In a kind of *Feminine Mystique* for the "aughties," echoes of the woes of the 1950s housewife reverberate from the lonely suburbs of *then* to the gentrified city of *now*. The film opens in Bali, where Liz (Julia Roberts), on assignment for a slick travel magazine, meets a wise old medicine man named Ketut, who sends her on a path of self-discovery. His advice: find balance. The action moves episodically to her house in New York, where we witness her growing discontent with married life, and to another place in New York, the apartment of the handsome struggling actor into whose arms she jumps to get free of her marriage. The rest of the movie takes place in Italy, where she eats, India, where she prays, and Bali, where she revisits the medicine man and, under his wing, learns—spoiler alert—to love again.

From one vantage point (and this was clearly the response of millions of people), what is not to love about this story? How can one not sympathize with an account of one woman's passage from misery to happiness, emptiness to fulfillment, anxiety to well-being, isolation to love? It is a classic tale of a person's awakening to feelings of profound unease after taking life just as prescribed by the dominant norms of her social set and her social setting. Finding that life sorely wanting, amid material comfort and even wealth, the protagonist suffers from impoverishment of a different sort.

From another vantage point, one could easily deride *Eat Pray Love*—as many have—as a now-familiar account of one person's encounter with what are sometimes uncharitably dubbed today "First World problems." In her new introduction to the tenth-anniversary edition of the memoir, Gilbert herself acknowledges that her book's detractors have a point. She is well aware, as many of them pointed out, that only someone of enormous privilege could have done what she did—taken a year to travel the world in search of herself. Floundering families, crumbling communities, and the suffering of others are, as we also know, too often the cost of following the therapeutic dream of self-fulfillment. Unleashing and validating one person's pent-up dreams and desires can come at the expense of long-abiding dreams and desires of another.

Is *Eat Pray Love* a deeply moving story of someone truly searching for how to live a meaningful life or just another individualistic liberationist narrative?

No matter how critically one might view the antics of its real-life protagonist, the story itself is an archetypical tale of spiritual quest, self-discovery, and fulfillment. A closer look at the crystallized version of the story as depicted in the movie can take us beyond easy praise or dismissal into new ways to think about the dilemmas of life it explores and the answers it gives. Prior to her awakening, Liz's social milieu dictated everything from her definition of success to her very self-definition. Then comes the dawning realization of being out of place, out of tune, and out of answers. The quest is joined, the odyssey begun. Adventures ensue. The stifling marriage falls away, and likewise her rebound romance, and soon we find ourselves enjoying the pleasures of Rome and the Italian countryside—lingering over good food, wine, and the loving embrace of new friends. Then comes spiritual pilgrimage and, eventually, a new relationship with a man who seems to embody all of these good things. It is an oft-repeated tale of spiritual longing and belonging.

Yet it also leaves us hanging and thus wondering. All is tied up neatly at the end, with nothing but happiness understood to come next. That is just the problem. It is not that the ending is too happy. It is the slippage, as the tale of spiritual longing *becomes* a tale of emotional belonging.

Near the end of the movie, it is not yet clear how things will turn out between Liz and her new love interest, a Brazilian entrepreneur named Filipe (Javier Bardem). To that point, the script had groaned a bit at times, but the landscapes and vicarious gustatory pleasures had kept the vessel afloat.

The moment of truth has come. Covering her eyes, Filipe leads Liz to the beach where he has packed for a boat trip to a nearby island for a few days and decides to pop the question, or rather, to pop *a* question. It is the closest thing to a proposal that can be imagined by a world-traveling professional in our times. He says that since his life is in Bali (he runs an import-export business) and her life is in New York, they could make a life together living part of the time in each place. Kind and gentle to this point, and unfailingly warm and sensual, he turns hard-edged when Liz freezes, unable, both figuratively and literally, to jump on board. With her doubt, expressed as much through Julia Roberts's body language as her lines, from which she seems strangely disconnected, Liz seems caught at a convergence of past, present, and future in the way we really are—or should be—at such times, asking what we knew and felt before, what we learned, and what we imagine might happen, not just what *we feel right now.* All she learned through her year of soul-searching seems to be trying to break through, but she is paralyzed. When Filipe throws down an ultimatum she is stunned and unable to reply: "Look me in the eyes and tell me: Do you love me or do you love me not? It's very easy. I know you feel the same way I do. Why can't you say it back?" Shaky and wide-eyed, she ekes out, "I don't know why! Why can't I?" He provides the answer. "Because you're terrified, my love."

Felipe does not back down. Against her lover's renewed and ever more forceful entreaties, she tries to express herself: "I found something! And I can't give it up! Trust me. If I did you wouldn't be so all in love with me."

Felipe: Ah, the balance thing. You've traveled all around the world to find your balance. And the balance that you think you've found is what? Meditating twenty minutes and going to an old medicine man? Listen, balance, my darling, balance is never letting anyone else love you less than you love yourself.
Liz: Listen to me! I do not need to love you to prove that I love myself.
Felipe: Run away from me and you're running away from all the great possibilities of your own life. I'm getting into the boat.

Liz storms off, but before leaving Bali she stops to see Ketut one last time. When he asks her whether she loves her boyfriend, she says, "I ended it. . . . I couldn't keep my balance." Now we see that the scene on the sand was not the real moment of truth, but this one is. The plot requires us to go back to the question of *what she feels right now.* "Liz, listen to Ketut. Sometimes to lose balance for love is part of living balanced life."

So that is it. The wisdom after a year of searching seems to bring her right back where she started, either propelled by infatuation into another misty dream or awakened to the reality of a loving relationship that will need tending just as her first marriage did.

It is a blissful ending. Or is it? Will it still be after the point where the movie leaves off? Beyond movie and book, anyway, the life of the memoirist must go on. In 2016, Gilbert made a public announcement that she had fallen in love with her best female friend of fifteen years and ended her marriage to the real-life version of Filipe.[32]

A couple of years earlier, she and her husband had put up for sale their yellow 1869 Italianate Victorian house in Frenchtown, New Jersey. In a YouTube video she made to sell the house, she asks cheerfully why someone would sell such a beautiful house after devoting so much care to it. Answering her own question, she says that she and her husband travel too much to keep it up and she just feels the need to move every few years. The video opens with her warm invitation: "Hi! I'm Liz Gilbert and this is my house and I'm selling it, for no particularly rational reason except that I love moving and I spent the last six years making this house really beautiful. So if you want it you can buy it. Come on in!" Her exuberant tone in videos, interviews, and memoirs has gotten across not only her love of moving but her clear love of conveying to others her love of moving, and all of the other loves in her life. Another place we might start is to reinhabit ourselves by retrieving a sense of privacy, or "boundaries," a self-help term. The movie version of *Eat Pray Love* manages to protect a sense of privacy, while Gilbert's memoir tells it all. She is up front and unapologetic about this. In her YouTube video to sell her house, she shows every corner of her "Skybrary," a top-floor study with hand-carved bookcases complete with secret drawers and compartments. After showing several of these, she laughs that some people say she should not show people her secret hiding places. "But I'm a memoirist. All I know how to do is reveal."[33]

A dictum today is that after a certain point it is "time to move on." In the case of emotional, psychological, or physical violence or abuse, any compassionate human being would understand that such conditions must be changed. No one can know the private life of someone else. The personal stories in *Eat Pray Love Made Me Do It* speak to a complexity that defies caricature. But in the movie, when asked why she left her husband, who was devastated by the divorce, Liz said she supposed they were too immature and grew apart. If that is the case, whether with her love interest at the start of the story or her love interest at the story's end, the task would seem to be the same: to grow *together*. And whether on one's own or with someone else, the task also remains: to learn how to live a life.

Greif touches on a couple of ancient schools of philosophical thought and world religions he thinks might have different answers. He alludes to alternatives to today's experience-fueled form of "eudaemonistic hedonism" in various Stoic or Epicurean strands present in yoga, meditation, and "some aspects of Christianity"—all of which offer a way "out of the lust for experience by denying and controlling it." But he dismisses them and returns to experience, though with "a set of solutions" that "tries to *radicalize* experience" by replacing the hedonistic, cumulative version with one both aesthetic and perfectionistic: "Aestheticism asks you to view every object as you would a work of art. It believes that art is essentially an occasion for the arousal of emotions and passions. You *experience* a work of art," whereas "Perfectionism, in contrast, puts the self before everything. It charges the self with weighing and choosing every behavior and aspect of its way of living."[34]

In what Greif sees as their proper form, both aestheticism and perfectionism assume that you can make yourself. He warns against "debased" versions, such as consumerism, in which you make yourself through aesthetic experiences you purchase, or self-help, in which you make yourself "normal," presumably after having been "wounded by experience."[35] It is not clear what would guard against such debasements, or even against sheer solipsism, which Greif acknowledges is an "obvious criticism" of what he is proposing. He suggests that "mature forms" would require us to be aware of other people similarly trying to make *themselves*. But if everyone is looking at everything in the world in terms of what it has to do with one's own self and one's own experience, it remains a mystery what might serve to support human connections, shared commitments, and any greater project beyond the individual. Yet Greif's recipe retains a pinch of older traditions of self-making, twice removed through his avatars Gustave Flaubert (of Epicurean aestheticism) and Henry David Thoreau (of Stoic perfectionism). He makes passing references to holding back as one part of self-cultivation and even expresses a desire for a kind of "modern transcendence," but the dish he serves up smells a lot like a stew made from familiar stock: the myth of mastery, pleasure seeking, and sky-is-the-limit self-creationism. A sense of human limits, and the humility it can inspire, is the missing ingredient—a key ingredient of more serious, sustained, and sustainable forms of self-cultivation.[36]

The problem with so many perspectives current today is that they share an emphasis on the lone individual. It is telling that both Greif and Gilbert elsewhere voice deep reservations and suspicions about marriage, he in a separate *n + 1* essay, for some reason not included in *Against Everything*, and she in a follow-up memoir, *Committed*.

Something precious is lost by staying on the surface when it comes to our profound ties to other people and communities and fixating on a mode of living as experienced by the individual apart from others. This is precisely where the frozen-over framework of individual experience leaves us. Greif reduces the grave existential fact of human isolation to "the frustration that no one will feel the way I do in the many various moments that affect me most deeply. No one knows 'what it is like for me.'" Experience becomes a way to understand another person, as people take turns sharing their own experiences: "You can hear it reflected in practically any intimate conversation you care to eavesdrop on: 'Ah, I can't say something exactly like that happened to me, but it does remind me of the time that I . . .' Two commiserators use each other as transponders of their own experiences, in their best shot at empathy."[37] The thought of conversation, or even intercourse in both old and new meanings, as nothing more than turn-taking recitations of individual experience, or expressions of "what it is like to be me," is an uninspired vision of what is possible between people. We can do better.

What this view lacks, almost ironically, is a deeper concept of the inner life. Like a star that cannot be seen unless the observer looks to the side of it, experience enhances life when not pursued in this way, *as* experience. Astronomers call this "averted vision."[38] Another way to live is not to attempt to attain and sustain unlimited highs but to cultivate the inner person in calm and contemplation. This is where schools of thought from antiquity can help as a lens through which to see our own pursuits, opening up possibilities for enrichment we did not know existed. Paradoxically, they do it by foreclosing possibilities, through self-discipline and the enjoyment of new depths—as well as the soaring heights—that discipline makes possible.

Modern Epicureans sometimes seem to think they were the first to discover the need for release and the joys of experience. This means the modern variant often borders on the very thing the ancients tried to dissociate themselves from: hedonism. Many long-standing traditions and practices, including ancient schools and movements such as Stoicism, Epicureanism, Cynicism, and Platonism, took as a given the overwhelming experience of being alive. Like many religious traditions, which they have informed in different measures at different times, they offer ways to live that encompass those extremes of emotion once deemed the *passions*. Like nature, fate, and other forces not entirely in the hands of humankind, the passions risk subverting our best intentions, hopes, and ideals at every turn. The task of living, then, is to navigate the powerful currents in both our internal and external worlds. But in contrast to the perspective of the various philosophical schools, the view from the twenty-first century often diminishes emotion, shrinking it to a mere experience, while claiming to give it free rein as never before. The view from antiquity reveals emotion to be the life-creating, life-altering, and life-destroying force it really is. It is not responsible, or even desirable, to live without limits on emotion, or, as under the current cultural dispensation, according to an imperative of limitlessness.

The ancient philosophical schools saw our yearnings—emotional, physical, intellectual, spiritual—in their full and potentially tragic proportions. What differentiated these systems of thought was their approach to what we do going forward. If we are to find workable answers to the questions that plague us, to meet even in part the hunger many people express today, we will need to recover a fuller sense of the different resources people have pioneered to come at these problems.

Eat Pray Love struck a chord, resonating in a culture in which the acoustics were already excellent for its purposes. The notion of life as a journey is age-old, yet different ages have had different ideas about what that has meant. Today, we frequently hear someone refer to "my journey." What is meant by *journey* in this context? What makes some such references sound more genuine, while others seem to summon up the form of a journey but content that has more to do with the time-bound precepts and formulas of our own therapeutic culture? As Greif writes, "Adventurers are always coming back to tell us the thrills of daring acts that recreate more of the same. 'I stood on the precipice and leaped!' 'Into what?' 'Into the known!'"[39]

An episode in the *Simpsons* television show, set in the fictional family's town of Springfield, comments on this bluster about personal improvement and such proclamations of total transformation. Cultural historian and media critic Paul Arras offers a cameo that captures both the hyperbolic promise and the underwhelming results associated with this mentality:

Springfield as a whole seems largely immune from America's therapeutic, self-help culture. Still, the residents of Springfield are highly susceptible to cultural trends and advertising's influence. When, for example, a self-help guru comes to town in "Bart's Inner Child" (season five, episode seven, November 11, 1993), the entire town embraces his advice and holds a "Do

What You Feel" festival. Quickly, as the consequences from the citizens neglecting their usual responsibilities become apparent, the festival descends into chaos and violence. Once things settle down and the town falls back into the comforts of its status quo, the Simpsons debate the lessons they have learned. Marge suggests, "The lesson here is that self-improvement is better left to people who live in big cities." Lisa protests, saying, "Self-improvement can be achieved, but not with a quick fix. It's a long, arduous journey of personal and spiritual discovery." Homer, misinterpreting Lisa's point, inadvertently describes the entire town's philosophy: "That's what I've been saying. We're all fine the way we are."

While *The Simpsons* often seems a cynical take on our times, Arras's deft analysis shows its evolution over time from a searing critique of the hypocrisy and materialism of bourgeois suburban life to a more nuanced portrait, with an increasing emphasis on community in the Simpsons' world.[40] The critique of the self-help culture writ large indeed often highlights the need for a world beyond the self.

GET THEE TO A GREEK ISLAND

Daniel Klein offers a close-up portrait of a deliberate attempt to live according to Epicurean principles in modern times. In his case, he seeks such an experience in order to learn to be at ease with aging or old age. It seems a good example of cultivating the inner person in calm and contemplation. In his *Travels with Epicurus: A Journey to a Greek Island in Search of a Fulfilled Life*, his subtitle tips us off to his goal and invites us in. Who can resist the promise of a journey to a Greek island, even if we must visit vicariously while he actually takes the trip? At a dentist's appointment, he learns he will need an expensive and time-consuming procedure if he desires to dodge the blow to his ego of dentures. Instead of spending the money on dental work, he decides to try to locate some deeper solace and source of meaning. He packs some of his philosophy and other books and heads to Hydra in the Aegean Sea.[41]

What Klein finds in Greece amounts to nothing short of an alternative approach to living. What he was fleeing from back home was not just the money and time commitment of the dental work. It was also the cult of youth all around him and what he calls a "forever young" mentality of even people his age. According to a "new old-age credo," someone "getting on in years" now hears a familiar refrain, "You're not old. You're still in your prime!" (6). This way of thinking encourages people regardless of their age "to keep setting new goals, to charge ahead into new ventures, to design new programs for self-improvement," chasing the promise of extending "the prime of our lives indefinitely" (6).

For many, this credo has translated into putting off retirement, working as hard as before, or transposing frantic work schedules to leisure-time activities, with "copies of *1,000 Places to See Before You Die* tucked in their backpacks." Back home, it means everything from breast implants for a female friend in her late sixties to a testosterone patch and Cialis for a male friend in his seventies. Aghast, Klein sets out to find a more "authentic" version of life as an old man, one based on an acceptance of facing honestly the reality of aging (6–7). So far, so good.

This embrace of old age is embodied in the figure of an old Greek man with a weathered face named Tasso, who lounges at Dimitri's Tavern in the village of Kamini, periodically sniffing a sprig of wild lavender he keeps behind his ear. Klein sits at another table reading *The Art of Happiness, or The Teachings of Epicurus*. Tasso engages with his tablemates in desultory conversation alternately with "leisurely, comfortable silences," as they watch the sun set over the ocean. Klein goes on to observe alluring aspects of island life, which launch charming meditations on topics like play and time (such as the slow tempo of the movements of the elderly).

Klein perceives fundamental contrasts between his previous life in the US and the patterns of everyday life he sees on Hydra: old age as "the pinnacle of life" (13) instead of something to run away from; walking at a "leisurely pace" rather than rushing around; "sitting still" in place of "super busyness" (49); "pure play" versus "keeping one eye on the scoreboard" and "sports as self improvement" (51); or a stroll versus a power walk as "another ambitious activity crammed into our schedules" (51). He remembers earlier in life seeing old French men playing *pétanque* (a game like bocce ball or *boules*), and experiencing a revelation as it occurred to him for the first time that one can be old and still have fun. Now in Greece, seeing old men playing cards moves him, as they lose themselves in the spirit of play, including in their words, ideas, jokes, and aimless reminiscences (59). Klein realizes he had been "ignoring my spiritual yearnings" (145), seeking distraction, newness, and busyness instead of living in the present—and even instead of living in the past. Ultimately, he concludes that it is "*accumulated experience* [emphasis in original]" that "an old person has available to him in abundance" (69). "The trick" is to be able to savor this by recalling these experiences and contemplating their meaning, "pondering the big questions" (111) and focusing at last "on the ultimate spiritual questions" (144).

While not religious to date, Klein feels an "inchoate yearning for some kind of enlightenment," a vague longing for "a transcendent dimension" (145). He gravitates not toward a transcendent divinity but "a spiritual *experience* [emphasis in original]" (146). Against the new atheists like Sam Harris, he does not have any response to the idea that such an experience is merely "wish fulfillment." He can still choose what he calls "embracing my yes" (147). The closest he comes is listening to music or observing nature in a way that causes him to lose track of himself. As a result, he concludes that Zen Buddhism might have the answer—"mindfulness"—to be "*fully* here now [emphasis in original]" (150).

Upon returning home, Klein asks himself if living the way he did on Hydra is compatible with a life of continual work. So he comes around to the idea that the answer to a fulfilling life lies in being "as mindful as we possibly can be of where we are in life right now" (161). This is as close as he gets to an answer to his quest for "a relevant philosophy of authentic old age" (161). In an anticlimax, he concludes that he needs to ask his wife, daughter, and friends for their "permission to become an old man" (162). His wife's response ends the book:

> She laughs, of course. "My permission? What for?"
> I laugh too. "I don't know. I guess I think you'd rather I stay young or at least *try* to stay young."
> "Permission granted," she says, smiling. "Anyway, I think it's too late—that sounds like an old man's question." (162)

Half memoir, half travel diary, *Travels with Epicurus* mixes philosophical reflection with autobiography in order to come to terms with old age in a way that attempts to go against dominant American cultural currents. In his exposure to the slower pace of life and the practice of savoring the moment, Klein finds in life among the old men on Hydra at least provisional answers to some of his yearnings for a more "authentic" old age, spiritual experience, and an understanding of the meaning of life. As such, it is a pleasant journey for the reader.

This is true to the school of thought Klein invokes. The Epicureans' focus on pleasure as the highest good seems to Klein closest to capturing what he finds on Hydra and the general approach he embraces by the end. He includes a brief overview of the ancient Epicureans near the start of the book, then goes on to touch on other philosophers, quoting or alluding to them on particular points, without getting into the details of their widely varied worldviews. In seeking reconciliation between his life on Hydra and back at home in Massachusetts, he poses the choice as between the "forever young" mind-set and one based on a blend of philosophies he has cited, as though they are one: "Is there an acceptable golden mean between the 'forever young' ethos and the Platonic/Epicurean/existential ideal of a fulfilled and authentic old man? Can we split the difference without compromising both extremes so much that we end up with a mushy philosophy of old age?" 160). Against the obvious answer of "no," he again plays our day's ace in the hole—mindfulness. But this ignores vital differences in philosophical outlooks and actually does end up a kind of mush that has less potential to go against the prevailing culture than Klein suggests.

Epicureanism is ultimately reconciled in Klein's book with the therapeutic culture, with its doctrine of personal fulfillment and authenticity. In this culture, these endeavors often become another form of self-directed "striving" (14). It is ultimately a counsel of escape—another form of distraction—from ethical commitments and communal well-being. Klein praises the "radical egalitarianism" of Epicureans, yet nearly all of the thinkers he cites are male, and he does not explain how society will remain egalitarian with its oldest and (in his view) wisest members so disengaged, living on islands for one. This shows the ease with which Epicureanism can be tailored to fit a modern individualistic ethos. Klein dedicates himself to what will make him feel better, which for him means feeling more authentic. It is not about changing society. Others rarely figure into the discussion except as a kind of backdrop for his own endeavors and desires.

The book has the imprint of the tourist, gazing upon another culture through a misty veil. All is happy on Hydra. Klein's discussion of the laid-back attitude in Greece is a generalization that might be applied to many an island vacation. As with *Eat Pray Love*, the question remains how to live after returning from the vacation. Ancient Epicureanism was not thought to be a part-time option, suitable only for old age.

Klein's brand of Epicureanism in the end leaves the modern therapeutic culture unchallenged. His need for "permission" to be old resonates with that culture's notion of giving oneself permission to give in to desires of all kinds. As we saw in the Introduction, the tension between permissions and restraints lies at the heart of Philip Rieff's view of culture. The therapeutic distorts this by validating only permissions. Supports for practicing restraint collapse as any transcendent notion of the good fades from view. Though claiming to be a synthesis of ancient philosophies, it becomes none other than the therapeutic synthesis. In this case, the therapeutic, in the guise of the new Epicureanism, seems to have triumphed over ancient Epicureanism and all of its rivals, ancient and modern.

There is a major difference between Plato and Epicurus on the issue of the transcendent. Klein's sleight of hand inexplicably throws them suddenly together. Klein reserves his only criticism for Stoicism, which stands out in what is basically an irenic, even sunny treatment of all other philosophies. Singled out, Stoicism falls short for reasons long the mainstay of modern culture since the 1960s: Stoics are in denial. Their philosophy comes down to an attempt to suppress their emotions. Unlike Epicureanism, which stresses emotion, Stoicism "feels more like denying pain than transcending it" (127). Klein briefly brings in the Stoics as needed to guard against "anticipatory depression" of "old old age [*sic*]" but then dismisses them (133). Denial is automatically opposed to authenticity, assumed here to be emotional experience.

What drops out of Klein's picture is the importance of virtue in the ancient philosophical views he cites. He embraces what he sees as "Epicurus's dictum that the happiest life is free from self-imposed demands of commerce and politics" (107). He sees Epicureanism as a call to scale down, a critique of consumerism. Yet the trip to Hydra must have cost something. At the end of the book, he admits he could not go so far as to live the life of an ascetic— even if it means having to answer his spiritual yearnings with a kind of spirituality lite.

Modern versions of Epicureanism often depart from the ancient school. Yet perhaps we can see where such versions fall short as not completely unrelated to the earlier ideas. The Epicurean view is in some ways instrumentalist. It casts pleasure and virtue as inseparable, yet with pleasure rather than the good as the highest end. Virtue can therefore become instrumental for pleasure. Although it is unfair to mistake Epicureanism for hedonism, Epicureanism might contain the seeds of hedonism on these grounds. As Epicurus's tenth maxim states, one should not oppose excess for its own sake but rather oppose it because it does not dispense with pain (10.150, p. 667). Epicurean doctrine has no airtight preventive against hedonism. Pleasure can involve virtue in Epicureanism, but Platonism offers more certain answers as to how and why, by keeping virtue and the good as the highest end, and pleasure as inherent in it—but suffering as well. Epicureans view suffering as a necessary by-product of the pursuit of pleasure—something to minimize by avoiding it whenever possible and by not focusing on it. Here, Epicureanism resembles Gnosticism because it casts knowledge as therapeutic. Knowledge of natural science reduces fear and anxiety. In this way, science becomes tied to pleasure. This fails to address knowledge that does not quell anxiety. Friendship is also instrumental, according to the twenty-eighth maxim, because it enhances our security more than anything (10.148, p. 673). According to maxim 31, justice is also expedient (10.150, pp. 673 and 675). It is merely the means of keeping one person from harming another. As we assess the consequences of this way of thinking, it helps to recall that in Greek mythology Hydra betokened less a vacation spot than a dangerous monster that snatched up hapless sailors at sea.

FOODIE CULTURE

Many Epicureans today use the word *epicurean* to mean the opposite of Epicurus's appreciation of a simple meal of "bread and water." The foodie culture can cross over many walks of life and economic levels. At the expensive end, though, it can soar into the stratosphere. The fear that Epicurean taste for the good life, as based on the experience of the senses, could devolve into hedonism has a history as long as the school itself. Diogenes Laertius mentions the accusations hurled at Epicurus that he was nothing more than a libertine. Oscar Wilde captured this tension in *The Picture of Dorian Gray*. In that novel, a beautiful young man sells his soul to remain as young and beautiful looking as a portrait painted of him. He goes on to live an indulgent, lawless existence until his sins catch up to him. He confesses and resolves to live a moral life, destroying the painting so that he himself will age. Instead, someone hears a crash and a cry, and when his servants go to his room "they found hanging upon the wall a splendid portrait of their master as they had last seen him, in all the wonder of his exquisite youth and beauty. Lying on the floor was a dead man, in evening dress, with a knife in his heart. He was withered, wrinkled, and loathsome of visage. It was not till they had examined the rings that they recognized who it was."[42] As Dorian Gray learned, the attraction to a life of pleasure can be fatal.

Modern versions exhibit this dichotomy intrinsic to Epicureanism. We might consider these poles an Epicureanism of excess versus an Epicureanism of limits. On the one hand, the word has come to mean self-indulgence, and on the other, the discipline of good taste.[43] Sometimes these opposite-seeming tendencies come together in strange ways. The gourmet revolution provides numerous examples. For instance, the most recent iteration since the 1960s of a centuries-old intermittent turn to new cooking, *nouvelle cuisine*, increased the size of plates and simultaneously shrank the size of portions. Some foodies relish the hunt for the best restaurants in the world—or at least the most expensive. This can mean waiting for months for a reservation, paying exorbitant prices, and tasting minute concoctions one at a time, like miniature works of art in an edible museum, savored during a slow-paced five-hour meal. Alongside the obvious self-indulgence, there is a kind of self-discipline in this pursuit if patience is always, as they say, a virtue.

A brief profile can give us a taste of this. A restaurant in Chicago called Alinea offers not just dinner but "experiences" with wine pairings each step of the way. Its sixteen- to eighteen-course dinner goes for $295–360 per person, or customers can order the Alinea Kitchen Table, its "highest dining expression," at an even higher price tag of $395 per person. The latter is the restaurant's "most intimate, immersive and cutting edge experience." Winner of several awards including a high rating in the *Michelin Guide*, Alinea promises customers that "dining at Alinea is not only delicious, but also fun, emotional, and provocative." Priding itself on its "innovative approach to modernist cuisine," Alinea does not accept reservations but instead sells tickets for those who click on a button on their website labeled "Book your Experience."[44]

Next to its three-star ranking of Alinea, the only restaurant in Chicago to achieve that mark as of 2019, the *Michelin Guide* offers a pithy notation: "Excellent cuisine, worth a special journey." It elaborates on what customers can expect:

> Dining here is partly theater and pure pleasure. Meals take advantage of every sense, so guests should expect scented vapors, unexpected tricks, sizzling charcoal and tableside preparations. The olfactory experience is vivid—if you keep your eyes closed, intense wafts of citrus or smoke will easily reveal what course was just served. This chamber is sure to be packed; yet it feels more like a party than a crowd. Service is remarkably knowledgeable, attentive and engaged, thanks to a staff that brings both humor and personality to the meal. Dishes are always whimsical and sometimes experimental. While dining on a duo of squid—one as an inky sauce and another with lemon-chili butter—a bowl of oranges on the table is simultaneously filled with liquid nitrogen for a profound complementary aroma. Langoustines are compressed into a sheet of paper and then melt tableside into a superb bouillabaisse. Dessert may arrive floating on a string, as in a green apple balloon of childhood fun.[45]

A restaurant review of Alinea describes the experience in detail, raving about the components and composition of courses that include delicacies from all over the world and end with these "edible helium-filled balloons."[46]

New interest in all things ancient takes many different forms. Jackson & LeRoy, a luxury builder of custom homes and remodeler in Salt Lake City, Utah, prides itself on offering "more than the mere construction of a home" but "homes that matter—to clients, to our environment, and to the community." Featured in numerous magazines and winner of prizes such as the 2016 Parade of Homes People's Choice Award, the company's work includes a project it calls "Ancient Modern," a house built in Highland, Utah. Photographs posted on the company website show a house reminiscent of "a home set in an English garden or countryside," for which the client pined.[47] Its elements include symmetry, simplicity, and order. It has the minimalism and grandeur of much modern architecture for upscale homes, with soaring ceilings, a spacious layout, expensive fixtures, and materials such as brass and granite. It attempts a human-sized organization of space and features that make it comfortable while striking a meditative mood with a narrow spectrum of whites, tans, grays, blue gray, green gray, and rooms free of clutter and bright pigments. Floors are wood and tile, sinks farmhouse style chastened with straight, even severe lines, with industrial design undertones common today. Stools at the sleek kitchen island have some of the only round shapes; whether intentionally or not, their seat cushions' extralong cloth ties wind around the stainless-steel chair legs like the leather sandal straps on the legs of a toga-wearing ancient. According to an upscale appliance company that gave it an award, the house measures 7,800 square feet, fulfilling "grandest desires" while keeping a "homespun comfy quality."[48]

Sub-Zero, a company established in 1945, pioneered in home refrigeration, Wolf in commercial cooking, and Cove in dish washing. All three have combined to offer in-person showrooms and online shopping. They offer various up-market appliances: a twenty-four-inch under-counter wine cooler at $3,775; a thirty-six-inch designer refrigerator/freezer drawer with ice maker at $5,145; a thirty-six-inch classic side-by-side refrigerator/freezer at $10,660; and a forty-two-inch classic French door refrigerator/freezer with internal ice dispenser at $12,470. Wolf ranges include a thirty-inch gas range with four burners and infrared charbroil listing at $7,830, and Cove dishwashers include a twenty-four-inch model (ready for custom kitchen panel doors) at $2,099. Wolf Gourmet Countertop Appliances offers a high-performance blender at $599.95, a programmable coffee system at $499.95, a four-slice toaster at $399.95, and a stand mixer at $899.95. The company even has a mobile app. The tagline on its home page is "Live deliciously." In nearly subliminal ghost-like lettering it adds, "We believe that a life lived well is a life lived deliciously." The words are superimposed over a looped video of a family toasting across a long banquet table.[49]

On a more modest scale, perhaps in part as a move away from such excesses in the pursuit of tastes, an article in *Taste* magazine describes a current back-to-basics trend in cooking. It regales readers with the launch of *Basically*, a new *Bon Appétit* website featuring recipes that simplify cooking for time-strapped home cooks by lowering the number of ingredients and steps. This new website "announced that, as ever, *Bon Appétit* had its finger pointed at the prevailing zeitgeist: a broader lifestyle-oriented movement toward minimalism." Other examples include the tiny-house movement, which embraces the simplicity of small living quarters; #vanlife, a social media tag celebrating living on the road in a van; *Kinfolk* magazine, which promotes the slow-living movement for young professionals; "whitewashed coffee shops that evoke both the Apple store and a Swedish sanatorium"; and Marie Kondo's *The Life-Changing Magic of Tidying Up.*[50]

In trying to account for the trend of simple cooking, the food studies scholars interviewed by Rebecca Marx attributed it to the ever-renewing search for new consumer trends, which swing like a pendulum between complexity and simplicity:

> And as in fashion, when a previously rarefied experience becomes available to the masses—when you're suddenly rubbing shoulders with tourists at Alinea—"you have to invent a new kind of sophistication, and that often is a complete return to simplicity," says Ken Albala, a professor of history and the chair of food studies at the University of the Pacific in Stockton, California. "It's finding something so beautiful and simple that you can't access it with mere money." None of this is new, of course: In the ancient Roman novel *Satyricon*, a nouveau riche character throws an elaborate banquet, only to be told by Rome's disapproving elites that it would be better to go to a farm and eat just-laid eggs and fresh vegetables. "You think, Oh my god, this was written yesterday," Albala says. "But it's 2,000 years old."[51]

Truer to the spirit of ancient Epicureanism is the slow food movement, which originated in Bra, Italy, in the late 1980s and went on to spread throughout the world. Founded by a grassroots group led by Carlo Petrini, slow food seeks "to defend regional traditions, good food, gastronomic pleasure and a slow pace of life." It advocates and models biodiversity, local sourcing, and other aspects of localism, such as "connections between plate, planet, people, politics and culture." Its principles have also inspired movements in other realms of life. It pursues related practices itself in the form of efforts such as the slow wine movement. Its website offers reviews of over 2,500 wines and three hundred wine cellars, taking an approach to wine criticism that rates wines for "wine quality, adherence to terroir, value for money and environmental sensitivity." One of its many collaborations close to home, together with the University of Gastronomic Sciences, resulted in the Wine Bank, which preserves wines from small producers throughout Italy organized in its wine cellar by region, helping to pioneer an attendant slow wine movement. With a broader devotion to a slow world, the slow food movement's philosophy reads: "Slow food stands at the intersection of ethics and pleasure, ecology and gastronomy. It opposes the standardization of taste, the unrestrained power of multinationals, industrial agriculture and the folly of fast life. It restores cultural dignity to food and the slow rhythms of conviviality to the table."[52] Epicurus would be pleased.

In another example of what appears to be a New Epicurean treatment, greater humility also comes into play. The Bollywood movie *The Lunchbox* draws us into scenes in Mumbai that juxtapose the modern blare of fast-moving traffic with close-up shots of traditional modes of bicycle delivery of large stacked containers filled with multiple dishes encased in cloth lunchboxes of all colors.[53] (See fig. 3.5.) In one kitchen, a frustrated wife tries to win back her husband's estranged affections through cooking, but the results of her efforts accidentally end up on the table of an equally lonely midlevel insurance manager on his lunch break. Through a twist of fate, her delicacies awaken the palette of this older widower, who has long since given up on human connection. The two lonely souls discover the mix-up and decide separately not to correct the delivery service. They communicate indirectly through the degrees of spiciness and amounts ingested or ignored and directly with notes enclosed in the lunchbox. When the woman's husband turns out to be having an affair, they feel a bit freer to take a chance and meet, but a number of things get in the way. This is certainly a movie about the pleasures of cooking and eating. Yet it is also a movie about holding back, preserving a space between people, and about the ways the world can enforce such spaces even when the longing to bridge them becomes overpowering. Colors, smells, textures, sounds, and tastes evoke a scene of loneliness and separation even amid millions of people, as well as the genuine fulfillment of just knowing the love of another, a mysterious gift bestowed by cosmic accident even if the protagonists, because of their circumstances, get to enjoy only a taste of true love—for now, anyway. The film's ending leaves the future open. And so we should leave its categorization as Epicurean open, since the reader might decide otherwise after chapter 5.

SUSTAINABLE SELF-MAKING

What is it now to "escape into the known," as Greif so engagingly puts it? The known these days is change, escape, motion, dissolution, disruption, starting over—so called "creative destruction." In this context, what would constitute a genuine adventure might instead be cultivating the art of return. An alternative ending to the film version of *Eat Pray Love* would be a reunion rather than a new relationship, an outcome described in many of the personal stories recounted in *Eat Pray Love Made Me Do It*. Sustaining relationships emerged continually as the hard-won achievement in personal stories of those so movingly affected by the book.

The German writer Peter Sloterdijk, a professor of philosophy at the Karlsruhe School of Design and author of *Critique of Cynical Reason* and the *Spheres* trilogy, writes that the nineteenth century's unifying worldview centered on work and production, while that of the twentieth century focused on reflexivity—a tendency toward self-referentialism. The twenty-first century, in Sloterdijk's view, will need to center on "practices," which he sees as assorted disciplines of self-making, many of which derive from religious traditions. This is a dire matter, even one of sheer survival. So that we might manage to face the prospect of environmental depletion, he writes, "Now is the time to call to mind anew all those forms of the practicing life," even if the religious and metaphysical foundations for these practices have fallen away. Sloterdijk hopes that such a return to the rich resources of past practices can translate into a collective one-world set of practices aimed at the shared goal of sustainability.[54]

The challenge of such an approach is that enduring social practices have historically been inspired and sustained by communities of people sharing transcendent commitments, a certain *telos*, and a particular content that gives meaning to the practice. Daily life entails navigating the choices we face within a particular context, in a particular place, surrounded by particular people. One of the reasons Gilbert could pick up and leave was, as she herself confides, that she had a great deal of money, time off to travel, and an extraordinarily large circle of supportive friends and family members. In the movie version hardly any appearances of or references to that entire social world surface. One of the ironies of the *Eat Pray Love* phenomenon is that this story of individualistic self-fulfillment is so often experienced in community, by sisters or mothers and daughters or in reading groups, church groups, tour groups, and many others.

A true alternative to the cult of commodified peak experiences for the individual suggests another kind of odyssey—one that begins where the voyage ends, which is exactly where the real demands come, in the course of daily life and amid the external and internal conflicts that threaten to shatter us individually and tear us asunder. In Carl Sandburg's poem, "The fog comes / on little cat feet. It sits looking / over harbor and city / on silent haunches / and then moves on."[55] The worth of mindfulness and other self-help philosophies often seems to be in the eye of the beholder, so varied (and variable) is the current self-help landscape, and we shall see whether they go the way of the latest failed therapies. In the meantime, the ancient schools of philosophical thought might be what remains when the fog "moves on." They have, after all, endured for some time. Their reappearance is a promising sight, but only if we still have eyes to see, along with the interest in looking beyond ourselves.

For it really to catch on, this art of return might need to give more sustained attention to different philosophical views from those that elevate experience over all, as if in compensation for deprivation of the resources needed for a soul to sit still and glory in the realization that a universe and a world of others exists that is external to us yet inextricably tied to our very being. We are born into a world we did not create. The art of return must also take seriously the notion of transcendent good, perhaps the only enduring answer to the question of how to live. It is not enough to call for balance or to invoke traditional practices for their instrumental value, holism for its liberating effects, mindfulness as another way to enhance individual experience, or self-expression as feel-good spirituality. To navigate the pull of the opposite tendencies in Epicureanism, from deprivation to plenty and back, such a clearer vision is a must.

FOUR

THE NEW
CYNICISM

All hope abandon, ye who enter here!
—*Dante*

On a frigid mountain outcropping, an adolescent boy in a loin-cloth stands barefoot in the snow at night. He turns his grim face toward the viewers, locking eyes with us. Suddenly, he jerks back to face an oversized wolf, eyes glowing yellow and mouth gaping to reveal massive incisors. The boy delivers the final blow with his spear. The camera pans to the full moon and the wolf's snarling growl turns into a dying howl. The fifteen-year-old (played by Tyler Neitzel) has proven himself and returns to Sparta to take on his role as king.

Thirty years after this rite of passage, an emissary of the Persian king (Peter Mensah) visits King Leonidas (Gerard Butler). When the king asks the messenger the reason for his visit, the messenger requests a sign of Sparta's submission to Xerxes, "Earth and water." They stroll together to a nearby watering hole, where Leonidas unexpectedly draws his sword. With the gaping well at his back, the visitor utters, "Madman! You're a madman!" Leonidas sneers, "Earth and water. You'll find plenty of both down there." In the escalating exchange, the messenger cries, "No man, Persian or Greek, no man threatens a messenger! . . . This is blasphemy! This is madness!" Right before the Spartan king kicks the man into the water to his death and the royal guardsmen plunge their spears into the rest of the Persian entourage, blood splattering everywhere, Leonidas asks, "Madness?" With eyes burning and his grimace as fierce as the wolf's in the earlier scene, he screams at the top of his lungs, "*This . . . is . . .* SPARTA!"

Thus begins the story of the Battle of Thermopylae in 480 BC, as told by the creators of the 2006 movie *300.*[1] Leonidas goes on to mount a fierce resistance to Xerxes, taking a noble last stand, where he and a small band of three hundred soldiers hold off the vast Persian army at a narrow mountain pass against all odds. Betrayed by a disgruntled would-be soldier who told the Persians of a back entry to the battleground via goat path, Leonidas and the Spartan soldiers meet their deaths, to a man. A gripping story with a basis in fact, the Spartan resistance speaks of what is possible when all faculties of the human person are fully engaged, mind, heart, and soul. Leonidas would not abandon his commitments— Spartan lands, loved ones, ideals—for anything. Courageous to the end, he was willing to give his life for what he saw as the higher good.

In transposing this episode in history to a fictional rendering on the screen, it might seem the history was tailor-made for a Stoic treatment. This is often the case with matters of war and soldiery, which demand courage and fortitude by definition. Yet for our purposes here, in this telling of the story, the movie *300* is instead a study in cynicism.

ONE NEED NOT GO VERY FAR TO ENCOUNTER THE observation that our times are awash in cynicism. For many observers, cynicism is the best way to characterize the present moment. For instance, Jeffrey Goldfarb sees the US as having a cynical culture.² To call someone cynical—including one's self—is commonplace. As with the schools of ancient Greco-Roman philosophy we have examined, there are differences between ancient and modern movements. In the case of Cynicism, the problem is compounded. Just as modern meanings of the word *stoic* can fall far from the tree of the ancient Stoa, in every tradition we sometimes encounter only attenuated connections with the original school. This is especially true of cynicism, which has a life of its own as a modern concept, often virtually independent of the ancient one.

The problem of sources further compromises the identification of the early tenets of Cynicism. Of all the ancient movements (Cynicism was not an actual school), this one has the fewest extant sources. Most of what is known about the earliest Cynics comes in the form of anecdotes and sayings recorded centuries later. If that were not enough to cloud the issue, the approach of the ancient Cynics tended to minimize the importance of written philosophy. The tradition of Cynic thought, then, is a tradition of a tradition. In a sense it is a case not of later reception and interpretation but of reception and interpretation *as* the original approach of Cynics to the art of living. One of the few tenets that runs across all versions is the questioning of tradition itself. Cynicism can therefore constitute a kind of tradition, but paradoxically one of oppositional or antifoundational thought.

ANTITRADITION TRADITION

Cynicism might seem to some readers a less viable approach to life than the others profiled in this book, more useful as an epithet for a pessimistic view of human nature leading to toxic dread and suspicion. Along these lines, a recent study claimed a link between cynicism and dementia.³ To others, it might seem like a commonsense response to the world as we know it. While not a formal school like Stoicism and Epicureanism, Cynicism had a significant and often underestimated presence. Revisionist scholars now consider it a cultural movement, yet one with an identifiable intellectual history as a coherent approach to living. Characterized and caricatured by both advocates and critics as denoting the simple life of Diogenes "the dog," the early Cynics include Antisthenes and Crates and others. While these pioneers cannot be studied through extensive original texts, they are accessible through a multitude of writings of others offering fragments and testimony. (See fig. 4.1.) On some of the conduits to the modern period, Louisa Shea's *The Cynic Enlightenment: Diogenes in the Salon* is particularly helpful not just in content but also in the form of the study, which, like this one, takes on distant eras while finding current relevance of ancient tenets.[4] Peter Sloterdijk's *Critique of Cynical Reason* focuses on key differences he sees between ancient and modern cynicism, and his dense doorstopper became a surprise best seller.[5] Like his, many other late twentieth-century works of social criticism picture European and American life as plagued by cynicism. However, few of those critics share Sloterdijk's unusual antidote: more cynicism.

While critics might lament the modern descent into the abyss of cynicism, many people actually wear the cloak of cynic without excuses, or at least refer to their cynicism as normal and understandable. Karen Salmansohn's numerous works, including *Instant Happy, Happiness in a Box, How to Be Happy, Dammit: A Cynic's Guide to Spiritual Happiness*, and *Enough, Dammit: A Cynic's Guide to Finally Getting What You Want*, present a mode of self-help designed for today's cynics. Shows like *Seinfeld* and movies like *The Matrix* articulate different forms of what we can fairly consider cynicism. Beyond existentialist and postapocalyptic genres, cynicism became a major preoccupation of movies as an art form generally, spanning decades and directors, from Federico Fellini to Woody Allen. Ingmar Bergman's classic *Winter Light*, about a man's struggle with his faith in God, and Sean Penn's later *Into the Wild* both consider an individual's opting out of society altogether. Numerous blogs have sprouted up, such as *The Cynical Sanctuary* and *Cynical-C*. How much does this modern designation have to do with the classical Cynics, who renounced worldly goods and preached a gospel of virtue and happiness? It is the goal of this chapter to find out.

At the heart of ancient Greek Cynicism lies the figure of Diogenes of Sinope. His memory, at least, if not his person and mind, became so central to later understandings of the Cynics that it causes one scholar to assert that "the reception of Cynicism in the Middle Ages and in modern times is, with few exceptions, simply the reception of Diogenes." Regardless of the veracity of particular details of his life and thought, by all reports Diogenes was a colorful character. He has gone down in history as the philosopher who divested himself of all of his possessions in order to live according to his philosophical principles. He dressed in minimal attire and slept in a wine barrel, performing all imaginable bodily functions in full public view. He is known to us for his quips and witticisms, bald and often offensive observations, and embedded puzzles and paradoxes. Some of his thoughts later meshed with other traditions, from early Christian fathers' commitments to asceticism and critiques of sinful excess to folkloric portraits of the "wise fool."[6] Intrinsic to the ancient lore of Diogenes are three anecdotes that are endlessly repeated. The first (above) involves his living in the barrel and defecating (among other actions) in public. The second involves his response to meeting Alexander, who sought out the philosopher and asked what he could do for him. Enjoying some sun at that moment, Diogenes replied that Alexander could "get out of my light." A third story has Diogenes carrying a lantern. When asked why, his cryptic reply that he was looking for (good) men, which implied that he could not find any. These anecdotes have provided the material for a variety of renderings, from the raucous to the reverent, in innumerable paintings, sculptures, and other forms.

Diogenes Laertius's *Lives of Eminent Philosophers* conveyed these anecdotes, along with many more, in the form of a minibiography.[7] This work was a famous history of philosophers published in the third century AD that profiled numerous ancient thinkers. Based on compilations of any available sources, Laertius's portrait thus assembles information that may have been based on hearsay or legend. Many of the anecdotes have not been definitively established as truth. Yet most scholars do not dismiss them because they still capture the spirit and tradition of Cynicism.[8]

Turning to the modern period, the German language now differentiates between ancient Cynicism, *Kynismus*, which refers to the specific views of the ancient Cynic philosophers, and *Zynismus*, which expresses the broader modern notion of "cynicalness." Between the eighteenth century and the early twentieth century, another term, *Cynismus*, came into use to denote a concept of cynicism that "showed a tendency to free itself from its connection to its ancient substrate and become independent."[9] In English, the distinction between ancient and modern concepts is usually conveyed only orthographically, with *Cynicism* referring to the ancient movement and *cynicism* with a lower-case "c" to the modern concept.[10]

In a review of W. Desmond's *Cynics* (2008), John Sellars poses the enduring problem of whether ancient Cynicism even constituted a philosophy or "merely a style of living." Doubting "the philosophical value of Cynicism" extends from at least the first century BC, when Diogenes's Roman follower Varro raised questions along these lines, and this debate continues today. In his 2010 review, Sellars remarks that it is thus time for a full assessment, which he hoped to find in Desmond's book. The classic overview of Cynicism to date is D. R. Dudley's 1937 *History of Cynicism* (since reprinted), but that work does not evaluate its philosophical standing. Recent work by Marie-Odile (Antony) Goulet-Cazé and others set the stage for such a reassessment. Sellars finds Desmond's book "so even-handed" as not to put forth "any firm interpretive conclusions at all": while giving praise where it is due, he states, "What we have here, then, is not a strong reading of the Cynics but rather a straightforward and balanced presentation of the ancient evidence, with readers being left to make up their own minds about how best to understand what the Cynics were trying to do." This matters for our purposes because even this leading scholar concludes by reiterating the long-standing question "Is Cynicism a real philosophy?"[11]

Despite the dearth of sources, philosophers and others have engaged with that key question over the centuries, particularly in the Renaissance, the Enlightenment, and the nineteenth century, and on up to our times. Nietzsche, Foucault, and Sloterdijk are just a few of the most prominent modern philosophers who have taken it up in a sustained way.

Goulet-Cazé calls ancient Cynicism not a school but a "philosophical protest movement," noninstitutional by intention. Rather than taking root in a particular location, like the other schools, with systematic instruction and a distinct lineage, Cynic philosophizing took place in public, "creating unrest in the streets, at crossings, in front of temples" or at stadium entrances. Of its original sources, "almost none" exist. Even the roots of the term *cynicism* are murky. By some accounts, the philosophical movement was named after the Cynosarges, a gym in Athens where a temple to Hercules stood and where Antisthenes, a pupil of Socrates, taught. By other accounts, the term came from *kýnes*, meaning dog, employed as an epithet. This nickname stemmed from the "candid" and "shameless" behavior of Cynic philosophers. In these two origin stories, Antisthenes is deemed the founder of the movement. In other versions, from late antiquity onward, Diogenes of Sinope is considered the founder. The Stoics drew a line of intellectual transmission from Socrates to Antisthenes to Diogenes to Crates to Zeno, the founder of Stoicism. Yet scholars suggest this might have emerged from the Stoics' desire to trace their own lineage back to Socrates. Further, the historical record is inconclusive about whether Diogenes, given his early exile, was influenced directly by Antisthenes in person. Goulet-Cazé's entry in *Brill's New Pauly* grants that Antisthenes clearly played a role but says "Cynicism as a movement was founded by Diogenes" and "he determined its essential features."[12] Whether or not it was founded by Antisthenes, and whether it initially took its name from the gymnasium or from the derogatory nickname, the movement came to be associated above all with "Diogenes the Dog." (See fig. 4.2.)

The early Cynic movement had two main heydays: the older Cynicism of the fourth and third centuries BC and Roman imperial Cynicism of the period from the first through the fifth centuries AD. Prominent in the ancient movement were not just

Diogenes but his student Crates of Thebes (husband of Hipparchia of Maroneia, also a Cynic), as well as Crates's students, Metrocles of Maronea (Hipparchia's brother), Monimus of Syracuse, Menippus of Gadara, Zeno of Citium, and Cleanthes of Assos. Although Hipparchia came from a comfortable family, she gave up everything to join Crates in the life of a Cynic. (See fig. 4.3.) As Diogenes Laertius recounts the story, Crates, out of respect for her parents, initially discouraged Hipparchia's love for him. Once he saw that she was unwilling to part with him, Crates took off his clothes to emphasize his Cynic way of life. Still not dissuaded, Hipparchia accepted his marriage offer and joined him in following the Cynic teaching of Diogenes.[13]

Subsequent figures included Bion of Borysthenes, Cercidas of Megalopolis, and the teacher Teles (the earliest practitioner of the Cynical-Stoical diatribe), Meleager of Gadara, and the Roman senator M. Favonius. Prominent in the imperial movement were Demetrius of Corinth (a friend of the Stoic Seneca), Demonax of Cyprus, Peregrinus Proteus, Oenomaus of Gadara, Maximus Heron of Alexandria, Gregorius of Nazianzus, and Sallustius.[14]

From the first century AD, the movement became "*the* popular philosophy *par excellence* [emphasis in the original]," according to Goulet-Cazé. While Cynicism at this time had prominent philosophers among its proponents, it was also "a popular philosophy" among slaves, poor people, and others. Its adherents sometimes embraced both Cynicism and Christianity, and observers have sometimes discerned similarities between the ascetic practices of the two movements. At other times, these movements stand out as starkly opposed, for instance in Crescens's persecution of Justin and in Augustine's criticism of the Cynics. Goulet-Cazé concludes that "this movement had neither dogmatic sources nor a philosophical system, but was based on a uniform ethical teaching that was expressed in an ascetic way of life." While there are almost no original sources of the earliest Cynics, she believes that the anecdotes and other observations about how Cynic philosophers actually lived do reveal a general philosophical approach.[15]

A close look at the Ur-text on Diogenes gives us a sense of his self-definition and ideas about how to live.[16] According to different accounts, either Diogenes or his banker father, Hicesius, "adulterated the coinage." In one rendering of this incident, Diogenes visited Delphi or the Delian oracle in his own city of Sinope to ask Apollo if he should "alter the *political* currency" [my emphasis] on behalf of workmen he was supervising. Having received permission, he interpreted it not figuratively as approval to resist the powers that be but literally as approval to deface the "state coinage."[17] In any case, after this he went into exile, whether by force or choice (2.20–21, p. 23; also 2.38, p. 39).

When someone later brought up that Diogenes had adulterated the coinage, he replied, "That was the time when I was such as you are now; but such as I am now, you will never be" (2.56, p. 59). Laertius says Diogenes encountered Antisthenes in Athens and persevered in becoming his pupil, but this appears doubtful.[18] Still, by all accounts Diogenes, like Antisthenes, "set out upon a simple life" (2.21, p. 25). He owned only a cloak, a "wallet" to carry his food in, and, after he became "infirm," a "staff." When he could not secure a cottage to live in, he famously took up residence in his legendary tub in public, begged for his food, and took care of bodily functions in full view (2.23, p. 25; also 2.69, p. 71). When Plato called him a dog, he did not object (2.40, p. 41). One poetic account of his death read, "Diogenes, a true-born son of Zeus, a hound of heaven" (2.77, p. 79).[19]

Self-righteously defending his shamelessness, Diogenes made a practice of mocking conventions of all kinds, whether social, religious, political, or philosophical (2.75, p. 75). Laertius adds other stories about his inversion of hierarchies. Alexander came and announced to him, "I am Alexander the great king," to which Diogenes snapped, "And I am Diogenes the Cynic." Laertius continues, "Being asked what he had done to be called a hound, he said, 'I fawn on those who give me anything, I yelp at those who refuse, and I set my teeth in rascals'" (2.60, p. 63). When Alexander asked him whether he was afraid of him, Diogenes asked him whether he was "a good king or bad." When Alexander replied, "A good king," Diogenes asked, "Who then is afraid of the good?" (2.68, p. 69).

Plato came in for special criticism by Diogenes, who objected to the eminent philosopher's abstract philosophical discussion (2.24–25, p. 27; 2.53, p. 55; 2.67, p. 69). Not only did Alexander respect Diogenes so much that he sought him out, but Philip II of Macedon released him when he was brought in as a prisoner of war—"After Chaeronea, he was seized and freed"—despite his acerbic response to Philip's question of who he was: "A spy upon your insatiable greed" (2.43, p. 45).

Bought by Xeniades as a slave, Diogenes became an invaluable member of his household, teaching his sons not only their studies but how "to ride, to shoot with the bow, to sling stones, and to hurl javelins," and his children respected Diogenes and requested him in particular (2.21, p. 33). His modus operandi was to demean and criticize. He showered nearly everyone and everything with invective. Yet Diogenes "was loved by the Athenians." For instance, Xeniades proudly told people, "A good genius has entered my house" (2.74, p. 77). Whenever a prankster vandalized the philosopher's tub, citizens provided him a new one. When he died, his followers fought over who would bury him and went on to erect statues with this inscription: "Time makes even bronze grow old: but thy glory, Diogenes, all eternity will never destroy" (2.78, p. 81).[20]

Diogenes's message was that philosophical principles were to be lived. Ideas had little worth if not put into action in everyday life. He formulated his defense of his performance of private acts in public as a logical proposition, explaining that, if they were worth doing, they were worth doing anywhere: "If to breakfast be not absurd, neither is it absurd in the market-place; but to breakfast is not absurd, therefore it is not absurd to breakfast in the market-place" (2.69, p. 71).[21] Diogenes opposed privacy as a kind of hypocrisy, which he abhorred. For other examples of two-faced behavior, he attacked those who criticized money but actually loved it and those who derived pleasure from attacking pleasure (2.28,

p. 31). He saw the battle for transparency as part of a war on hypocrisy. Overall, Diogenes intended his actions as a demonstration of the need to live well, meaning according to nature and virtue. His simple living as a critique of frivolity, excess, and artificiality became the subject of many later portrayals. (See fig. 4.4.)

Diogenes's philosophy focused on the question of how to live and found the answer in the simple life. According to Laertius, "He would continually say that for the conduct of life we need right reason or a halter" (2.24, p. 27). Without reason, a halter would presumably serve to force a person, like an ox or horse, to rein in his or her actions. Diogenes supposedly drew a lifelong lesson from watching the behavior of a mouse: "Through watching a mouse running about . . . not looking for a place to lie down in, not afraid of the dark, not seeking any of the things which are considered to be dainties, he discovered the means of adapting himself to circumstances." His observation about how little a mouse needs supported his decision to divest himself of all but the barest necessities. Along these lines, he got rid of his drinking cup when he saw a child cupping his hands to drink water, and his bowl when he saw another using a hollowed-out piece of bread to scoop up his lentils, declaring, "A child has beaten me in plainness of living" (2.37, p. 39). Plain living would free people of distractions and enticements and other things that infringed on their freedom. Self-sufficiency was mandatory for maintaining this cherished state.

The anecdote about the child bore the mark of another theme, which is that the humble may someday be high. To the question of how he would like to be buried, he answered,

> "On my face."
> "Why?" inquired the other.
> "Because," said he, "after a little time down will be converted into up." (2.32, p. 33)

When he was bought as a slave by Xeniades, Diogenes instructed his master, "Come, see that you obey orders" (2.36, p. 37).

Besides plain living, discipline topped Diogenes's list of priorities: "Nothing in life . . . has any chance of succeeding without strenuous practice; and this is capable of overcoming anything" (2.71, p. 73). He praised "gymnastic training" and "the manual crafts and other arts," such as flute playing, for instilling virtue and skill through "incessant toil." He judged this development of skill a counterpart to "the training of the mind" (2.70, p. 73), while criticizing attention to athletic contests over other pursuits.[22] He lauded discipline and high standards, believing attention to both "mental and bodily" training essential (2.70, p. 71). Pursuing the musical metaphor further, he compared holding high standards to a conductor's practice of tuning on the high end so the chorus would not slip into a flat note (2.35, p. 37).

The Cynic philosopher saw his own role as teaching his listeners the ability to live according to these standards. When Diogenes was initially put up for sale as a slave, the auctioneer asked him what he could do, and he retorted, "Govern men" (2.29, p. 31). Living according to these philosophical principles was necessary to bring the soul in harmony with one's way of living (2.65, p. 67; 2.27–28, pp. 29–31). His prescription and social critique were connected, as he saw moral hypocrisy as a rampant problem of the times. Studying philosophy helped one focus on the beauty of the soul rather than on "bodily charms" (2.59, p. 61): It was preparation for life, whether good or bad (2.63, p. 65). Before him, Antisthenes supposedly declared that the advantage of philosophy was "the ability to converse with myself" (1.6, p. 9). Laertius relates another story, this time about Diogenes's definition of virtue: "When someone declared that life is an evil, he corrected him: 'Not life itself, but living ill'" (2.55, p. 57). Only plain living could bring harmony between one's moral precepts and practice.

Besides the goal of a peaceful accord between philosophy and life, forsaking unnecessary work and cultivating few wants would ensure that Diogenes would suffer no restraint on his open expression. Laertius said this was what Diogenes prized above all: "Being asked what was the most beautiful thing in the world, he replied, 'freedom of speech'" (2.69, p. 71). Living on the streets was no sacrifice because he received so much in return: free rein of his own mind and the entire city. He did not consider himself homeless; rather, all Athens was his—and beyond. His status as an exile early on and later as a person with no fixed residence was the basis for a strain of cosmopolitanism in his thought: "Asked where he came from, he said, 'I am a citizen of the world'" (2.63, p. 65). Only a self-sufficient, disciplined person could remain free in that sense (2.31, p. 31). This fit with the simple life, as paring down answered the critique of excess and distraction. It also fit with the inversion of hierarchies, which placed the philosopher over everyone, including the most powerful politician: "All things belong to the wise" (2.37, p. 39).

The tradition of Cynic philosophy connected Diogenes's reversal of the order of things and questioning of handed-down assumptions to the literal act of defacing the coinage. His contortion of common knowledge was the philosophical equivalent of adulterating the currency. Diogenes's ruminations on pleasure show how this worked. Though he praised discipline and hard work, he condemned "useless toils" for making people miserable. Instead, he counseled being in tune with nature. Reducing one's needs could result in pleasure in a much more simple and straightforward fashion. As Laertius writes of Diogenes,

> For even the despising of pleasure is itself most pleasurable, when we are habituated to it; and just as those accustomed to a life of pleasure feel disgust when they pass over to the opposite experience, so those whose training has been of the opposite kind derive more pleasure from despising pleasure than from the pleasures themselves. This was the gist of his conversation; and it was plain that he acted accordingly, adulterating currency in very truth, allowing convention no such authority as he allowed to natural right, and asserting that the manner of life he lived was the same as that of Heracles when he preferred liberty to everything. (2.71, p. 73)

Relinquishing possessions and the desire for wealth, reputation, and other external rewards allowed one to be free of the treadmill of needless work and the complications of artificiality.

In a way, the lack of original sources for Diogenes might not have mattered to later interpreters as much as for other philosophers because his whole point was that he lived his philosophy. He and his followers conveyed the Cynic ideas by giving publicity to private life, toppling hierarchies, and questioning convention. At the core of Cynicism lay a proud shamelessness, a value at odds with Athenian society, given its emphasis on custom, the *polis*, norms, and laws.[23] Philosophical elements emerge in the tellings and retellings of how Diogenes spoke and lived, with his life an object lesson for his maxims and inversions. In his arguments, he emphasized being self-sufficient and free and open. To match these words, his manner of living was transparent. He used ridicule and criticism of others to point out flaws in other people's arguments and freely hurled belittling insults. Later on, instructors drew on the Cynics' tradition to teach rhetoric because of these methods. The art of debunking, by pointing out logical flaws, was his métier.

THE ANTIART OF LIVING

This approach is a strange blend of shamelessness and shaming. Diogenes's own attack on shame threatened to erode the basis for his exposure of the hypocrisy of others through the act of shaming them. He proclaimed self-sufficiency while being a beggar at the mercy of others. His main recurrent gambit was to mount a powerful attack on the way most people lived. This was at times humorous and at times bitter. One of his favorite motifs was to question the very designation "man," judging many to be unworthy of the honor while he himself behaved scandalously. In Diogenes's thought and practice, what justified and smoothed over these contradictions was his universal rejection, a cosmic *no*.

Diogenes put forth what was basically an antiart of living. While taking umbrage with hypocrisy, ancient Cynicism had a share of its own. Its leader touted virtue yet seemed to flout it. He collapsed the public/private distinction and turned any sense of status or decorum—seen as a vital constituent of virtuous behavior at the time—on its head. His own behavior and his vociferous verbal assault on norms raised the question of what he thought virtue really was. In Laertius, it remains unclear.

If the art of living is about reason "or a halter," for a person as for a stallion, then abandoning all halters means we are thrown on our own resources, armed with reason alone. Diogenes thought reason sufficient. Instead of using reason to help us control our emotions and desires, as the Stoics taught, and walking an inner tightrope by using our personal powers of self-control, Diogenes suggested triumphing over our emotions and desires by reducing them. Once minimized, they are easy to satisfy, literally according to how and when nature calls.

On the surface, the answer to the question of how to live was self-control. Yet beneath ostensible discipline in some areas, such as getting rid of one's possessions, lay a notable lack of discipline and self-sufficiency in others, such as begging for food on principle even when one possessed enough resources that one did not need to beg. It is not difficult to understand Plato's description of Diogenes as "a Socrates gone mad." With the abandonment of convention, philosophy actually means nothing at times while appearing to mean everything. The radical transparency of Cynicism pulls the veil off everything. All withers before the public gaze, as though society were nothing but a ruse. The Cynic's rootlessness is at once geographic and philosophical. It is a kind of role playing because it places the emphasis on a personal way of life *as* philosophy, while claiming to strip off all masks and forsake all roles.

This disposition has become so widespread today that it is sometimes invisible, just part of the air we breathe. Though it can include an "anything goes" mentality, it does relativism one better. It is more a view of "everything goes," yet with the opposite meaning of "goes": not "everything is accepted" but "everything is cast aside." While Cynicism can lead to an ascetic critique of materialism, it can also border on nihilism.

Cynicism continues today, not just by accident but as a self-chosen identity. Modern cynics' interpretations vary greatly, some fitting Diogenes's ethos and some not. We can locate it in a widespread intellectual disposition, apparent in such phenomena as a notion of "radical honesty," a "hermeneutics of suspicion," radical relativism, a cult of transgression, and a general demeanor of debunking, unmasking, and bitter irony.[24] In many ways, cynicism has made a comeback as a predominant aspect of postmodernism. This is clear in the example of Deconstruction, a movement in philosophy that was taken up in a wide variety of other fields, from literature to art. In looking at two sources, one sympathetic and another critical, we can see how some artifacts and aspects of this movement belong to the New Cynicism.

Modernists and postmodernists alike have lamented the unmooring and malaise of the modern individual at the same time that many have participated in ways of thinking that exacerbated them. They share a distrust of inherited ways of making sense of the world, whether institutionalized religion or grand narratives. Like Nietzsche, they take as self-evident that culture has collapsed but differ on the question of how and what to do about it. Martin Jay's *Songs of Experience* describes how many twentieth-century thinkers rejected the phenomenon of the self altogether, faulting the mind-body division of Enlightenment rationalism for underwriting hostile and inhumane conditions. Reason had devolved into the destructive rationalism of industrialization and the fascist war machine alike. Critical theorists associated these vast historical developments with a view of the self as coherent, autonomous, and in possession of free will, arguing that the self is undesirable or, even further, nonexistent.

DEATH OF THE SELF

After illustrating the "fracturing" of the notion of experience "into discrete subcategories" in the eighteenth and nineteenth centuries, Jay turns to what he sees as "the most provocative twentieth-century attempts to rethink the category of experience."[25] He explores twentieth-century thinkers who sought an "undoing of the radical modalization of experience" (260).[26] Besides a search for unity of experience, these thinkers sought "a way to get beyond or restore a position preceding the fatal split between subject and object" (265). They aimed to find an alternative to traditional notions of experience that had presumed "an integrated, coherent, and more or less autonomous subject" (264), with the capacity for conscious free agency. Uniting movements as varied as pragmatism, Marxism, and postmodernism is what Jay sees as a continuous "new, postsubjective" thread. Thus he discusses William James's notion of "prereflective immersion in the flux of life" and celebration of "pure experience" (286) and John Dewey's communalist devotion to "a post-individualist overcoming of self-interest" (295).

In response to the disenchantment and alienation of modern life, thinkers like Walter Benjamin embraced the redemptive potential of alternative forms of experience. This led to everything from a celebration of children's use of color and language in his early writings to the apocalyptic view of redemption through destruction that he put forth later on. He was open to a "magical" view of a language of nature, religious mysticism, drug use, and astrology, graphology, and other pseudosciences as ways of "experiencing the world that had been all but lost in modernity" (325).

Jay shows how Benjamin's friend and correspondent Theodor Adorno both drew on Benjamin and differed notably with him on key points. For one thing, Adorno lacked Benjamin's "ambivalence" about "the decay of experience," seeing it as "only a source of lamentation," not potential renewal: Adorno did not share Benjamin's "wishful thinking about the opportunities opened up for radical renewal" in cultural collapse (344). For another, while Adorno saw aesthetic experience as providing a glimpse of "unalienated existence," his own gestures toward the reclamation of a fuller experience respected the integrity of the traditional boundaries of both subject and object. Throughout his survey, Jay reserves special mention for defenders of the autonomy and integrity of each of these separate entities while also striving to overcome the fragmentation of life. Dewey, for instance, lauded the benefits of aesthetic experience as the essence of experience itself—"fulfillment of an organism in its struggles and achievements in a world of things" (164)—but insisted on the independent existence of the aesthetic object rather than holding a view that beauty is created solely by the beholder's powers of perception. Similarly, Rudolf Otto emphasized religious experience as an understanding provoked by God as separate from humankind rather than as primarily a subjective emotional state (116–17).

Despite such interjections, Jay does not openly endorse Adorno's view of experience over Benjamin's—in fact, Benjamin's "desire to overcome the modalization of experience into its component parts and heal the split between subject and object," Jay writes, "might well be called the most complex and lyrical song of experience in the long history we have been following in this book" (314).

Jay does subtly communicate reservations about the so-called "linguistic turn" in poststructuralist theory. In the work of historian Joan Scott and philosopher Richard Rorty, Jay seems to see a kind of reductionism or determinism whereby no objective reality appears to humankind "unmediated" by language (and the conceptual apparatus it implies), so that language thus actively constitutes experience itself. Beginning in the 1980s, Scott's views in part responded to the emphasis on workers' experience as the primary and most telling subject of historical inquiry—as the main agent of historical change—by earlier social historians like E. P. Thompson. Rorty also criticized the celebration of experience, a reaction to the absence of foundational beliefs in objective or universal truth, as a "pseudo-solution, a kind of crypto-foundationalism for thinkers who lacked the courage to live without one" (302), in Jay's words. Instead of relying on experience as a basis for any notion of truth or verification, Rorty urges an acceptance of the contingency of truth and belief, famously counseling "ironic skepticism" about human experience itself as something separate from language (307).

THE LIMITS OF EXPERIENCE

Jay's book culminates in his discussion of what he sees as the survival—or revival—of a notion of experience in the life and work of certain poststructuralist or postmodernist thinkers. Poststructuralism's celebrated hostility to assertions of truth or reality—its questioning of transcendent or universal bases for knowledge or belief as well as its dismissal of the very notion of the subject—has led to the assumption that its adherents uniformly reject the notion of experience altogether.

Jay grants that some, like Paul de Man and Jacques Derrida, "welcomed, even sought, what one observer has called 'the demise of experience'" (364), associating it with such useless and retrograde notions as rationality, meaning, reality, and the "centered subject" (364). Traditional concepts shared the problem of phenomenology, the philosophical study of conscious phenomena and lived experience, with its misguided "metaphysics of presence" (364). But Jay sees others, like Georges Bataille, Roland Barthes, and Michel Foucault, as exemplars of "a complex and often positively inclined attitude toward something that they explicitly called experience" (365), an attitude that links them more to previous thinkers than commonly assumed.[27] Jay argues that some postmodernists still hold onto a sense of the importance of experience.

Jay describes these other postmodernists as deeply concerned with the question of whether there existed some kinds of "experiences without the robust, integrated subject, which deny presence, plenitude, interior depth, and narrative completion" (367). In response to the restrictions and sameness of modern life, Bataille embraced the notion of the extreme "inner experience"—a flight into forms of ecstatic self-immolation, similar to mystical rapture but missing the aim of unity with God, revelation, confession, or "anything reassuring," in Bataille's words. Jay writes of Bataille that any view of inner experience as "a deliberate project" implied intention or reflection, which adhered to "a traditional notion of the self able to undergo a cumulative process of formation or cultivation (*Bildung*)" (374, 369), rather than a "willingness to live life as a radical experiment" (370). That kind of experience as experiment "is never beholden to another authority beyond itself" (377). It did possess a communal dimension, but one that lacked grounding in or association with any social institution, even language. Following Bataille, Barthes also linked repetitive acts of sexual excess with the intensity and self-erasure of mysticism, as distinguished from the religious experience of Christianity, which he thought mistakenly emphasized redemption and other purposes.

Anonymity, Jay writes, furthers the desired forfeiture of self in Barthes's schema, calling into question any "controlled order" (386).

Foucault also believed in transgression as the ultimate experience—Jay calls his view an "erotics of disruption." After Bataille, Foucault argued, in Jay's words, for "ecstatic self-denial that culminates in sexual excess, madness, and the limit-experience that is death" (394). During a set of 1979 interviews Foucault praised writers like Nietzsche and Bataille for attempting "through experience to reach that point of life which lies as close as possible to the impossibility of living, which lies at the limit or the extreme. They attempt to gather the maximum amount of intensity and impossibility at the same time."[28] Foucault admired these figures for their rejection of phenomenology's search for the integrated subject of mundane existence in favor of the self's "annihilation" or "disassociation." Foucault praised this "limit experience" for successfully "tearing" the "subject from himself."[29] He considered all notions of truth as constructions of inherited discourses, merely manufactured expressions of power, calling experience "always a fiction, something constructed."[30] Since Foucault nevertheless acknowledged the reality of experience prior to its linguistic reconstruction, stopping short of claiming that language was prior to or constitutive of all of human experience, Jay thinks Foucault held onto a meaningful concept of experience. The question for us is whether that is enough.

THE AGE OF LIBERATIONISM

In his exhaustive biography *The Passion of Michel Foucault* (1993), historian James Miller established the degree to which Foucault pursued this notion of the limit experience in everyday life.[31] Praising Miller's substantial care in writing the book, as well as the worth of Foucault's own oeuvre, philosopher Alasdair MacIntyre invoked the way in which some forms of dissent—he uses the case of the Cynics—actually serve "the agencies of normalization": "Complex social orders sometimes provide space within which ritualized dissent and rebellion are not only permitted, but tacitly encouraged. . . . Impulses to dissent, by being expressed in this harmless way, are prevented from becoming a danger to the conventional order." Our contemporary ethic of emotivism, as MacIntyre showed in *After Virtue*, severs the individual from any source of meaning outside the self and its own impulses, portraying moral choices as an expression of personal creativity. This cult of free choice, "characteristic of advanced capitalistic modernity . . . provides a reinforcing counterpart to the bureaucratized careers of its elites, one which enables individuals to think of themselves as independent of their socially assigned roles, while they live out what is in fact one more such normalizing role."[32]

In his work overall, MacIntyre argued that contemporary views of experience lack any kind of moral vocabulary in which to make sense of our existence. While Jay's analysis is attuned to the moral dimension of experience—his section on religious experience bears this out—the question of experience as a whole versus its various parts has pride of place. While not condemning "modalization" altogether—Jay says specialized examination helped sharpen the views of aspects of experience—he sets his sights on "the desire for a more all-encompassing notion of experience" (403). While he is attuned to the widely different connotations of *Erlebnis* and *Erfahrung*, his working notion of "holistic" seems to blend cognitive and sensory dimensions yet does not offer a clear resolution to the tension he sees between them.

Open to a wide range of definitions and approaches, Jay gives the impression of likening the quest for the "limit experience" to earlier attempts to plumb the depths of human experience from Montaigne onward. For all their talk of annihilating the subject, his postmodernists do not strike him as cultivating mere *Erlebnis*—construed as fleeting sensation—or as giving way to a narcissistic conflation of subject and object.

While the notion of holism or totality has some interest, it cannot do the heavy lifting required to bring together views as different from one another as those of the exemplary postmodernists and Montaigne's.[33] For the reduction of the notion of lived experience into momentary sensory excitement, as separate from reflection, does not fully capture the current crisis in experience, which is one of quality as well as type. Jay's book helps show that we do not merely face an *Erlebnis* society, in the sense of an arena for free play of the senses; we even have some thinkers providing the reflection, theory, or worldview to back it up, even if their narrative is an antinarrative or their theory reduced to a power play or language game. As Philip Rieff suggested in his *Triumph of the Therapeutic*, even the anticulture—the idea that there are no valid limits on impulse—eventually becomes the new culture.

Today's search for ways to obliterate the self is the logical outgrowth of a view in which nothing is certain but the individual, and at the same time sources of meaning for the individual have fallen away. Jay sees Montaigne's thought as prefiguring modern views of experience in part because the latter acknowledged death as the limit of experience. Where postmodernists exhibited "a restless desire to push the boundaries as far out as possible," Jay seems bemused that Montaigne appeared content—"cheerfully resigned to what life as he knew it might provide"—thus falling short as a "model for modern man at his most restless and ambitious" (28).

Jay compares Montaigne's discussion of death with the fascination Bataille and others had for death as a "limit experience." But the difference could not be more palpable. Montaigne says, "For my part then, I love life, and cultivate it, such as it has pleased God to bestow it upon us." He treasures human appetites as natural and God-given, properly embraced with moderation, humility, and gratitude. If he is not in search of transcendent truth, it is because it is assumed. His "holism" is a balance not between mind and body but among mind, body, and soul: "Let the mind rouse and quicken the heaviness of the body, and the body stay and fix the levity of the soul. . . . In this present that God has made us, there is nothing unworthy of our care."[34]

Montaigne's views in "Of Experience," in fact, take up explicitly the very subject that gives Bataille and Foucault such a thrill—the mixing of pleasure and pain. But Montaigne's view of the subject is quite different: "I enjoin my soul to look upon pain and pleasure with an eye regular . . . and equally firm; but the one gaily and the other severely, and, so far as it is able to be as careful to extinguish the one, as to extend the other."[35] Jay argues that some postmodernists still hold onto a sense of the importance of experience. His protagonists, however, deliberately sought a form of experience beyond morals and coherence.

RETURN OF THE SPARTANS

Unlike Montaigne's essays, which praised simple pleasures, the movie *300* is life stripped bare. It removes all adornments, reducing everything to a war for survival. On the surface, it seems to draw an invidious contrast between the Greeks as paragons of strength and beauty, with their bulging abdominal muscles bared even in battle, and the Persian fighters, who wear identical masks, all frozen into the same ghoulish grimace. As perverse and impotent as Xerxes appears, King Leonidas appears valiant and virtuous. Were *300* a sociological or historical study, it would be discounted as biased to the point of ethnocentric deformity. It is easy to understand criticism of the movie for its stereotypes and simplistic East/West dichotomies.[36]

When we turn to the realm of the imagination, however, it is more difficult to know what to make of characterizations such as this one. After all, there is a long-standing debate about how literally we should interpret creative works. Literary critics remind us that were we to take such works at face value as literal depiction, and depiction as endorsement, we would miss the point of many literary styles, devices, and genres—satire, caricature, humor, irony, just to name a few.[37] Cynics are known as progenitors of the genre of satire and diatribe.[38]

The Spartan soldiers do not exactly represent the height of individuation themselves. With bodies exercised to the identical muscle-bound state and facial features largely obscured by helmets, they give the overall impression of regimentation and uniformity, not freedom and individual bravery. Beauty might technically be on the side of the Spartans in *300*, but only if one dismisses any notion of individualized identity and character.

300 stands out not only for the number of violent scenes, which of course are common for a war movie of the combat variety, but for the macabre way in which such scenes of violence—and the pre- and postbattle scenes as well—are depicted. The movie uses special effects to slow down the actual act of brutal killing, as if to allow viewers to savor it more than they would if it were in real time, and to allow for numerous instances of violent dismemberment. Instead of a recognizable theater of war, between such combat scenes and those of grisly and unconscionable treatment of the countless corpses appearing continually on the screen, stacked and strewn like so much garbage, this resembles nothing so much as a holocaust.

To display such horror without providing a clear sense of what to make of it leaves viewers to their own devices. Were this a time of moral certitude, with signs everywhere of the successful inculcation of moral conscience, and not the time of Abu Ghraib and shootings in American schools, malls, and workplaces, the audience could perhaps be counted on to react with loathing against the Spartans, whose inhumanity seems to exceed by far the brutality appertaining, by its very definition, to war. But the filmmakers skip over lurid scenes without any final commentary about this violation of all known morals, norms, and customs of warfare, according to which countless combatants and nations have sought to limit the bestial tendencies to which humans are prone to revert in a time of extremity. The continued focus on King Leonidas's wife and son at the movie's end, as at the beginning, asks the viewer still to be sympathetic and to consider Leonidas a great, fallen hero. This makes it seem that the message of all the violence is that it is all part of war and that war is dark and inhuman of necessity. It begs the question of whether war is ever this dark and inhuman without becoming something else: the radical evil of a Hitler or a Stalin. Even in the case of *Gladiator*, which does have a clear moral to the story, at one point, from the gladiators' arena, amid the ravages of the blood sport, Maximus asks, "Are you not entertained?" That question applies not only to ancient but to contemporary audiences watching the same spectacle, even if at a remove that allows modern viewers a kind of guilt exemption.

War, more than death, may properly be seen as the true opposite of life. In peacetime, there can be a peaceful, timely death.
In battle, death becomes the forceful violation of the life-force and
the destruction of living beings. The complete overturning of the
ideal of harmony that is thought to order everyday life in local
communities—the replacement of humanity with inhumanity—
makes even those wars fought for the worthiest causes tragic.

Numerous movies have captured the tragedy of war. *The Thin
Red Line*, for instance, takes a very different tack from *300* as it
portrays a US army rifle company engaged with Japanese soldiers
in Guadalcanal, a key episode in the Pacific theater during World
War II.[39] This 1998 film directed by Terrence Malick and based on
a novel by James Jones is also extremely and graphically violent,
and, as is the case in many war movies, one side (the Japanese, in
this case) is not as fully drawn as the other (the Americans). Japanese soldiers are rarely even seen, and when they are, they are
not featured enough to be grasped as individuals, while the American characters deliberately draw viewers in, raising the emotional
stakes when so many of them meet their deaths. Despite the context of the "Good War," which so much of contemporary American culture celebrates as righteous and necessary, *The Thin Red
Line* unequivocally addresses the way that warfare brutalizes both
sides: not only does it cause human suffering and loss of life, but it
inevitably triggers emotional crisis and poses the ultimate test to
participants' sanity. Without suggesting that it was undesirable
that the Americans stopped the advance of the Japanese, the movie
aims to capture the grim realities and human costs of war. Unlike
300, which gives no hint of what to make of scene after scene of
bloodshed, *The Thin Red Line* depicts fresh, youthful soldiers
bravely risking their lives and just as bravely confronting the way
in which the experience of battle threatens to sap meaning from
everything they once held to be true. Private Witt, played by
James Caviezel, regularly goes AWOL, wandering through local
villages and observing the ways of the island's native inhabitants.
In a voice-over, we are privy to his thoughts: "This great evil.
Where does it come from? How'd it steal into the world? What
seed, what root did it grow from? Who's doing this? Who's killing

us? Robbing us of life and light. Mocking us with the sight of what we might've known. Does our ruin benefit the earth? Does it help the grass to grow, the sun to shine? Is this darkness in you, too? Have you passed through this night?" Witt, a gentle and sensitive soul, ends up using his last minute of life to wander out into an open field, with Japanese soldiers encircling him, to draw fire to his own body to provide a warning for the rest of the company stationed down the river so that they may survive.

Where *The Thin Red Line* has soldiers questioning war, however, a realistic depiction of the Spartans might be woefully anachronistic in imputing such doubts to combatants trained from birth to embrace battle as the ultimate proving ground and the battleground as the suitable and desirable place to die. If this is the implicit assumption behind *300*, it is very difficult to make it out; the movie's fantastical style and hyperbolic technique frustrate any attempt at realism. Its glaring lack of dialogue only makes the task of interpretation harder. This is philosopher Richard Rorty's recommended posture of postmodernist "ironic detachment."[40]

THE PRICE OF UNMASKING

In 2007, Damien Hirst, the British artist best known for suspending dead animals in formaldehyde, produced a new masterpiece: a human skull cast in platinum, studded with diamonds. The piece, entitled *For the Love of God*, includes over 8,500 jewels and cost about $28 million to produce. A consortium of investors, including Hirst himself, purchased the skull for £50 million (about $100 million). Since its sale in 2007, the piece has remained hidden away, rarely brought out for public exhibition.[41]

What is wrong with productions like Hirst's ornamented skull, and with so many other objects and images that pass for today's masterworks of both high and popular culture? What is it about them that makes them seem obscene? This is the subject of Philip Rieff's book *My Life among the Deathworks*. This book was not Rieff's first tour de force, but it was the last to be published in his lifetime.[42] The sociologist died in 2008. His life among the deathworks ended, but the deathworks live on. His book is one of the most direct attempts to confront the sources and costs of a cynical modernity. Even when it came in the guise of a seemingly benign therapeutic culture, he asked us to look beyond the surface to the substance of the kind of person wearing the mask. This included those claiming to be engaged in the pursuit of unmasking. The paradox of the unmasking was that the wearers of the mask had nothing underneath, not unlike Hirst's smiling skull.

Rieff's 1959 biography *Freud: The Mind of the Moralist*, followed in 1963 by his ten-volume edition of *The Collected Papers of Sigmund Freud*, established him as one of the keenest and most original of Freud's interpreters. Rieff's brilliant book bore down on the tensions between ethics and psychoanalysis—the persistence of a moral outlook in Freud's thought at the same time that Freudian theory represented a new sensibility in revolt against nineteenth-century moralism, especially in the realm of sexuality. In Rieff's account, psychoanalysis sought to apply "aseptic rationalism" to love and sex, shining the light of science into the darkest corners of the psyche. Its method of therapy required the breakdown of the traditional social space between analyst and patient—the sharing of personal, even unconscious life, over which the patient had no control and therefore no responsibility. "By waiving the restrictions of conventional logic and prudery, the therapeutic hour provides the patient with a model refreshment," Rieff wrote. "It puts an end to decorum, providing a private time in which anything may be said—indeed, in which the patient is encouraged to say everything."[43] Rieff did not look kindly upon these releases from traditional restraints.

An intellectual biography of uncommon suppleness, and a genuine literary achievement, *Freud* concludes by heralding the arrival of a new human type that Rieff memorably calls "psychological man." Forever anxious and insecure, psychological man eschews political and religious commitments, and even economic calculation, for an obsession with self that is unprecedented in human history. He is "anti-heroic, shrewd, carefully counting his satisfactions and dissatisfactions, studying unprofitable commitments as the sins most to be avoided."[44] He is driven by the "ideal of insight" and "self-contemplative manipulation," and his interest resides only in himself.[45] The new mode deforms inwardness.

In 1966, Rieff probed more deeply into the implications of psychological man in *The Triumph of the Therapeutic: Uses of Faith after Freud*, his most influential and eye-opening work, mentioned in the Introduction of this book. A study of Freudianism in its larger cultural and intellectual contexts, it established him as one of the great critics of modern life. Rieff emphasized the post-Freudians' misuse of psychoanalytic insights for grandiose plans for social or personal regeneration, which he opposed to Freud's Stoic wisdom, his sense of the limited and therefore tragic ramifications of his theory. Where *Freud: The Mind of the Moralist* was steadfastly focused on the man and his ideas, *The Triumph of the Therapeutic* was a study of the Freudian aftermath, of Freudianism as a kind of civil religion—of how the breakdown of reticence, convention, and social distance promoted the treatment hour into an emblem of society at large, as everyone learned to live like analysands and analysts, laying bare their lives for public consumption. *My Life among the Deathworks* was joined by four other posthumous books: the other two volumes in the trilogy *Sacred Order/Social Order*, edited by Kenneth S. Piver, which is begun by *My Life among the Deathworks*; a study of charisma, long in the making; and a new edition of *The Triumph of the Therapeutic*.[46]

DEATHWORKS

For Rieff, a deathwork is "an all-out assault upon something vital to the established culture."[47] Much of today's cultural expression, in his view, consists of deathworks aimed at destroying not just an older traditional culture but also the foundation of culture itself. Rieff's complaints are very large. He believes that in America transgression has now replaced creation as a cultural ideal: that what passes for creativity in our time has more to do with the urge to destroy. *My Life among the Deathworks* is a major work of social criticism that offers a profound assessment of the historical developments that have brought us to this anguished moment. With the intellectual courage that made his earlier work so vital to readers in a wide range of fields and walks of life, Rieff urges us to train our sights on the void itself.

Consider some of the images that illustrate Rieff's complaint. Robert Mapplethorpe's *Self-Portrait*, from 1978, signifies for Rieff the extent to which art gave way over the course of the twentieth century to transgression for transgression's sake. The photograph, in which the photographer poses with a whip inserted into his anus, seems designed to arouse not only a dark kind of violent lust, reminiscent of a scene with Spartan ephors (priests) cast as leering and depraved old men in *300*, but also a sense of spiritual desolation—a feeling of having fallen so low that there is no way out. The photograph seems to recommend this pain. And this is only an extreme example of the lurid fixations in the popular culture that have metastasized to vast proportions. There is also, to choose from many instances of nihilism in popular culture around the time of the publication of *My Life among the Deathworks* and since, the video game *Grand Theft Auto*, in which players beat prostitutes to death after having sex with them; Eminem's rapping about raping and murdering his mother; the graphic violence of Madonna's wildly popular video "What It Feels Like for a Girl"; the website gorezone.com, which shows scenes of accidents, torture, and mutilation; the television commercial for Starburst candy that depicts a man reaching into a boiling vat of what looks to be acid, only to have his arms dissolve. Rieff does not argue for censorship. He argues for concern. And he asks what it means for an entire culture to be beset by such motifs. He looks beyond excessively violent or sexual imagery to the question of the culture as a whole, offering a theory and a method of viewing cultural artifacts as well as the unconscious expressions we use in everyday life.

My Life among the Deathworks is a hauntingly beautiful blend of poetry, ethical inquiry, and lament. Upon opening it, however, readers familiar with the early work, or even those for whom this work is their introduction to Rieff, may well want to close it. It is a difficult, even turgid book, and its endless allusions and impacted erudition sometimes threaten to stifle sense. It is peculiar to write an urgent polemic in an arcane style. Rieff ought to have forsworn the jargon and the esotericism to which so many contemporary academics are prone; but *My Life among the Deathworks* veers perilously close to the style of the postmodernist professor who seems to aim at obscurantism rather than illumination. Rieff even presents a vocabulary of his own: "pop" stands for "primacy of possibility," a cult of the primordial (49); "via" for "vertical in authority," a kind of moral stairway leading to the heavens, our position on which determines our identity (13); and so on. What can be done with a sentence such as this: "Every via in all second worlds is there to organize the lifespace of agents moving freely in that space, or fatefully in competing first world vias" (13).

Rieff says that his method is one of collage: he aims "to take the reader behind and beyond contemporary reality by juxtaposing events and works that do not appear, on first reading, to be related" (18). He adduces many "image entries," which are "sorties into an otherwise invisible sacred order," in order to examine, as if under a microscope, works of art and other cultural expressions from many different time periods, here described as a "whirling contemporaneity" (18). This bears some similarity to some postmodernist techniques of collage and random juxtaposition yet contains a searching critique of precisely their method of fracturing the world into small pieces and rendering it incoherent.

At the crux of the book is the notion of culture as "world-creation": "the arrangement or order of words, images, bodies, of all social relations," which amounts to "the making of the world each new day." Rather than a benign lifestyle choice, Rieff sees culture as highly serious, "the continuation of war by other—normative—means." We struggle internally with our baser impulses, which threaten to lower us on the vertical in authority. The result of this struggle establishes where we end up morally, what will be our inner makeup, since for Rieff we are "constituted by where we are in sacred order." Likewise, this struggle carries over onto public terrain, "where the fighting continues" (2).

Rieff offers a typology of human experience as divided into first, second, and third worlds. These designations correspond roughly with historical epochs: first, ancient civilization, which was devoted to "mythic 'primacies of possibility' from which derived all agencies of authority, including its god-terms" (5); second, the era of Judaeo-Christian culture in the West; and third, our own times. The third world's "recycling" of the first world's aesthetic troubles Rieff deeply, for it renders primordial various facets of identity, such as race, ethnicity, or sexuality, while emptying identity of any meaningful content and transforming it into mere role playing. The sense of the self and its needs as primordial obscures any boundaries between the self and the real world. A pretense of creativity hides a practice of destruction, as others are no longer respected as persons in their own right, as beings independent of the self and its own picture of itself and its wants.

Rieff makes no secret of his affinity for the second world. Lacking the "metadivine and impersonal" aspects of the first and third worlds, the second is rooted in a humbling faith in ultimate authority, the specificity of which rules out primordial fantasies and abstractions of the self (5). With nature deemed created and not a divine force itself, the possibility for taming it exists. And the concrete sense of the divine in the Judaeo-Christian tradition lends itself to a view of the human person as inviolable because "the superb thing in creation is the human" (55).

As Rieff showed in *The Triumph of the Therapeutic*, authority traditionally worked through moral interdiction and culture's provision of legitimate releases. Remissions were expected and accepted. But as he argues in *Deathworks*, the elites of the third culture took a "radically remissive" stance, attacking their culture head on. Replacing traditional authority with a new antiauthoritarianism that cast all interdiction as intolerable restraint on individual freedom, the third world then constituted an anticulture, replacing humility with a sense of unlimited possibility and the everyday reality of restraint and satisfaction with the gospel of self-fulfillment through personal experience, "always ending in the name of a better world elsewhere" (6).

Contemporary culture, for Rieff, aims at little more than the demise of the second world. Where Freud, in Rieff's earlier account of him, appeared to be on the fence between the dying and the emergent cultures, in *My Life among the Deathworks* he now joins the "great negational theorists and artists," having played a role in ushering in an amoral universe in which "everything supporting ascents to a higher, more human life" is actively suppressed (8). That a way of life devoted solely to the freeing of the individual actually deprives people of the sources of freedom of self-creation, which is a moral endeavor, is the bitter irony of our age. In the absence of legitimate authority, power alone dictates, which can only lead to a cult of "creative destruction"—to deathworks. Here, Rieff and Foucault would agree, but they would differ over why and where we should turn—Rieff to meaning through common interest, Foucault to freedom through radical dispersion of truth.

Through his readings of artworks and artifacts, Rieff's view of what is missing from contemporary life emerges. While he sees third-world motifs in early modern as well as modern and contemporary works, he argues that these motifs have now become dominant. The inventions that he analyzes range dramatically in style, medium, and historical circumstance. They include Marcel Duchamp's *Fountain* (1917), Piero Manzoni's *Artist's Shit, no. 31* (1961), and Andres Serrano's *Piss Christ* (1987). But some of the objects of Rieff's wrath are more surprising. The painting *Summer* by Giuseppe Arcimboldo, from 1573, which depicts a man's face composed of seasonal fruits and vegetables, attacks the second world's sacred order by taking one of the prime symbols of humanity—the human face—and deconstructing it: the devotion to a coherent, created reality, in which the integrity of the human person was a foundation, falls prey here to the "doctrine of decreation in which the new world is a series of more or less horrible or at least horribly clever pastiches and negations" (26). Michelangelo's *Rondanini Pieta* merges persons unduly; his *Roma Pieta* overeroticizes the mother-son relation. Vermeer's *Girl Interrupted at Her Music* depicts a violation of propriety. Picasso's *Les Demoiselles d'Avignon* is "the founding transgressive image of modern art," with what Rieff furiously denounces as its "dog-faced defecating woman" (107). All these masterpieces are also deathworks "against the sexual self-control of second cultures" (86).

For Rieff, the space between beings represents the distance necessary for the inviolability of the self and the maintenance of the proper relation between self and others. Thus Michelangelo's *Cre-*

ation of Adam on the Sistine ceiling is an exemplary second-world creation, with its void between the divine and the human, "the space in which all humanity lives" (45). The distance between lovers is what makes love possible, as it maintains the integrity of each individual necessary for any sense of relation. But the third culture tries to close "the distances between any desire and its object," to deliver instant gratification, and to merge the self into everything outside of itself. When the self becomes nothing but its desires and its impulses, liberation seems to demand the eradication of all obstacles between the "I" and the "not-I" (175). Human beings are experienced only as objects in the self's quest for gratification and eventually are turned into trash. In the rush to battle, combatants cannot even wait for dust to become dust; in the case of the heaps of dead bodies in *300*, soldiers are denied the honor and dignity of a proper burial, just decomposing into the soil on which the next battle is waged.

This obliteration of both the self and others through the destruction of boundaries prepares the ground, Rieff insists, for an erotics of destruction. Without legitimate limits on desire, aggressive impulses often take over. This is why, in Rieff's view, the ultimate deathworks were the Nazi death camps. Suggesting a link that may offend some readers, Rieff writes that works such as Duchamp's *Étant donnés* (with its peephole into a shimmering landscape featuring a naked and mutilated female corpse) and the death camps bear a deep resemblance: both violate "the temple of God, the body" (111). It is a coarse comparison, but it is based on an idea worth taking seriously, which is that art cannot be entirely severed from morality. The rendering of corpses as beautiful—or murders as artistic or masterful or efficient—is part of the third culture's "negation of life itself."

There is much fodder for controversy in these pages, not least Rieff's opinions on homosexuality and bisexuality, which in his view run against the commanding truths of the second culture. Rieff is also quick to say that he does not regard his own criticism as the last word. Even the "commanding truths" are not rigid; they are constantly reinterpreted by generation after generation. He stands firmly against today's forms of religious extremism and against any attempt to reimpose an older religious order, regarding fundamentalism as another example of the disastrous cult of primordial identities. With its consistent defense of democracy and the individual and its strict criticism of consumer capitalism, Rieff's work can hardly be subsumed under any political umbrella. His work can be read as one of the strongest defenses of the inviolability of the individual imaginable.

While Rieff can be dismissed as a disgruntled reactionary on some counts, this criticism of modern culture for its objectification of human beings joins concerns of progressives for its threat to society's vulnerable groups. It preys upon people whose position is already tenuous and seemingly expendable, so depictions of the virtual violence against them is not discontinuous with actual violence they face in real life, or, if not violence, then the omnipresent sense of danger that any security they experience can be taken away. When not aimed directly at vulnerable groups, the reduction of the human body to the status of a thing indirectly expanded the groups of the vulnerable. Stuart Ewen's work has brilliantly dismantled the advertising industry's hidden psychological scaffolding. He has shown definitively the deliberate strategy of advertisers to arouse anxieties in potential customers that their products would then fulfill. In essence, they sold anxiety in order to create a perpetual market of consumers made vulnerable to their suggestions.[48] In other settings this might be considered behavioralism or even brainwashing. The deceptive guise of consumer choice softens it.

Feminist critics have focused on the uses of the objectification of women. The documentary film *Killing Us Softly* looks specifically at the portrayal of women in parts.[49] Ads show women as represented by only one part of their body, or in positions of violence. Images of destruction proliferate in modern marketing. Portraying the human body or face in deliberate shards, to take the feminist critique further to join with Rieff's, is more than a problem. It is part of an antiwoman assault. The feminist critique helps us take seriously his critique. His criticism of Marcel Duchamp's *Étant donnés* could be classified as feminist analysis.

On the other hand, the device of synecdoche is a valid artistic technique. What is the dividing line between synecdoche and the destructive creations Rieff warns against? It is not the technique itself but whether the work is good, in both senses of the word, moral and aesthetic. Part of the modern quandary has been a move away from matters of judgment, which has reduced everything—history, film analysis, literary criticism—to discussions of technique or individual genius, forsaking more difficult discussions of *moral worth*.

While Rieff's view of our contemporary situation is grave, his jeremiad reveals a certain degree of hope. He calls for more careful readings of cultural expressions that are attuned to the whole as something sacred. He distinguishes between a performative or critical intellect, which only dissects and destroys, assuming that there is no truth or reality and so canvassing the cultural scene for texts and traditions to debunk, and a "feeling intellect," which continues to seek out truths through a combination of all the human faculties rather than a rationality shorn of the insights of the heart and the soul.[50]

A CYNICAL MOMENT

German philosopher Peter Sloterdijk's *Critique of Cynical Reason* (*Kritik der Zynischen Vernunft*) was published originally in German in two volumes in 1983. In its first few months it had already sold over forty thousand copies. Andreas Huyssen writes in the English version's "Foreword: The Return of Diogenes as Postmodern Intellectual" that it offered "German intellectuals a master lesson in the pleasures of the text." Because of the book's critique of the Enlightenment, the Left sought to consign it to "the dust bin of history," while liberals hailed its author as another Nietzsche, Spengler, or Schopenhauer.[51] Sloterdijk's controversial work, equal parts cultural criticism and work of philosophy, describes contemporary culture as awash in "a universal, diffuse cynicism."[52] Modern cynicism took hold in the "disillusionment with

Enlightenment," the twilight of "naïve ideologies" in the 1960s and 1970s, and the ensuing exhaustion of critique (3, 6). The mood is dark: "In the new cynicism, a detached negativity comes through that scarcely allows itself any hope, at most a little irony and pity" (6). The characteristic approach of the New Cynicism is "critique-through-unmasking," and he begins the book with eight paradigmatic forms of critique in this spirit: critiques of "revelation," "religious illusion," "metaphysical illusion," "idealistic superstructure," "moral illusion," "transparency," "natural illusion," and "the illusion of privacy" (22–75). He proceeds, back and forth through time, with a dizzying survey in a self-professed "pastiche" of the context, causes, and consequences of the new cynical mode.

Louisa Shea notes that Sloterdijk's *Critique of Cynical Reason* sold more than any philosophical work in Germany since World War II and galvanized German intellectual circles. Sloterdijk, she writes, describes the Enlightenment's contribution to a diffuse modern cynicism characterized by "moral disillusionment and political disaffection."[53] He now wants to revitalize the Enlightenment's "unfinished project," following Kant's "critical impulse," and return to ancient Cynicism (131).

Shea writes that after Cynicism's heyday in the eighteenth century, it experienced a "fall from grace," shifting to its current definition, "an attitude of disillusioned self-interest" (132). Hegel dismissed Cynicism, which helped sideline it as a serious philosophical school of thought (133). In the post–World War II era, Cynicism experienced a revival in German thought. Foucault separately noted this revival yet had not read Sloterdijk's work before he delivered his five lectures on Cynicism at the Collège de France in March 1984 (131–32). In her survey of the reception of Cynicism, Shea notes that writers from theologian Paul Tillich to Klaus Heinrich took a new look at ancient Cynicism as a worthwhile form of social criticism in contrast to modern cynics' creed, which was simply the "freedom of rejecting whatever they want to reject" (135).

Shea presents a reading of Sloterdijk that clarifies his critique of modern cynicism as an attack on a certain modern self, a form of subjectivity autonomous and embattled, riveted above all on self-preservation. The traits of the modern self include paranoia, "pragmatic opportunism," self-satisfaction, and the drive for self-advancement (146–47): "This paranoia manifests itself on the political front in the arms race: taking the nuclear bomb as the symbol of the cynic self, Sloterdijk confronts his reader with a concrete image of the danger cynic subjectivity poses to itself and the world" (153). As a solution to this "cynic egoism," writes Shea, Sloterdijk proposes a kind of demilitarization within; he "calls on us to disarm the subject and urges the softening, or 'liquefaction' (Verflüssigung), of our egos (C 379; K2: 695)" (153).

Shea points to Sloterdijk's unusual employment of meditation as a key to this new self's "liquefaction" and argues that the Buddha comes "to replace Diogenes as the central model of Cynic consciousness" (156): he contends that "ancient cynicism is best understood as a form of Buddhism" (156). While Sloterdijk does not identify specific points of overlap between Cynicism and Buddhism—his style strikes her as more "*satura*, or potpourri" than logical argument—Shea does not see the analogy as flawed in itself. She alludes to legitimate scholarship linking "Greek Cynicism and Asian religious traditions," though she says scholars generally find the evidence inconclusive. Sloterdijk's "interpretation of ancient Cynicism as meditation" retrieves ancient Cynicism's focus on "clarity of mind," which she sees as a vital part of ancient Cynicism nearly absent in understandings of the Cynicism of the figures she examines, such as Diderot, d'Alembert, and Rousseau (157). Drawing on the conclusion of Claire Muckensturm that an encounter between Onesicritus and Indian sages in 326 BC yielded "an *interpretation graeca* that transformed the Indian sages into model cynics,"[54] Shea thinks Sloterdijk basically "turns the tables on Onesicritus and posits an 'Eastern interpretation' that transforms the Cynics into model Buddhists" (158). This fits with the work of those scholars who have argued for either direct intellectual influence or philosophical parallels.[55] She reviews work by Thomas McEvilley that lays out the specific points of comparison, including a shared aim of "clearing, or silencing, the mind" (158). Other scholars have even drawn a comparison between the Cynics and a Hindu sect "known for their habit of imitating dogs" (159).

For our purposes, it is especially interesting that what Sloterdijk proposes sounds like a kind of cynic's therapy through renewed and revamped Cynicism. But he emphasizes that the problem is modern cynicism, not Cynicism itself. To make a distinction between what he criticizes and what he advocates, he uses the German spelling to refer to the ancient philosophical movement of Cynicism: *Kynismus*. Against the modern mode he proposes a revival of the ancient, which he envisions as a practice capable of withstanding today's assault on all of the old certainties, from self and soul to truth and reality. He taps ancient Cynicism as a possible resource for resistance against the incursions of both dehumanizing institutions and the defeatism of the modern intellectual culture.[56]

The New Atheism fits the movement of the New Cynicism, expropriating the role of making the scales fall from the eyes of the benighted populace.[57] In a more lighthearted nod to the New Cynicism, we can see in the advice literature of Karen Salmansohn, which she addresses to cynics, a sense of the personality her self-help was up against.[58] Unfortunately, her advice participates in more cynicism, if only in the guise of solving problems essentially by putting on a smiley face. Critics see positive psychology's histrionics of optimism as a sign not of hope but of a culture that has given up.[59]

Cynicism has gotten a lot of play in recent years. A kind of Neo-Cynicism had a heyday in the Enlightenment period and has continued as a main current ever since, bubbling up at some moments more than others.[60] The aftermath of the First World War, for instance, saw traditional sources of meaning emptied out. In *The Great War in Modern Memory*, Paul Fussell wrote of the way in which World War I made everyday words, such as *honor*, ring hollow, completely inverting the psychic order.[61] A cynical posture seemed to go hand in hand with aspects of modern life, from total war to life in the nuclear age, the 1960s distrust of authority, the credibility crisis of Watergate, the fall of the middle class, and other developments. One of the aspects of this cynical valuation—whether partial cause or central symptom—has manifested itself as a crisis in the very notion of truth.

As early as the 1950s, exposés in the form of historical and sociological studies revealed the growing use of psychology in politics and advertising.[62] The television series *Mad Men* later joined this chorus through its fictional treatment of an ad man whose aggressive self-interest in personal and work life alike brought him to a very low point.[63] Manipulation of the individual's wants and perceived needs, public opinion, mass tastes, and political behavior drafted truth claims into the service of mobilization of judgment and sentiment from which there has not yet been any significant demobilization. Techniques of manipulation of words and images became a weapon not only in war and political machinations—from the rise of fascist dictators to wartime propaganda abroad and at home—but in supposedly peaceful postwar consumerist pursuits in the economic colonization of corporate capital. While critics, many of them inspired by the Frankfurt School's warnings about the various dangers a consumerist society posed to the individual, subjected cultural systems and expressions to stringent analysis for the ways they represented and purveyed the interest of political and economic regimes, some saw danger to standards of taste and excellence in the rise of mass culture and its tendency toward homogenization and catering to the lowest common denominator. Others defended the new media and expressions as democratic forms worthy of taking seriously or enjoyed as entertainment.[64] Disagreement over form, content, and degree split the critical movement against modes of manipulation. If these two camps had not diverged over whether the new media were good or bad, perhaps there would have been a more serious assault on manipulation itself. Losing sight of the line between manipulative and nonmanipulative communication removes the basis for distinguishing between propaganda and education. This leads to a new cynicism as all words become suspect. Everyone seems out to manipulate.

THERAPY AS TRUTH TELLING

A key example of the New Cynicism is the final lecture course of Michel Foucault, as presented some two decades after his death in a still-influential book, *The Final Foucault*. Foucault aimed to reveal the hidden workings of power in modern life by laying out the systems of domination in institutions and institutionalized practices that changed in the aftermath of the Enlightenment, from bodily punishment to internalized psychological pressures. In his histories of the insane asylum and the prison, he traced the emergence of self-imposed disciplinary practices as part of the modern disciplinary apparatus of states and societies to uphold particular power relations. Although modern forms of social control appeared more salutary—jail time aimed at rehabilitation versus execution and torture in public squares—they could now intrude into individuals in the endeavor to control their behavior. Older forms of punishment gave way to modes of discipline that ruled out opportunities for freedom and resistance.

As a philosophical spokesman and hero for the emerging gay liberation movement, Foucault's ideas inspired a cottage industry of criticism in literary studies and other fields that often reduced them to the ideological position that everywhere, at all times, power controls everything, co-opting every opportunity for resistance. This bleak view had a certain allure as a radical posture in the post-1960s era. Although Foucault himself sought to confront and change the systems of oppression he saw, most of his acolytes applied his theories to literary analysis and cultural studies.

Followers signed on to what amounts to a caricature of Foucault, whether in sympathy or critique. Yet, as with any original thinker, Foucault's thought did not remain frozen. In particular it evolved with his engagement with ancient Greek and Roman philosophers. He saw in their thought and in their lives an arena with more room for freedom than was true in twentieth-century life, and he drew on their teachings and example for an approach he thought relevant to modern struggles. For the tiny elite of ancient intellectuals, in his portrait, philosophy was a way of life that provided alternatives to prevailing social norms and even space for self-creation. In contrast, at most other times and for most other groups, norms became encrusted and inescapable, a process he called "normalization." The whole modern project of constructing a self—"subjectivation"—came under suspicion for its inculcation of relations of domination. Foucault thought domination inevitable but imagined alternatives to rigid structures that left no room for fluidity and freedom of self-chosen roles.[65]

In 1987, the journal *Philosophy and Social Criticism* published an interview with Foucault that took place shortly before his death in 1984, along with a set of essays on the evolution of his thinking in what turned out to be his last years. Now published in book form, *The Final Foucault* illustrates his evolving ideas, capturing crucial nuances that help soften some of the hard edges of the caricature of his view as one of all power all the time. In one essay, Thomas Flynn gives an account of some of the central themes of the last course Foucault taught at the Collège de France. Drawing on his class notes, Flynn offers a portrait of Foucault as "parrhesiast," or truth teller, of a type most akin to that of the ancient Cynic. After lecturing on "parrhesia as a political virtue" the prior year, Foucault in this course addressed "truth telling as a moral virtue."[66] Given his lifelong attack on modes of self-constitution as mechanisms of enforcing particular regimes of power, Foucault's "increased focus on the subject, the agent and self-constitution" seemed surprising, but Flynn points out that Foucault maintained his emphasis on power and truth in what he called "techniques of domination," which played themselves out in the construction of the subject. While it might seem "as if Foucault's polemic with the humanists had turned into dialogue," Flynn concluded that "there is no indication that this was the case; he was not growing soft on subjectivism" (115).

In the fourth century BC, *parrhesia* entailed courage, as the truth teller stated what he genuinely thought to be true and risked violence from the one listening (103). According to Flynn, Foucault saw four different modes of truth telling: the prophet, who was concerned with "destiny"; the sage, concerned with "being"; the "teacher-technician," concerned with *technē*; and the parrhesiast, concerned with "ethos" (104). The prophet speaks of the future in opaque ways, the sage of principles about how the world is, the teacher-technician of knowledge and skill, and the parrhesiast of the "individual and the present situation." The teacher risks nothing, because there is a bond between teacher and student, but the parrhesiast risks everything, because his truth "divides, even as it may bind and lure" (104).

Different "regimes of truth," as Foucault put it, emphasized different modes of truth telling. For instance, the "university tradition focused on the sage and teacher," and "political revolutionary discourse emphasized the prophetic and the parrhesiastic"—the "politics of truth." The latter was "obviously one he favored," according to Flynn (105). Foucault became interested in a new form of ethical parrhesia appearing in Plato but emerging afterward in different form, lacking Plato's focus on the soul. Instead of truth telling's role in the formation of the soul in light of "essence or form," what interests Foucault is "a relation between one's self and the logos one proclaims," or the question of the way one lives and its relation to his philosophical views, the "**harmony** [bold in original] that obtains between his *logos* and his *bios*, his doctrine and his life." This practice of truth aims, not at contemplation of the soul, but at "a certain **style of existence** [bold in original]" (109). For Foucault, Flynn writes, this made life an aesthetic endeavor: "The *bios* can be a beautiful work," separate from metaphysics and the more dominant Platonic "care of the soul" (109).

Foucault thought, according to Flynn, that in Socrates, truth telling and the notion of a "beautiful existence" came together in a mode of "care of the self"; "the art of existence **is** [bold in original] truth-telling" (109). Foucault thought this approach rarely reappeared in the Western philosophical tradition—except in Cynicism.

The Cynics, Flynn writes, were the ultimate parrhesiasts. Having freed themselves from the pressures of social convention, they "made of their lives a liturgy of truth-telling" (110). Cynic philosophy has less to do with doctrine and theory than with "a way of life" passed down through stories of the "philosophic hero." Such exploits of everyday living depicted the "true life" (*alétheia*) of the Cynics, equating truth telling with an authentic life itself (110).

The notion of *alétheia* was multidimensional, including what was unhidden, pure and unmixed, correct and unchanging: "Accordingly, 'true life' for Plato meant: one not dissembled with regard to its intentions or ends; a life without mixture of virtue and vice; a life of rectitude, lived in accord with norms and rules; one that escaped corruption or fall and hence one not divided in itself" (110). The Cynics turned the Platonic notion of the true life on its head, by taking it to what appeared to be its logical extreme, making a movement out of the idea of "**life as the scandal of truth** [bold in original]" (110): "For the Socratic 'other world' they substituted an 'other life,' the truly philosophical life, the 'true life'" (110). Flynn sees the importance of the Cynics to Foucault as providing an alternative to Platonism's emphasis on the soul and notion of another world, "a kind of carnivalesque grimace toward the Platonic tradition" (110):

> Specifically, the Cynics' understanding of the true life entailed a point-by-point inversion of the Platonic view just enunciated, namely: (1) absence of dissemblance to the point of dramatization—their notorious "naturalism"; (2) lack of admixture of virtue and vice as exemplified in their poverty (an inversion of Stoic indifference), which led paradoxically to dependency, mendicancy, and dishonor [*adoxia*]; (3) rectitude understood as life according to the natural demands of animality, including the rejection of social conventions and taboos; and (4) self-possession and sovereignty pushed to the extreme of claiming a militant kingship which fights against customs, institutions, personal passions and vices to restore us to our natural state. (110–11)

That natural state was somewhat different for the Cynics.

Since Foucault's argument was a critique of Enlightenment and scientistic reason as well as Platonism, he has been attacked on the grounds that his critique of reason undermines his own reason-based critique. Flynn defends Foucault against such attacks by arguing that he suggests, not that we can never know anything, but that the question of "homogeneous reason and univocal truth" allows for "a plurality of counterpositions, of points of resistance, of styles of life—of 'truths'" (112).

As we saw in chapter 2, John Sellars understands the philosophical project as directed toward the question of how to live.

His view parallels Foucault's: both see theory and practice as reconciled by technique. Sellars writes, "It is of course a commonplace to proclaim that in antiquity philosophy was conceived as a way of life. To be a philosopher in antiquity—a Platonist, a Stoic, an Epicurean, a Cynic, a Neoplatonist, even an Aristotelian—meant that one would live in a specifically philosophical manner."[67] Sellars acknowledges that modern philosophers interested in this conception of a philosopher draw on the ancient Stoics. But Sellars's own interest is in "the *relationship* between an individual's philosophy and his or her way of life" (50). Foucault came closest, Sellars thinks, with his idea of "the art of living, the *technē tou biou*" (57n9). While the phrase does not appear in ancient philosophy, what does appear is a "τέχνη περί τὸν βίον, an art concerned with one's way of life." This phrase, or a version of it, appears most often in the thought of Sextus Empiricus, a Pyrrhonian Skeptic who lived in the second and third centuries AD and wrote against the idea of an art of living.[68] "Latin equivalents would be *ars vitae* and *ars vivendi*" (5n27), as in Cicero and Seneca respectively. Sellars responds to Martha Nussbaum, who criticizes Foucault's emphasis on techniques of the self on the grounds that this emphasis makes philosophy and religion difficult to distinguish, since both traditions involve such techniques. Sellars defends Foucault against the charge that techniques of the self undervalue philosophy's mode of rational analysis, which Sellars insists remains central for Foucault (116–17).[69]

Sellars may be constrained, even in trying to bridge the two elements of Stoicism, by our own culture's division of theory and practice, knowledge and application, and by the modern connotations of the derivatives—current overreliance on words with the root *techne* and the developments to which they refer. It seems he holds back from grasping the content of the knowledge as the key that connects the two. His discussion of the way of life of a philosopher as the expression of that philosophy has a modern feel to it, as though we are trying to get hold of something ever receding, trying to pin down the precise difference between their view and ours, something lost in translation. Cynicism might best be understood as negation. Giving up on both as a way to bridge this difficult gap between ideas and living—an all-bets-are-off response—seeks to unveil the emptiness of everything as mere artifice and ungrounded social constructions.

Referring to the different styles of facial hair sported by members of the different schools, Sellars concludes that "one can begin to see how different types of beard might not merely indicate visually to which school an individual belonged, but actually *express* the philosophical positions held by that school" (19). He uses this as an example of those philosophers who had a conception of philosophy that was not merely theoretical, as captured in Socrates's phrase, "deeds not words" (20). This leads them to place emphasis on life itself: "In antiquity the word βίος (bios) or 'life' referred to an individual's way of life or manner of living and was distinct from the merely biological connotations of being a 'living being,' for which the Greeks used ζῷον (Zoon)" (22). We see this in the interest in biography, anecdote, stories, and the like, as in Xenophon, Plutarch, Diogenes Laertius, and Porphyry. Studying philosophy was about changing one's life (23), including one's mind or character, νόος (nous), and soul, ψυχή (psyche). But by his own admission, Sellars notes that the beard styles came later than the first Athenian schools.[70] Was the main point not that these schools *were* different approaches to how to live but that that was their very subject? They were clearly interested in the differences among them. Sellars emphasizes the importance of the biographical in philosophy. But given the imprimatur of our own times we might fear that those differences could be trivialized into *only* differences of external style, projected image, and outward identity as a matter of choice. Contemporary ways of living focus almost completely on those more superficial kinds of differences, on the "lifestyle" of the individual. This is almost the opposite of the art of living, which is neither how you project yourself as detached from character nor the mere application of the philosophical principles of a particular school of thought. In the Golden Age of Hellenistic philosophies, living philosophically was not an a priori choice but a result determined by action. It took ideas seriously as the internal counterpart to the outer life—it presupposed an inner life (30).

As his interest in Greco-Roman philosophy deepened, Foucault showed an increasing interest in the moral subject, which so much of his earlier work had undermined. Holding a chair in the "History of Systems of Thought" at the Collège de France, Foucault helped recruit philosopher Pierre Hadot for a chair there in the "History of Hellenistic and Roman Thought" in 1983, from the position he had held in Latin Patristics at the École pratique des Hautes Études. In a piece on the two philosophers called "The Joy of Difference," Cory Wimberly writes that "Foucault was struck by Hadot's characterization of ancient philosophy as a way of life—a spiritual practice of self-transformation that was more than just an assemblage of truths, it was a practice of continual improvement of oneself and one's world." While they shared a view of "philosophy as a way of life" that "might occasion personal and social transformation," they differed on what that entailed. For Foucault, philosophy meant liberation from the power/truth nexus through difference. For Hadot, it meant movement toward unity and the Universal.[71]

ALL ABOUT ME

In *The Care of the Self*, Foucault describes what he saw in the first couple of centuries of the new millennium as a "cultivation of the self": "The art of existence—the *technē tou biou* in its different forms—is dominated by the principle that says one must 'take care of oneself'" (41–43). He quotes an aphorism from Seneca that urges an individual to "spend your whole life learning how to live" (48). At the crux of Foucault's argument lies his interpretation of the Stoics, in particular, appearing in a crucial section of *The Care of the Self* that spells out exactly what he means by these philosophers' focus on "the cultivation of the self." While he suggests antecedents and parallels among Platonists and Epicureans, their schools of thought receive only brief attention in paragraphs introductory to Foucault's close reading of the Stoics. The approach to the self that interests him had long been embedded in Stoicism: "Taking care of one's soul was a precept that Zeno had given his disciples from the beginning, and one Musonius was to repeat, in the first century, in a sentence quoted by Plutarch: 'He who wishes to come through life safe and sound must continue throughout his life to take care of himself.'"[72] Foucault does not grasp the irony of using a quote about care of the *soul* to support "care of the *self.*"

Foucault cites the importance Seneca placed on a certain aim: "*sibi vacare,*" which Robert Hurley translates as a man's imperative "to make himself vacant for himself" (46). Hardly a vacation in the usual sense, this involves an urgent and intense project: one must "lose no time and spare no effort in order to 'develop oneself,' 'transform oneself,' 'return to oneself'"—all of which Foucault sees as "different forms" of taking "care of the self" (46). He interprets a quote from *Meditations* as Marcus's call to take care of himself, arguing that "Marcus Aurelius also feels the same haste to look after himself" (46–47). This is reminiscent of the modern misinterpretation of the first-century BC Roman lyric poet Horace's famous line about *carpe diem* as a call to purloin everything we can get hold of rather than to fulfill the real requirements of the day.[73] Seneca is talking about the need to "return to oneself" and Marcus to "rescue yourself," which are very different activities from merely "caring" for oneself, although the latter may serve as a toehold in the climb toward that higher ground (46–47).

It is revealing that for Foucault the version of Stoicism put forth by Epictetus exhibits "the highest philosophical development of this theme" (47). Foucault's reasoning helps flesh out what he thinks this care of the self entails. It begins and ends with the human capacity for reason, instilled in our very nature by Zeus, which allows us and requires us to take care of ourselves (47). Foucault sees this as "a kind of permanent exercise" (49), as important for older adults as for those just embarking on their mature lives. The care of the self involves "*epiméleia*" (ἐπιμέλεια, attention), not a vague orientation to self-care and "not just a preoccupation but a whole set of occupations," including daily "introspection," morning and night, as well as more extensive retreats (50–51). It entails a rigorous routine, based on the analogy between "the medicine of the body and the therapeutics of the soul" (55). Any successful treatment needs to begin with "the establishment of the relation to oneself as a sick individual" (58).

To Foucault, the ultimate goal of this practice is self-knowledge leading to a "conversion to self." While the notion "has a Platonic cast," Foucault sees Epictetus's version as "considerably different," as a pivot to "the relation of oneself to oneself." The upshot comes as some surprise in an oeuvre dominated by dark themes. "The relation to self" allows "one to delight in oneself" (65). For Foucault, then, the end of self-care is not just self-control but a kind of self-possession that allows the individual to enjoy himself as "an object of pleasure." He thinks Seneca describes the ideal state of mind, in which self-possession and freedom from inner disturbance lead to joy. Foucault translates Seneca's use of the words *gaudium* and *laetitia* to connote a form of pleasure deriving from oneself as opposed to *voluptas*, a form of pleasure based on things outside oneself.[74] For Foucault, Seneca's remark that one "pleases oneself" means being satisfied with only what is within one's control and dismissing the rest. At the heart of this "ethics of pleasure" lies the cultivation and formation of the self through self-knowledge: "The task of testing oneself, examining oneself, monitoring oneself in a series of clearly defined exercises, makes the question of truth—the truth concerning what one is, what one does, and what one is capable of doing—central to the formation of the ethical subject" (68). It is knowledge that sets the individual free—to be dominated only by himself. For what? Pure pleasure. How to get there? *Techne*.

Foucault sees "the question of truth and the principle of self-knowledge" as joined together in what is a *techne* of living. Given Foucault's role as an astute analyst of the precise vocabularies of certain modern discourses, such as those around madness or punishment, it is worth pinning down his notion of this approach as *techne*. On the surface, Stoic self-examination "appears to constitute a sort of small-scale judicial drama" (61): one analyzes every aspect of one's thoughts and actions, in the presence of an inner judge who evaluates the evidence of the antics of the self with an accusing eye. But Foucault settles on the role of "inspector," or "a master of a household checking his accounts," because it is more "a kind of administrative review." A person carries out this internal inventory not to determine guilt or stir remorse but "to commit to memory, so as to have them present in one's mind, legitimate ends, but also rules of conduct that enable one to achieve these ends through the choice of appropriate means" (62). Epictetus likens the self to a "'night watchman' who checks the entries at the gate of cities or houses" or "a 'tester of coinage,' an 'assayer,' one of those money-changers who won't accept any coin without having made sure of its worth" (63). The self needs to engage in a constant "screening of representations" (63) to determine their worth: "You see in the matter of coinage . . . how we have even invented an art, and how many means the tester employs to test coinage—sight, touch, smell, finally hearing: he throws the denarius down and then listens to the sound and is not satisfied with the sound it makes on a single test, but, as a result of his constant attention to the matter, he catches the tune, like a musician."[75]

The contrast between Epictetus's notion of the inner self as a "tester of coinage" and the Cynic lore of Diogenes as defacing the coinage helps underline the difference between the Stoic role, which Foucault renders sympathetically, and the Cynic's rejection of roles altogether. But Foucault reconciles Stoic and Cynic roles in an interpretation of Epictetus's portrait of the ideal Cynic. Discussing the Stoics' support for matrimony and the Cynics' general disregard for all social ties, Foucault also renders the Cynic sympathetically. Both seem to endorse Cynicism in a roundabout way by suggesting that what necessitates the Cynic's renunciation of social ties is the current state of the world and not something intrinsically wrong with the institution of marriage and community. Epictetus casts the Cynic as "the man who makes a profession of philosophizing, who must be the common pedagogue, the herald of truth, Zeus' messenger to humans, who goes on stage to challenge men and to reproach them for the way they live," in Foucault's paraphrasing of passages in the *Discourses*.[76] Epictetus's Cynic rejects marriage only because he is concerned with the state of all of humanity. If all were wise, "there would be no further need of these men who are sent by the gods and who, unburdening themselves of everything, rise up to awaken others to truth."

Foucault explains: "Everyone would be a philosopher. The Cynic and his rude profession would be unnecessary" (159).

This passage helps reconcile Foucault's seemingly sympathetic view of the new marital ideal of the Romans and the whole task of the formation of ethical selfhood, on one hand, with his life-long criticism of the very notion of the modern self as a bastion of bourgeois individualism, a tool of control and discipline. We should note that the Stoic self amounts to a self-chosen practice of freedom and self-control, aside from the workings of the state and other forms of power and hierarchy. If all could live *this* way, there would presumably be no need of the Cynic's antics. The Cynic speaks the truth about the world as a kind of Stoic self-examination writ large. There is a key difference. Speaking the truth externally is the Cynic's task. Speaking the truth internally is the Stoic's task.

The Cynics represented the polar opposite of the Stoics' version of cultivating the self. Their notion of speaking the complete truth out loud, and supposedly living it, is directly opposed to the self-disciplined practices of the Stoics. This difference hinges on the stark difference between letting it all out and holding it all in. But if we accept Foucault's interpretation of the Stoics, they too were devoted to the truth in their quest for self-knowledge. Like the Cynics, they were suspicious of surfaces and first impressions. They were concerned with how philosophy was lived—thus their dramatic acts in service of calling attention to the truth of things. The Cynics, however, wore their self-consciously fashioned selves in the same way as those they attacked and ridiculed. They presented themselves as anticonvention, but their theatrical totalizing view of society, as in total dismissal of society, was just as much of a convention of self-presentation, shorn of deep examination of the world outside the self and its image. This was the world reduced to a mirror.

Foucault's interpretation of the Stoics fits best with the codified *Handbook* of Epictetus, though he misses the point that even in tough Stoicism the search is for the "music" that the pure coin makes, not its monetary value. If anything, Foucault's view has shades of Epicureanism with his emphasis on pleasure. It might be an "ethics of pleasure" of a sort, but it falls short of the art of living. What he describes is not the art of living but the technique of living.

What is missing in Foucault's account is a full sense of the moral dimension of the art of living, and the way in which the philosophers he examines situated the human person in a world, physically and spiritually—in a veritable universe. Their search for truth did not stop at the self, nor did it end at the question of control. "Control" is an inadequate translation of the Stoics' famous directive to determine which things are and are not "up to us." This means not only what is or is not in our control, but what ultimately matters—and what exists besides us. The relevance of an idea or action to the formation of the individual's moral character is the only meaningful measure. The Stoics cannot be understood without granting their agreement with the Socratic notion that knowledge and virtue are inextricable. To depict the ultimate achievement of their exercises as pleasure or to associate it with a "stylistics of living"—"lifestyle," in today's parlance—is to fail to grasp their interest in the world beyond their own heads.[77] They sought a way to live in the world, not in terrain coterminous with themselves.

Foucault went on to become a household name, at least among academics of critical and, Sloterdijk would say, cynical propensities. In the late twentieth century, Foucault's earlier studies had a towering impact on literary studies and beyond, encouraging a multitude of works of lesser subtlety and range than his. A rigid application of his theories as a formula for power's operation everywhere at all times furthered a generalized suspicion of all traditions and institutions, as though society itself inevitably resulted from conspiracies of domination. A fair interpretation of much of Foucault's message, this reductionist reception neglected his more nuanced ideas about possible resistance as well as his larger social vision. What would have happened if the ideas of Hadot, and not Foucault, had captured the limelight? As important as he was to Foucault and many others, Hadot's work, and that of others who had more in common with him, did not get the same play. But if we are granted a breather from the cynicism of the moment, we might see that change. In chapter 5 we will see signs that it already might be happening. Hadot's specific response to Foucault's renderings of the ideas of the ancient philosophers offers powerful foreshadowing of our final school of thought.

FROM PLEASURE TO JOY

While Pierre Hadot's idea of ancient philosophy as a way of life—*bios*—was a major influence on Foucault, Hadot thought it meant something very different.[78] In *Philosophy as a Way of Life: Spiritual Exercises from Socrates to Foucault* (1995), Hadot explicitly takes issue with Foucault's characterization of ancient philosophy. What Foucault calls "practices of the self" (*pratiques de soi*), "arts of existence," or "techniques of the self," Hadot had defined as "spiritual exercises." According to Hadot, while "the ancients did speak of an 'art of living,'" this was very different from what Foucault has in mind: "It seems to me . . . that the description M. Foucault gives of what I had termed 'spiritual exercises,' and which he prefers to call 'techniques of the self,' is precisely focused far too much on the 'self,' or at least on a specific conception of the self."[79] Hadot's specific disagreement centers on Foucault's portrait of ancient philosophy as "an ethics of the pleasure one takes in oneself" (207). Hadot points to the wording in Seneca's twenty-third letter, which is pivotal to Foucault's reading of ancient philosophy as centered on the pursuit of pleasure. Foucault's translation of Seneca's words *voluptas* and *gaudium* as "pleasure" was not, in Hadot's view, just a mistranslation but showed "a great deal of inexactitude":

> In Letter 23, Seneca explicitly opposes *voluptas* and *gaudium*—pleasure and joy—and one cannot, therefore, speak of "another form of pleasure," as does Foucault (*Care of the Self*, p. 83) when talking about joy. This is not just a quibble over words, although the Stoics did attach a great deal of importance to words, and carefully distinguished between *hedone*—"pleasure"—and *eupatheia*—"joy." No, this is no mere question of

vocabulary. If the Stoics insist on the word *Gaudium*/"joy," it is precisely because they refuse to introduce the principle of pleasure into moral life. For them, happiness does not consist in pleasure, but in virtue itself, which is its own reward. Long before Kant, the Stoics strove jealously to preserve the purity of intention of the moral consciousness. (207)

Even more crucial is the basis of the joy involved in Stoicism. Rather than finding "joy in his 'self,'" as Foucault suggests, Seneca finds joy in the very opposite, "in the best portion of the self, in 'the true good.'" Hadot continues: "The 'best portion of oneself,' then, is, in the last analysis, a transcendent self. Seneca does not find his joy in 'Seneca,' but in transcending 'Seneca'" by discovering he is part of "universal reason" (207). Hadot reads the Stoic exercises as spiritual practice that leads to self-transcendence: "Seneca sums it up in four words: *Toti se inserens mundo*, 'Plunging oneself into the totality of the world'" (208).

According to Hadot, Foucault's advancement of a mode of living he calls "an aesthetics of existence" stemmed from the "more or less universal tendency of modern thought" (208) to abandon universals.[80] Universals represented efforts to oppress individuals and groups—especially those not in sync with dominant norms or otherwise in the minority vis-à-vis the mainstream or powerful ingroups. As 1960s social movements later became institutionalized in the academy, increasing attention went to the differences among groups, between people, and eventually even within an individual.

Hadot made a towering contribution in his life's work in a number of ways on numerous themes. One of the overarching themes of his oeuvre was his view that ancient philosophy was above all "a way of life." Rather than separate philosophical theory from practical application, Hadot argued that Greco-Roman philosophy, in its intention, literary genres, discourse, and pedagogy, wedded the content of its claims about the world with the living of a human life, forming a set of "spiritual exercises." Rather than "teaching an abstract theory," ancient philosophy entailed "the art of living" (83). This art consists of "a concrete attitude and determinate lifestyle," in translator Michael Chase's wording, that involves not just discourse and exegesis but existential matters "of the self and of being," and that possesses therapeutic ends. Philosophy "causes us to *be* more fully, and makes us better": "It is a conversion which turns our entire life upside down, changing the life of the person who goes through it." While the Stoics and Platonists figure prominently in Hadot's evidence for this understanding of philosophy, he considered this function of philosophy as "a therapeutic of the passions" to be something the schools of thought shared: "Each school had its own therapeutic method, but all of them linked their therapeutics to a profound transformation of the individual's mode of seeing and being" (83). This was achieved not only through cognition but through other modes of perception and means of uniting "imagination and objectivity" to intuition and inner vision. Practices included meditation, memorization, reading, dialogue, research, and other exercises designed to change habits of thought, feeling, and action (86).

Analytic philosophy, which dominates academic philosophy today, primarily explores precisely defined questions through logical and semantic clarification rather than philosophy's connection to daily life. Some find the notion of ancient philosophy as an art of living compelling but would disagree with Hadot's characterization of that art as involving "spiritual exercises." In his *Pursuits of Wisdom*, a crucial contribution to the understanding of philosophy as a way of life, John Cooper profiles five schools of thought in meticulous detail and accessible prose to a wide readership crossing over the usual public/academic divide.[81] Rather than see one overarching art of living cultivated by ancient Greco-Roman philosophy as a whole, he details the different modes advocated by the different schools. Cooper's work poses a fundamental challenge to Hadot's notion of "spiritual exercises." Instead, ancient philosophy's practice involved its paramount commitment to reason, which Cooper sees as a very different commitment from spiritual practice.[82]

While Cooper and other critics have cast doubt on the usefulness of the idea of philosophy as involving spiritual exercises, we can see some important overlap between Cooper and Hadot. Both point to the importance of practice in understanding ancient philosophy, and to its fundamental blending of reason and morality. Yet both, too, face the challenge of coming up against the problems with the concept of technique, which can function as a wall it takes the most exquisite care to surmount. Each does manage this feat. Foucault does not. This is the key problem with the practical application of philosophy, as we saw in Sellars's book. It is most apparent in—and may be seen as a trait of—Cynicism itself. Here is where Foucault's ideas can once again put him in the camp of the Cynics, even if his emphasis on pleasure might seem to place him with the Epicureans.

While Hadot and Foucault had mutual respect for each other's work, their main difference, which might be simplified as an understanding of the art of living as based on pleasure versus joy, amounts to an unbridgeable chasm between the perspectives of a Cynic and a Platonist. For Foucault, truth ultimately came down to pleasure; for Hadot, truth, an intrinsic attribute of the good and beautiful, resided with the divine.

Foucault, with his emphasis on pleasure, might seem more akin to the Epicureans, but pleasure can be a theme of any school of thought. Hadot says it is surprising that Foucault did not write more about Epicureans given that "Epicurean ethics is, in a sense, an ethics without norms" (208), thus outfitted perfectly for the "modern mentality," which is how Hadot characterizes Foucault's view. A rendering of philosophical practice as concerning the self's concern with itself and its pleasures does not describe Epicureanism. For Hadot, Epicureans too engaged in philosophy as "spiritual exercises." While they did not share the notion of "nature or universal reason," neither did they adhere to a philosophy that referred purely to the individual self. While they did see the world as created by chance, they acknowledged that a person required a world of other people and things for basic needs to be met, as well as for pleasure: the individual needed food, love, community, and a physics to guard against "fear of the gods and of death" (208). Beyond this, Epicureans "needed the imaginative contemplation of an infinite number of universes in the infinite void, in order to experience what Lucretius calls *divina voluptas et horror*"(208–9), translated as "a sort of divine delight" and "a shuddering."[83] This "immersion in the cosmos" is the fundamental element of Hadot's own view.

Hadot argues that Foucault's portrait of the "philosophical practice of the Stoics and Platonists was nothing but a relationship to one's self, a culture of the self, or a pleasure taken on itself" (208). Instead, Hadot sees the relationship of the self with something beyond the self as the point of ancient philosophical practice: "In my view, the feeling of belonging to a whole is an essential element: belonging, that is, both to the whole constituted by the human community, and to that constituted by the cosmic whole. Seneca sums it up in four words: *Toti se inserens mundo*, 'Plunging oneself into the totality of the world.' In his admirable *Anthropologie philosophique*, Groethuysen pointed out the importance of this fundamental point. Such a cosmic perspective radically transforms the feeling one has of oneself" (208).

Hadot points to the example of ancient "spiritual notebooks" or *hypomnemata* used to record the thoughts of others. Foucault sees them as a sign of an eclectic gathering of ideas from different schools of thought, and as a set of personal choices, thus composing a means of "construction of the self." But eclecticism was used only as a way to gain converts, not as "an art of disparate truth," as Foucault argues (210). Hadot insists that the aim of this practice "is not to forge oneself from one's individuality" (210). Instead of "writing oneself," "writing, like the other spiritual exercises, *changes the level of the self*, and universalizes it" (211). For St. Antony, a monk whose writings both Hadot and Foucault discuss, Hadot says that writing allows one to apply reason by examining oneself through the eyes of others: "What was confused and subjective becomes thereby objective" (211).

Hadot agrees with Foucault that the practices of the Platonists and Stoics do involve "conversion toward the self" in the sense of being free from outside attachments, gaining self-mastery, and finding "one's happiness in freedom and inner independence" (211). But the self is not the end point. Instead of turning one permanently toward an interior world, this philosophical practice allows one a deepened connection to the "world beyond."[84] For

Hadot, "This movement of interiorization is inseparably linked to another movement, whereby one rises to a higher psychic level, at which one encounters another kind of exteriorization, another relationship with 'the exterior.' This is a new way of being-in-the-world, which consists in becoming aware of oneself as a part of nature, and a portion of universal reason. At this point, one no longer lives in the usual, conventional human world, but in the world of nature. As we have seen above, one is then practicing 'physics' as a spiritual exercise" (211).

While his analysis seems to border on other schools of thought, representing a departure from the approach of his earlier work, Foucault's view ultimately hews most closely to that of the Cynic. The Cynic's flouting of convention and devotion to the "truth" is a parody of this spiritual practice. Interiorization—the journey into the interior—ends by bringing a person out of the self into a new experience of the external world, into a feeling of attachment to it not as an emotion but as a reasoned understanding of one's unity with it, with something vastly larger than the self and all-enduring. The Cynic instead voyages without, in the external world, and in an everyday drama *en plein air* performs private acts, unmasking what he considers others' hypocrisy and demonstrating his own moral superiority. Rather than experience the humility of being part of an external world, Cynics claim this superiority over others on the basis of their special insight that questions all human convention as unreasonable. Cynics' conversion is only a halfway stop. The destination is the self, on display for all to see, an inward-facing externalism. It deliberately tries to attract attention, to make an object of the inner world—of inwardness—as something that is just as visible and transparent as the external world. Rebuking surfaces—declaring that things are not what they seem—ends up reinstating them by replacing the old with a new surface to present as the remedy: "Look at me" versus "Look within." In place of a doorway within to everything else that is not the self, the Cynic builds a glass house, demystifying the inner life by showing it all. The end point becomes one and the same with the technique for getting there: exposure. Truth is what is seen.

Thomas Flynn compares and contrasts Foucault and Hadot in an essay that links the project of philosophy as a way of life to existentialism. For Flynn, the focus on philosophy as a way of life is an "existential revival," in which the question of philosophy's connection to living is receiving renewed attention, in spite of a philosophy profession dominated by the pursuit of knowledge separate from any such practical application.[85] Flynn sees an analogy between Foucault's view and a nontheist existentialism like that of Jean-Paul Sartre, even though Foucault bristled at such a comparison, and sees an analogy between Hadot and the theist existentialism of Kierkegaard. Yet Flynn points to Hadot's parting of ways with the Christian existentialism of Kierkegaard in his differentiation between spirituality and religion. Hadot argues for the relevance of spiritual practices even in a secular age, on the grounds that these exercises allow those who are not religious "the possibility of choosing a purely philosophical way of life."[86]

Flynn reviews Hadot's objections to Foucault's notion of ancient philosophy as practical through certain "techniques of the self," emphasizing Hadot's criticism of Foucault's overemphasis on "the 'self' as individual and self-constituting." Foucault's notion of philosophy as an "art of living" construed it as an aesthetic project, as though the individual created him or herself rather than connecting to others and the universe through reason-based truths concerning justice.[87]

A further criticism of Foucault, for Flynn, is Foucault's separation of Cartesian reason from the concept of care of the self. "'What is the price that I must pay to gain access to the truth?' Foucault challenges. 'What is the labor I must undertake on myself. . . . What is the modification of being that I must set about to gain access to the truth?'"[88] Flynn continues, "Here Foucault introduces the expression 'the condition of spirituality for access to the truth.'"[89]

Foucault's formulations suggest an instrumentalism of truth by overconnecting truth to life. If the point is to live a certain life, then in the absence of an outside, transcendent referent what is to prevent an instrumentalizing of truth in the service of practical exigency? Foucault's view of ethical truth is too manipulable because it mocks all outside authority beyond the self. For this reason Habermas viewed Foucault's notion as anarchism.[90]

As Flynn suggests at one point, Foucault's work as a whole was part of a critique of Enlightenment rationalism. Foucault could not embrace Hadot's enthusiasm for universal reason in light of its dangers. Yet Hadot's work speaks precisely to this by suggesting a transcendent referent. The problem is neither reason nor emotion, but the instrumentalizing of either. Thus it becomes imperative that any conception of philosophy as a way of life guard against the instrumentalizing of truth. Cynicism cannot.

As Hadot points out, Foucault's notion of "techniques of the self" is "focused far too much on the 'self'" (206–7), yet the problem does not stop there. It is also the focus on technique that falls short, something to guard against in the notion of a practice as well. To characterize Stoics' practices as "spiritual exercises" might fit, but when it comes to Plato and the Neoplatonists, to single out practices from their larger view risks privileging process over content, one of their fundamental caveats. This focus has led to mischaracterizations of figures as mystics rather than as Platonists who hew to a particular philosophy in which such separation of means from ends would be meaningless. Platonism stands out from all the schools precisely for its insistence that ends—content, meaning, idea—never become detached from means and process. When they do, we are left with mere technique. It was not the technique of living that interested them.

Sloterdijk differentiates between ancient "kynicism" and modern "cynicism." It is clear that he admires the figure of Diogenes, praising ancient kynicism as "cheeky," which he means as a compliment. Ancient kynics' "provocative gestures" represented their core belief that philosophy should be "embodied": "For the philosopher, the human being who exemplifies the love of truth and *conscious* living, life and doctrine must be in harmony" (101). Sloterdijk sees the antics of Diogenes as a kind of "low theory" as opposed to the high theory of Plato: Diogenes "starts the *non-Platonic dialogue*" (102). To Sloterdijk this translates into a dedication to truth telling that makes Diogenes even more important for truth than Plato. But it seems unlikely. Unlike Platonism, Cynicism has no system for telling the difference between truth and untruth. Cynicism is about truth telling, that much is true, but it has little to go on when it comes to truth.

WHAT IS MISSING FROM POSTMODERN VERSIONS OF experience or most contemporary versions is a sense of the capacity of everyday experiences to inspire flights of joy and profound gratification that can both involve and outlive moments of sensory exhilaration and also withstand the application of the mind's reflection and find meaning. This notion—of the sacredness or inherent integrity of the ordinary—is a theme noticeably underrepresented in postmodern thought as in our times overall.

As in all times in human history, our age has its share of threats to the mundane rhythms of life and everyday satisfactions. Montaigne knew these threats firsthand—from the religious violence and epidemics around him to the intense personal pain of the kidney stones he was forced to endure—and counseled a virtuous discipline against complaint and dissatisfaction: "We must learn to suffer what we cannot evade."[91]

The ruthless assault on the self and its invaluable connections with others—from omnipresent flickering images of people and things in compromised positions, from the routinization and bureaucratization at work and beyond, from huge state machineries and faceless terrorists, domestic and foreign, from ways of life that promise plenty but deny basic satisfactions, from an economy and culture obsessed with superficial pleasures—has helped phase out truly alternative traditions of experience. The fascination with near-death experiences—in sadomasochism, extreme tourism, survival themes in reality television shows—speaks to an inability to find excitement and fulfillment in everyday life. Cynicism is not the answer.

At a time when everyday life can be so violently disrupted, we might well remember Montaigne's delight in and sense of the intrinsic worth of everyday life. Now views like Montaigne's—renewed over time by Tolstoy, Emerson, the political philosopher Jean Bethke Elshtain or the poet Wendell Berry in our own time, along with so many others—form a countertradition, living in the interstices of an economy, politics, and culture that have little use of the ordinary or the limited. Friendship, love, conversation—these are some of the subjects most fondly discussed by such writers, for whom aversion to pain, whether self-inflicted or induced by others, is a given. Without the moral grounding that reminds us of such givens, it is all too easy to lose sight of the multitude of satisfactions inherent in regular association with others, which alone makes life worth living.

FIVE

THE NEW
PLATONISM

Architecture is frozen music.
—*Goethe*

Here we are in the dreaded void. At terrifying speed, a rocket
penetrates the deepest recesses of outer space, parting a path
through clouds of meteors. They stream by in lines of light, then,
closer now, clouds become clods and thud off of the sides of the
ship, which is later catapulted into a black hole. You yourself
are expelled from the broken vessel and cast out into the great beyond, a wall-less cavern of nothingness, loneliness, and meaninglessness.

Yet in this last instant you see something. In place of your life
passing before your eyes, you glimpse one brief and specific moment of your life so clearly it must be real. It is a moment you regret above all others, when you took a step with the assumption

that in the unfolding of a life there would always come more opportunities for the ultimate love.

Implausibly, here it all is again right before your eyes, despite
your loss. You see the bookshelf in the bedroom of your ten-year-
old daughter, and you are her astronaut hero of a father, absent
from her so long that she is somehow also an adult in the same
room. Your inspiration to do good, to scope out other possible
galaxies in order to rescue humanity from a dying planet, was impossible to distinguish from your own ambition, and rocketed you
into space for all of her growing-up years, almost entirely cut off
from her except for some Skype communications. Your wife had
died and no love anchored you, or so you thought. As year after
year went by, the weight of your decision cracked you open, the
broken love bond shattered your self and soul into shards.

Impossibly, you get another chance.

ARCHITECTURE AMID THE STARS

Out of the gloom come random flashes of light of varying intensities, from blinding sun-force to gentle eye-floaters, those specks
of light sometimes glancing across our field of vision. Your boots
clang on a metal grill, and you are falling at great speed through a
shaft until your body emerges into a kind of room somehow built
in the midst of the nothingness. You yourself are floating now, suspended in a special time-within-time and space-within-space, cor-
doned off from the night sky with shafts of light of all colors
speeding by horizontally and vertically all around you, thick ones,
thin ones, resembling those light beams, nicknamed "God's light,"
that shine out from clouds at sunrise or sunset or filter through
window slats. They seem immaterial like light yet material like the
particulate matter illuminated by light, rushing by like water, a
combination of every play of light you have ever seen—equal parts
rainbow and moonbeam—and yet a form of light you can reach
out and touch, be submerged by, live within. It becomes books,
bookshelves, and all they contain. The special time and space turn

out to be all times and all spaces. And here you are, miraculously, to experience it, not dead but as alive as it is possible for any human being to be, suspended within the glory and terror of this astonishing beauty.

Your daughter is on the other side of the bookcase, the same age as when you left her, and in other views an adult now. If only she can read the signs—dogged and determined as she always was, able to intuit the most imperceptible utterances of the universe—you might be able to send her a message. Even up against ridicule and discouragement, she never could be dissuaded from her powers of perception and precocious self-possession. You find a way to knock a book off the shelf. By some miracle father and daughter manage to be reunited in the end. Not only that, your new love interest awaits you on another planet with the not-too-onerous task of repopulating the universe.

Besides the tricks of Hollywood screenwriting (as a Cynic might say), how exactly was this big save accomplished? What far-fetched possibility, latent in that convergence across a seemingly unbridgeable chasm, challenged the very facts of human existence? The answer is found in the esotericism of the newest New Science of our day, an arcane loophole that only life-and-death desperation wrenched open.

As the intellectually inquisitive asked all along, the spiritually daring assumed, and the brokenhearted hoped against hope, human life turned out to have another dimension. Our experience was hemmed in by the three dimensions of space that made our bodies able to inhabit the earth—height, length, and width, or line, plane, and cube—with just a fourth dimension thrown in gratuitously by some cruel miser, catapulting our bodies on a mad course of unilinear time, straitjacketing not just our individual life course but all of human history. Instead, there *is* a fifth dimension. As the daughter suspected, enchantment governs the universe, and as the father needed to be the case, the fifth dimension brings them back together, belatedly, generations later, answering the child's forsaken tears and prostrate begging, emotional suffering she had unknowingly passed like a baton to her father. What was the ultimate mystery, the one and only thing that could win out over fatal human blindness, hubris, and error, and triumph over the entire space-time continuum?

For anyone who has seen *Interstellar*, the answer is known.[1] But even those who have not seen it might have a guess. The answer is, quite simply, love.

This is as Platonic as it gets. Witnessing on the big screen the now-famous climactic scene of *Interstellar* calls to mind inspired passages of the *Enneads* of the first great Neoplatonic philosopher Plotinus, in which he conveyed a state of mind in physical imagery of color and light. This chapter juxtaposes them in order to suggest a new way of coming at some of the abiding questions we face about our condition and circumstances as humans in this world, especially about how and why we as individuals think of ourselves in relation to others and the physical world, how and why we live in a common world with others.

The idea that love can be such a powerful force it can overcome time and space is not so far-fetched. We have encountered it in love poems, love songs, and in everything from tragic tales in theater and opera to real life. From world-historical acts of creation and destruction to so-called random acts of kindness that knit together our world, cultural expression over millennia, and civilization itself, are unthinkable in the absence of the human capacity to love. It is everywhere and always. You need only be rewarded or disappointed in love, or experience either one vicariously, to know that we are virtually ensconced, enclosed, enfolded—or smothered, as the case may be—in love and its infinite progeny.

Like all human creations, science is inextricably entwined with love. The creators of *Interstellar* knew that. It turns out that the artistry of the bookshelf scene was woven through with real developments in science, informed by a delicate dance between real questions and speculative answers. But for our purposes here, the climactic scene described above serves as a portrait of a phenomenon that weds the real and imagined in a way that is highly suggestive for thinking about an element often missing from many discussions of the state of community and society today and the quest for a public or practical philosophy of living.

Interest in Platonism today takes many forms. Along with Voegelin, who also wrote on Plato, just a handful of modern thinkers influenced by Platonism include Hannah Arendt, Iris Murdoch, Leo Strauss, Simone Weil, and Alain Badiou. Catherine H. Zuckert has charted the influence of Platonism on the thought of Nietzsche, Heidegger, Gadamer, Strauss, and Derrida.[2] In *Diotima at the Barricades,* Paul Allen Miller explores the reception of Plato in the work of feminist thinkers Simone de Beauvoir, Hélène Cixous, Luce Irigaray, and Julia Kristeva.[3] English theologians John Milbank, Catherine Pickstock, and Graham Ward's movement of Radical Orthodoxy presents a postmodern critique of modernity. Blending Christianity and Platonism, they publish a journal, *Radical Orthodoxy: Theology, Philosophy, and Politics.* The International Society for Neoplatonic Studies, founded in 1973, holds conferences and publishes the *International Journal of the Platonic Tradition.*

Platonism does not appear immune from incursions from New Age spirituality and the Gnostic sensibility explored in chapter 1. Professor of computer science Bruce J. MacLennan writes on a website called wisdomofhypatia.com that he "offers regular workshops on Neoplatonic spiritual practice, Pythagoreanism, theurgy, and related subjects." Author of a book by that title, he offers a nine-month "virtual course in philosophy, well-being, and divine union," which serves as "an essential and practical introduction to the ancient wisdom of the West." According to his online course materials, he offers "guided visualizations including an eight minute Platonic ascent and descent" and other eyes-closed activities. Plato can apparently also be enlisted to further business.[4]

ANCIENT PLATONISM

Platonism is rooted in the thought of one of the most famous philosophers across time and the globe, Plato (428/7–348/7 BC). (See fig. 5.1.) It is in part because of Plato that this period was considered the golden age for thought that it was. Thanks to Plato, we have his own ideas and the ideas of his illustrious teacher, Socrates, which were not written down. Plato's lifelong engagement with the teachings of Socrates found an echo in his student Aristotle's lifelong engagement, in turn, with the teachings of Plato.

Plato came from an aristocratic family that could claim ancestry of a mythical king and Athenian poet and lawmaker Solon. His father was Ariston, his mother Perictione, and his brothers Glaucon and Adeimantus. He was taught by Cratylus, a Heraclitean, until becoming a student of Socrates when he was twenty. While many details of his life are difficult to confirm, it is thought he began writing in 399 BC, the year Socrates died, and that from 390 to 388 BC he traveled to Egypt, Cyrene, Lower Italy, and Syracuse, meeting philosophers and political figures, including Dion, the brother-in-law of Syracuse's tyrannical Dionysius. He may have been sold into slavery but later set free. In 388/7 BC, he founded the Academy northwest of the gates of Athens. It went on to offer instruction in many subjects, especially math, and many great philosophers taught there alongside Plato. In 367 BC, when Syracuse's Dionysius I died, Dionysius II showed an interest in Platonic philosophy. Persuaded by Dion, Plato moved to Syracuse to influence hoped-for reforms, which did not come about. Conflict between Dion and Dionysius made the situation precarious. Plato did not support Dion's military action against Dionysius because he thought Dionysius had saved his life. After a second stay, and obstacles and threats, Plato could finally leave Syracuse in 360 and return to Athens.[5]

According to *Brill's New Pauly*, all of Plato's works or those attributed to Plato are preserved, including the *Corpus Platonicum*—thirty-four dialogues, the *Apology of Socrates*, and thirteen letters—as well as six short dialogues not considered authentic in antiquity and a collection of *Definitions*. In addition, there are two other letters, a collection of *dihaereses* (logical definitions through division of types) in Diogenes Laertius, thirty-two epigrams, and a poem fragment. The works came to be arranged in nine tetralogies. Over the centuries, much controversy surrounded, and in some cases continues to surround, the dialogues' chronological order and the authenticity of particular works. There is an extensive indirect tradition of his thought, as recorded by Aristotle and other students such as Speusippus, Xenocrates, Hestiaeus, and Heraclides.[6]

Plato's Academy, which persisted for at least three centuries, was founded in Akademeia, a park named after Akademos or Hekademos (Academus or Hecademus in Latin), with a gymnasium and places of worship. The Academy had elements that distinguished it from other schools:

(1) the absence of tuition fees; (2) a philosophical community (πολλὴ συνουσία, τὸ συζῆν [pollè synousía, to syzên] Epist. 7,341c 8–9); (3) common school festivals (Apollo's birthday) and symposia; (4) numerous researchers and teachers; (5) out-of-town "branches" of the Academy (such as in Atarneus and Assus); (6) provisions for the continuation of the school beyond the founder's death; (7) the objective recognition (ἐπιστήμη; epistémē) of justice and the good (instead of rhetorical lobbying) as a basis for the school's political claims; (8) the importance of mathematics and cosmology; (9) a belief in the immortality of the soul.

The school resembled the Pythagorean communities Plato had encountered on his educational journey, without their "dogmatism and secrecy." People were allowed to disagree. The Academy encouraged "a tolerant diversity of opinion" and an "open-minded spirit." The Academy had high stature even in Plato's lifetime, with brilliant students and scholars and research on math, zoology, botany, logic, rhetoric, and astronomy. It was also highly respected for its political philosophy.[7]

Upon Plato's death in 347 BC, Plato was considered "the 'divine' son of Apollo." His nephew and student Speusippus succeeded him, and then another student, Xenocrates. Under Xenocrates, Aristotle, who went on to be the most famous student of Plato's, left and founded his own school circa 335 BC. Polemon the Athenian, then Crates, were the subsequent heads. A student of Polemon was Zeno, the founder of the Stoa.[8] Aristotle, who lived from 384 to 322 BC, built on Plato's thought yet differed from his teacher on many matters, including the value the student placed on empiricism over the teacher's theory of ideal forms.

Scholarch from 268/4(?) to 241/0 BC, Arcesilaus questioned the notion of "certain truth," and in the second century BC this skeptical turn grew under Carneades (156/5–137/6 BC) and the rise of the New Academy. The Stoic Chrysippus refuted Arcesilaus's ideas. Carneades then responded to Chrysippus. Part of the Athenian philosophical delegation to Rome in 156/5 BC, Carneades spoke there both for *and* against justice.[9] He held that "certainty in knowledge is unattainable" but that "one could ascertain the 'probable' through systematic argument." Some successors were strict Skeptics, but others merely saw Skepticism as a tool "in the fight against the 'dogmatists.'" Philo, a Hellenistic Jewish philosopher, went into exile in 88 BC when Athens sided with Mithridates of Rome. In 86 BC the Academy's grove was cut down, and there is no evidence of the continuation of the Academy "as an institution." Philo's student Antiochus of Ascalon argued with his teacher about Plato's positive teachings. Antiochus considered Plato a "dogmatist" and deemed the Academy's teachings "compatible with those of the Peripatos and the Stoa." Engagement with Plato's thought continued—in the first century AD, Plutarch studied under a Platonist in Athens. Marcus Aurelius established in AD 176 teachers for the main philosophical schools, including Platonism as well as Aristotelianism, Stoicism, and Epicureanism. Plotinus taught in Rome from AD 244 to 270, and others were non-Athenian—Porphyry of Tyre, Iamblichus from Syria, Aedesius from Cappadocia, Theodorus from Cyrene in northern Africa.[10]

NEOPLATONISM

The term *Neoplatonism* was originally applied in the nineteenth century to the movement from the third to the fifth century AD. It is more widely used to refer to Plato's ideas as taken up and often reinterpreted by later adherents. Movements sprouted up in Rome, Athens, Alexandria, Apamea, and other places, sometimes institutionalized as schools and at other times studied and practiced independently or outside a formal context.

The Neoplatonist school in Rome was founded by Plotinus in AD 244, after he studied in Athens under Ammonius Saccas. Plotinus's students included Amelius Gentilianus and Porphyry. Porphyry's students included Iamblichus and Theodorus of Asine. Iamblichus founded a school in Apamea in Syria. His disciple Sopater of Apamea was executed by Emperor Constantine. Iamblichus's student Aedesius started a school in Pergamum, helping spread Iamblichus's ideas throughout coastal Asia Minor. Aedesius's students included Emperor Julian. Eusebius, another student of Aedesius, also instructed Julian, as did Aedesius's students Chrysanthus of Sardis and Maximus of Ephesus.[11]

In the late fourth century, Neoplatonism came to Athens. Plutarch (d. AD 432), a wealthy Athenian, was considered the founder of the school there. "Life of Proclus," by Marinus of Neapolis, and "Life of Isidorus," by Damascius, have provided details on the school. Plutarch's successors were Syrianus, a student of Plutarch's, and Proclus (AD 412–85), who was Syrianus's student in turn. Plutarch's students also included Hierocles. Proclus's students included Hierax, among others.[12]

The Neoplatonist school that emerged around AD 410 and ran until about 530 began the "Platonic succession." The Platonists once again owned the grounds of the Academy, but they taught in "a private house on the southern slope of the Acropolis." Proclus's commentaries on Plato marked the high point. The school was "a center of intellectual opposition against politically triumphant Christianity." In AD 529 Emperor Justinian forbade its scholars from teaching. In AD 532 seven Platonists appealed to the Persian king Chosroes (Khosrow I). While they could not keep the school alive, they settled in Persia at his invitation and then moved to Harran, where they established a school. After this, Simplicius wrote his commentaries on Aristotle, "perhaps because Platonic topics were now prohibited."[13]

The Alexandrian School of Neoplatonism of the fifth to the sixth centuries AD most likely, according to Pierre Hadot, did not differ greatly from Athenian Neoplatonism.[14] According to

I. Hadot, in her *Le problème du néoplatonisme alexandrin*, Alexandrian Neoplatonism was not a separate school from the Athenian one.[15] Not only did it lack an institutional structure and a succession, but there were also continuous exchanges between the Athenian and Alexandrian Neoplatonists. Damascius taught in Alexandria before heading the Athenian school, and Simplicius studied with Damascius in Athens after beginning under Ammonius in Alexandria. Some key members of the school in Alexandria, all economically independent, were Hypatia, Hierocles, Hermias, Ammonius, David, and Elias.[16]

Starting with Iamblichus, who lived from AD 245 to 325 and was a biographer of Pythagoras, Neoplatonism became a theology with *theurgic* aspects (communication with the divine spirits, or worship through rituals sometimes considered sorcery) and *hieratic* aspects (sacred writings or traditional priestly practice).[17] It became extremely systematic under Proclus in the fifth century AD. But according to Pierre Hadot, Neoplatonists "aimed higher" than theology, which "can only speak of god." They desired "to be in direct contact with the deity."[18] Plotinus experienced oneness with God, as did Porphyry. According to Hadot, Iamblichus and his students even gave primacy to hieratic goals, while Plotinus and Porphyry and others still accorded primacy to philosophy. Platonism and Christianity have been closely intertwined in intellectual history, and at times, in certain thinkers, have converged. The church fathers—for instance, Eusebius of Caesarea, Basil of Caesarea, and Gregory of Nyssa in the fourth century—were greatly influenced by Neoplatonism, especially by Plotinus and Porphyry. Later on, Pseudo-Dionysius the Areopagite (likely AD 650–725) employed Proclus's categories for "a model for a Christian hierarchy of heavenly beings."[19]

In the fourth and fifth centuries Neoplatonism reverberated in the Latin part of the Roman Empire, both pagan and Christian. This influenced the Latin Middle Ages, especially Johannes Scotus Eriugena (ninth century) and the School of Chartres (twelfth century). Yet Plato's texts were scarce there for roughly a millennium. In the Arab world they continued to be passed down, so when interactions with Europeans in the medieval period increased, the texts came into circulation in the West. A key figure in making this possible was Avicenna (Ibn Sīnā, 980–1037). A prolific writer, philosopher, and scientist—the most famous intellectual in the medieval Islamic world—he drew on Aristotelian and Neoplatonist traditions. He lived in what is now Iran near the beginning of the Islamic Golden Age, and his work in medicine, astronomy, and many other subjects went on to influence Thomas Aquinas (1225–74) and other medieval Scholastics and later Renaissance thinkers. One of Avicenna's accomplishments was his engagement with ancient Greek texts, which helped ensure their survival and their influence on future generations. A precocious genius, Avicenna began studying Hellenistic texts at a young age, and they remained central to his various studies throughout his life.[20] Later, Averroës (Ibn Rushd, 1126–98) advanced Aristotelianism and the role of philosophy and reason in Islam. Critical of Avicenna and Neoplatonism, Averroës was criticized by Aquinas and other Catholics. Yet translations of his work, especially commentaries on Aristotle, helped stir up interest in ancient philosophy.[21]

The thirteenth century brought a vibrant fusion of the Arabic tradition of Greek texts ("Theology of Aristotle," which was Platonism) and the Latin texts. Neoplatonism went on to exert a great influence on the Renaissance, Early Modern, and Modern periods in the West as well as in intellectual traditions and the work of individual thinkers throughout the world.[22] Platonism informed the content and form of movements from Renaissance humanism and seventeenth-century Cambridge Platonism to strains of modern analytic, moral, and Continental philosophy as well as poetry, music, math, architecture, and many other fields of endeavor. In the mid-seventeenth century the Cambridge Platonists, such as Henry More and Ralph Cudworth, explored the connections between Platonist philosophy and everyday life. Platonism influenced analytic philosophy through the work of Bertrand Russell, W. V. O. Quine, and others, and constitutes a school of thought in the philosophy of mathematics, as in the work of Kurt Gödel.

Perhaps Plato's most famous work in modern times is one of his dialogues, the *Symposium*, the story of a dinner party. At one of their evening gatherings, the participants decide to give speeches on love, and an elaborate conversation unfolds, with each layer peeling off to reveal another. Each layer has its own integrity, as the speaker makes a strong case for a particular way of looking at love. Then the next speaker makes a similarly strong case, but for a completely different view. Finally, when it is Socrates's turn, his speech outshines all the rest, making it the very center of the dialogue. Its view triumphs over the chaos of competing perspectives before it.

To simplify here, we will not linger long over each speech except that of Socrates. Although the narrator nods to the existence of other speeches not recalled, seven are recounted. Phaedrus begins: "Love was a great god, among men and gods a marvel," the source of "all of our highest blessings."[23] He describes the practice of at least some Athenian aristocrats whereby an older man (the lover) pursues an adolescent boy (the beloved), an act now deemed repugnant and condemned by law.[24] Phaedrus praises the practice, seeing it as a path to "a comely life" of honor, a motivator of "noble deeds." In his view, love becomes a "guiding principle" and "a power," for it inspires both the lover and beloved to the greatest heights of accomplishment because each person seeks to avoid shame in the eyes of the other. The best and strongest city or army would be "composed of lovers and their favorites," because it would result in "a mutual rivalry for honour" (178 C–E and 179 A, pp. 101–3).

Next up, the lawyer Pausanias objects to this unrelieved praise of love, given that there are very different versions of love, one praiseworthy in his eyes but another undeserving of the eulogy Phaedrus has delivered (180 C, p. 107). There are two loves, one "Popular" and one "Heavenly." Since activities are not good in themselves, only according to how they are done, loving can be shameful or noble, depending on whether the intentions of the lover and beloved involve only lust or lifelong commitment. The doctor Erixymachus also draws a distinction between Heavenly and Popular love but argues that the difference is whether the particular love is good for your health or makes you ill (in body and spirit). The comic dramatist Aristophanes goes on to paint a visual portrait in an origin story in which humans used to consist of two beings joined together. Because they attempted to climb Mount Olympus, Zeus split them in half and consigned human beings to lives of longing for their other half. Each person engages in a prolonged search, sometimes lasting a lifetime. Some are lucky enough to find the self's other half, some are not (189 C–193 D, pp. 133–47).

Finally, in Socrates's speech, we encounter a vision of love that eclipses all of the others. While continually displaying humility and doubts about his own abilities, Socrates goes on with stunning eloquence to summon a timeless vision. In a fascinating twist, he declares that his version of love is not really his. Rather, he encountered a Mantinean woman named Diotima, who shared with him her intricate vision of love and life. He takes pains to note her extreme intelligence. At one point, he says she answered one of his questions "like our perfect professors" (208 C, p. 197).

In Socrates's account, his conversation with Diotima begins with much give and take, as they basically revisit and dismiss each of the previous speeches. Then she delivers a long speech of her own. Thus it turns out that Socrates's speech is actually a speech within a speech: Socrates's speech is really Diotima's. Using the same method of questioning used by Socrates (hence the Socratic method), Diotima first establishes, with his agreement, that men love the good and want it to be theirs forever (206 A, p. 189). She then ventures that the "method" and "behavior" of love is "begetting on a beautiful thing by means of both the body and the soul" (206 B, p. 191). When Socrates says he does not understand this, she embarks on a detailed explanation of how "all men are pregnant, Socrates, both in body and in soul: in reaching a certain age our nature yearns to beget" (206 C, p. 191). Pregnancy is the best way to understand it. Even so, it applies equally to men and women: "It is a begetting for both" (206 C, p. 191). This creation of new life requires beauty, because begetting can take place only in the beautiful. This is because "it is a divine affair" and only "the beautiful is accordant" with the divine (206 C, p. 191); "Thus beauty presides over birth" (206 C–D, p. 191). Diotima corrects Socrates's assertion that "love is of the beautiful." Instead, she says, "It is of engendering and begetting upon the beautiful" (206 E, p. 193).

Diotima goes on to spell out the source and ramifications of this vital and fateful distinction. "This engendering and bringing to birth" is, for a human being, "an immortal element in the creature that is mortal" (206 D, p. 191). The impetus for this creativity is our yearning for immortality, which in turn comes from love's desire to possess the good forever. Longevity comes to a being through "generation," the only way to "leave behind it a new creature in place of the old" (207 D, p. 195). Besides wanting to hold onto the good and to replace the old with the new, another motive for creating is that people seek "immortal distinction" (208 D–E, p. 199). Those who give birth physically produce children. But "engendering" takes place not in the body alone but also in the soul. In the case of the latter, this kind of creative person receives even more acclaim, as in the case of the great poets and inventors. Diotima goes on to describe just how this happens. Her description comes in the famous passage that envisions for us a "ladder of love." It begins when a person falls in love with a particular body and its beauty.[25] This makes one see the beauty in another body, then in all bodies, as one becomes "a lover of all beautiful bodies." From this revelation, one grasps the value of the beauty of souls as even higher than that of the body. As we ascend the ladder, the beauty of "our observances and our laws, all connected in kinship and fellowship," and "branches of knowledge" dawns on us (210 B, p. 203). Finally comes the view from the top.[26]

Right before getting there, Diotima says, a person who turns to "the main ocean of the beautiful may by contemplation of this bring forth in all their splendour many fair fruits of discourse and meditation in a plenteous crop of philosophy." Then, at the summit, one can find "a certain single knowledge connected with a beauty which has yet to be told" (210 D–E, p. 205). This opens up into a unique, eternal, and "wondrous vision" (210 D–E, p. 205), combining body, mind and soul in a grasp of the true essences of things beyond illusion and in a love for ideas, concepts, and philosophy itself. Love becomes one with beauty as external measures fall away and all that is left is the inner beauty of the soul. This is mortal humans' taste of the divine, eternal, "intelligible world," the one way we can participate in this realm. Although we continually fall back down the ladder, we are capable of climbing back up again.

The inability of words to capture the vision at the summit is made clear by the choice to use negatives to describe what it is not. More formalized notions of *apophatic* or *negative theology* in a range of religious movements and ensuing Neoplatonist thought suggested a way to express or describe what defies the human capacity to express or describe.[27] The great mystery is evoked here by *not* spelling out the specifics. But the idea is clear. We can grasp the one and only beauty of which all things beautiful partake.

To get the full effect, it is helpful to read it in the words of two different translations. At the top of the ladder, we have moved beyond attachment to a single body and instead find ourselves in the realm of the soul. Referring to the person ascending to the top, Diotima asks, "What if he could behold the divine beauty itself, in its unique form? Do you call it a pitiful life for a man to lead . . . ?" (211 E and 212 A, p. 207). A person witnessing this carries this vision with him or her always. It is the ability to go beyond illusion to truth. One "sees the beautiful through that which makes it visible to breed not illusions but true examples of virtue, since his contact is not with illusion but with truth" (212 A, p. 207). In the more recent translation by Alexander Nehamas and Paul Woodruff, the passage reads: "When he looks at Beauty in the only way that Beauty can be seen—only then will it become possible for him to give birth not to images of virtue (because he's in touch with no images), but to true virtue (because he is in touch with the true Beauty)."[28] This description rules out interpretation of a reductionist dichotomy between real and ideal. Instead of counterposing reality and the ideal, this passage emphasizes illusion versus truth. The illusion-reality poles are more suited to Gnostics' unveiling of all of our reality as illusion. In stark contrast, Plato clearly seeks the basis for looking beyond illusion to find what is true about our world.

SYMPOSIUM FOR CHRISTIANS

The reading of Plato that we find in the work of the early church father Origen (ca. 184–ca. 253) helps foreground the tight connection in Platonism between the spiritual and the bodily. In a direct reference to Plato's *Symposium*, Origen draws our attention to one of the central tensions readers encounter in his *Commentary on the Song of Songs*. Writing about Greek philosophers who have explored the nature of love, he refers to tracts, for instance, composed "in dialogue style" about "a banquet not of food but of words."[29] These philosophers say that love "is the power that leads the soul from earth to the lofty heights of heaven" (219). Origen acknowledges that readers of such works on love have misunderstood them to condone abandonment to "the sins of the flesh and the precipitous paths of lewdness." He concedes that readers of the Song of Songs are capable of using the text in parallel fashion as a springboard for dissipation. However, Origen's reasoning for why this response rests on a misguided interpretation on the part of some readers is unmistakable. Reading, as much as writing, consists, for Origen, in grasping the spirit of the text as much as the surface details, "lest we also should in any way offend against what was written well and spiritually" (219).

Many, if not most, modern scholars deduce that the distinction at the heart of Origen's normative stance—his judgment of what constitutes a good or bad reading of such texts or a good or bad behavioral response—is the familiar dualism that constitutes an undeniable part of the Western intellectual tradition. John Dawson points out, however, that such a view does not hold up to a careful reading of Origen. Focusing on Origen's use of allegory, Dawson shows that, rather than presenting the worlds of bodily and spiritual experience, expression, and longing as opposed, Origen sees these as intricately entwined. Body and soul, to Origen, are in close connection. Furthermore, the relation is not one-way but circular. It is not simply that the body is shed as the spirit is fulfilled but that each is necessary for the fulfillment of the other. Rather than merely a disease-prone appendage, though sometimes appearing as such in his pages, "Origen's category of body appears as a complex and rich psychosomatic medium of a person's divine transformation."[30]

We can glimpse the relation between the material and spiritual in several stirring passages in Origen, as in his discussion of the places in scripture where "the names of the members of the body are applied to the members of the soul" (221): physical sight is parallel to spiritual insight in Ecclesiastes ("The wise man has his eyes in his head," 2:14); ears can hear the divine; hands can write, moved by spirit; feet stumble or walk on the path of righteousness; the throat "is an open sepulcher (Ps. 5:9)." What is more, the pathway to God wends through the epiphany and intense suffering of love. To be lovestruck by the material world and by the divine is one and the same: "Therefore, if anyone has been able to hold in the breadth of his mind and to consider the glory and splendor of all those things created in Him, he will be struck by their very beauty and transfixed by the magnificence of their brilliance. . . . And he will receive from Him the saving wound and will burn with the blessed fire of His love" (223). These are the words of someone who, rather than rejecting the physical, sees the spiritual as something as real as that which we can apprehend through everyday use of our bodily senses. That those senses are our *only* conduit to the divine, along with the lived experience of suffering and decay—necessary for but also constitutive of spiritual transformation—is clear in Origen. The time-bound depths of human suffering are intrinsic to the experience of the heights of awe, love, and wholeness.

LOVE IN THE COSMOS

The first major Neoplatonist philosopher, Plotinus (AD 204/5–270), inspired by Plato's views on all matters, elaborated his own poetic philosophy with beauty at its center. (See fig. 5.2.) Plotinus disagrees with inherited Greek and Roman notions of beauty as having to do mainly with "being well-proportioned and measured."[31] According to this definition, only composite things can be beautiful, and only a whole can be. This is not logical for several reasons. First, if the whole is beautiful, then all of the parts must be. Second, some things are not composite or divisible. By that definition, the sun or the stars would be "excluded from beauty," and that is absurd; and anything else not beautiful because of symmetry, proportion, and measure would not qualify as beauty. Only things with parts and complexity will qualify for the traditional definition, while Plotinus sees beauty in simple elements as well: "And in sounds in the same way, the simple will be banished, though often in a composition which is beautiful as a whole each separate sound is beautiful" (1.6, p. 235). Third, the same thing can be beautiful at times yet not at other times. A face can be beautiful at one time and ugly at another, so it must be that beauty is not just appearance. And when it comes to beautiful propositions, the beauty cannot derive from proportion and symmetry, because if two propositions agree, they can still be ugly or bad. Virtue is beautiful but is not necessarily "well-proportioned" (1.6, p. 237). Beauty is something we recognize immediately, and so is ugliness.

In Plotinus's writings, love comes up in the third ennead in his discussions of the universe. In *Interstellar*, love is a dimension. As we have seen, the film depicts love in terms of time, place, and the universe. Plotinus's conception of love helps identify the problem with the prevailing notion of love today, which in certain ways celebrates love but in other ways diminishes it. The separation of love from vast and enduring questions ends up severely underappreciating its importance. Porphyry explains cryptically: "We placed the treatise *On Our Allotted Guardian Spirit* in the third ennead because the subject is treated in a general way and the question is one of those which people consider when dealing with the origins of man. The same applies to the treatise entitled *On Love*."[32] Plotinus's student Porphyry, also an important Neoplatonist philosopher, is responsible for the dominant organizational schema of Plotinus's oeuvre still used.[33] No matter what he would think of the arrangement of his works overall, Plotinus clearly saw love and the nature of universe as inseparable.

DESPERATELY SEEKING PLATO

Turning to our own times for signs of a New Platonism, we can find a range of critical works and scholarly studies, but works that advocate it outright are more scarce. As we saw earlier, the tone and tenets of a therapeutic sensibility are embedded in our culture, purveyed in everything from popular culture to self-help and our other institutions, so hegemonic as to be almost impossible to counter. Whether or not one accepts modern culture's characterization as a New Gnosticism, we might consider whether any of the old schools help suggest a way out of the hold that the therapeutic seems to have on our selves and, some say, our souls.

Because the explicitly political writings of Plato draw attacks for being elitist and antidemocratic, some well founded and others questionable, the Platonic tradition is often eclipsed when democratic theorists and practical philosophers recall other Greco-Roman philosophies and find them relevant to our own times. Yet places like *Interstellar*'s five-dimensional tesseract in space resonate with what we might call Plato's socio-aesthetic themes and melodies conducive to democracy.

In our own day, there is renewed interest in Plato, though in some cases it really turns out to be interest in his teacher, Socrates, who has perennially enthralled observers. Rebecca Goldstein, author of *Plato at the Googleplex*, self-consciously takes on the persona of Plato. Literally, in her own words, she "impersonates him."[34] This is apparent in an interview she did with Nick Romeo for the *Atlantic*. Romeo asked Goldstein, who says she speaks on Twitter as Plato, what Plato would think of TV, movies, celebrity culture, today's Olympics, and contemporary novels. The way she decides whether Plato would approve or disapprove stems from a particular interpretation of Plato. For instance, when asked what movies he might like, she includes *Eternal Sunshine of the Spotless Mind* because of its shift in the position or perspective of the narrator, as occurs in Plato's *Phaedrus*. Although *The Matrix* and *The Truman Show* bring to mind Plato's cave allegory, she says that he would not approve of those movies because "they're playing with cool ideas rather than sending us into a tailspin of questioning our assumptions about the way we're living our lives."[35]

Goldstein says Plato would consider something "meaningful entertainment" if it spurred "good philosophical discussion." When Romeo asks her what Plato would think if his dialogues were put into movie form, she says, "That would be terrific. As long as there's interesting dialogue going on, and not just an on-slaught of images." When Romeo asks whether that means Plato would reject movies based on only "special effects and spectacle," she answers, "Right." Plato would approve of "movies with dialogue that would awaken in us a kind of inner drama that makes us ask important questions, like 'What are we doing with our lives?' He would like that."[36] If anything, her depiction better fits Socrates, with her stress on asking questions.

Goldstein seems to overlook the content of Plato's view. Her time-traveling Plato could be any philosopher and resembles today's philosophy professor more than the Plato of the dialogues. In his chosen literary form, however, he presented distinct views, as he raised particular questions and explored all of the possible an-swers; he was not just asking questions for the sake of asking ques-tions. Aware of the full array of professions and practices, he envis-aged them as embodying philosophical principles, such as aiming at excellence and virtue. The closest Goldstein comes to a view on content is when she stereotypes his views on music as rooted in fearing the elevation of emotion over reason, "like a crotchety old man talking about the kind of music kids like today."[37] Goldstein thinks that Plato would have approved of social media and the internet in their early days as one big conversation, before they devolved into silos of the like-minded. She reads the cave allegory as a basis for why a Plato transplanted to our own day would re-spond with suspicion to TV, for making people passive, since for her Plato stands for actively talking and questioning. She seems to take observations in the dialogues at face value as his views, pure and simple, finding solace only in the way he "changed his mind constantly." Reading the dialogues as if each time someone speaks in the dialogues it is Plato, then the next speech is him changing his mind, is a common misreading of the genre.

There is a fine yet crucial distinction to be made here about the blended philosophical/literary enterprise. Goldstein operates under the assumption that novels are a way of "producing philosophy as an artistic form," and movies and other genres just another way of "doing" philosophy. The tendency to see philosophy as a technique or process surfaces in other attempts to make philosophy relevant or applied, presenting a chronic challenge for the search for a usable philosophy. In an article about Iris Murdoch, who engaged deeply with Platonic ideas, humanities scholar Alan Jacobs explores this tension between philosophy and literature. Murdoch produced scores of novels and three volumes of philosophical essays. She found the nineteenth-century novel generally more conducive to philosophical inquiry than twentieth-century novels about philosophical ideas or journalistic novels of social commentary. Murdoch thought there was a "poverty of concepts" plaguing modern philosophy and also a loss of "persons" in modern novels.[38]

Pushing back against any notion of philosophy as technique, Plato stands out for prizing content as well as form. More than mere philosophical discussion, Plato's dialogues take the reader somewhere new. The dialogue form existed, not for its own sake, but to get at certain ideas and values. In Diotima's speech—and other such high points, including the cave allegory—the attainment of philosophical truth is creative, generative, and sublime. It cannot be dismissed in modern notions of disembodied intellect, technique, rationality, or a form of reason separated from emotion. Instead, it is our taste of immortality, the closest we mere mortals ever come. The vision at the top is one of unparalleled inspiration, with love, beauty, and wisdom all coming to mean something other than their customary meanings. It is a linking of the bodily or physical with the ultimate intellectual and spiritual experience of the cosmos and everything in it in a glorious oneness. It centers upon virtue. Plato's personae believed in such a thing as the good, and Plato's work is an unmitigated and elaborate defense of the existence of the good and its relevance, appropriateness, and necessity in individual and common life. The dialogues ask, above all, What is the good? We get sidetracked by the formula "Knowledge is virtue," but the point is that the knowledge is of the good.

A view that emphasizes Socratic questioning in itself ignores the time and space needed for the practice of contemplation. The need for contemplation lies at the heart of Plato's message, the dialogue form, and Socratic teaching. Socrates is frequently waylaid purely by his own thoughts. In the *Symposium*, he is an invited guest who in turn invites Aristodemus, but Aristodemus must forge ahead and arrive at the party alone because Socrates has stopped for contemplation. Agathon relieves him of his embarrassment right away by saying he meant to invite Aristodemus, but it *is* embarrassing. Later, Alcibiades refers to a time when Socrates stopped to think and continued all day and night. At the end of the *Symposium*, Alcibiades is upset that he cannot get Socrates to make love with him. To end the dialogue by suggesting Socrates did not give in to bodily passions underscores Diotima's vision of the spiritual nature of wisdom. Some of the asides also suggest that the sublime involves something beyond physical union. Plato's treatment takes into account suffering, given the depth of emotion people can experience. Rather than presenting a pure coping strategy, it argues for the desirability of a higher ideal—the ultimate consolation—which is a stronger elixir than the fleeting rewards of pleasure and vanity. It is a vision of unparalleled beauty that takes us into a realm of truth as opposed to illusion.

This point about truth versus illusion is lost on modern critics who see the idea of universal truth as anathema—as a reason to dismiss Plato altogether. But in a world beholden to image, the idea that truth *does* exist, and can even be glimpsed by us, is a valuable countertradition. It rests on the distinction between truth and illusion, not truth and experience. This is the source of a hope that there *is* meaning, unity, and good. This is a path, perhaps the sole path, beyond the relativism—our modern sophistry—of philosophical discussion in which all sides are of equal standing, and beyond emotivism and its leveling of all judgments into matters of personal preference. In Plato's works, we encounter the basis for the idea that value judgments are possible. The dialogues wed poetry and philosophy in defense of the very existence of *value*. The loss of this conviction would dismay Plato. He would have us search in our practices for rays of light, for ways of reaching to the truth of ideals, our capacity for judgment, and the value of value. That is the vision that has inspired so many since who have been moved by Plato and have felt their experience on earth transformed. The lives saved from the abyss of hopelessness by the idea that the good not only exists but can be intuited by a person—as in the excellent, virtuous, beautiful—would be impossible to count.

What is timeless about beauty, and love, is the goodness of the real thing. What is truly good stands opposed to the false or illusory. Contrary to Goldstein, who opines that Plato would understand the pursuit of fame, Plato's work offers a basis for a wholesale *condemnation* of the celebrity culture—of a focus on image and externals over inner beauty and earnestness. It is crucial to remember he was writing against the Sophists.

THE WORLD ACCORDING TO PLOTINUS

As one of the most important interpreters of Plato, Plotinus helps point to crucial aspects of Platonism. We can locate signs of a New Platonism in the renewed attention to Plotinus's ideas. The revisionist scholarship helps highlight aspects of his thought that can allow us to mount a resistance to the problems of modern Gnosticism and Cynicism that we have been exploring. Unlike those postmodernist theorists such as Jean-François Lyotard who, whether triumphantly or critically, emphasize splintering of the self or dissemblance, admittedly privileging the parts over the whole, Plotinus holds unity in the highest regard. Everything in existence is at its best when in harmonious connection to the great whole of which it is a part. The partial for him is always less than the complete, as he points out in the *Enneads*: "Let us state that there are some things which are primarily divisible and by their very nature liable to dispersion: these are the things no part of which is the same as either another part or the whole, and the part of which must necessarily be less than the all and whole. . . . But there is another kind of being, opposed to this one, which in no way admits division, is without parts and cannot be divided into parts" (4.1.1, p. 9). Unity is the ultimate, the sine qua non of truth, beauty, goodness, and all being and nonbeing; for Plotinus, God is "the One." The One is what inspires—literally what breathes life into—all of the created world, whether objects or living things. This univalent divinity is not itself created but rather exists for all eternity: infinite, causal, elemental. It was there before us, will remain after us, and, in fact, is us—if we are fully alive, that is. Although the One lies beyond the grasp of sense perception, it is all that is truly real.

So much of Plotinus's thought would no doubt strike today's readers as hopelessly idealistic and overly mystical. To turn what is truism today—that what is most real are those things that are most tangible, physical, and accessible to the five senses—and argue, as Plotinus does, that it is rather in the inner life that reality lies would likely draw ridicule and hasty dismissal in many circles or just strike listeners as strange. But Plotinus presents this argument with great care and gravitas.

This school of thought offers something vital to our current void. It is a much-needed alternative to atomistic individualism and the proliferation and leveling of views to such a degree that any common ground or shared vision threatens to slip away. This work seeks to bring Plotinus's voice more fully into a rich and exciting conversation currently taking place among scholars across several subfields and disciplines as well as the wider public today. This conversation is timeless in that it revolves around enduring questions about the experience of being human, but at the same time is extremely urgent and time-sensitive. At its heart is the question of why today, even in parts of the world supposedly most blessed by the fruits of human progress, profit, and innovation, there seems to be so much wrong at the levels of the individual and the community.

In the context of communitarian critiques of the centrifugal tendencies of modern life, Plotinus's systematic argumentation can help us explore underlying suppositions and propose alternatives to embedded predispositions, with his vision of human interiority and its implications for the quality of human life. Taken together, his observations present a strong counterargument to much of what comes down to us as inherited wisdom, forcing us to re-examine our assumptions at the most fundamental level. Not only does Plotinus deem unity sacred and the sacred a unity, but he also reasons, in engaging philosophical treatises that constitute a genre unto themselves, his *Enneads*, that humans have access to this sacred reality: not via any external pathway, but through a kind of secret doorway within. By means of our inner life, we can reach a state of unity that weds entities usually held to be irreconcilably opposed: affect and intellect, subject and object, body and spirit.

Plotinus's poetic reconciliation of immanent and transcendent realms belies much of today's presumptive common knowledge about Platonism. It points to sources of coherence and coalescence that Philip Rieff, Alasdair MacIntyre, and others find alarmingly lacking, presenting a vision of ecstasy that is not only compatible with thought but inextricably intertwined with it. Despite the centuries of social, political, and cultural change that intervene, Plotinus's words seem almost crafted with us in mind. Revisionist currents in Plotinian scholarship, not ordinarily brought into assessments of the condition of our own society and culture, help highlight aspects of his thought that are relevant to our contemporary quandaries.

"THE BODY'S RAGING SEA"

Plotinus and other early thinkers powerfully influenced by Plato have often been assumed to adhere to a radical dualism that pits body and mind against one another as enemies beyond reconciliation in this world. In studies of ideas and practices concerning the body in late antiquity, a number of recent scholars have pointed to the fallacy of such assumptions, foregrounding the ambivalence about embodiment. While not all would deliberately adopt the mantle of Platonist, added together their various defenses contribute to the observable reenvisioning that constitutes a New Platonism.

Plotinus no doubt saw bodies as a fundamental problem for their possessors. His famous ennead "On the Three Primary Hypostases," meaning foundations or essences, leads off with the question of what has made humankind forget its ties to the divine, answering: "The beginning of evil for them was audacity and coming to birth and the first otherness and the wishing to belong to themselves." Passage after passage describes the temptations, distractions, and corruptions arrayed from the start, in the natural order of things, against all attempts to lead a virtuous or holy life. His works are veritable studies in the catalog of emotions we would now dub, with unintentional understatement, negative: jealousy, deceit, guilt, rage, lust, greed, hate, despair. Attachments to the external world trigger these ignoble responses, which then dominate daily experience in the form of "the body's raging sea" (5.1.2, p. 15).

Writing on providence, for instance, Plotinus presents his attempt to grapple with the perennial question of why evil exists if there is a good creator of all (the enduring theological question of theodicy). His sustained rumination on the taking of human life indicates a clear tendency to see humanity as divided into good and bad. "Then, too, a wicked ruler might do the most lawless things; and the bad get the upper hand in wars, and what crimes they commit when they have taken prisoners!" Plotinus exclaims. "All these things cause perplexity about how they can happen if there is a providence." Though his answer has many complexities, it hinges on the fact that we are "mixed" beings—part matter and part spirit—so that we can never achieve the purity or wholeness of pure spirit: "First, then, we must understand that those who are looking for excellence in what is mixed must not demand all that excellence has in the unmixed, nor look for things of the first order among those of the second" (3.2.6–7, pp. 63–65).

The material portion of human beings threatens perpetually to draw them into the shady "substratum." As religious studies scholar Patricia Cox Miller writes, Plotinus calls attention to "misdirected sight, that is, a form of attention that fixates and fragments the soul"—as it does in the Narcissus myth—"into a congeries of its own grasping desires." Allowing that "Plotinus often linked this kind of woeful particularity to human physicality," she points to his view that "the body hinders thought and fills the soul with negative emotions."[39]

In tandem with other revisionist scholars such as Sara Rappe, Miller offers a compelling interpretation of Plotinus's distaste for the material as only one side of the story. While his adherence to the Platonic dichotomy between the sensible and the intelligible realms "seems undeniably dualistic," she clarifies, his concern with the fragmentation attendant upon too much attention to the pull of the material does not hold up to characterization as "a spiritual flight from the merely physical."[40]

Pierre Hadot baldly challenges the portrait painted by Porphyry in claims such as "Plotinus resembled someone ashamed of being in a body."[41] Not only was Plotinus merely reflecting a tradition still dominant in his time that blamed the body as a "tomb and a prison," but he had far too subtle and even mystical ideas to be taken as a cold rationalist with no sympathy for human feeling. Like Miller, Hadot sees that "it is not out of hatred and disgust for the body that we must detach ourselves from sensible things." The physical is not inherently evil, but it becomes so when it cuts a human being off from access to the divine. An inheritor of the Platonic intellectual tradition, Plotinus sees humans as between the material and the spiritual, prone to degradation yet remarkably endowed with a soul, which, "passing beyond all this, can fix herself in the Principle of all things."[42]

Hadot joins Miller and Rappe in qualifying Plotinus's dualism, emphasizing, like them, that, while it has been a fixation of many interpreters hence, Plotinus's original concern lay elsewhere. Plotinus abhorred the wasted potential of genuine beauty in the stunting of selfhood—the fragmentation of the person into jarring spangles rather than coalescence into a pure and solid gold, a metaphor he uses frequently. Failure to experience union was, in all seriousness, a fate worse than death. In the best of conditions, our lot is replete with unfulfilled longing, painful loss, and dogged meaninglessness. With no hope for transcendence, there is no sense, no answer to the question of evil. Our lot becomes a living death. Plotinus describes the path to union as a coming to life, an awakening to joy and meaning, a reconciliation between disparate parts of experience. In particular, he focuses our attention on the connection and compatibility between emotion and intellect.

Plotinus is concerned with no less momentous a task than soul-making. One scholar called his treatises "spiritual exercises in which the soul sculpts herself," calling attention to one passage in the *Enneads* (5.3.17, p. 133) that likens this act of creation to child-birth.[43] This has echoes of Diotima. What is the soul? At the most hopeful points in Plotinus, Miller shows us, it is the realized self, a self fulfilled—neither antecedent nor subsequent to physical reality—in which material and spiritual are reconciled. Thinking becomes being. Plotinus, she writes, "believed that the soul was a principle of self-cohesion anchored in a stabilizing, transcendent reality."[44] Richard Wallis emphasizes that this creation is very much an experience in the *Enneads*, a transition from the realm of discursive thought, which involves "both reasoning from premises to conclusion and simple transition from one object of thought to another," to a wondrous realm in which transcendent meaning comes to the fortunate beholder no longer in parts but as a totality, enshrouded in "radiant luminosity." Further, the observer no longer observes: "No longer is there a spectator outside gazing on an outside spectacle."[45] The illumination is not outside, beyond, or separate from us; rather, it is from within, and it is indeed purely within that we experience this vision.

Plotinus describes this experience, phenomenon, or process—it is difficult to find the right words for it (see chapters 3 and 4 for my reservations about calling it "experience")—at key places in the *Enneads* as an overcoming of the separation between subject and object, showing that what he has in mind is a form of consciousness uniting the everyday and the divine, the material and the intellectual and the spiritual. When one experiences the world in this way, one moves beyond surfaces to inner depths that are then illumined. "All is colour and beauty to its innermost part," observes Plotinus: "There is no longer one thing outside and another outside which is looking at it, but the keen sighted has what is seen within. . . . One looks from outside at everything one looks at as a spectacle. But one must transport what one sees into oneself, and look at it as one and look at it as oneself" (5.8.10, p. 273).

Plotinus describes a way of seeing oneself and other objects of knowledge as other than objects—a way of "belonging to ourselves" (5.8.13, p. 281). This is how suffering and alienation, our "walking on alien ground" (5.3.8, p. 99), are overcome, as beauty is discovered within and deemed worthy of awe and love.[46] Only through this is anything else understood or loved, and through this encounter emotion and intellect become part of the same mode of apprehending both the universe within and the universe without. It is a mode of existence that allows us to transcend the disruption of separation: of material and spiritual; of bodily and intellectual; of subject and object; of part and whole; of internal and external; and of all of the other severances that cause such pain, isolation, agony, self-loathing, lack of understanding, agitation, irresolution, disappointment, and disorientation—the "birth pangs," perhaps, of the soul.

Running through the writings of Plotinus is a deep preoccupation with the split between subject and object that is at the heart of nearly all of human thought and activity. Language itself inscribes this division. The sentence's two parts, subject and predicate, seem to represent a propensity for dualism at the root of the Western intellectual tradition—and even life practices—that is almost inexorable. The intellectual and the affective, mind and body, are usually considered separate faculties. Much follows from this, including our understanding of the intellect, heart, and soul.

Plotinus shows that this separation, far from being inevitable, is not actually the way things are. The divisions of self and other, internal and external, observer and observed, are aspects of the material and everyday intellectual realms. His point is that these realms are not the beginning and end of reality. Rather, referring to Plato's forms, he says that they only bear "traces" of another realm in which the gap between parts vanishes. Truth can only be glimpsed as a unity, but even further than that, the faculty that glimpses and that which is glimpsed become a unity. Even the word *becomes* does not quite capture Plotinus's point, for he describes a state of understanding in which the seer and seen *are* one: "illumination gives the soul a clearer life, but a life which is not generative; on the contrary it turns the soul back upon itself and does not allow it to disperse, but makes it satisfied with the glory in itself . . . at once illuminating and illuminated, the truly intelligible, both thinker and thought, seen by itself" (5.3.8, p. 99).

Michael Sells posits that Plotinus evokes "a kind of apophatic pact between the text and the reader" according to which the reader sets aside propositions "with the expectation that their meaningfulness will be retrieved in a nonreferential or transreferential mode of discourse." Critique of ordinary language constructions is both form and content of Plotinus's work, as "discursive reason [to Plotinus] reflects alienated consciousness." Only *nous* (usually translated as spirit or mind) allows the individual to transcend the "dualisms of subject-object, cause-effect, origin-goal."[47] Sells shows that inactivity is necessary for this sort of nondualistic contemplation, which fits the emphasis in Plotinus on quietude and passivity versus action and movement.

Sara Rappe also sees the theme of subject-object division as having a vital importance for Plotinus that crosses over linguistic presentation into the content of his metaphysical views: "Plotinus thinks that language fails as a vehicle for conveying metaphysical truth since words necessarily refer to entities standing outside of the linguistic system, whereas truth is both self-certifying and self-revealing." Rappe dwells fruitfully on observation and the crucial metaphor of light and illumination and transparency, centering on the difference in Plotinus between "looking outside and seeing inside."[48]

Pierre Hadot takes us even further, beyond the metaphor of sight. In an intriguing interpretation, he perceives in Plotinus's phrasing what we might see as an inextricable term, neither love, nor an apprehension of truth, nor ecstasy, but a blend of these. "Plotinian love," he writes, "waits for ecstasy, ceasing all activity, establishing the soul's faculties in complete report, and forgetting everything, so as to be completely ready for the divine invasion."[49]

The idea of waiting runs against the grain of much of the way everyday life is now structured. But the need for preparation is a practice that requires a plentitude of focus to keep us busy, even if it is a practice based on not being too busy to fail to recognize this "invasion."

STOIC IMPRACTICALITY

Let us now return, *pace* Philip Rieff, to a basic paradox of modern life: the more American culture has become fixated on individual therapy as the primary concern, the less relief seems attainable even from the stresses and strains we can expect to encounter on an everyday basis, let alone life-altering trauma and crisis or political breakdown. Coping is all that can be imagined. Once the therapeutic culture has no outside referent, it seems it cannot deliver on its own promise. With all of its bluster, and its displacement of all other ways of thinking about being in the world, it turns out it is not even therapeutic. Further, the individual loses the central inner resource necessary for self-respect and self-development: the ability to recognize the good. By abandoning the notion of relations free of manipulative pressures, people lose the basis for grasping beauty as goodness, for trust, and for love. What does that leave? Through a brief sketch of a contrasting way to approach some of the issues raised by the thought of Plotinus, the current work hopes to suggest what a new Platonism might offer those sensitive to, even suffering from, the fractured therapeutic lens as a worldview.

A reinvigorated search for a practical philosophy manifests itself today in a number of places, such as Jules Evans's *Philosophy as a Way of Life and Other Dangerous Situations: Ancient Philosophy for Modern Problems*. As we saw in chapter 2, much of this new interest has so far centered on Stoicism. Richard Sorabji, one of the academic scholars whose new Stoicism was profiled there, noted the relation between cognitive behavioral psychology and Stoicism.

Far from attempting to popularize such prescriptions in any kind of simplistic fashion, Richard Sorabji draws vital distinctions among particular philosophers and philosophical traditions, articulates the nuances of their arguments, puts them in historical context, and splits hairs about what he sees as valuable and what he does not. As we noted in chapter 2, he differentiates the Aristotelian "tradition of moderation" of emotion or *metriopatheia* from the Stoic "tradition of eradication." While advocating Stoicism, at one point he openly states reservations about the Stoic doctrine of *apatheia*—"the eradication of emotion":

> I am against the Stoic thesis of indifference, and I find this an unattractive side of their philosophy. It is better to treat the welfare of our loved ones as something very much more than rightly preferred, even though the Stoics are right that this means incurring the risk of loss and desolation. . . . None the less [*sic*], as already remarked, we can learn from the Stoics in treating unwanted emotions, without agreeing that none should be wanted. Not only are emotions quite often unwelcome: they are also quite often counter-productive. Anger or anxiety may be what is preventing us from getting what we want.[50]

In Sorabji's hands, Plotinus's view of emotion combines moderation and eradication, placing them at different "stages of progress" of the self from "ordinary civic virtue" to "purified virtue." He argues that the Neoplatonists went on to "exploit" Stoic ideas, such as the notion of involuntary "bodily shocks," in order to suggest how emotional experience can indeed occur, even while the soul achieves *apatheia*. Emotional experience can occur through pains and "bites," for instance, in the form of "sensations of movement in the chest." Plotinus, writes Sorabji, concedes that the body alone may "receive shocks" and suggests that the soul's triumph over unwilled sensations can have the effect of mitigating or even eliminating "pain, fear, or anger." These shocks, writes Plotinus himself, "will be few and promptly dissolved by the soul's proximity." Similar shocks do occur during spiritual experiences, as in the profoundly moving mystical apprehension of beauty, but these bring a "blow without harm," a notion with echoes in St. Augustine's evocation of "the light of God's wisdom striking him."[51]

While adopting the notion of "shocks," Plotinus found much with which to disagree in Stoicism. Some of these disagreements are helpfully discussed in the early twentieth-century writings of William Ralph Inge, Anglican priest and professor of divinity at Cambridge University, as well as dean of St. Paul's Cathedral. In one of his many studies, precisely by elaborating Plotinus's points of difference with the Stoics, Inge addresses the delicate relation in the *Enneads* between unlike realms of experience, illustrating the manner in which Plotinus's thinking on the physical and the spiritual resists simplification into dualism.

Inge writes that Plotinus inverts the Stoic hierarchy of reality and unreality, objecting that in its focused attention on physical or material being, "Stoic doctrine gives the first place to that which is only potential, whereas the possibility of passing into activity and actuality is the only thing that makes Matter respectable." Given the sacred hierarchy, matter cannot be "anterior to Soul" and thus cannot be "the first principle"; it must be acted upon to be brought fully into existence. Inge writes that, from a Plotinian perspective, "while professing to be materialists," the Stoics "slide into pantheism." This slippage comes from their view of matter as "the only evidence of real existence," capable of "inner development, without being acted upon by anything from outside." Hence their materialism. However, for Plotinus, Stoicism's concept of matter leads them astray. For him, matter is something quite different. In essence, matter is not so much physical reality but "all things," which are contingent upon being infused with energy, made into something, existing only by virtue of inspiration from the higher reality of intellection.[52]

Inge clarifies that modern notions of matter work for the Stoics but are insufficient for understanding what Plotinus had in mind. Our scientific view, as he puts it lyrically, regards matter as "the texture out of which objects perceived by the senses are woven, the substance which physicists classify as consisting of this or that 'element.'" Modern physics, in Inge's view, keeping in mind that he was writing over a century ago, casts the constituent components of matter as increasingly miniscule, divided into "atoms, corpuscles, and electrons, until they are on the point of vanishing altogether except as subjects for electrical energy." This is like the general ancient notion of matter, Inge contends, which is not, however, that of Plotinus, for the latter's beliefs are not consistent with his other ideas: energy cannot move mere energy, as opposed to something. Instead, matter is "infinite in the sense of indeterminate"; in itself it is not nothing, but rather "no thing," which is not the same. It is "potentiality without any potency." As Inge explains, "Its nature is to be the recipient of forms." Matter exists in relation to a principle above it that gives it "form, meaning, and definite existence." While Inge concedes that there are many complexities and nuances to the notion of matter in Plotinus, and that indeed some passages do cast matter in a negative light, he asserts that it is of crucial importance that we see, in the *Enneads*, that matter is not always negative but primarily, or only, when lacking form.[53]

To return to our own day, it might seem that the proper response to the excesses of the therapeutic sensibility is a kind of Neo-Stoic resurgence. Critics like sociologist Digby Anderson argue just that. In an engaging discussion of the "the therapeutic cult" at the root of contemporary culture and behavior, he identifies several social developments as culprits, including the mushrooming of sentimentalism in all realms. A key example for him appears in medical practice, where even patients diagnosed with a fatal disease commonly deny this fact. This amounts to an act of "willful self-deception," to Anderson's mind, which he distinguishes from courage. "The result of denial," he writes, "has been a sentimental culture in which it is asserted that every health problem must have a cure if only we fight hard enough or spend lavishly enough." What is more, this denial quickly becomes, of necessity, collective, embedding us in "a histrionic world of pretense." Yet what Anderson prescribes has the greatest relevance here: "Sentimentality ousts a stoicism necessary where disease is concerned. By contrast, stoicism is a neglected virtue. People used to have an unfussy attitude toward their health, but the media culture has encouraged self-pampering until this has become endemic." He attacks not only the therapeutic culture but additionally the practices of psychotherapy and counseling, seemingly wholesale.

Within these "phony" occupations, "confessional" approaches simply constitute "an excuse for indulgent personal reverie." Anderson continues: "Professional help is a sentimental concept: it is a private shirking of responsibility combined with a public display of cheap compassion." The antidote to all this sentimentality is "realism."[54]

This tendency—to blame the therapeutic sensibility on an excess of emotion—has shades of the Stoic "eradication" of emotion. And we hardly need to remind ourselves that emotion has been exploited for the purposes of profit making. Anderson draws an unflattering portrait: "A preoccupation with myself, a wish, even a need to talk about myself and my problems, a predisposition to think such problems happen to me and an aversion to assume responsibility for them, perhaps a view of myself as a victim with rights denied, and a belief that talking is the first stage to curing the problems together with a government and a range of policies which endorse such tendencies: this sort of culture is what might be termed therapeutic."[55]

It is difficult to argue against the idea that a healthy dose of Stoicism is in order. However, Plotinus's view of the limits of the Stoic view should give us pause. The problem with the modern therapeutic is neither too much emotion, with too strong a pull of the material realm, nor too little reason, with too weak a pull of the mental realm, but precisely the dualistic presuppositions that divide them. While the Stoics promote individual flourishing of all kinds—physical, mental, spiritual—their fundamental emphasis is on how to live, while Plotinus calls forth a vivid vision of not only how but *why* we should.

Epictetus's recommendations involve the rejection, or we might say, in Anderson's word, denial of inconvenient, distracting, and counterproductive feelings. In their heartfelt generosity, the Stoics hope that we will not have to suffer from risky, hurtful experience. Plotinus, on the contrary, takes intense suffering as a given, as the entire basis for our participation in the divine through our spiritual intuition cultivated in contemplation. Further, he describes the suffering as intently as he does the elation that ensues upon overcoming it. The transcendent is for him the reward of the sufferer.

This calls to mind Rieff's explanation of the way in which what we sacrifice in terms of our short-term gratification in order to partake in community and culture is "given back bettered."[56] We move ourselves beyond emotion pure and simple not for the purpose of protecting our limited and fragile bodily selves but rather to allow us to sustain cataclysms of insight equal to those that bring us to the depths of physical pain but of a completely different kind. These cataclysms fill us with splendor and beauty. They deliver the euphoria of communion, unity in multiplicity, the divine "blow without harm." This is precisely what the modern therapeutic culture cannot deliver. Its fault is not that it tries—to console, to comfort, to ease our suffering—but that it fails.

PLATONIC PRACTICALITY

Plotinus also differentiated his thinking from Gnosticism with points of criticism that allow us to begin to sense a new Neoplatonist alternative to the therapeutic, sharpened by our previous discussion of the limits of the New Stoicism. How to live is inextricably connected to the question of how we worship—what and when and how and why we worship. One place we can best see what is at stake is in the encounter between Platonism and Gnosticism. It is easy to confuse or conflate them. There are overlapping elements between Christianity and Gnosticism, as there are between both of them and other religions. But there are essential differences. Plotinus's criticism of the Gnostics blended concerns about both form and content, associating their way of conveying ideas with the ideas themselves. On the ideas side, he refuted the Gnostics' description of the composition of the self, the divine, and the nature of consciousness, based on the doctrine of the One—an indivisible, ultimate, and infinite "principle of the good." And just as the divine could not be split, it made no sense to Plotinus to conceptualize the Intellect as multiple. Imagining a kind of infinity mirror of self-consciousness, he suggests that this shows that the notion of one thinking of oneself thinking in no way implies more than one entity: "If one even introduced another, third, distinction in addition to the second one which said that it thinks that it thinks, one which says that it thinks that it thinks that it thinks, the absurdity would become even clearer. And why should one not go on introducing distinctions in this way to infinity?" (2.9.1, pp. 54–59).

Everything else in Gnostic thought presupposes this division of entities, with one divine force all good and another responsible for a world full of disorder and evil. Gnostics "disapproved of this universe," believing it was created "as the result of moral failure." While this might sound like the same distinction between the realms of the ideal and the real, Plotinus emphasizes that it could not be more different. Those who criticize the world in this fashion exhibit an idealism gone awry or a misplaced idealism; they have too high a standard, forgetting that the world is not the same as the intelligible world but "an image of it" (2.9.4, p. 25). Thinking about it "too highly" makes them see the real world as greatly flawed. A different presupposition—the oneness of the divine or a sense of sacred unity—shows the universe to be a good and beautiful place.

As much as the Gnostics' metaphysical beliefs, Plotinus faults their sensibility and their manner of expressing their views. He finds their jargon pretentious, aimed at attaining the status of a school. He objects to their tendency to ridicule Greek philosophers in order to prove them wrong, even while drawing on their ideas. Gnostics chase fame. In place of calm and dignified argumentation, they put forth "arbitrary, arrogant assertions" and use "magic chants" to dazzle their converts with special powers, with no actual evidence of curing disease. It is a show anyone could pull off.

Connecting their ideas and their disposition, both the content and form of their movement, Plotinus singles out the significance of their arrogance. In their dim view of the universe, they believe they alone have understood "the intelligible nature but he [Plato] and the other philosophers had not" (2.9.6, p. 245). They claim that they alone possess "special secret knowledge" with the "power to save" (2.9.15, p. 283n2). To place oneself above Intellect is, to Plotinus, to reveal that one is not exhibiting the genuine article, for its vital prerequisite is not to put oneself above other men and gods (2.9.9, p. 261). Humility is the necessary precondition of genuine insight.

Some of Plotinus's most striking observations come, as with his other *Enneads*, in the form of a paean to the created world itself. The Gnostics "disapprove of the universe," fault the "director of this universe" (2.9.6, p. 247), "blame the soul for its association with the body," and persuade converts "to despise the universe and the beings in it" (2.9.15, p. 283). They claim to have special access to the divine. To Plotinus, it does not make sense that someone who has supposedly seen the higher world would not find the universe beautiful (2.9.16, p. 289). In criticizing the Gnostics for failing to see the world as it is, Plotinus delivers a rhapsody on the wonder and glory of the universe worth quoting here at some length. He refers to the Platonic notion of the intelligible world, a nonmaterial world of ideal forms of the real versions we encounter in our daily lives. While critics have used Plato's forms to dismiss Platonism as antimaterial, Plotinus gives us a vivid vision to counteract such an interpretation of the intelligible world:

> It is not the part of an intelligent man even to enquire about this but of someone who is blind, utterly without perception or intelligence, and far from seeing the intelligible universe, since he does not even see this one here. For how could there be a musician who sees the melody in the intelligible world and will not be stirred when he hears the melody in sensible sounds? Or how could there be anyone skilled in geometry and numbers who will not be pleased when he sees right relation, proportion and order with his eyes? For, indeed, even in pictures those who look at the worlds of art with their eyes do not see the same things in the same way, but when they recognize an imitation on the level of sense of someone who has a place in their thought they feel a kind of disturbance and come to a recollection of the truth; this is the experience from which passionate loves arise. But if someone who sees beauty excellently represented in a face is carried to that higher world, will anyone be so sluggish in mind and so immovable that, when he sees all the beauties in

the world of sense, all its good proportion and the nightly ex-cellence of its order, and the splendor of form which is mani-fested in the stars, for all their remoteness, he will not thereupon think, seized with reverence, "What wonders, and from what a source?" If he did not, he would neither have understood this world here nor seen that higher world. (2.9.16, pp. 289–91)

It would be impossible to read this praise of the real and ideal worlds and their intrinsic relation as antimaterial or dualist. It is a declaration of love for the real as having shades of not only the ideal but the divine. Further, the worldview of the Gnostics, through the eyes of Plotinus, has no place for virtue. They do not write about it—another thing distancing them from ancient Greek philosophers. If you say you follow God but give no sense of how to live, which is what virtue gives us—ways to live—you end up espousing belief in God without embodying what that means: "God, if you talk about him without true virtue, is only a name" (2.9.15, p. 285). "Despising the universe and the gods" is not the way of "becoming good" (2.9.16, p. 285). A view that despises the created world and lacks a sense of what the divine means for liv-ing every day can lead to one of only two extremes: pleasure or re-nunciation. Accordingly, some Gnostics are extreme in their as-ceticism, and others, espousing the ideas of Epicurus, take them to their extreme and abolish and make fun of self-control (2.9.15, p. 283). Plotinus demurs. "Surely, what other fairer image of the intelligible world could there be? For what other fire could be a better image of the intelligible fire than the fire here? Or what other earth could be better than this, after the intelligible earth? And what sphere could be more exact or more dignified or better ordered in its circuit [than the sphere of this universe] after the self-enclosed circle there of the intelligible universe? And what other sun could there be which ranked after the intelligible sun and before the visible sun here?" (2.9.4, p. 239).

It takes arrogance and impiety to dismiss all of the beauty and order of the universe. The foundation of virtue is insight into the good. Only someone who is without that faculty could fail to be "seized with reverence" (2.9.16, p. 291).

In his *Confessions*, Saint Augustine of Hippo (AD 354–430) employs spatial metaphors to articulate a distinction that is at once delicate and subtle and a critical foundation stone of his materialist spiritualism. (See fig. 5.3.) Without the metaphor of physical location and the closely associated metaphor of sight as a way of apprehending the location of key entities such as God and the self, Augustine's references might be so elusive as to be nearly indescribable.

Throughout Augustine's narration of his life events and his peculiar interpretation of them, it becomes clear that he opposes one way of inhabiting his physical body and advocates another. It is not just the eschewing of bodily pleasure for higher, spiritual pursuits; Augustine makes no secret of his disdain for the consuming passion he felt for sexual intercourse with women. A large share of the relief he sought as he anticipated conversion, and the relief he found once he finally experienced it, involved summoning strength to overcome his "sexual habit" and to replace licentious pursuits with those that honored his beliefs and commitments.[57] Brian Stock's attention to the "aesthetic" approach Augustine says he took toward reading in his early years, "a type of reader's response in which the pleasure of the text is an end in itself," versus the "ascetic" approach, which "assumes that the text is a means for attaining a higher, more pleasurable end," presents a parallel.[58]

However, there is another, less easily recognizable yet equally important point made by Augustine that prevents readers from being left with a sense of radical alienation between the body and the heart-mind-soul constellation. Augustine writes that when he was in a period of terrible suffering, he allowed himself to be seduced by the "bold-faced woman . . . in Solomon's allegory" because "she found me living outside myself" (3.6.11, p. 43). He associates his sorry state with his misconception that "for me 'to see' meant a physical act of looking with the eyes" (3.7.12, p. 43): grieving the loss of an unnamed Catholic friend, "My eyes looked for him everywhere, and he was not there" (4.4.9, p. 57). Augustine could see neither God nor himself using ordinary sight. Addressing God, he asks, "Where was I when I was seeking for you? You were there before me, but I had departed from myself. I could not even find myself, much less you" (5.2.2, p. 73). Yet a moment of spiritual vision comes over him: "At that moment I saw your 'invisible nature understood through the things which are made' (Rom. 1:20)" (7.17.23, p. 127).

Later, reading the Psalms made Augustine so filled with love for God and with anger and pity for the adherents of Manicheanism, he admits to wishing they could hear his rhapsodic comments, then corrects himself: "But in truth I would not have said those things, nor said them in that kind of way, if I had felt myself to be heard or observed by them. Nor, had I said to them, would they have understood how I was expressing the most intimate feeling of my mind with myself and to myself" (9.4.8, p. 160). This passage alludes to a way of inhabiting one's physical body that is completely different from usual, which renders one an object either by presenting oneself to others as if playing a part or by observing oneself from without. Both cause alienation from oneself, leading one to look with the eyes but never see, to fail to fill in the empty space within the body's four walls, like a book with literary style but no content (3.3.7, p. 39). Waxing rhapsodic about the perfect repose of spiritual ecstasy, Augustine describes the experience as one in which self-objectification is finally overcome. God and self are located spatially and finally seen, but seen by the same entity that is doing the seeing; deadening self-consciousness falls away and one is living from within. At this moment, Augustine writes, "The very soul itself is making no sound and is surpassing itself by no longer thinking about itself" (9.10.25, pp. 171–72). On the way to self-inhabitation is a phase of self-conscious seeing of the self. Eugene Vance's discussion reveals a fascinating dynamic in an autobiographical work that, by nature of the genre, consists of "a dialectic between the converted self and the unredeemed self-as-other" as "the 'I' of the narrative past catches up with, and becomes identical to, the 'I' writing the text."[59]

In book 10 of his *Confessions*, Saint Augustine takes what seems like an abrupt departure from his autobiographical narrative. He confronts head on epistemic, metaphysical, and moral agonies, raising such questions as "Is the mind, then, too restricted to compass itself, so that we have to ask what is that element of it-self which it fails to grasp? Surely that cannot be external to itself; it must be within the mind. How then can it fail to grasp it?" (10.8.14, p. 187). From the mysterious parts of the mind that can-not be grasped by itself, cannot even be located, Augustine moves on to ask, "As I rise above memory, where am I to find you? My true good and gentle source of reassurance, where shall I find you? If I find you outside my memory, I am not mindful of you. And how shall I find you if I am not mindful of you?" (10.17.26, p. 195). From the search for God in the mysterious parts of the mind, Augustine asks, "Is not human life on earth a trial in which there is no respite?" (10.28.39, p. 243).

Book 10 is a veritable pelting, addressed to God himself, of the deepest questions that face humans in the course of their lives. It ranges vastly as it covers themes from memory and reason to emo-tion and appetite. It takes up the theme of self-indulgence, which was the focus of so much of the earlier narrative. Gradually weav-ing before our eyes a rich tapestry out of searching question after searching question, Augustine presents a way of living that allows us to confront and transcend a sinful kind of self-indulgence, trad-ing it in for a type of self-discipline that wondrously allows for the greatest pleasures of all.

Brian Stock argues that Augustine explores these themes through the overarching trope of reading, suggesting that the em-phasis on reading in his confessions and ultimate conversion paves the way for the exegetical final chapters. What Stock calls "the para-dox of memory"—the limits of memory's ability to contain events while also being a container of events, the only way our minds have to try to contain events, in fact—is like human life, with its temptations to self-indulgence, its overflowing urges.[60] Both "memory and continence" serve in the *Confessions*, according to Stock, to draw together into a single unity "disordered experi-ence."[61] The paradox is resolved only through the deep emotional-intellectual spiritual experience of the divining Augustine de-scribes, which is based both on recognition of our own limits and on access through meditation to what is beyond us: "For the analysis of memory and the command to remain celibate have this in common: they demonstrate in different spheres that man's inability to contain himself can be overcome only with the help of God."[62]

Augustine's confrontation of his past through his searching examination of his earlier habits, still with him in the upsetting form of his unconscious life—nighttime dreams of sexual intercourse that he cannot banish and over which he has no control—is intertwined with present longings for comprehension and completeness. His desperate queries thus link the existential with the epistemological in his presentation of the crisis of individual life as he tries to redirect the excruciatingly painful, uncontainable desire for exuberance, unity, and fulfillment from the material to the spiritual—for him, the real. He achieves this through a grasp of the parts of the self inaccessible to memory, those almost glimpsed by memory but prior to our own specific memories, as he seeks to reorient everyday behavior, through religious practice, to ecstasy regained.

Augustine was profoundly influenced by reading Plato and Plotinus.[63] To return to Plotinus allows us to see the influence of a certain kind of approach that influenced Christianity and both vied with and fused with Aristotelian conceptions of virtue more familiar to us now. As we have seen, Plotinus is surely, like Rieff, greatly concerned with separation, division, and fragmentation and the emotional, intellectual, and spiritual illnesses they cause. While Plotinus presents a vision of transcendence that is irresistible, it is precisely his unwillingness, or perhaps a constitutional inability, to sacrifice the complexity of either the human or the divine to achieve it that has such allure. His notion of oneness never gives up the reality of loss, longing, and pain. It is a state of mind that is at once yearning, suffering, and searching, and yet deeply reverent, grateful, and liberated, able to lose itself to an incomparable love that is neither all body nor all mind but a strange blend of the two. This love is all that is truly real.

Poetry is essential for man's survival. There is a need for such poetics in our philosophies. Camus is helpful here because, as he contrasts the two movements of Neoplatonism and Gnosticism, he achieves a poetic reconciliation between Greek philosophy and

Christianity. Even if more recent scholarship would see his view as simplistic, science, music, and drama all once came to us through poetry. Practical philosophy must put poetry and philosophy back together.[64]

CAMUS'S AFFECTIVE PLANES

When Augustine read Plato and Plotinus, their ideas precipitated a mental revolution, in the literal sense of a rotation, of his entire inner world. While modern political philosophy is indebted to Augustine, his own indebtedness to Platonism often remains in the background. Scholars such as Henry Chadwick demonstrate the impact of the ideas of Plato and Plotinus on Augustine's thought.[65] The twentieth-century existentialist philosopher Albert Camus sees this influence as vital.

Possibly the least known work of Camus is his earliest, *Christian Metaphysics and Neoplatonism*, although its themes reemerged later in his most famous works. The book distinguishes between the tradition of Greek thought and Christianity, identifying what was distinctive or even "irreducible" in each but also what they shared.[66] Neoplatonism contributed to Christian inwardness, contributing a form specifically designed to handle desire. Arguing for the central role of Neoplatonism in the emergence of Christianity, *Christian Metaphysics* provides a helpful glimpse of Augustine, the end point of the study and arguably the beginning of modernity.[67] For our purposes, Camus's work helps identify the points of divergence between Gnosticism and Neoplatonism and assess what he thought was at stake.

Camus defined the task as a matter not of comparing Christian dogma with Greek philosophy but of envisioning the birth of a whole civilization as involving a "changing of planes and not a substitution of systems" (39). Greek philosophy shifted onto a new plane in Christianity, a "sentimental" or "affective plane" (39). Turning to this plane foregrounds tensions with the Greek system of thought, revealing that "Christianity is not a philosophy that is opposed to a philosophy, but an ensemble of aspirations, a faith, that moves to a certain plane and seeks its solutions within that plane" (39–40). These are simplifications, as Camus admits. Yet they also are *arguments* about the nature of large structural changes and their spiritual implications, so to evaluate them purely for their historical details misses the mark.

Just as Philip Rieff chronicled the rise of "psychological man," from "economic man" of the eighteenth century, "religious man" of the Judaeo-Christian tradition, and "political man" of the Greeks, Camus traces in the early centuries of the Common Era the replacement of "Greek Man" with "Christian Man."[68] In a classically simple structure of four chapters, he begins with early evangelical Christianity, then moves to two attempts to synthesize Greek thought and Christianity, Gnosticism (the one that failed) and Neoplatonism (a success), and ends with Augustine's launching of a fully developed Christian doctrine. Writing before the explosion of interest in these themes in the late twentieth and early twenty-first centuries, he gestures to a more complicated story yet seeks to draw a "simple comparison" (131). Here, his particular focus on Plotinus helps us identify a certain understanding of inwardness shared by the two traditions of Christianity and Greek philosophy and lying at the heart of the Neoplatonist synthesis.

As Ronald Srigley points out in his introduction, the ancient/modern quarrel lay at the center of Camus's interest in this early work and throughout his writing life. In this work we see what Camus thought was at stake—the version of inwardness at the nexus of Christianity and Greek philosophy. He tried to get at irreducible elements of each as well as places where they came together, comparing and contrasting the movements' views on, among other topics, virtue, evil, history, and the relation of humans to the world. Camus helps foreground the vital difference he sees between Gnosticism and Neoplatonism. At the heart of Camus's sweeping view of the Greek philosophical tradition is, unsurprisingly, the connection between reason and virtue, and a definition of evil as the absence of both. For the Greek philosophers, to be knowledgeable and to be good were one and the same, as Socrates taught. This is what impelled those in the Socratic tradition to follow passionately their different schools of thought.

Because man's natural state entailed the capacity to be rational, a person could learn virtue and improve morally. Philosophical contemplation thus played a key role in life, as the path to wisdom and away from evil and ignorance. For early Christians, virtue could not be earned or learned. Original sin had naturalized evil as part of the state of human beings. The only path to anything better was through grace. Only the person of Christ, whose coming was the sole way man might become free of sin, could achieve this. Incarnation, Camus writes, is thus the "irreducible originality" of Christianity, whereas for the Greeks it was metaphysical speculation. Camus sums up the move from the Greek to Christian worldviews as a move from "Good" to God, and from contemplation to the imitation of God, from understanding to loving (42–43). In Jesus's death, "man has paid for his sins. The incarnation is at the same time redemption" (53).

Camus locates the difference between Greek and Christian culture in their ways of bridging the distance between man and God. For the Greeks, knowledge fills that gap, while for the Christians, it is the grace of God that connects human beings with the divine: "Plato, who had wanted to unite the good to man, had been constrained to construct an entire scale of ideas between these terms. For that he created knowledge. In Christianity, it is not reasoning that bridges this gap, but a fact: Jesus is come" (53). We can witness a remarkable reconciliation between the two overarching traditions of thought in the expressions of the early church fathers, who were educated in the Greek philosophical tradition, yet were Christian believers. For those sages, reason and faith were not contradictory.[69]

Camus sees Gnosticism as an important and major early attempt to reconcile Greek thought and Christianity through a combination of knowledge and faith. Looking at Christians' criticism of the Gnostics allows the difference between Christianity and Gnosticism to emerge directly. For Christians, Christ is the "Emancipator as much as Redeemer," through unearned grace (76). For Gnostics, he is the Emancipator, through knowledge. Moreover, the particular manner in which knowledge, for the Gnostics, is attained is through initiation. In Gnosticism, between man and God there is a whole set of intermediaries, an entire "Christian Olympus" (76). The Gnostics' view of the creator God as evil leads them to despise all of creation: "The rule of life that Marcion proposes is ascetic. But it is a proud or arrogant asceticism. One must scorn the goods of this world out of hatred for the Creator. One must give as little influence as possible to his domination. This is Marcion's ideal" (75).

In his chapter "Mystic Reason," Camus argues that Neoplatonism was another attempt to reconcile Greek philosophy and Christianity, but this one worked much better. In Plotinian philosophy, Camus finds both immanence and transcendence. Both centered on a *desire* for God, for what we do not have (103–4). Neoplatonism entails a certain kind of inwardness, giving Christianity a structure and universalizability through the influence of metaphysics. Inwardness is how we confront desire for what we cannot possess yet can be absorbed by and participate in. This union, even of what we cannot own or overtake—*because* we cannot—can paradoxically cause spiritual ecstasy. Camus points to Plotinus's vivid description of this event, which values humankind as part and parcel with God but not by confusing or collapsing them:

> In order to ascend to God, one must return to oneself. Carrying within itself the reflection of its origins, the soul must be immersed in God. From God to God, such is its journey; but it must be purified, that is to say, it must be cleansed of what is bound to the soul during generation. It must not cling to what is not the soul, but must return to that homeland, the memory of which occasionally colors our souls' restlessness. The soul, to that end, is destroyed and allows itself to be absorbed into intelligence, which dominates it, and intelligence in its turn endeavors to disappear in order to leave only the One that illuminates it. This union, so complete and so rare, is ecstasy. (105–6)

Camus's paraphrasing points us to the quality of meditative inwardness that paradoxically, in turn, leads us outward to unity with and adoration of the world: "Solitary meditation, in love with the world to the extent that it is only a crystal in which the divinity is reflected, thought wholly penetrated by the silent rhythm of stars, but concerned about the God who orders them, Plotinus thinks as an artist and feels as a philosopher, according to a reason full of light and before a world in which intelligence breathes" (106).

Camus charts the tremendous influence of Neoplatonism on Augustinian thought even while acknowledging the differences between Greek thought and Christian theology. There were many contrasts: incarnation versus contemplation, as we have seen, and the significant role of virtue in Augustine's sense of the limits of philosophy (116). But Neoplatonism softened the faculty of reason for Christianity, thus influencing it and contributing a metaphysical orientation that launched the formalization of the tradition of Christian doctrine in the form of Augustinianism (129). This whole movement was not the Hellenization of Christianity, according to the thesis popularized in the nineteenth century by Lutheran theologian Adolph von Harnack, who famously argued that accretions of Greek elements degraded Christianity, but the Christianizing of Hellenism (132). Camus holds Neoplatonism and Gnosticism up against each other, which helps us see the irreplaceable *elements* of the Platonist view.

KNOWINGNESS

It is easy to ridicule a movie like *Interstellar* by accusing it of sentimentalism, quasi-scientific pretensions, and a UFO-believer brand of superstition in place of faith. Like movies claiming to be historical in some way, those nodding to real science lend themselves to long lists of gaffes and inaccuracies. Obligingly, one YouTube video examines *Interstellar* in granular detail, pointing to everything from events that could not have happened in real life to errors in timing and inanities in dialogue. The reviewer speculates on what was sacrificed in order to serve which exigency: film production, plot, or emotional appeal. So far, so good; all in good spirit. But, looking further, points of criticism range from gratuitous to more off key than any original blunder. In one scene, the YouTube video questions a rocket ship scene from *Interstellar* in which one NASA astronaut instructs another in how a wormhole works. He takes a sheet of paper to depict the normal spatial layout of the universe, then folds it over and sticks a pencil through it to illustrate how a black hole is made. The YouTube video ridicules this scene on the grounds that NASA scientists would already know such a basic fact.

This might be, yet it is a perfect example of a certain tone of sophisticated knowingness, which often drives this kind of critique more than the aim of merely identifying factual inaccuracy. Instead, accumulating absurdities often aims to glorify professional expertise, the special status of the specialist, and knowledge assumed to be more advanced because it is harder to understand, to the exclusion of other forms of knowledge. The difference between esotericism and knowingness is that the former is merely complex, the latter exclusive. If nothing else is learned from the Greek philosophers who took all of life as their subject, we should at least note their love of clarity. Classical simplicity often makes complexity comprehensible and communicable. Without the capacity to go beyond complexity, to see our way through to the other side, we are fated to miss everything of importance, from truth to goodness and beyond—to forget to feel the awe and grandeur of life itself.

Everyone from poets to scientists has made such a brief, and anyone trying to weigh in on a truly crucial question knows it is precisely the simplest possible terms that are required in the end. So many times the simplest possible terms are excruciatingly complex, so there is no way to reduce them. When complexity owns the day, though, as the be-all and end-all, it is not *necessary* complexity but obfuscation.

This kind of confusion swirls around John Keats's poem *Ode on a Grecian Urn*. The stanzas describe the urn itself and the scenes depicted upon it in heartbreaking detail, musing on the meaning of such a relic for those living now. The poem ends with the famous lines "Beauty is truth, truth beauty,—that is all / Ye know on earth, and all ye need to know." The poem's ending polarizes readers and critics, with some finding the poem sentimental and simplistic and others one of the deepest and most beautiful ever written.[70] Whatever the reader's view, the lines are reminiscent of Platonism. They offer one of the most clear and succinct descriptions of it.

Plotinus's mode of affective apperception stands in stark opposition to this knowing pose. Instead, he counsels receptivity and a special mode of listening. The Plotinian position is an openness to the way the world is, throwing open a window onto possibilities new to us. The forms are fixed and eternal, which allows us entry into a complexity unconfined, a boundless expansiveness. Only through discipline can we find freedom, and through finitude our taste of the infinite. The French painter Philippe de Champaigne's *Saint Augustine* (ca. 1645–50) depicts the theologian in his study, in a moment of illumination, surrounded by books and papers. In one hand he holds a quill pen and in the other a heart on fire. His mouth is slightly open, perhaps in a sudden gasp of awe, and his gaze is fixed on a ball of gold light at our upper left in the midst of which we can discern the word *veritas* (truth). The flames of the heart and the light of truth make a path that meets at his head, which gives off a halo of flames. The painting captures a moment of illumination through its evocation of an inner epiphany in terms of a special light that seems to suspend Augustine within it. The light in *Interstellar*'s tesseract scene likewise transforms an everyday space into a site of revelation.

As stated at the outset of this chapter, the *Interstellar* scene was informed by real science, in a delicate interplay between established fact-based knowledge and educated speculation, the proven and the envisioned. It is ultimately, though, a work of imagination, a rendering of the inner psyche dramatized and depicted before our eyes in which a fictional world could bend to our selective suspicions and desires. Such efforts, whether successful or not, attempt to bring poetry back to science, and science back to poetry, where they belong. In the chamber in distant space, the tesseract (a four-dimensional cube, or "hyper-cube"), we witness a reunion of two people but also the overlapping of huge parts of our own interior and exterior worlds, which we keep or allow to be sequestered only at our loss.[71] It makes possible a magnificent reconciliation of

the binaries that are at once essential for a human being's recon-
noitering of the world and navigation of the life course and at the
same time the bane of human existence: science and religion, romance and reality, time and space, desire and fulfillment, fact and
belief, body and mind, life and death, loss and love, and the transcendence of beginning and ending through being and becoming.

The tesseract depicts interior reality *as* reality. It shows a way
that interior and exterior reality are sometimes conjoined. This can
occur through communion with another soul in the universe. That
moment of poignant, exquisite, awe-inspiring connection is spirit-
saving.

The image of the tesseract offers a visual architectural image as a
way to imagine the unimaginable, to catch a glimpse of that transcendence to which we are heir, if only we are patient enough to
open our senses and ready ourselves. The most utilitarian among
us will prove that it cannot be. The most love-besotted will know
that it must.

HIDDEN FIGURES

While not consciously casting itself in the role, another recent film,
Hidden Figures, shows traces of a kind of socio-aesthetic Neoplatonism. (See fig. 5.4.) The film centers on math in the way *Interstellar* did science. Here we encounter a woman meticulously
coiffed and dressed in what passes for professional attire for that
rare black American woman in a mid-twentieth-century white-
collar workplace, an A-line dress. Katherine Johnson (played by
Taraji P. Henson) was told to wear a string of pearls on the job, yet
her neck is bare. With a quiet dignity, she nudges her glasses higher
on her nose and climbs a ladder next to a wall-sized chalkboard.
The room is full of white men with their hair cut short, clad in
starched white shirts and dark ties. She perseveres. The men sit at
separate desks yet work as a team under the supervision of the
boss, who can see everything from his raised glassed-in office. In
neat, humble, and highly legible handwriting, she begins at the
top left corner to fill the board with mathematical notation. Since

beginning work here, her few breaks in the workday involve making her own coffee in a coffee-pot labeled "colored" and running in her heels a quarter of a mile because she cannot use the whites-only bathroom. Yet she perseveres. She is one of a small group of female African American mathematicians who each work as a "computer" in the nation's space program before that word came to refer to an inanimate object. The machine on deck in the back room awaits its debut, poised to take over the calculations, but in the meantime, human beings of rare aptitude became a national treasure, people whose abilities involved both extraordinary exactitude with formulas and calculations and true originality. She is demeaned in the workplace as in the wider society, with the civil rights movement only beginning to topple de jure let alone de facto segregation. And yet, she perseveres.[72]

By the time Katherine has reached the bottom right-hand corner of the board, the whole room full of men is watching, including the floor supervisor, who confirms on the spot that she is right. Her calculations are not just correct but brilliant. It dawns on her boss (played by Kevin Costner) that she is a mathematical genius. Further, she is proficient in the very fields they need if they are to launch a man in space to answer Sputnik. Buckling under Cold War pressures, his men are forced to give her a chance. The capsule they built is failing its tests, its shingles flying off in the testing chamber and bouncing violently off the observation window where the engineers look on with horror. Katherine saves the day, managing to calculate the exact trajectory of John Glenn's Mercury spacecraft and thus prepare the US for competition with its greatest foe, the only other world power in postwar America. In the course of their work together, her boss removes the "colored" label from the coffee pot and takes a sledgehammer to the "colored bathroom" sign, declaring to the entire workforce that from now on, all bathrooms are open to all. Everyone at NASA, he says, "pees yellow."

Katherine Johnson's intelligence, acknowledged only because of fears for national security, helps level the barriers facing her, which would otherwise stand in the way of both her success and the country's. In the escalation of anxiety about annihilation, Americans suspect outer space is a possible launching pad for nuclear missiles. The country's very existence seems to rely on her genius, which means all barriers to the full play of her powers must topple.

It is difficult not to be moved deeply by the movie, even with its limits and simplifications. We root for the underdog—of course we do—and end up feeling a little sheepish, asking ourselves how good the movie really was. The protagonist's tic of adjusting her glasses countless times plays to stereotypes of the "geek," and there are many other such clichés. From the vantage point of the twenty-first century, a period that witnessed the monumental achievement of the first African American president, the movie cannot help but resonate. And discoveries of Russian hackers' tampering with the 2016 US presidential election help. Oppression based on race has hardly gone away either, with NFL players taking a knee to protest police brutality, nor has oppression based on sex, with the #MeToo movement unveiling case after case of sexual harassment and assault. The costumes and props used in the movie are those of the early 1960s, but the injustices are those still present in some places today. The injustice that someone so smart and valuable to the country must endure humiliation and discrimination on a daily basis lies at the heart of the movie. In one scene, a presumably racist white policeman who comes upon Katherine's broken-down car ends up insisting on giving her a police escort to her job. National security clarifies, crystalizing higher priorities. Merit seems to conquer all.

Yet there is another element at work here, which emerges as Katherine is immersed in the act of writing down her calculations on the board. Her advanced math is applied in this case, but in the moment, it harkens even to a hidden past of her male coworkers, whose jealousy and resentment fall away along with their sexism and racism. There is a purity and a passion to advanced math, as there is in every serious pursuit. This plays an essential role in the movie, as if a second plot is trying to break through, less bound by the political and social realities of both the era depicted and the era in which the movie was made. It is as if the numbers speak to us from another world with almost sacred undertones. Especially when combined with the allure of explorations in the great mystery of space, the miracle of numbers seems to become literally our pathway to the heavens.

We find this kind of scene in many other movies, so much that it requires only a brief gesture in *Hidden Figures*, even if it leaves math lovers thirsty for more. A well-known earlier movie, *A Beautiful Mind*, contains many such scenes.[73] And of course, it is not always math that is the superhuman, almost magical expertise in question, though it is usually an area associated today with unique and unusual genius like physics, philosophy, or poetry. In the place of the chalkboard, there can be an instrument, and the notes of a brilliant concert pianist.

Our culture's shorthand for all of this is encapsulated in one word, Einstein. Einstein's brilliance is legendary, his name a household word. His pithy sayings—such as "Pure mathematics is, in its way, the poetry of logical ideas"—appear on coffee mugs. T-shirts printed with $E = MC^2$ abound. It is a rare mathematical formula that has such cachet. In their ability to illuminate small corners of the universe's infinite mysteries, such virtuosos give onlookers a vicarious experience of the extraordinary.

Hidden Figures primarily plays on the meritocratic narrative. No one so competent should suffer such discrimination. Merit should triumph, or so goes a dominant American argument for equal treatment. Yet the movie also nods to this other narrative, in which genius suspends time and place and transcends all other particulars. Its beauty is exquisite and gives us a taste of perfection by association. We are paralyzed, suspended in the moment, as when we encounter one of the earth's great wonders. It is the human person at his or her best, humankind operating in an ethereal realm of staggering mystery.

This kind of excellence is something in its own right, existing apart from and above all of our more mundane concerns. Our experience of it is transformative. In the single moment of ecstasy and awe, we feel our life to be changing. As in a religious revelation, we cannot imagine ever going back, ever being the same again. It is a recognition of the coexistence of the extraordinary and the ordinary in human life, the humanist sublime.

The movie is thus about more than its stated themes of racial justice and the rights of the deserving, or the equalizing imperatives of intelligence. It is also about transcendence attainable through our ideals. Entrance into a world of our experience and ability that seems to defy reality, the limits of everyday life, evokes the divine. Our ideals make us reach for unreachable things. In reaching, we can get so close that the gap between us and the divine is nearly imperceptible.

RECOGNITION

Given our separateness, all communication is translation. The reality of ignoring inwardness and failing to cultivate the inner life as our sole basis for connection makes translation impossible. Being open to influence but impermeable to manipulation lays pathways to deep involvement, to the inseparable intertwining of our minds and our lives. It starts with acknowledging our coexistence. The irony is we think we want everyone to speak our own language. We want to feel comfortable in the world and try to surround ourselves with people like us. Communication with those like us can be harder than with those not like us because we fail to see this challenge. We are all discrete beings.

In *Interstellar*, the act of communication was an act of translation from the past to the present. Humans supposedly needed a third party, extraterrestrial beings who could operate outside of our normal dimensions, to make this communication possible. Yet the film also presents the basic, mundane longing that we have for particular people and places in our past. While cloaked in the form of sci-fi adventure, with a future-oriented sensibility of progress, the story is all about conserving. It centers on the problem of how to preserve humanity itself. *Arrival* (2016) is another movie along these lines. For Hans-Georg Gadamer, the act of cultural influence is itself an act of translation of the intellectual and artistic tradition.[74]

"Recognition elicits the permanent from the transient," Gadamer writes in "The Relevance of the Beautiful."[75] The tesseract in

Interstellar is reminiscent of Gadamer's mention of André Malreaux's museum without walls, an imaginary museum where all of the world's great works would coexist in one place and time.[76] Even if not of the caliber of the greatest works of all time, movies like *Interstellar* and *Hidden Figures* can also give us a feeling of Platonic wonder. All we need is one such experience to open us to an infinity of others, to plant the seed of recognition of the beautiful, not just in art, but in everyday life.[77]

Readying ourselves means living a certain kind of life in which we are open to subtle cues and silent communications, redefining self-fulfillment as a mode of inhabiting the very moment in which we find ourselves at any given time by honoring its connection to all others, past and future. It means living in one place by honoring *its* connection to all others as well. Everything is more interdependent than it appears when viewed from the vantage point of the lone individual, and more mysterious than it seems when viewed from the vantage point of knowingness and total human mastery. To usher in better ways to live together that locate, retrieve, conserve, and create what we need for our own flourishing, a practical philosophy is necessary for any kind of follow-through on our commitments. Discipline and practices are in turn necessary for any kind of practical philosophy. Yet it is some kind of vision of beauty that is necessary for any form of discipline and practice. Such depth of devotion is impossible without contemplation of the ideal, which animates our striving.

Today's culture operates on a soul-diminishing basis of appearance as a stand-in for beauty, for "goals," with superficial, fleeting outward images bearing no resemblance to inner reality or quality. Chasing after apparitions starved of meaning has proven to pave the way only to despair and unhappiness. Any hope we might have for a better life would need to rejoin beauty and truth, retrieving meaning through hope for transcendent, immanent fulfillment of longings that can otherwise destroy us. Given our need for love, which is as painfully real as can be, anything less would be impractical.

For Plotinus, love was about the *recognition* of the inner beauty of others.

Being in the tesseract is both fleeting and forever. Our greatest heights of experience could never have been imagined if we were not creatures who suffer and die. There are times the toxic can be taken away by the cleansing tide, to join all the other things only the great infinity of the ocean can wear soft. Would we really rue the day? All the beauty around us would never have materialized before our eyes if we had never been in dire straits. Suffering makes us reach for one another, hoping for recognition, as does love.

LIVING FROM WITHIN

Desperate spiritual and emotional need, intense longing, painful desire, crushing and debilitating loss, disappointment and disenchantment, nausea—they give the unsought gift of a pathway, albeit one through real threats to body and mind, to illumination and incandescence. There exists a kind of beauty that cannot be looked at head on because it is like nothing we have ever known, as if all were present at once, part of just one enduring moment. That is what the tesseract scene gestures to, with all of its bars of light and bookcases and books imbued by a love so strong and powerful it can reach across all of the dimensions, including time.

This is not to suggest that one must embrace *Interstellar* as a film and judge it excellent as such. It is legitimate to worry whether, taken as a whole and placed in today's dominant tropes, its larger message fits with the Gnosticism of our times, with Gnosticism's ghastly boast of "freeing ourselves from finitude."[78] It is this context that sets out the task before us. We have the perennial job of intricately separating out the strands that distinguish ideas, practices, and traditions from one another, the only method by which we have ever effected a stay from the course that would plunge us into terror instead of wonderment. We might consider whether there is another scene—perhaps from a different film, book, painting, musical composition, or even real-life experience—that invites us into another close reading of this sort, giving rise to such questions. It takes a different state, more contemplation than mass entertainment. Our study of all things broken, internal and external, is transformed completely when informed by an acquaintance with the sublime. What this book is suggesting is that this ancient conversation, in the form of our modern meditations, can return us to ourselves. This can prepare us for the momentous question of how we might inhabit our beautiful universe and provides ever-renewing answers to the question of why we might want to.

Plotinus's notion of "belonging to ourselves" provides a vision of a way of life we might call *living from within*. In a time overtaken by image and illusion, beholden to mirages and mirrors, it signals an alternative—the choice of reinhabiting our very selves. The soul is the integrating part of the self. It answers to the postmodern notion of the self splitting into fragments. Acknowledging the limits of our own embodiment, we could practice ceasing to look at ourselves from outside, as objects, and manage to refrain from subjecting other people to that same objectifying gaze.

Einstein's comment blending math and poetry and logic originated in a miniobituary presented as a letter to the *New York Times* in 1935 upon the death of the Jewish émigré mathematician Emmy Noether. Dismissed from the University of Göttingen when the Nazis took power, she subsequently taught at Bryn Mawr College. Einstein's moving words drew a portrait of a person not in thrall to the world of externals but committed to something else:

The efforts of most human-beings are consumed in the struggle for their daily bread, but most of those who are, either through fortune or some special gift, relieved of this struggle are largely absorbed in further improving their worldly lot. Beneath the effort directed toward the accumulation of worldly goods lies all too frequently the illusion that this is the most substantial and desirable end to be achieved; but there is, fortunately, a minority composed of those who recognize early in their lives that the most beautiful and satisfying experiences open to humankind are not derived from the outside, but are bound up with the development of the individual's own feeling, thinking and acting. The genuine artists, investigators and thinkers have always been persons of this kind. However inconspicuously the life of these individuals runs its course, none the less the fruits of their endeavors are the most valuable contributions which one generation can make to its successors.

The coffee mug quote came from Einstein's praise for Noether's distinction and algebraic discoveries: "Pure mathematics is, in its way, the poetry of logical ideas. One seeks the most general ideas of operation which will bring together in simple, logical and unified form the largest possible circle of formal relationships. In this effort toward logical beauty spiritual formulas are discovered necessary for the deeper penetration into the laws of nature." If we stop with the quotable mug, we miss his own poetry in the elegiac memorial to Noether's everyday efforts in mathematical discovery and teaching and the sense of connection he saw between "logical beauty" and "spiritual formulas."[79]

BELOVED COMMUNITY

Why all this talk of love? What use are these visions today, from Plato's "ladder of love" to Plotinus's "radiant luminosity," and from Botticelli's *Primavera* to the tesseract scene in *Interstellar*? Much of these ideas might strike our contemporaries, at least the skeptics or cynics among them, as mystical or at least overly idealistic. Ideal spiritual love might seem irrelevant to our times and unconnected to concerns about democracy, equality, and justice.

But many of the pioneers in just these movements of justice, equality, and democracy would think that to ignore them is to abandon the very reservoir from which we need to drink if we are to make a better world. Martin Luther King Jr., for one, was profoundly influenced by Plato, Plotinus, and other philosophers, ancient and modern. On the night before he was assassinated, nervous and exhausted after receiving numerous death threats, he delivered his mountaintop speech. In words that reverberate across the generations, he fused religion and theology with classical imagery and personal experience.

And you know, if I were standing at the beginning of time, with the possibility of taking a kind of general and panoramic view of the whole of human history up to now, and the Almighty said to me, "Martin Luther King, which age would you like to live in?" I would take my mental flight by Egypt through, or rather across the Red Sea, through the wilderness on toward the promised land. And in spite of its magnificence, I wouldn't stop there. I would move on by Greece and take my mind to Mount Olympus. And I would see Plato, Aristotle, Socrates, Euripides and Aristophanes assembled around the Parthenon as they discussed the great and eternal issues of reality. But I wouldn't stop there. I would go on, even to the great heyday of the Roman Empire. And I would see developments around there, through various emperors and leaders. But I wouldn't stop there. I would even come up to the day of the Renaissance, and get a quick picture of all that the Renaissance did for the cultural and aesthetic life of man. But I wouldn't stop there. . . . Strangely enough, I would turn to the Almighty, and say, "If you allow me to live just a few years in the second half of the twentieth century, I will be happy."[80]

In his struggle for civil rights King returned again and again to the redemptive power of love and the notion of "the beloved community." Even in his time of tribulation, with forebodings that his life could be cut short, he failed to indulge in escapist fantasies that denied the beauty and meaning of the one place and time in which we are fated to live. Love stood at the center of his thought and his inspired oratory.

With his words, Martin Luther King Jr. was able to get millions of people to picture in their own minds a better place for us all to live. In part, this was because he was not alone. He was standing on the shoulders of others, black and white, women and men, who were more than ready for the moment of change and had paved the way through their own struggles and achievements.[81] He was walking alongside others, from leaders like Fanny Lou Hamer to members of the New Left's Students for a Democratic Society, who also mentioned love in their founding Port Huron Statement as the driving force of their vision of a truly participatory democracy. At a fiftieth-anniversary gathering of SDS members, another national treasure, Todd Gitlin, also spoke in lyrical terms of the love powering the movement, the ideal those young students shared with the civil rights movement of "the beloved community—the kernel of a moral awakening that would put intelligence to work in behalf of transcendent values."[82] Theirs—ours—was and is a vision enshrouded in "radiant luminosity." Reverend King's inspiring vista from the highest reaches of the feeling intellect, as captured by Romare Bearden, is reminiscent of the view from Diotima's ladder. (See fig. 5.5.) Without such inner vision, without the frozen music that is architecture—our making of a habitable world—our happiness can remain nothing but a vain pursuit.

MUSIC IN THE COSMOS

When we forget ourselves, and stumble and even fall, we might do well to listen to the refrain of another poetic voice leading us back to basics, that of the Irish singer-songwriter Van Morrison in his song "I Forgot That Love Existed." The song opens with ripples of pain and turmoil conveying the recurrent heartbreak that subsides only when illumination strikes him in the form of a real world of other people who restore his spirits. Invoking Plato and Socrates by name, for holding love in the highest esteem, the song ends by imagining a way we might remember to remember what is "truly real." This would involve using our usual faculties in a new way that unites capacities we have but often keep apart: "If my heart could do the thinking and my head begin to feel." When we forget a basic fact of our existence, such as the existence of love, and discount its reality, we are lost. Yet the saving grace is not luck or accident or limerence—as in *falling* in love—but instead *remembering* that love exists, as it did long before us. As in so many of his other compositions, Van Morrison's lyrics blend seamlessly into the meditative instrumentals of guitar and piano, leaving the listener with reverberations of stillness.[83] Another twentieth-century composer put to music Diotima's vision of love in a piece for violin, string orchestra, harp, and percussion. In 1954, the composer and conductor Leonard Bernstein wrote an orchestral piece modeled on Plato's *Symposium*, with a separate movement for each speaker's discourse on love. A few bars from Socrates's speech shed light on how brilliant a vision it offers.[84]

After the moment of silence between movements—in this case between those of "Agathon" and "Socrates: Alcibiades"—a gong sounds, and the strings start the music off with a mood of interior excitement, like shivers down the spine. Their loud chords announce a presence, then suddenly become quiet to allow the violin to state its melody, which begins on an F and climbs two octaves over several measures, and even higher momentarily before returning and slowing down from "*a tempo (al cadenza)*," to *Adagio*, with instructions in the sheet music, *teneramente*.

Then begins a new sound. Marked *Poco meno mosso*, both violin and other strings play *dolcissimo*. The violin begins with a half note on high A, declining to a flat, back to a natural, then F sharp, then natural, held for three beats, in preparation for F sharp, G sharp, A, back to F sharp in preparation for one of the most exquisite measures in modern music. (See fig. 5.6.) The strings hold a chord while the violin soars, finally joining the strings in a chord by striking G and holding it with the greatest delicacy, *lunga*. Breaking the mood, sudden loud notes ring out full force as Alcibiades crashes the party, and the key changes dramatically, as does the tempo. The violin must contend throughout the rest of the serenade with the newly assertive strings, now playing in a variety of modes, including a jig.

Watching Bernstein's piece performed by a virtuoso violinist conveys the range and depth of emotion, from sorrow and pain to love and beauty. Each note climbs ever more reverently, the violin's infinitesimal whisper capturing the dawning view from the ethereal heights of Diotima's ladder. In the space of one measure, the notes keep us suspended there, both elevated and abject, humbled and elated, feeling everything at once, in the infinity of a moment.

WOULD IT BE NICE SOMETIMES TO HAVE HAD CERTAIN events occur at very different times in very different ways and have other constellations of all kinds made possible beyond the particularities and limits of our own embodied existence? Would that not almost always be the case—no, always? The human, material world has its accidents, wrongs, crimes, and imperfections. Yet the equally human world of the spirit has access through intuition to the realm of perfection not in spite of but because of that suffering. In that realm, all sources of separation from complete satisfaction are removed. It is a delicate and rare thing to live in constant awareness of this. And yet it is a human possibility, to live in the eternal moment, in the eye of the sacred, flooded by warmth, struck to our core by the humbling ecstasy of human connection, at home in the universe, in peace. Returned, to ourselves.

CONCLUSION
Philosophia

> Love is the most durable power in the world.
> —*Martin Luther King Jr.*

Our philosophies of life pervade all we do. The problem is not this or that approach but the day-to-day structure in which each approach is presented and considered. The current structure allows for a sphere free of concern about the meaning of life, a bifurcation of our selves into economic versus emotional, exploitative versus empathetic, body versus soul. We allow the humanities—the traditional repository of deeper wisdom about our condition and the art of living—to wither away. In their place remain only slogans and lists. A generalized discontentment, resentment, and sense of victimization pit us against one another, while satisfaction of our needs and wants eludes us even in the flood of self-help offerings, New Age therapies, and consumer choices that nearly drown out all alternatives and our inner lives in the process.

What we need is a new structure. We need a framework of understanding that allows us to contain and make sense of the conflicting advice dispensed. Calls for meditation abound. Meditation may clear our minds, but contemplation redirects us to what fills them. There needs to be some order to our thoughts, a common framework sufficiently durable and expansive as to allow for the flourishing of a conversation in which particular schools of thought are considered, spiritual seeking is not cut off from the rest of life, and such a fragile and evanescent-seeming phenomenon as our general disposition is appreciated as formative and constitutive of all of our experience, what we create, and what we are able to contribute. Everyone is his or her own philosopher; like a writer or artist in residence, our philosopher interprets life as it is being lived. This can be anything from paralyzing to fortifying. It all depends on the content of the philosophy being dispensed by ourselves or others.

Self-appointed experts claim to have the solution. But the word *solution*, when applied to human beings, should always have shades and shadows of danger. The word *final* accompanies it for anyone living after World War II, and even in its more benign forms it should raise suspicions. If there was a "solution" for human living, there would not be a need for life itself: the only final solution for life is death. A humble way to live acknowledges that we are all seekers in need of a way to contain and steer our seeking into safe and renewable, sustainable and meaningful pursuits. We need a world that is safe for our self- and soul-making. While we talk a lot about sustainability today, we think mainly of the inanimate resources around us. Yet these are related to the personal and interpersonal resources needed for sustainable human bonds. We should be careful what we wish for. We do not need a solution but a mode of living. The art of living involves physical needs and desires but takes seriously our intellectual and spiritual ones equally.

PRACTICAL PHILOSOPHY

The therapeutic culture aims at the physical and the mental but lacks a sense of the existence of a transcendent good beyond the individual, or of the existence of good as something transcendent. To live without manipulating others or being manipulated oneself is only part of it. In addition, we want and need trust, respect, integrity, and dignity for our human connections and democratic community.

The paradigmatic relation, perhaps the only true opposite of manipulatable social relations, is one of love. Feelings or reasons that emerge in the context of nonmanipulable social relations possess a different nature, character, or quality from those in the context of social relations based on manipulation. Art, music, religion, and poetry are just some of the ways we know such a way of being in the world exists. When we suspect an idea, feeling, or person is being used for ulterior purposes, hope for a better world evaporates. In *Self and Soul: A Defense of Ideals*, Mark Edmundson calls for a pedagogy that brings ideals into the equation.[1] Rita Felski is another pioneer who argues for a form of literary criticism that goes beyond deconstruction. Her *Limits of Critique* is a manifesto for a move beyond the "hermeneutics of suspicion" explored in chapter 4.[2]

With no vision of the good, we are lost and bereft. All our projects become self-serving. Yet serving our own ends for the sake of serving our own ends can never serve our ends. We are creatures capable of goodness. Only living a life turned toward goodness will fulfill our cravings and humanity. Aiming at the good takes us out of ourselves. If we are too internally focused, with ourselves as the boundary of our loyalty and commitment, we never really enter into the world of others. We cannot know other people or the divine.

Cultivating emotions like empathy and compassion seems like a desirable way to address self-interest, whether of the overly emotional or overly rationalist variety. Narcissism manifests itself as a disorder, while rationalism appears sane, a calculated and functional choice. To persuade people temporarily not to act in their self-interest, we turn to arguments based on reason such as precedent or numbers or harm; or else we try to appeal to their emotions, especially through such mechanisms as compassion or empathy. Reason and emotion have a much too complicated relation to use one against the other, and both can be enlisted on behalf of pure self-interest. It is a certain relation between them that is the dysfunction of our epoch. Many accept that both reason and emotion should serve the self's motives, desires, and aims, not only to the exclusion of others', but to the exclusion of what is good. The problem is always a question of the nature, character, and quality of what is being served and why.

The instrumentalization of people to serve someone else's interest changes everything. The tenor of human relations changes, resulting in an expansion of self-interest to such a degree that it ends up in no human being's interest at all. It creates the conditions for an inhumane social world, a world inhospitable to human flourishing or even self-maintenance. The spiritual discipline of living in community with others, versus merely functioning within a society, is a discipline not against emotion, or against reason, but against the instrumentalization of both in the service of either the individual or the collective. Ferdinand Tönnies captured this distinction in the difference he drew between *Gemeinschaft*, or relationships formed out of family ties and friendships, and *Gesellschaft*, relationships formed in the practice of functioning within a (modern, capitalist) society.[3]

THE USES OF USELESSNESS

The real therapeutic paradox is that what is truly therapeutic is not inherently designed to be therapeutic: what is most useful is what is not inherently meant to *be* used. Those who lose themselves in a practice or activity for the sake of the highest standards of excellence, teaching and learning for joy and enrichment, and the satisfaction of being useful without being used, know firsthand what it means to inhabit a sphere free of manipulation. This is captured in the notion of grace. When we give up on the existence of such a sphere, everything from individual freedom to democratic self-governance can evaporate.[4] In the absence of countervailing forces, power devours everything in its path.

Practical philosophy is also at its very core paradoxical. It could even be dismissed as an oxymoron. Isn't the very definition of philosophy that it is not practical? Friedrich Nietzsche wrote that "philosophy is distinguished from science by its selectivity and its discrimination of the unusual, the astonishing, the difficult and the divine, just as it is distinguished from intellectual cleverness by its emphasis on the useless."[5] This comes in his *Philosophy in the Tragic Age of the Greeks*, in which he gives brief profiles of prominent pre-Socratic philosophers and places archaic Greek philosophy on a pedestal.[6] He praises Thales, known for his proposition that water is the source of everything, for neither seeing this as an allegory (resorting to "fantastic fable") nor ultimately explaining it away through science and logic. Thales embodies (demonstrates) the meaning of *sage*, a word Nietzsche traces to the verb *sapire*, to taste. "The peculiar art of the philosopher" presupposes tasting, "savoring," "selecting," and making distinctions: "Science rushes headlong, without selectivity, without 'taste,' at whatever is knowable, in the blind desire to know all at any cost. Philosophical thinking, on the other hand, is ever on the scent of those things that are most worth knowing, the great and the important insights" (43).

Alongside this praise for philosophy's uselessness, Nietzsche amplifies on the theme of the importance of philosophy in a certain kind of everyday living. Nietzsche starts the work by holding up the culture of the ancient Greeks as a model of a "truly healthy culture," introducing the health metaphor in his very first paragraph. Nietzsche depicts modern German culture at the time he was writing in the 1870s as one in which philosophy has no place: "There are people who are opposed to all philosophy. . . . The physicians of our culture repudiate philosophy" (27). To those critics, defending philosophy would require showing "to what ends a healthy culture uses and has used philosophy" (27). If a culture is already healthy, that is one thing, but if it is not, philosophy cannot be *used* to heal it: "If philosophy ever manifested itself as helpful, redeeming, or prophylactic, it was in a healthy culture. The sick, it made ever sicker" (27). A healthy culture, for him, possesses some basis of coherence. Devoid of this "unity of style," Nietzsche writes, "philosophy could never re-integrate the individual into the group" (33) but would, rather, "isolate him still further" and go on "to destroy him through that isolation" (27–28).

Nietzsche proceeds to the proper attitude toward philosophy taken by his ideal culture: "The Greeks, with their truly healthy culture, have once and for all justified philosophy simply by having engaged in it, and engaged in it more fully than any other people" (32). They did not reserve philosophy for times of difficulty but engaged in it early on and continued into old age, while others reserve philosophy for times of duress, in an individual's or a culture's development, and hold no central place of honor for philosophers. Greeks had sages as others had saints (32). (We have mainly celebrities.) When a "genuine" culture does not exist, Nietzsche goes on, a philosopher is "a chance random wanderer," consigned to exile—"a comet, incalculable and therefore terror-inspiring." When such a culture does exist, the philosopher "shines like a stellar object of the first magnitude in the solar system of culture" (34). To Nietzsche, these conditions prevailed for philosophers up to Socrates, but "beginning with Plato" the philosopher became a lone soul in exile. In those later times, philosophy no longer had such a central place in daily life. Nietzsche observed that, by the nineteenth century, "No one may venture to fulfill philosophy's law with his own person, no one may live philosophically" (37).

On the contrary, we live philosophically in spite of ourselves. His other views aside for our present purpose, what if Nietzsche is right that the truly therapeutic is that which is not explicitly aimed at therapy? If philosophy is called in belatedly as a remedy for personal ailing in a sick society, it loses its capacity to induce health. As soon as it is valued for its uses, as a means to this end, it loses its ability to achieve this end. The health-inducing properties do not come from employing it as a tool toward some other definition of flourishing—wealth, entertainment, consumption, fame—but from a definition of flourishing in which philosophy is already an intrinsic component. We are social creatures, yet we are also creatures of *philosophia*, the love of wisdom, and literature, religion, music, art, architecture, and other deep and sustained pursuits. These pursuits structure the *enhanced* version of living.

Using philosophy to live versus *living philosophy* is thus a distinction necessary for redefining the notion of a practical philosophy. The most practical philosophy might paradoxically be the most impractical, the most useful might be the most useless, the most applied philosophy might be that which cannot—merely, belatedly, superficially, deceptively, instrumentally—be applied. A commitment to this practical impracticality would keep a school of thought from the jaws of the market, the therapeutic, or any other ideology. The case against instrumentalism is that it makes us lose our concept of *noninstrumentalism* and the capacity to tell the difference between means and ends, falsehood and truth. When these lines become blurred, there is no basis to keep from becoming an instrument—of others and even of ourselves. A practical philosophy must allow for the flourishing of the individual *and* the shared world. Philosophy is practical if it is not purely personal but ties our personal strivings in a meaningful way to the world of others.

A workable public philosophy does not end questions but questions ends. It admits that we are beings in progress with decisions to make every day. The problem with today's answers, whether popular or academic, is not that they are simple and direct but that they give a set of precepts for living that already assume the answers. This is a framework of expertise or knowingness, the main trait of the culture of Gnosticism, a violation of a revelatory approach to learning and nonmanipulative communication.[7] That is the very opposite of practical.

Determining what is practical depends on one's idea of what it means to be human, what our lives can and should be about, and what we think about the world around us, our relations with other people, and the best way to live. That is not something any human knows. To pretend we do brings untold dangers. As we have seen, the Greeks had a word for the perils of excess knowingness: *hubris*. It is the impulse behind movements such as the Cultural

Revolution in China, or cultural adjudication in Stalinist Russia, for two extreme examples. Though it comes in a softer form in American academic expertise and self-help nostrums, it deprives the individual of the deepest joy of living—learning. Knowingness destroys revelation, and revelation is the necessary ingredient to transform the constitution of a self to a soul.

THE NEW ARISTOTELIANISM

Today's cultural ethic of market growth, careerism, personal gain, and consumerism has outright defenders in philosophies based on everything from classical liberalism to Ayn Rand objectivism. A very different modern movement has challenged that orientation toward individual rights, privileges, and even entitlements. In the late twentieth century, Amitai Etzioni, Michael Sandel, and others provided alternative bases for a revivified public philosophy that emphasized the responsibilities, not just the benefits, of citizenship. Mary Ann Glendon's book *Rights Talk: The Impoverishment of Political Discourse*, published in 1991, epitomized this shift.[8]

Earlier, in the mid-twentieth century, British philosophers Philippa Foot and Elizabeth Anscombe made similar appeals beyond the self-interested individual, in a philosophical movement that became known as virtue ethics. The dominant philosophical influence on recent and contemporary virtue ethics, particularly now through the work of Alasdair MacIntyre, has been Aristotle. In turning to Aristotle for a foundation for a critique of the modern order, including the chaos of social and moral life, philosophers pointed to the need for a basis of shared commitments, a rationale for taking the path of what was morally good, the good to be found in community and practices, a foundation for the "moral ought." The answer to the question of why a person should act morally was found in Aristotle's notion of *eudaemonia*. In his *Nicomachean Ethics*, Aristotle argues that a final end of human life—a goal or *telos*—is happiness or well-being.

Coming with a similar set of concerns, because of his "identification with the Platonic and Augustinian ethical traditions," scholar Matthew D. Mendham presents an alternative guide for ethical philosophy to MacIntyre's Aristotle: Plato. MacIntyre assumes a dichotomy between a foundation for morals based on *eudaemonia* and the chaos of "stifling duties, neglected virtues, or arbitrary wills" that constitutes contemporary culture. Eudaemonism provides a way of reconciling the pursuit of self-interest with concern for others by connecting what is good for the self with virtuous action, by definition that action which is good for others. The classical liberal defense of the virtuous nature of self-interest on the grounds that it is good for everyone rests on the assumption that it is in the individual's own interest to allow others to pursue their self-interest. This is an instrumentalist notion that behaving in a virtuous manner toward others is in one's own interest: treating others well is for the purpose of serving one's self, so the good action is an instrument aimed at promoting the good of the self, and other people can even be treated in an instrumental fashion. In today's more informal terms, people are being used, but it is all right because they are using others. In this magical thinking of enlightened self-interest, the good of the whole is somehow served and everyone feels good in the end.

Crucial in MacIntyre's view, *pace* Aristotle, is the harmonizing of individual interests with good treatment of others, but without any instrumentalism. As Mendham puts it, MacIntyre has shown how eudaemonism "can support the profound human conviction that virtuous behavior and affectionate dedication to others should be performed for their own sake." Mendham explains that this version of eudaemonism rests on the notion that it is a basic structure of the human being "to pursue her own good, the attainment of which is only possible through non-instrumental dedication to the virtues and to a generous communal life." Aristotle's underlying assumption is that one's own well-being relies on knowing one is acting virtuously. The place of this knowledge of virtue in the very definition of human happiness is the crucial element that keeps one from using others to pursue one's self-interest.[9]

Yet that knowledge is no match for all of the urges of the human body and soul. It is not that we treat others well so we will be treated well, a bargain of temporarily suspended self-interest in service of a self-interested outcome, but that well-being entails overcoming self-interest itself. As Socrates put it simply, virtue is knowledge.[10] That virtuous knowledge is happiness. We are happy when we are living a life of virtue. This is Aristotle's view of the *telos* of a human life. Whether our character is morally good or bad remains a mystery until our lives are complete. It is only on our deathbed that we know.[11]

Mendham agrees that "harmonizing self-interested desires with virtue and common goods is central to the morally and experientially good life."[12] However, he helps us identify a vital, if elusive, point. Mendham questions the eudaemonism of the Neo-Aristotelian position. Drawing on the later ideas of ethical obligation and action of Saint Anselm of Canterbury, John Duns Scotus, and Immanuel Kant, Mendham proposes that their view of virtuous behavior is "more rationally and phenomenologically plausible."[13] These thinkers add the element of difficulty into the equation, which puts virtue, and the link between virtue and happiness, to the test.

To these philosophers, virtuous behavior happens when something is "done for its own sake under difficult circumstances." MacIntyre poses an ethics founded on eudaemonistic assumptions as the alternative to today's complete moral chaos. Calling on us to go back further than Aristotle and his focus on individual well-being, Mendham sees in "Platonic alternatives" a better option. These Platonic alternatives are based on "phenomenological insights such as behaving rightly for its own sake."[14] Even for the most adverse conditions, such as the last hours of Socrates's life, this choice could apply. With his execution imminent, Socrates is still happy. Before Aristotle, Plato accepted the root of eudaemonism, the idea that "the rigorous moral life" is also "ultimately the most rewarding." Yet for Plato, morality extends beyond any form of "self-interested calculation." Logic and reason are neither logical nor reasonable if employed in service to nefarious ends, not because they are not *virtuous* but because they are not *good*. Plato's lifework continually redirects every discussion to a consideration of the good involved: "Across his career Plato showed this dedication to a distinctive and radically prioritized moral good, which was perhaps seen as sufficient for happiness."[15]

THE LOVING OUGHT

Mendham's best example is Plato's description of unselfish love. Mendham identifies "secondary noneudaemonistic appeals" in Plato's thought, "such as condemning self-excepting self-interest as the source of all evil, and insisting that the self was made first for the sake of the universe, not vice versa."[16] Mendham goes on to draw a distinction between Platonic and Aristotelian visions: "The Platonic focus upon the love for various ends instantiated in different ways of life, as well as the various sources of moral norms, suggests different avenues for reflection than the Aristotelian focus on proper habits and virtues serving as means to the single end of happiness."[17]

Mendham sees a clear contrast in the views of Aristotle and Plato on the topic of both means and ends in morals: Plato allowed for a plurality of moral goods and the ways we attain them, while Aristotle focused single-mindedly on virtue as the one path to happiness, the ultimate human good. Mendham highlights the ideas of John Rist as providing a Platonic revision of the Aristotelian position, a "'metaphysical background eudaemonism': That doing what we ought to corresponds with our advantage, even though we are not to do it merely or foundationally because it is to our advantage; that we are obligated to pursue virtue for its own preeminent sake even while we recognize its ultimate utility; and that knowledge of the Good, itself the highest enjoyment, reveals irreducible obligations."[18] We must note that it is knowledge of the *good* (an end), not of virtue (a means).

In Mendham's phrasing, Rist argues that Plato "is not urging us to be good *because* it pays to be good, whether in this world or in another—though as a matter of fact it does—but because we are made to conform ourselves to the goodness of the gods."[19] In sum, Mendham writes, Rist "maintains that Platonic obligation is moral in a manner not reducible to enlightened self-interest."[20] Rist is one of a few recent Platonists returning to Plato not for political but for other reasons.

THE BEAUTIFUL LIFE

The question of how to live and why (whether to live in a certain way and even to live at all) is the overarching preoccupation of political philosophers such as Alasdair MacIntyre, Martha Nussbaum, and Charles Taylor. How does a movie like *Interstellar* possibly relate to questions of political philosophy? Some of the most compelling recent and current philosophical positions can be roughly gathered together under the umbrella of moral philosophy. In a critique of modern individualism, some writers focused on the need for a greater emphasis on community and civil society, even before the ugliness of the most recent divisions manifested themselves in the 2016 presidential election. They argued that individual rights, liberties, and privileges needed to be countered by a sense of duty and obligation. Many in the movement of virtue ethics drew on Aristotle to argue for community and responsibility. Yet all forms of community are not of equal value. How do we promote those forms of community worthy of our best strivings? For that we must rely on Plato.

So what does Platonism have to offer that has not already informed moral philosophy, communitarian thought, and virtue ethics? Practical philosophy has also had a resurgence, and schools of thought such as Stoicism seemed to be another pendulum swing away from selfishness and self-indulgence. Gnosticism and Cynicism are all-pervasive and offer no way out. Epicureanism is all-pervasive, yet in a form that has lost sight of its ancient focus on virtue. Of all of the major schools having a resurgence today, Platonism is the one most missing. Yet it is the one perhaps most needed. This is because Platonism helps us see questions of value as paramount. Virtue ethics mainly concerns the *means* of living a virtuous life. Plato always brings us back to *ends*.

A disciplined life of virtue requires a heightened sense of right and wrong. As we saw in Philip Rieff's view, culture itself rests on the notion that some things are allowed and some forbidden. Virtuous behavior, in this view, usually means not giving in to certain emotions and desires, as we saw in Stoicism. What is often lost sight of is the good—the point of the virtuous behavior in the first place. Truth rings true as in beautiful.

In answering the critique of the therapeutic culture and the hyperindividualism of the late twentieth and early twenty-first century—from the Me Decade and the Culture of Narcissism to the "I, me, mine" mind-set of ecstatic capitalism and the money and celebrity and consumer culture, the critics' challenge put forth a creed that placed community over the individual. Its warning of the risks to the polity of what Sandel called "the unencumbered self" is validated by evidence even further of the reign of the rapacious self exposed by the Me Too movement.[21] The return of white nationalism and other deeply antisocial assaults on individuals and groups adds more evidence. Total relativism supports total shamelessness—everything goes—which dons the mantle of complete self-acceptance and toleration of others but incidentally paves the way for raw power, in the form of a culture of bullying, incivility, and violence. Shame and guilt presuppose a notion of the good, grasped through conscience. The shamelessness of the Cynics presupposed virtue and the good, but today's shamelessness does not.[22]

In place of the grasping and rapacious self, following its own interests wherever they lead, whether in career accomplishment and the amassing of wealth or in the liberated libido and unrestricted desire or in outright violence, some philosophers put moral obligation and virtue ethics. In place of what I *want* to do, writers like Charles Taylor, Alasdair MacIntyre, Cornel West, Mary Ann Glendon, and Jean Bethke Elshtain speak of the importance of what I *should* do. Virtue should overcome not only unlimited self-expression and reckless personal hedonism but also corporate greed and political corruption.

Adding Platonism into the picture takes this cultural conversation a step further. In moral thinking, we hear about serious matters in tones both sobering and wise: obligation, duty, consideration of the community more than the self. Albeit somber, much of this writing inspires those who already find virtue and community uplifting and devotion to the good life a worthy ethical goal. That term, *the good life*, captures both meanings—*good* as in "Life is *good*" and *good* as in "*We* are good." The good life as elaborated on by Aristotle included finding the mean between different urges to attain balance and to serve the good life in both of these senses. Though they provided very different answers, all of the ancient schools of Greek thought took up this question.

Today, problems in the nation and world clearly threaten well-being: depression, anxiety, fraying families and communities, addiction, and suicide rates are all evidence of this. Much can be seen as an embodiment crisis—difficulty managing being in a body and all that it brings with it—desire, instinct, urges, emotions, pain, suffering, hunger, thirst, love, loss. Platonism and Aristotelianism have historically served as influences at times within Abrahamic religions—Judaism, Christianity, and Islam—a profound point of commonality we ignore at our loss.[23] Platonism, often the assumed but unspoken background of Aristotelianism and the other schools of thought, and such a major influence on Augustine and Christianity more broadly, as well as other world religions, points us to an element often missing in discussions of our public philosophy. Rather than stop at the good life, it sets our sights higher, on the beautiful life. But the Platonist notion of beauty is unlike that which prevails today—external, image oriented, fleeting, superficial, and illusory. Instead, beauty is a moral phenomenon, category, or reality, like the good life, only better. It is more than a call for obligation, responsibility, limits, and sacrifice, which are all well and good for those already converted to those goods—for preaching to the choir of the communally minded. A focus on the good life teaches us *how* to live, while a notion of the beautiful life inspires us with a vision of *why*.

We do not need to agree on the precise contours of the beautiful life, only that the beautiful life is what we should strive for. An ongoing public conversation must take place as the way of working out what that means as new events occur. If we cannot agree that it is better to be good, living among others will not be possible except by force, manipulation, or coercion. Everyone need not agree on the details, but we must agree on the need for good ends: justice, human dignity, and the inviolability of the human person. Ideals animate moral principles with a vision of the beautiful. The conversation about these philosophies serves as a bulwark against manipulation because it creates an expectation of inwardness, determining one's inner life by tilting it toward the good.

THE QUESTION OF VALUE

What the imagination seizes as Beauty must be truth.
—*John Keats*

Platonism is the philosophy of value par excellence. It is not just a vision of the good life that we need, but a vision of what it means to lead a beautiful life, not just the aesthetic lifestyle of Foucault. Today we find such images, themes, and concepts in movies from *Interstellar* to *Hidden Figures*. It is often in the case of math or science, including computer technology, where such visions are articulated. Only in the rarified air of the outer recesses of the universe or an artificial world do we still seem to find any order, purity, beauty, or even divinity. By contrast, these values might seem impossible to find in everyday life. Even words seem to have played themselves out, bygone relics of a confining vocabulary that is now exhausted. Only the numerical universe seems to possess the capacity to gesture toward perfection, to inspire awe, as we saw in *Hidden Figures*. Yet this is not the case. We can find sources of renewal, not just in numbers and stars, but also in the staggering mystery and beauty closer to home, including in ideas and words and the human beings capable of embodying them.

PLATONISM AS PRACTICAL PHILOSOPHY

How can Plotinus help with a practical philosophy for our own time? It is precisely in his commitment to philosophy *not* as practical but as an end in itself. So even to ask the question this way is both modernist and anachronistic: How can we use the philosophy of Plotinus to apply it to our lives, to pluck it from the tree of philosophical traditions, and put it to use in our current context? This would be meaningless to Plotinus, for whom philosophy *is* life. In the Western intellectual tradition, Plato is the major source for noninstrumentalist thinking. The good is, in content and form, anti-instrumentalist. It is a delicate task to wed an idea and an application: the need or imperative to use the idea can distort any truth it might hold. What happens when what is needed is something other than the true, or the right, or the beautiful? Socrates would think this impossible, since for him the truth *is* virtue. So trying to articulate a practical philosophy risks many things—getting ideas wrong or inaccurate for reasons ranging from being selective for one's needs to taking ideas out of context, applying ideas in a way they were never meant to be applied or in a way they were intended but that is dangerous or wrong. Using an idea as a tool or weapon is also instrumentalism; it violates the idea itself and those in the situation who are being wronged by the manipulation of truth.

The overarching mistake is to reduce a set of complex musings to simple directives that preclude a fuller conversation. Complexity is not the answer so much as intricacy—the qualifications and considerations of multiple perspectives and dimensions—in which moral reflection occurs and virtuous action arises. These intricacies *are* the content of inwardness. The overly hasty search for a quick fix makes us act on impulse, whether affective or cerebral, forecloses alternatives prematurely, and reduces thought to *rule*. Rules then often preclude further thought. Rules, standards, and precepts are vital but either just the beginning or else a premature ending. We must live life in the interstices between these births and deaths, beginnings and endings. The consideration of the rule in light of a given situation is the inner conversation that needs to be part of decisions to act. Inwardness is the space—the gap between people—where we process this intricacy, not just to accept or get over our fears and anxieties, but to figure out how they can best inform and fill our lives.

Maybe this is the litmus test for self-help approaches: which ones foster lifelong practices of self-making toward nonmanipulable relations and self-transcendent ends of the good and beautiful as expressed in love. As Joseph E. Davis puts it so eloquently: "The cultural challenge of minding our minds, then, of leading more reflective lives, is both a matter of reducing the overload and filling an absence—the cultivation of those loves that can order our attention and intensify our connection to the good beyond ourselves."[24]

WHOM DO YOU LOVE?

The bare-all, share-all culture of advertising, entertainment, political discourse, and social media has a rationale that goes something like this: open-ended self-expression brings the catharsis necessary for health, happiness, and self-confidence. Confession of one's innermost feelings is not only accepted but expected. Yet however pleasant or freeing its short-term effects, the confessional mode does not work. Radical transparency has not proven to draw people together. Even when everything is said, total self-disclosure does not ensure closeness, or even the sense that we know one another at all. The poet, novelist, and essayist May Sarton drew a distinction, in *Journal of a Solitude*, between the painful solitude of loneliness and a generative form of solitude that gives rise to love and gratitude.[25]

In the first half of his book *Love and Human Separateness*, philosopher Ilham Dilman presents a sustained critique of the Cartesian self, drawing on the critique of Ludwig Wittgenstein. Wittgenstein argued that we respond to other people in the context of our embodied existence. This runs against René Descartes's notion that at best all we can know of another person derives from our observation of a physical body, from which we can infer the existence of a mind. Instead, Dilman writes, we see a "live human being" and so "our responses, our whole orientation, are those that have a human being as their object." This orientation to others constitutes "an attitude toward a soul." We do not respond to another person because we have a notion that he or she exists, based on our knowledge of the existence of our own mind—"I think, therefore I am"; rather, we respond to a person's embodied being.[26]

Even though we need not doubt the existence of other people, that does not mean we can easily know them. Dilman's exploration of the question of whether we can ever know another person allows us to see a very different kind of inwardness and the interpersonal relations it allows. Dilman's discussion recalls Rieff's vision, explored in chapter 4, of the necessary sacred space we must maintain between us. The notion of the *intermundia*, which appeared in the Epicurean texts discussed in chapter 3, can give us a poetic metaphor for this.

Dilman asks, "What is it to *know* a person?" (emphasis in the original). This question, and the implied sister query of whether we ever can, gets us back full circle to the problem of the nature of the separateness of human beings. Are we separated from one another by a "distance or a gulf"? Is this gap inherently unbridgeable or can we overcome it under certain conditions? (3). Dilman explores novels for notions of separateness as well as works of philosophy. He takes seriously Sartre's portrait of lovers who are doomed to conflict because of their separate existence, and Proust's illustration of the way in which separateness keeps people apart even when they are in love. Ways of thinking about our separateness range from the "classical solipsism" of Proust's narrator Marcel, who holds it as a philosophical position, to the "affective solipsism" of Rosamond in *Middlemarch*, who believes people "exist for her convenience." Both deny the reality of other people (4). In Dostoyevsky, in contrast, Dilman sees a glimpse of a possibility for human contact (5).

In Dilman's view, precisely what separates us ends up bringing us together. The way we know another person is contingent upon our preserving the space between us. Rather than collapsing that distance, we need to acknowledge the reality of our basic separateness while grasping it as the basis for our uniqueness and our love for someone not ourselves. This is the condition for a separate self that can love and be loved. Dilman describes the way that love transforms the potential for separation into a benign separateness through a form of inwardness directed toward finding and sustaining our connections with others.

To Dilman, we begin as separate, unique beings, and this separateness is "part of the framework" in which we interact. Even if we interact with others, this does not mean we naturally or easily "make contact" with them. That would require coming to know them. If we make no contact, "each remains alone in the relationship" (159). To make contact we must see a person "for what he is and this involves appreciating his character and understanding his motives." Without knowing the other person in this way, "one's interaction with him will not amount to contact" (5).

Knowing another person is the way that human separation turns into separateness. Dilman argues that separateness is necessary for intimacy and knowledge between people. In this way, the inwardness of separation in which we all find ourselves can become the very mechanism by which we come to know other people: "The separateness I have been commenting on, far from being a gulf between us, unless of course we make it so, is in fact a necessary condition of friendship, love and human give and take. . . . I cannot really love someone with whom I have identified myself to the extent that I do not feel her to have an identity apart from mine. The wonder of friendship and the magic of love depend on the separateness of friends and lovers; it is this which make their response to one another a gift" (105–6). What leads people to know one another in the way that leads to genuine contact has nothing to do with the quantity of self-revelation but the quality, not only the sharing but the receiving. What determines whether interaction amounts to contact is how we approach our separateness. Thus the gap between us becomes not only bridgeable but the very source and subject of our connection. The bridge is our disposition: "The attitude of those involved to that separateness, therefore, affects the character of the interaction, and so determines whether or not it amounts to contact" (159). We can choose estrangement. Or we can choose love.

A BOOK LIKE THIS ONE CAN DO NO MORE THAN HINT, gesture, and whisper of the subject it has taken up, *ars vitae*. It is intended as a small contribution to a vast, ongoing conversation.

Yet it is *the* human conversation, to which all others are in some way connected. It is a conversation that everyone is a part of by definition, whether through words and actions or inaction and silence. Everything we do or do not do, everything we think or do not think, everything we imagine or fail to imagine, everything we create or destroy, speaks of a philosophy of living sometimes barely audible and at other times roaring like an ocean. This book is merely an attempt to chart some of the sounds—notes, themes, motifs, riffs, symphonies—that have reached one person's ears, in hopes it may help even one fellow human being hear still others. We sorely need to tune our ears, eyes, or any other sense available to us to the important things. The most important things include the beauty and love all around us. These are the things that make it possible to endure all of the rest.

EPILOGUE

Once

The world of dew
Is the world of dew
And yet, and yet . . .
                    —*Issa*

A young boy runs out into the path of what at first looks like his father and his entourage, returning from war. All is aglow with glory, and the anticipation of reunion. The sun shines in the son's eyes. His mother smiles in anticipation. They shield their eyes from the blinding light. But as the thundering hooves grow louder, then suddenly deafening, we realize it is Commodus's men, and they are not going to stop.

This scene in the movie *Gladiator* captures the fragility of life. It draws a sharp distinction between peace and war, innocence and knowledge, the particularity of life and the faceless machinery of death. It speaks to something shared, gesturing to aspects of what it means to be human—which entails both attachment and alien-ation, creation and destruction, love and enmity. Our existence is painfully contingent on the constellation of people, places, and things all around us, and their behavior in time, random or in-tended. The thinness of the line between life and death, whether spiritual or biological, staggers the mind. As Bob Dylan put it, "He not busy being born is busy dying."[1] Locating that line and spin-ning that gossamer thread into a capacious space for life—creating the architecture Goethe describes as "frozen music"—is the art of living.

Later, after learning of the death of his wife and son, Maximus loses heart. Suffering from a wound on his arm from his would-be executioner, from whom he has now escaped, he loses conscious-ness. He is flat on his back, having been captured by new masters, when we encounter him again. We wonder whether he still has the will to live. The first words Juba says to him, as he tends to Maxi-mus's wound, are "Not yet." Later, Juba repeats this several times at key moments of crisis. And after Maximus dies at the end of the movie, the last words we hear are Juba's: "Now we're free . . . and we'll see you again. But not yet. Not yet."

The scene with Maximus's wife and son captures this moment of "Not yet," and the way time and space combine in the way we experience it. The space between the boy and Commodus's men is the time between his life and his imminent and inevitable death if the horses do not stop. It captures the space-time continuum at its easiest to grasp, where the physical space *is* the duration of our lives. Distance becomes time's measure. The preservation of that distance is life giving. This moment-space—this space-moment—is all we have. Our life is lived in this interstice, in this fleeting inter-val. It is precisely this fragility and evanescence that delivers our only glimpse of something beyond us. Milan Kundera writes, "There is a certain part of all of us that lives outside of time."[2] The only way we know this time out of time and place out of place comes from that other part of us that lives inside it. To the mantra of "Not yet," Juba reels Maximus back in from certain death, as much from the loss of the will to live as from his bodily wounds—the dark night of the soul. Both our physical self and the spirit that animates it must be quickened for us to inhabit fully the moment we are given.

In the scene from *Gladiator*, the gap is temporarily salutary. At other times distances between us are not. When what lies at a distance is not an inanimate object but a living being, the gap can be both a source of agony—the gap of time and space that keeps us apart—and the only chance for connection. All of the means we seek for collapsing this distance or filling it with distractions from the pain it brings remove our ability to participate, human animal that we are, in the divine. Unless we protect that moment as something sacred, the moment of listening and of self-creation, we cannot know one another. To love is to maintain and respect that distance, however imperceptible, as vital for the very constitution of each unique self. Time can be a metaphor for the space between us. Only by honoring that uniqueness can we find unity. Our particularity is the source of each of us, responsible for all of our worst pain and loneliness and the best and utmost pleasure of connectedness.

This positive and compelling philosophical paradox could serve to replace the exhausted therapeutic paradox of a culture in thrall to therapies that are not therapeutic. The paradox of philosophy is that we can never possess knowledge, but we can love it all the more for that. We do not ever know everything about another person, who does and should have an inviolable inner life. We do not know the other person in the sense of seeing the whole person. That is a conceit—and an invasion.[3] Instead, we might love any knowledge we have of the good in another person, which is better.

The connection between space and time becomes all too real in the case of natural disaster. The eruption of Mt. Vesuvius in AD 79 lays bare their reality for us, or rather, what remains of the people who lived and loved in nearby Pompeii and Herculaneum. Waves of hot lava moved so fast that they caught people's expressions as they fled—the complete terror of having time and space suddenly come crashing in, colliding with one another, the collapse of their world inscribed on the bodies of those in its path. Time was up. There was no place to go. At one point in *Gladiator*, in a scene on a rooftop, Juba speaks to Maximus of his own family:

JUBA: It is somewhere out there, my country, my home. My wife is preparing the food. My daughter is carrying water from the river. Will I ever see them again? I think not.

MAXIMUS: Do you believe that you will see them again when you die?

JUBA: I think so, but then, I will die soon. They will not die for many years. I will have to wait.

MAXIMUS: But you would . . . wait?

JUBA: Of course.

MAXIMUS: You see, my wife and my son are already waiting for me.

JUBA: You will meet them again.

With a gentle smile, Juba adds, "But not yet. Not yet." As much as he misses his family, Juba signals that he hears other drummers too, beating the varied rhythms of his day-to-day existence. His own living counts too. It is not up to him to take on the role of a god. Captured in those two words, enhanced by the glint in Juba's eyes, lies the whole world that is a human life, that speck on the Stoic's time line pointing both ways toward infinity.

That speck—just a point in time and space—is where we live. Yet it is not all that we are. Once the spirit—*anima* in Latin, ψυχή (*psyche*) in Greek—leaves the body, we join that fast-flowing stream of time. But not yet.

AND YET

In the epigraph of this chapter, the Issa haiku bears a resemblance to Juba's mantra.[4] The intricate simplicity of poetry captures the difference. Here, in the alteration of a single word from "Not yet" to "And yet," we can grasp a world of difference. The "Not yet" is all we have, it seems, but when enlivened by the "And yet," we find there is another direction beyond the infinity of the past and future, and that is the infinity of the present. The poets, painters, and philosophers of the inner life, working in all genres from music to mathematics, from architecture to astronomy, sometimes harken to an indescribable phenomenon—an infinity within.

Stephen Greenblatt's *Swerve* argues that the essence of modern life can be found in ancient atomism, as propounded by Lucretius, through logic and rationality. Building on the atomists, the ancient poet spelled out the brilliant reasoning for why everything must be made up of minute particles. This came long before humans invented the technology to measure them: it seemed blatantly absurd to think that this minute building block of everything could keep dividing itself infinitely. That logic holds when applied to physical bodies. But when it comes to the entity animating them, we *can* imagine an infinity within. This is the special character of our moment here on earth. It is animated by something intangible, beyond understanding, outside the purview of our knowledge. But we are creatures endowed with understanding. As long as we are still capable of an inner life—a form of inwardness sturdy enough to allow us to draw on it again and again ad infinitum—our "Not yet" includes the mystery and ecstasy only to be found in the "And yet." The "Not yet" is our affirmation that we are alive. The "And yet" suggests there is something more to life than meets the eye, an infinity of reasons for living.

While a life can bring innumerable reasons to be alive, in a given moment all we need is one. And it is one that has everything to do with quality, not quantity. The movie *Once* captures this.

ONCE

The movie *Once* explores these subtle themes through the story of two people who meet at a time when both are separated from their respective partners in long-term relationships.[5] It opens with a young man (played by Glen Hansard) suffering the indignities of being a street performer as he plays a beat-up guitar for spare change in a Dublin square. His tunes draw the notice of a young woman (Markéta Irglová) of similarly humble appearance who is allowed to play the piano during lunch breaks in a music store.

They strike up a friendship, and more. Just how much more is precisely the question of the movie, and of the two people involved. It is clear to them both that all of the ingredients for love are present. Each confides in the other that the true state of their previous relationship is unresolved. The man's girlfriend back in London had an affair, and though she did not pursue it, he left her to return home, where his mother had recently died, to live with his father (Bill Hodnett). He now works with his father in his vacuum repair shop. His new female friend, having left her husband, has emigrated from the Czech Republic and lives in Dublin with her mother (Danuse Ktrestova) and young daughter. Both relationships had become strained, and the outcome of the challenges each face is unclear for most of the movie. Although they exchange few words on the subject, the new love they share is palpable. The plot weds their musical dreams with their exploration of what direction their personal connection will take. With minimal dialogue confronting the question directly, the choice they face comes through their demeanor and music. They decide to record a few songs together. They apply for a bank loan, talk other street musicians into joining them, and win over the studio engineer (Geoff Minogue), who starts out too cool for these amateurs and ends up in thrall to their work ethic and music. His eureka moment is our own, as the tentative sketches come together in passionate lyrics and melodies.

After the climax of producing the music together, the question of whether their love will find consummation resurfaces. It seems no longer the painful matter of before in the calm and clarity of the dénouement. They leave the agony of their new love behind and choose to return to their earlier loves and the lives they had embarked on before they met. It is as though cutting those ties would actually threaten to sever their new one. While counterintuitive, finding a way through the challenges and back to an earlier love emerges as the best, or only, way to honor what they too share. Acting any other way would violate loved ones as well as the truth and reality of love itself.

When they are just getting to know each other, in perhaps the most famous scene, the protagonists sing "Falling Slowly," winner of an Academy Award for Best Original Song. Later, in the real piano store where it was filmed, so many people played the song on the pianos for sale that management banned it. (See fig. E.1.)

In this scene, the man and woman begin to get to know each other by way of a musical conversation, their first time singing together. In the piano store, she plays him one of her original tunes and he joins in on guitar. The notes begin shakily then find their way. The tentative melody mirrors their hesitant introduction to one another. The song captures the allure of attraction to someone new, then ventures into the complexity and ambiguity of their respective situations. At one point, it seems to recommend returning to their old relationships with the metaphor of a ship's return voyage. Then it moves to their decision between old and new loves, mentioning hope yet leaving it ambiguous, as though hope applies equally to the old relationship and the new: "Raise your hopeful voice, you have a choice / You'll make it now." Musically and lyrically, hope seems to transcend the particular situation and time, as though uniting past, present, and future.[6]

At another moment, the song seems to embrace moving on. Ultimately, it ends with a resolution that begs the question of resolution altogether. The refrain of the song's title returns as the two musicians gently surrender to the way things are, slipping into the very sounds they are making, melding with the music and meeting again through their music-making. That might be the only possible answer, no matter what the decision. In other words, the decision does not involve whether to embrace the old or the new but whether to embrace the good in both. It does not try to do away with the pain but turns it into music—discovering a way to handle suffering. "Falling Slowly" suggests that one must protect something inviolable between people, which then provides consolation for what must be reined in. The real choice seems to be whether to turn pain into poetry or be beaten down by the pain of living.

Identified in the liner notes of the CD and the film credits as "Guy" and "Girl," the protagonists have a love that finds consummation in their music. At the end of the movie, before he leaves Dublin and returns to London, he enters the piano store, and later we see a piano being delivered to the woman's apartment. After she has a happy reunion with her husband and her mother and child, we are left with a vision of her at the piano, glimpsed through an open window of the apartment. Only her last wistful glance speaks of the whole world that was her love with the man— a love that was not permitted to take precedence over all previous ones. In its apparent denial, it allowed the hopes and dreams of all involved to be sustained. We might call this kind of sacrifice— whether for personal relations, the *polis*, or the planet—a *lifework*. Not only does it refuse to tear down what they have contributed to building, but it refuses to violate its own essence. This is love as more than momentary feelings of romance, infatuation, and excitement—as the enduring passion capable of finding, preserving, and sustaining the truth of feeling in all of its repleteness. This goal reaches beyond happy versus sad or having versus not having. It points to the infinity of actions—and at times, inaction—that allow it to keep its integrity. It catapults us beyond even virtue and character to the reasons for their existence—presence and nurturance of the original spirit of all good things.

This movie conveys all this not only through the story but through the music and camera shots, which convey the humble beauty of the characters' predicament and everyday lives. The viewer can almost feel the comforting roughness of the oversized sweaters protecting them from the raw air, and the elation of all of the notes and rhythms coming together. What stands out is the vast palette of the emotions, like the subtle colors, words, and exchanges between characters. Through a focus on a single note and its meticulous modulation, we can feel everything from the anguish of longing to the rage at the betrayals and shortcomings of the previous partners. But what is astonishingly beautiful is the way the songs do not clearly apply to either the new or the old love. Instead, the music seems to suspend time and envelop us in a moment and a place where the past and present come together. Flashbacks to videos of the man's girlfriend dancing with him in delight, dappled in light and laughter, remind us of the truth that their relationship too contained love. That truth is easily disregarded in the overlayering of new passions, but *Once* refuses to let us do so. In merging past and present, the songs skip forward to the future, when we could imagine the rigors of day-to-day life interfering with the new relationship in turn. That the movie and play and CD choose to return us to the earlier love is a bold move in our liberated times. Cultivating current loves that have crumbled rather than seizing every chance for new ones, in the hopes of finding true mega-love, or so the narrative goes, is not what usually grabs audiences today. It is a hard sell.

Yet the art of living at the very least involves navigating this "raging sea" that is our embodied existence, and the judgments of our minds, often seemingly in conflict with our bodies. Once we surrender to our status as neither all body nor all intellect but an infinitesimally fine instrument that records the movements of both, the task before us looks substantially different. It becomes less a chore of balancing between those competing claims than a task of bringing them into harmony, less about achieving balance between entities inexorably at odds than about attaining the fullest life given the limits and gifts of our embodied whole. To do this has struck many as involving faith in a transcendent element, animating all of our faculties and bringing them together in concert in the unity needed for a life—the way in which our soul is forged.

A richly multilayered word, *once* means both that something happens only one time and that something happened in the past, as in once upon a time. It is definite yet wistful, declaring with certainty that there can only be one occurrence of a thing and dreamily reflecting on a time gone by. It gives the same sense of fulfillment of the promise of a moment as of one human life. Like the word, the movie *Once* is a self-contained whole. This is one way we can tell if a work—just think of Tolstoy's *Anna Karenina*—reaches excellence in its given art, its *telos*. It becomes a world, an existence, a presence, almost a living being. The best works of art are so in part because they are capacious enough to contain the full range of possible approaches to our quandaries, our archipelago of sensibilities, and put them into conversation with one another. They soar, not because they lead us deeper into our own concerns, but because they lead us deeper into our own concerns to lead us out of them again into the world of others. They help us develop a life-saving inwardness. True, a slogan on a mug may not be a good life companion, but if it is a quote from such a work it may be. If a piece of advice lacks nuance, intricacy, and coherence, it cannot serve us well. It needs to emanate from and pertain to a world. We should not settle for fragments when we deserve to partake in the whole of which we ourselves are a part.

Issa's haiku acknowledges the reality of the physical world as fact. Ending with "And yet . . . ," the poet opens the door to the mystery of something more, something beyond what meets the eye. In the absence of mystery, we have already decided what we think and what we know—what we think we know about other people and our world. This brings knowingness, which shuts down channels of communication by judging all questions closed and all answers given. When knowingness is applied to human beings, it means the end of curiosity about another person. It spells the passing of enchantment and awe, of the capacity for surprise. Listening is no longer needed because judgment has occurred. An attitude of prejudging—literally prejudice—against the other person suggests that the person is known, with no room for change. We can move on.[7] Fully transparent, one person becomes interchangeable with another. Embarking on romantic and other relationships brings an initial sense of mystery. The newness wears off when it seems there is no longer anything to learn. Knowingness precludes inwardness, where one's uniqueness continues to arise in an individual's encounter with the ever-unfolding moment.

Against this mood of jaded disenchantment, we must cultivate an earnest openness that keeps alive the opportunity to learn but also to unlearn. Only with an openness to learning about the good and unlearning the bad do we really listen, and only by really listening do we continue to get to know other persons as they continue to become who they are. All of this presupposes that we are creatures capable of observing, sustaining, and living suspended in the fragile beauty of the world around us, within us, and beyond us.

N O T E S

INTRODUCTION

1. Marcus Tullius Cicero, *De finibus bonorum et malorum (On Ends)* 3.2.4, trans. H. Rackham, Loeb Classical Library (Cambridge, MA: Harvard University Press, 1914, 1931), 220.

2. Anthony Birley, *Marcus Aurelius: A Biography* (1966; repr., New York: Barnes and Noble, 1987), 195, 286n30. He established chairs in Platonism, Aristotelianism, Stoicism, and Epicureanism.

3. Aristotle, *Nicomachean Ethics* 1.1–8, trans. H. Rackham, Loeb Classical Library (Cambridge, MA: Harvard University Press, 1926, 1934), 3–69.

4. Epictetus, *Encheiridion* 3, in *Discourses, Books 3–4. Fragments. The Encheiridion*, trans. W. A. Oldfather, Loeb Classical Library (Cambridge, MA: Harvard University Press, 1928).

5. As of this writing, the mug is for sale at Zazzle: https://www.zazzle .com/epictetus_png_coffee_mug-168278386246607669.

6. John Kaag, "Need a New Self-Help Guru? Try Aristotle," *New York Times*, January 23, 2019; Edith Hall, *Aristotle's Way: How Ancient Wisdom Can Change Your Life* (New York: Penguin Press, 2018).

7. Carlos Fraenkel, "Can Stoicism Make Us Happy?," review of *How to Be a Stoic: Using Ancient Philosophy to Live a Modern Life*, by Massimo Pigliucci (New York: Basic Books, 2017), *Nation*, February 5, 2019, https://www .thenation.com/article/massimo-pigliucci-modern-stoicism-book-review.

8. Simon Critchley, *Tragedy, the Greeks, and Us* (New York: Pantheon, 2019); Catherine Wilson, *How to Be an Epicurean: The Ancient Art of Living Well* (New York: Basic Books, 2019); Seneca, *On Anger*, trans. James Romm, *How to Keep Your Cool: An Ancient Guide to Anger Management* (Princeton, NJ: Princeton University Press, 2019).

9. Gerald Howard, "Reasons to Believe," *Bookforum*, February/March 2007. In this fine profile of Philip Rieff, book editor Howard writes that Rieff's theory of the triumph of the therapeutic and psychological man "is one of the most durable concepts we have for grasping the inner dynamics of our culture."

10. For an investigation into the origins of the "Serenity Prayer," see Fred R. Shapiro, "Who Wrote the Serenity Prayer?" *Chronicle of Higher Education*, April 28, 2014, https://www.chronicle.com/article/Who-Wrote-the-Serenity-Prayer-/146159.

11. Lawrence C. Becker, *A New Stoicism* (Princeton, NJ: Princeton University Press, 1998).

12. Daniel Wickberg, "What Is the History of Sensibilities? On Cultural Histories, Old and New," *American Historical Review* 112, no. 3 (June 2007): 661–84.

13. The epigraph to this section is from Marcelo Gleiser, "Meaning in a Silent Universe," *New Atlantis*, no. 47 (Fall 2015): 76–86.

14. Philip Rieff, *The Triumph of the Therapeutic: Uses of Faith after Freud*, 40th Anniversary ed. (Wilmington, DE: ISI Books, 2007), x.

15. P. Rieff, *Triumph of the Therapeutic*, 3.

16. P. Rieff, *Triumph of the Therapeutic*.

17. Kathryn Schulz, "The Self in Self-Help," *New York*, January 6, 2013.

18. Schulz, "The Self in Self-Help."

19. Howard Thurman, *Jesus and the Disinherited* (New York: Abingdon-Cokesbury Press, 1949), 29.

20. P. Rieff, *Triumph of the Therapeutic*; Philip Rieff, *Freud: The Mind of the Moralist*, 3rd ed. (New York: Anchor Books, 1979). Others have contributed greatly to our understanding of the therapeutic sensibility, including Peter Berger, Tom Wolfe, Christopher Lasch, Christina Hoff Sommers, Sally Satel, and Wendy Kaminer, among others.

21. P. Rieff, *Triumph of the Therapeutic*, 1–54.

22. Alasdair MacIntyre, *After Virtue: A Study in Moral Theory*, 3rd ed. (Notre Dame, IN: University of Notre Dame Press, 2007), 23–24. "For what emotivism asserts is in central part that there are and can be no valid rational justification for any claims that objective and impersonal moral standards exist and hence that there are no such standards" (22). For MacIntyre's inspired discussion of the Aristotelian notion of *telos* and its connection with *eudaemonia*, see especially 146–50.

23. For example, Christopher Lasch, *The Culture of Narcissism: American Life in an Age of Diminishing Expectations* (New York: Norton, 1978); T. J. Jackson Lears, *No Place of Grace: Antimodernism and the Transformation of American Culture, 1880–1920* (New York: Pantheon Books, 1981); and Stuart Ewen, *Captains of Consciousness: Advertising and Social Roots of the Consumer Culture* (New York: McGraw-Hill, 1976).

24. Catherine Tumber, *American Feminism and New Age Spirituality: Searching for the Higher Self, 1875–1915* (Lanham, MD: Rowman and Littlefield, 2002), 173.

25. P. Rieff, *Triumph of the Therapeutic*, 8–10.

26. Jonathan Imber, ed., *Therapeutic Culture: Triumph and Defeat* (New Brunswick, NJ: Transaction, 2004). Imber went on to edit *The Anthem Companion to Philip Rieff* (London: Anthem Press, 2017), a collection of essays on Rieff's contribution.

27. Ellen Herman, *Romance of American Psychology: Political Culture in the Age of Experts* (Berkeley: University of California Press, 1996); James Davison Hunter, *Death of Character: Moral Education in an Age without Good or Evil* (New York: Basic Books, 2001); James L. Nolan Jr., *The Therapeutic State: Justifying Government at Century's End* (New York: New York University Press, 1998), 2. Nolan's first chapter, "The Therapeutic Culture" (1–21), is an excellent introduction to the concept and critique.

28. Frank Furedi, "The Silent Ascendency of the Therapeutic Culture in Britain," in Imber, *Therapeutic Culture*, 24; Frank Furedi, *Therapy Culture: Cultivating Vulnerability in an Uncertain Age* (London: Routledge, 2004).

29. James L. Nolan Jr. and Sandra Davis Westervelt, "Justifying Justice: Therapeutic Law and the Victimization Defense Strategy," *Sociological Forum* 15, no. 4 (December 2000): 617–46.

30. Niquie Dworkin, "Rieff's Critique of the Therapeutic and Contemporary Developments in Psychodynamic Psychotherapy," *Journal of Theoretical and Philosophical Psychology* 35, no. 4 (November 2015): 230–43.

31. Emotion-based claims and reason-based claims can both be valid, but their arbiter cannot be themselves or one another. An emotion-based claim cannot be bested by a reason-based claim by definition. Nor can a reason-based claim be bested by an emotion-based claim. Emotion and reason can be employed separately as means but can never by themselves get at ends. Both emotion and reason operating in tandem are needed to get at ends.

32. Boris Kachka, "The Power of Positive Publishing: How Self-Help Ate America," *New York Magazine,* January 6, 2013, 1.

33. Kachka, "Power of Positive Publishing," 5.

34. Kachka, "Power of Positive Publishing," 5.

35. Mark Greif, *Against Everything: Essays* (New York: Pantheon, 2016), 95.

36. Greif, *Against Everything*, 12.

37. Greif, *Against Everything*, 13–14.

38. Natalia Mehlman Petrzela and Christine B. Whelan, "Self-Help Gurus Like Tony Robbins Have Often Stood in the Way of Social Change," op-ed, *Washington Post*, April 13, 2018.

39. Ewen, *Captains of Consciousness*; David Bell, *The Cultural Contradictions of Capitalism* (New York: Basic Books, 1976).

40. Ilham Dilman, *Love and Human Separateness* (Oxford: Basil Blackwell, 1987), introduction and chap. 1.

41. Dilman, *Love and Human Separateness*.

42. Martha Nussbaum, *Therapy of Desire: Theory and Practice in Hellenistic Ethics* (Princeton, NJ: Princeton University Press, 1994), 3. Subsequent page citations are given parenthetically in the text. See also Nussbaum's *The Fragility of Goodness: Luck and Ethics in Greek Tragedy and Philosophy* (1986; repr., Cambridge: Cambridge University Press, 2001) and many other works for a sustained meditation on the ways ancient philosophy continues to speak to our times. Her sensitive close readings of ancient works and nuanced interpretations are a major inspiration for the current work.

43. Plato, *Phaedrus* 246b, trans. H. N. Fowler, Loeb Classical Library (Cambridge, MA: Harvard University Press, 1914, 2006), 471–73.

44. Robert E. Cushman, *Therapeia: Plato's Conception of Philosophy* (Westport, CT: Greenwood Press, 1976).

45. Aristotle, *Poetics* 6.21–28, ed. and trans. Stephen Halliwell, Loeb Classical Library (Cambridge, MA: Harvard University Press, 1995, 1999), 47, 49.

46. Plato, *Gorgias*, trans. Donald J. Zeyl, in *Plato: Complete Works*, ed. John M. Cooper (Indianapolis, IN: Hackett, 1997).

47. Paul Woodruff, "Sophists," in *Encyclopedia of Classical Philosophy*, ed. Donald J. Zeyl, Daniel Devereux, and Phillip Mitsis (Westport, CT: Greenwood, 1997).

48. For an overview of the historiography of the "Third Sophistic" from a scholar who argues against the periodization, see Lieve Van Hoof, "Greek Rhetoric and the Later Roman Empire: The 'Bubble' of the 'Third Sophistic,'" *L'antiquité Tardive* 18 (2010): 211–24.

49. Daniel T. Rodgers, *Age of Fracture* (Cambridge, MA: Harvard University Press, 2011).

50. Jean-François Lyotard, *The Postmodern Condition: A Report on Knowledge* (Manchester, UK: Manchester University Press, 1984).

51. Rod Dreher, *The Benedict Option: A Strategy for Christians in a Post-Christian Nation* (New York: Sentinel, 2017).

52. Charles Taylor, *Sources of the Self: The Making of the Modern Identity* (Cambridge, MA: Harvard University Press, 1989).

53. See David Riesman's description of the difference in cues for how to act from inner direction versus other direction in *The Lonely Crowd: A Study of the Changing American Character* (New Haven, CT: Yale University Press, 1950), 30–31.

54. Martin Bernal, *Black Athena: The Afroasiatic Roots of Classical Civilization*, 3 vols. (Piscataway, NJ: Rutgers University Press, 1987–2006). Critics attacked an interpretation they thought warped by the so-called political correctness of a new progressive/radical orthodoxy, and defenders, sympathetic to the book's suspicion of the impact of nineteenth-century racism on earlier scholarship and lingering ethnocentrism or myopia about cultural cross-fertilization, viewed this as political reaction. See the subsection "Egyptian Sources and Influences," in Richard H. Popkin's introduction to part 1, "The Origins

of Western Philosophic Thinking," in *Columbia History of Western Philosophy*, ed. Richard H. Popkin (New York: MJF Books, 1999), 3–5.

55. For instance, classical thinkers were foundational to the work of Leo Strauss. The more he engaged with the ancients, the more he found their writings fruitful and indeed essential for understanding politics, humanity, and even reality itself. See Timothy W. Burns, ed., *Brill's Companion to Leo Strauss' Writings on Classical Political Thought* (Boston: Brill, 2015). See especially Burns's introductory chapter, "Leo Strauss' Recovery of Classical Philosophy," 1–32.

56. A rich work introducing this thriving field is Anthony Grafton, Glenn W. Most, and Salvatore Settis, eds., *The Classical Tradition* (Cambridge, MA: Belknap Press of Harvard University Press, 2013). Grafton has been a leader in this field.

57. William Cook and James Tatum, *African American Writers and Classical Tradition* (Chicago: University of Chicago Press, 2010); Caroline Winterer, *The Culture of Classicism: Ancient Greece and Rome in American Intellectual Life, 1780–1910* (Baltimore: Johns Hopkins University Press, 2001) and *The Mirror of Antiquity: American Women and the Classical Tradition, 1750–1900* (Ithaca, NY: Cornell University Press, 2007); Patrice Rankine, *Ulysses in Black: Ralph Ellison, Classicism, and African American Literature* (Madison: University of Wisconsin Press, 2006); Robert G. O'Meally, *Romare Bearden: A Black Odyssey* (New York: DC Moore Gallery, 2007); Michele Valerie Ronnick, "Twelve Black Classicists," *Arion: A Journal of Humanities and the Classics*, 3rd ser., 11, no. 3 (Winter 2004): 85–102; Emily Greenwood, "Re-rooting the Classical Tradition: New Directions in Black Classicism," *Classical Receptions Journal* 1, no. 1 (2009): 87–103, notes that "Classica Africana" was formally designated a field in classics in 1996.

58. On Du Bois's classical education, see Francis L. Broderick, "The Academic Training of W. E. B. DuBois," *Journal of Negro Education* 27, no. 1 (Winter 1958): 10–16; and for more on his education philosophy, see Lauren A. Wendling, "Higher Education as a Means of Communal Uplift: The Educational Philosophy of W. E. B. Du Bois," *Journal of Negro Education* 87, no. 3 (Summer 2018): 285–93.

59. Greenwood's "Re-rooting the Classical Tradition" provides an excellent introduction to the field and overview of key works.

60. Marty Beckerman, "Millennials Are the Most Cynical Generation Ever, Study Finds," MTV News, September 4, 2014, www.mtv.com/news/1920597 /millennials-cynical-study/.

61. Henry F. De Sio, "Stop Blaming Millennials for Being Disillusioned," *Newsweek*, November 1, 2018; Rhiân, age twenty-eight, as told to Radhika Sanghani, "How It Feels to Have 'Millennial Burnout,'" BBC 3, February 27, 2019.

62. Neohistorism–New Classic Architecture, Flickr, https://www.flickr .com/groups/neohistorism.

63. For the Instagram account, see https://www.instagram.com/newclassi calarchitecture; the Twitter feed is at https://twitter.com/NewClassicism; the Pinterest board is at https://www.pinterest.com/newclassicism. Two architects working in this tradition are Ethan Anthony, president of HDB/Cram and Ferguson, and Duncan Stroik, professor of architecture at the University of Notre Dame School of Architecture and founding editor of *Sacred Architecture Journal*.

64. Kathleen Quigley, "Inside Architecture's New Classicism Boom," *Architectural Digest*, August 7, 2018.

65. See the Design in Mind film series (Institute of Classical Architecture and Art, 2018). The first film in the series is *Robert A. M. Stern: Always a Student*, dir. Robert A. M. Stern (Institute of Classical Architecture and Art, 2018).

66. *On Location with James Ivory*, dir. James Ivory, Design in Mind film series (Institute of Classical Architecture and Art, 2019); Mitchell Owens, "How James Ivory's Love of Architecture Impacts Cinema History," *Architectural Digest*, August 9, 2019.

67. Rick Noack, "Panoramic Views of the Ancient World—in Modern Day Germany," CNN.com, January 13, 2012. Some of his work includes exhibitions of Rome 312 in Leipzig (2005–9), Dresden (2011–12), Pforzheim (2014–18), and Rouen (2014–15, 2018–19).

68. Allison Malafronte, "Patricia Watwood: 'Venus Apocalypse,'" *Fine Art Today* (weekly newsletter from *Fine Art Connoisseur Magazine*), May 23, 2013. Another 2013 exhibit, *Compulsions*, at the Mark Miller Gallery, displayed works by Diane Corvelle such as *Engagement*. Another exhibit, California Arts Club's 102nd Annual Gold Medal Juried Exhibition, highlighted this style. It included works by Warren Chang, Max Ginsburg, John Nava, Alexey Steele, Ignat Ignatov, and Tony Pro. Brandon Kralik, "Contemporary Classical Painting Is Still Growing," *Huffpost*, June 4, 2013, https://www.huffpost.com /entry/contemporary-classical-painting-is-still-growing_b_3370484.

69. https://modernclassicisms.com.

70. Helen Roche and Kyriakos N. Demetriou, eds., *Brill's Companion to the Classics, Fascist Italy and Nazi Germany*, Brill's Companions to Classical Reception Series, vol. 12 (Leiden: Brill, 2017); Johann Chapoutot, *Greeks, Romans, Germans* (Berkeley: University of California Press, 2016).

71. http://pages.vassar.edu/pharos/.

72. Margaret Talbot, "Whiteness in Classical Sculpture," *New Yorker*, October 22, 2018; Sammy Feldblum, "Myth Appropriation," *Baffler*, September 21, 2018; Emma Yeomans, "The Far Right Is Using Antiquity to Rebrand Itself—but Classicists Are Fighting Back," *New Statesman America*, July 4, 2018.

73. Mary Beard, *SPQR: A History of Ancient Rome* (New York: Norton, 2015), *Women and Power: A Manifesto* (New York: Norton, 2017), and *Confronting the Classics: Traditions, Adventures, and Innovations* (New York: Norton, 2013).

74. Charlotte Higgins, "The Cult of Mary Beard," *Guardian*, January 30, 2018.

75. Review of *Pompeii: The Life of a Roman Town*, by Mary Beard, *Current World Archaeology* 32 (November 4, 2008).

76. Michael Deakin, "Hypatia," in *Encyclopedia Britannica Academic*, accessed March 1, 2019, https://academic.eb.com.

77. *Agora*, directed by Alejandro Amenábar (Focus Features, 2009).

78. "Hypatia at *The Dinner Party*," Brooklyn Museum, n.d., accessed January 13, 2020, https://www.brooklynmuseum.org/eascfa/dinner_party/place_settings/hypatia; Judy Chicago, *The Dinner Party: A Symbol of Our Heritage* (1979; repr., New York: Penguin, 1996).

79. Arthur Herman, "The Personality Divide: Are You More Like Plato or Aristotle?" *Signature*, November 14, 2013, https://www.signature-reads.com/2013/11/the-personality-divide-are-you-more-like-plato-or-aristotle [no longer available online].

80. Lloyd P. Gerson, *Aristotle and Other Platonists* (Ithaca, NY: Cornell University Press, 2005). In this and his larger oeuvre, Gerson presents detailed descriptions of different varieties of Platonism as groundwork for Aristotle's Platonism.

81. Mantha Zarmakoupi, *The Villa of the Papyri at Herculaneum: Archaeology, Reception, and Digital Reconstruction* (Berlin: Walter de Gruyter, 2010), vii–viii.

82. Nicola Davis, "Ancient Scrolls Charred by Vesuvius Could Be Read Once Again," *Guardian*, October 2, 2019.

83. Jess Walter, *Beautiful Ruins: A Novel* (New York: Harper, 2012).

CHAPTER ONE

1. Dan Brown, *The Da Vinci Code* (New York: Doubleday, 2003); *The Da Vinci Code*, directed by Ron Howard (Columbia Pictures, 2006).

2. D. Brown, *Da Vinci Code*, 44–45. Brown writes that, "considered the most anatomically correct drawing of its day, Da Vinci's *The Vitruvian Man* had become a modern-day icon of culture, appearing on posters, mouse pads, and T-shirts around the world. The celebrated sketch consisted of a perfect circle in which was inscribed a nude male. . . his arms and legs outstretched in a naked spread eagle" (45). The *Mona Lisa* is of course another such "modern-day icon."

3. Hans Jonas, *The Gnostic Religion: The Message of the Alien God and the Beginnings of Christianity*, 2nd enl. ed. (Boston: Beacon Press, 1963), xiii.

4. A miniature *Da Vinci Code* cryptex is available on Amazon starting at $39.99. *The Da Vinci Code* Cryptex 1:1 Scale Prop Replica, which has a real wooden box inlaid with the rose that plays so meaningful a part in the story as the symbol of the divine feminine, sells for $195.

5. For coverage of the controversy leading up to the film's release, as well as the filmmakers' efforts to address the outcry, see Nicole LaPorte, "Furor Feeds 'Da Vinci': Pic Bucks Controversy to Attract Huge Public Interest," *Variety*, May 15, 2006.

6. James Davison Hunter, *Culture Wars: The Struggle to Define America* (New York: Basic Books, 1991).

7. *The Matrix*, written and directed by Lana Wachowski and Lilly Wachowski (Warner Bros., 1999).

8. Lewis Carroll, *Alice in Wonderland*, ed. Donald J. Gray, Norton Critical Edition, 2nd ed. (New York: Norton, 1992).

9. The website for Gnosis—Quetzalcoatl Cultural Institute is at https://www.samaelgnosis.us; that for Gnostic Teachings is at http://gnosticteachings.org; for the book *The Gnostic Path to Oneness*, by Robin Sacredfire, see http://books.google.com/books?id=yrhKDgAAQBAJ; for the Gnosis Archive, see http://gnosis.org; for the website of the Gnostic Center of Long Beach, see http://gnosislongbeach.com; for classes at the Denver School of Gnosis, see http://gnosticstudies.org/index.php/our-studies/welcome/classes/; for the blog *The Negative Psychologist*, see http://www.thenegativepsychologist.com; for the website of the EOC Institute, see http://eocinstitute.org/meditation/how-to-reach-gnosis; for GCOL's website, see www.assemblyoflightbearers.org; for Free Will Astrology, see http://www.freewillastrology.com.

10. Christoph Markschies, *Gnosis: An Introduction*, trans. John Bowden (New York: Continuum Books, 2003), originally published as *Die Gnosis* (Munich: C. H. Beck, 2001); Karen L. King, *What Is Gnosticism?* (Cambridge, MA: Belknap Press of Harvard University Press, 2005); David Brakke, *The Gnostics: Myth, Ritual, and Divinity in Early Christianity* (Cambridge, MA: Harvard University Press, 2012); Michael Allen Williams, *Rethinking "Gnosticism": An Argument for Dismantling a Dubious Category* (Princeton, NJ: Princeton University Press, 1996); R. Van Den Broek, "The Present State of Gnostic Studies," *Vigilae Christianae* 37, no. 1 (March 1983): 41–71.

11. Jonathan Cahana, "None of Them Knew Me or My Brothers: Gnostic Antitraditionalism and Gnosticism as a Cultural Phenomenon," *Journal of Religion* 94, no. 1 (January 2014): 49–73.

12. Marvin Meyer and Elaine H. Pagels, introduction to *The Nag Hammadi Scriptures*, ed. Marvin Meyer, International ed. (San Francisco: HarperCollins, 2007), 1–13. One of the most famous of those who attacked Gnosticism as heresy, the second-century church father Irenaeus (ca. 125–202; bishop of Lugdunum in Gaul, which is now Lyons, France), cited a text called *The Gospel of Truth* as being by Valentinus (31).

13. Valentinus, *The Gospel of Truth*, trans. Einar Thomassen and Marvin Meyer, in Meyer, *Nag Hammadi Scriptures*, 31–47. All subsequent citations to this work are given parenthetically in the text by page number.

14. From one vantage point, this vision of the world as illusory and deficient, and of human beings as empty, ignorant, broken vessels, is desolate and frightening. But from another, through the eyes of those who belong to divine perfection, it is a vision of sensory seduction and fulfillment. Eating the fruit of the tree of knowledge brings union with the divine, and at different points in the document this evokes satisfactions of smell, sound, flavor, sight, and touch. For example, those who return to the Father, who "assigned their destinies," "embrace his head, which is rest for them, and they hold him close so that, in a manner of speaking, they have caressed his face with kisses" (47).

15. Jonas, *Gnostic Religion*, xvii. Jonas proceeds: "That there was such a gnostic spirit, and therefore an essence of Gnosticism as a whole, was the impression which struck me at my initial encounter with the evidence, and it deepened with increasing intimacy. To explore and interpret that essence became a matter, not only of historical interest, as it substantially adds to our understanding of a crucial period of Western mankind, but also of intrinsic philosophical interest, as it brings us face to face with one of the more radical answers of man to his predicament and with the insights which only that radical position could bring forth, and thereby adds to our human understanding in general" (xxxiv).

16. Adolph von Harnack, *History of Dogma*, trans. Neil Buchanan (New York: Dover Publications, 1961), vol. 1, quoted in Jonas, *Gnostic Religion*, xvi. Christoph Markschies provides a helpful explanation of the term and its various uses and requisite qualifications in "Does It Make Sense to Speak about a 'Hellenization of Christianity' in Antiquity?" *Church History and Religious Culture* 92, no. 1 (2012), 5–34.

17. See Edward W. Said, *Orientalism* (New York: Vintage Books, 1978), for a complete discussion of the concept's manifestation in a wide array of other contexts.

18. Jonas, *Gnostic Religion*, xvi.

19. Ellis Sandoz, introduction to Eric Voegelin, *Science, Politics, and Gnosticism* (1968; repr., Wilmington, DE: ISI Books, 2004), xiv.

20. See also Ellis Sandoz, *The Voegelinian Revolution: A Biographical Introduction* (Baton Rouge: Louisiana State University Press, 1981).

21. Voegelin, *Science, Politics, and Gnosticism*, 16. All subsequent page citations to this work and to its introduction by Sandoz (ix–xx) are given parenthetically in the text.

22. "And indeed, Platonic-Aristotelian analysis did not in the least begin with speculations about its own possibility, but with the actual insight into being that motivated the analytical process. The decisive event in the establishment of *politike episteme* was the specifically philosophical realization that the levels of being discernible within the world are surmounted by a transcendent source of being and its order. And this insight was itself rooted in the real

movements of the human spiritual soul toward divine being experienced as transcendent. In the experiences of love for the world-transcendent origin of being, in *philia* toward the *sophon* (the wise), in *eros* toward the *agathon* (the good) and the *kalon* (the beautiful), man became philosopher. From these experiences arose the image of the order of being" (Voegelin, *Science, Politics, and Gnosticism*, 14).

23. This calls to mind William James's "Will to Believe" (first published in *New World* 5 [1896]: 327–47), which defended religious belief as reasonable even without evidence.

24. Voegelin goes on: "Hegel conceals the leap by translating *philosophia* and gnosis into German so that he can shift from one to the other by playing on the word 'knowledge.' This wordplay is structurally analogous to Plato's in the *Phaedrus*. But the philosophic wordplay serves to illuminate the thought, while the Gnostic wordplay is designed to conceal the non-thought. This point is worth noting because the German Gnostics, especially, like to play with language and hide their non-thought in wordplay" (*Science, Politics, and Gnosticism*, 32). Whatever one thinks of Voegelin's Hegel, Voegelin's remarks seem prescient more generally, given the increasingly obscure jargon and fascination with a particular kind of wordplay cut loose from content that came to plague literary studies and other fields in the late twentieth century.

25. Another symbolic complex was the symbolism put forth by Joachim of Flora in the twelfth century to counter St. Augustine's philosophy of history, which saw life since Christ as the *saeculum senescens*, or senility of mankind, waiting for the end of history. Joachitic symbolism included a belief in perfectionism in this life (immanent); a third realm or era of perfection; a *Dux* or superman, who would usher in this new era; and a "free community of autonomous persons without institutional organization" (Voegelin, *Science, Politics, and Gnosticism*, 74).

26. This theme inflects Philip Rieff's *Charisma: The Gift of Grace, and How It Has Been Taken Away from Us* (New York: Pantheon Books, 2007); Elisabeth Lasch-Quinn and Matthew D. Stewart, "Philip Rieff as Social/Cultural Theorist," in *The Anthem Companion to Philip Rieff*, ed. Jonathan B. Imber (London: Anthem Press, 2018), 117–29.

27. We see this in what appear to be more complex theories, such as the Realist school of international relations, which, in the tradition of Thucydides and Machiavelli, finds the only possible motive to be aggressive competition. Rational self-interest is just a positive spin on Hobbesianism, making it sound as if the only reasonable option is self-interest. W. Julian Korab-Karpowicz, "Political Realism in International Relations," in *Stanford Encyclopedia of Philosophy*, summer 2018 ed., ed. Edward N. Zalta, https://plato.stanford.edu/archives/sum2018/entries/realism-intl-relations/.

28. Elaine H. Pagels, *The Gnostic Gospels* (London: Phoenix, 2006). As Pagels recounts, in 1945 an Arab peasant, Muhammad 'Alī al-Sammān, dug up

a tall jar in Upper Egypt. Fearing it might hold a *jinn* but hoping it contained some valuable treasure, Muhammad 'Alī broke the jar, finding what would become known as the Nag Hammadi texts, named after the nearby town. Muhammad 'Alī, under investigation for the revenge killing of his father's murderer, lost or burned a few of the texts and sold others on the black market. By 1952, the Coptic Museum in Cairo had gathered the manuscripts but, aware of their enormous value, restricted access to the documents. Finally, in 1972, through pressure from international scholars and the United Nations, the first of ten volumes of the library was published (xiii–xxxii). Pagels writes that her own interest lay in how these sources might affect the state of scholarship on early Christianity. Her project in comparative history supported her argument that we can understand early Christianity's political and institutional context by contrasting it with Gnosticism. Yet she did cast Gnosticism in a positive light, as something in tune with late twentieth-century movements.

29. See also Karen King, *Images of the Feminine in Gnosticism* (Harrisburg, PA: Trinity Press International, 2000).

30. This has shades of the Epicureans' view. Pagels, *Gnostic Gospels*, 86–87. Subsequent page citations to this work are given parenthetically in the text.

31. While Catholics sought to include the many, Gnostics instead preached a gospel that a brotherhood existed among a small elite. Gnostics thought human nature one and the same with the nature of God (Pagels, *Gnostic Gospels*, 116) while the orthodox acknowledged "the limits of human understanding" (114). The Gnostics thought only the few were in the know, while "most people live, then, in oblivion—or, in contemporary terms, in unconsciousness" (125).

32. Harold Bloom, "New Heyday of Gnostic Heresies," *New York Times*, April 26, 1992.

33. For example, see Wouter J. Hanegraaff, *New Age Religion and Western Culture: Esotericism in the Mirror of Secular Thought*, Studies in the History of Religions (Leiden: Brill, 1996).

34. April D. DeConick, *The Gnostic New Age: How a Countercultural Spirituality Revolutionized Religion from Antiquity to Today* (New York: Columbia University Press, 2016). Subsequent page citations to this work are given parenthetically in the text.

35. Besides Voegelin and Bloom, see Cyril O' Regan, *Gnostic Return in Modernity* (Albany: State University of New York Press, 2001); and Thomas Pfau, "The Philosophy of Shipwreck: Gnosticism, Skepticism, and Coleridge's Catastrophic Modernity," *MLN* 122, no. 5 (December 2007): 949–1004.

36. See also Wilfred McClay, "The Strange Persistence of Guilt," *Hedgehog Review* 19, no. 1 (Spring 2017): 40–55.

37. For a review that criticizes DeConick's ahistorical methods, see Michael A. Williams, review of *The Gnostic New Age: How a Countercultural Spiritu-*

ality Revolutionized Religion from Antiquity to Today, by April D. DeConick, *Catholic Historical Review* 103, no. 2 (2017): 321–23.

38. Bloom, "New Heyday."

39. For an excellent overview, see Joseph Dan, "Jewish Gnosticism?," *Jewish Studies Quarterly* 2, no. 4 (1995): 309–28.

40. Harold Bloom, "Kabbalah," *Commentary*, March 1975.

41. Christina Nielsen, "The Da Vinci Code and Modern Therapy," *Good Therapy Australia*, March 2, 2005, https://www.goodtherapy.com.au/flex/the -da-vinci-code-and-modern-therapy/447/1.

42. Mindell quoted in Nielsen, "Da Vinci Code."

43. Wilber quoted in Nielsen, "Da Vinci Code."

44. Roberto Assagioli, *Psychosynthesis: A Manual of Principles and Techniques* (New York: Hobbs, Dorman, 1965), 6, quoted in "Da Vinci Code."

45. Nielsen, "Da Vinci Code."

46. Nielsen, "Da Vinci Code."

47. Red Pill Junkie, "Take the Red Popcorn: Gnosticism in Cinema," *Mysterious Universe*, October 27, 2014, https://mysteriousuniverse.org/2014/10 /take-the-red-popcorn-gnosticism-in-cinema.

48. *Dark City*, directed by Alex Proyas (New Line Cinema, 1998); *The Truman Show*, directed by Peter Weir (Paramount Pictures, 1998); *The Thirteenth Floor*, directed by Josef Rusnak (Columbia Pictures, 1999).

49. Red Pill Junkie, "Take the Red Popcorn."

50. Douglas L. Cairns, "*Hybris*, Dishonour, and Thinking Big," *Journal of Hellenic Studies* 116 (1996): 1–32.

51. Plato, *Republic* 7.514–18. "But this is how I see it: In the knowable realm, the form of the good is the last thing to be seen, and it is reached only with difficulty. Once one has seen it, however, one must conclude that it is the cause of all that is correct and beautiful in anything, that it produces both light and its source in the visible realm, and that in the intelligible realm it controls and provides truth and understanding, so that anyone who is to act sensibly in private or public must see it." Plato, *Republic* 517b–c, in *Complete Works*, ed. John M. Cooper (Indianapolis, IN: Hackett, 1997).

52. *Groundhog Day*, directed by Harold Ramis (Columbia Pictures, 1993).

53. Alex Kuczynski, "Groundhog Almighty," *New York Times*, December 7, 2003.

54. Elizabeth Stamp, "Billionaire Bunkers: How the 1% are Preparing for the Apocalypse," CNN Style, August 7, 2019, https://www.cnn.com/style /article/doomsday-luxury-bunkers/index.html.

55. Robin McKie, "No Death and an Enhanced Life: Is the Future Transhuman?," *Guardian*, May 6, 2018. The article cites Mark O'Connell, *To Be a Machine: Adventures among Cyborgs, Utopians, Hackers, and the Futurists Solving the Modest Problem of Death* (London: Granta, 2017).

56. https://humanityplus.org.

57. Francesca Ferrando, "Towards a Posthumanist Methodology: A Statement," *Frame: Journal for Literary Studies* 25, no. 1 (2012): 9–18.

58. For example, Raymond Kurzweil, *The Singularity Is Near* (New York: Viking, 2015).

59. Zach Guzman, "Meet the Company Offering a Chance at Immortality for $200,000," CNBC.com, April 26, 2016, https://www.cnbc.com/2016/04/26/meet-the-company-offering-a-chance-at-immortality-for-200000.html.

60. G. C. Stead, "The Valentinian Myth of Sophia," *Journal of Theological Studies* 20 (1969): 75–104.

61. Stephy Chung, "Meet Sophia: The Robot Who Laughs, Smiles, and Frowns Just Like Us," CNN.com, November 2, 2018, https://www.cnn.com/style/article/sophia-robot-artificial-intelligence-smart-creativity/index.html.

62. Jennifer R. March, "Gaia or Ge," in *Dictionary of Classical Mythology*, 2nd ed. (Oxford: Oxbow Books, 2014), 200–201.

63. The Gaia Theory was developed by British scientist Dr. James Lovelock in the 1960s, and microbiologist Lynn Margulis and others including Vaclav Havel and Al Gore have embraced or been inspired by it. For an overview of the theory and its relation to environmentalism, see the website Gaia Theory: Model and Metaphor for the 21st Century, at http://www.gaiatheory.org.

64. Rosemary R. Ruether, *Gaia and God: An Ecofeminist Theology of Earth Healing* (San Francisco: Harper San Francisco, 1992).

65. Eric Owen Moss and Brad Collins, *Gnostic Architecture* (New York: Monacelli Press, 1999), 1.12 (chap. 1, p. 12; pagination restarts at 1 with each chapter).

66. Percy Bysshe Shelley, *The Complete Poetical Works*, ed. Thomas Hutchinson (Oxford: Oxford University Press, 1925).

67. Moss and Collins, *Gnostic Architecture*, 1.3. Subsequent citations to chapter and page number are given parenthetically in the text.

68. Tony Perrottet, "The Man Who Saved Havana," with photography by Néstor Martí, *Smithsonian Magazine*, May 2018.

69. Tumber, *American Feminism*, 1.

70. Tumber, *American Feminism*, 173.

71. Tumber, *American Feminism*, 2.

72. Anthony Grafton, "The Millennia-Old History of the Apocalypse," *New Republic*, November 8, 1999. See also Christopher Lasch, "Gnosticism, Ancient and Modern: The Religion of the Future," *Salmagundi* 96 (Fall 1992): 27–42.

73. Denise R. Letendre, "Divine Feminine Spirituality," in *Encyclopedia of Gender and Society*, ed. Jodi O'Brien (London: Sage Publications, 2009), 206–7.

74. E. L. James, *Fifty Shades of Grey* (New York: Vintage Books, 2011); *Fifty Shades of Grey*, directed by Sam Taylor-Johnson (Universal Pictures, 2015).

This controversial book-movie phenomenon centered on sadomasochism. The movie, largely panned by critics, and faulted for everything from violent and pornographic scenes to promotion of violence against women, was banned in many countries.

75. There is a lively debate over the supposed feminism in *Da Vinci Code*. While some adherents of the divine feminine say yes, some say no. The Gospel of Thomas is actually antiwoman, according to Philip Lee, who quotes a particularly egregious passage from *The Gospel of Thomas* ("Jesus said, 'I myself shall lead her, in order to make her male, so that she too may become a living spirit, resembling you males, for every woman who will make herself male will enter the Kingdom of Heaven'") and adds: "Somehow Dan Brown missed this passage in his effort in *The Da Vinci Code* to divinize Mary Magdalen as the focal point of the sacred feminine." Ken Myers, "An Ancient Modern Confusion," *Mars Hill Audio*, February 13, 2006, http://marshillaudio.org/addenda/ancient-modern-confusion; Philip J. Lee, *Against the Protestant Gnostics* (New York: Oxford University Press, 1993), 138.

CHAPTER TWO

The epigraph is from Hannah Arendt's *The Life of the Mind*, vol. 1, *Thinking* (New York: Harcourt Brace Jovanovich, 1978), 193.

1. They appeared recently as the title of a book by Mary Beard, *SPQR: A History of Ancient Rome*.

2. David Rieff, "Victims, All? Recovery, Co-dependency, and the Art of Blaming Somebody Else," *Harper's Magazine*, October 1991, 49.

3. D. Rieff, "Victims, All?," 54.

4. Peter Vernezze, *Don't Worry, Be Stoic: Ancient Wisdom for Troubled Times* (Lanham, MD: University Press of America, 2005); Thomas V. Morris, *The Stoic Art of Living: Inner Resilience and Outer Results* (Chicago: Open Court, 2004); Ronald W. Pies, *Everything Has Two Handles: The Stoic's Guide to the Art of Living* (Lanham, MD: Hamilton Books, 2008); Keith Seddon, *Stoic Serenity: A Practical Course on Finding Inner Peace* (Barking, England: Lulu, 2006); see also William B. Irvine, *A Guide to the Good Life: The Ancient Art of Stoic Joy* (Oxford: Oxford University Press, 2009).

5. Tom Wolfe, *A Man in Full: A Novel* (New York: Farrar, Straus and Giroux, 1998).

6. William O. Stephens, "The Rebirth of Stoicism," *Creighton Magazine*, Winter 2000, 34–39.

7. *Gladiator*, directed by Ridley Scott (Universal Pictures, May 5, 2000).

8. John McCain's autobiography mentions Stoicism expressly, and numerous people have associated him with it. He is not alone among presidents or presidential candidates, as Barack Obama has also been called a Stoic. John

McCain and Mark Salter, *Faith of My Fathers* (New York: Harper, 2008). See also James B. Stockdale, *Thoughts of a Philosophical Fighter Pilot* (Stanford, CA: Hoover Institution, 1995).

9. Jules Evans, "The Re-birth of Stoicism," *Philosophy for Life* (blog), November 30, 2012, www.philosophyforlife.org/blog/the-revival-of-stoicism?rq=stoicism.

10. According to www.modernstoicism.com, Stoic Week is a "global online experiment" in living stoically, aided by a handbook of exercises for individuals to follow, synchronized each year with an international conference or Stoicon, and smaller concurrent programs held throughout the world.

11. See his blog, *Philosophy for Life*, at www.philosophyforlife.org.

12. Donald Robertson, *The Philosophy of Cognitive-Behavioural Therapy (CBT): Stoic Philosophy as Rational and Cognitive Psychotherapy* (London: Karnac, 2010).

13. Jules Evans, *Philosophy for Life and Other Dangerous Situations: Ancient Philosophy for Modern Problems* (Novato, CA: New World Library, 2012), 25–73, 271.

14. The Stoic Registry, www.thestoicregistry.org.

15. David Sedley, "The School, from Zeno to Arius Didymus," in *The Cambridge Companion to the Stoics*, ed. Brian Inwood (Cambridge: Cambridge University Press, 2008), 26.

16. Sedley, "School."

17. Sedley, "School," 10–13.

18. Sedley writes, "According to Aristo, the term 'indifferent' must be taken at face value: since health or wealth, if badly used, does more harm than illness or poverty, there is *nothing* intrinsically preferable about either, and typically Zenonian rules such as 'other things being equal, try to stay healthy' damagingly obscure that difference." Sedley, "School," 14.

19. Christopher Gill, "The School in the Roman Imperial Period," in Inwood, *Cambridge Companion*, 47n52. One of the other works that informed this background section is Pierre Hadot, *The Inner Citadel: The Meditations of Marcus Aurelius*, trans. Michael Chase (Cambridge, MA: Harvard University Press, 1998), 73–100.

20. Brad Inwood, "Stoicism," in *Brill's New Pauly*, Brill Online Reference Works, 2006, http://dx.doi.org/10.1163/1574-9347_bnp_e1123400.

21. "Act with good reason in the selection of what is natural." Diogenes Laertius, *Lives of Eminent Philosophers* 7.87, trans. R. D. Hicks, vol. 2, Loeb Classical Library (Cambridge, MA: Harvard University Press, 1925, 1931), 197.

22. Well after Plato, the Academy founded in 387 BC became skeptical in 266 BC under Arcesilaus up until about 90 BC. See the entry "Academy" in Simon Hornblower and Antony Spawforth, eds., *The Oxford Classical Dictionary* (Oxford: Oxford University Press, 1999), 2.

23. Everything has a *pneuma*, or active principle, that makes it what it is, with each level defined by "its highest level of being": "Stable inanimate objects are held together by their mere disposition, living things by nature, animals by soul, and rational animals by reason." Inwood, "Stoicism."

24. Inwood, "Stoicism." Also helpful for this overview was Tad Brennan, "Stoic Moral Psychology," in Inwood, *Cambridge Companion*, 256–94.

25. Inwood, "Stoicism." Also helpful for this overview was Malcolm Schofield, "Stoic Ethics," in Inwood, *Cambridge Companion*, 233–56.

26. Richard Sorabji, *Emotion and Peace of Mind: From Stoic Agitation to Christian Temptation* (Oxford: Oxford University Press, 2000), 2.

27. Sorabji, *Emotion*, 17.

28. Sorabji, *Emotion*, 2, 17.

29. Sorabji, *Emotion*, 29. Also invaluable is Sorabji's *Self: Ancient and Modern Insights about Individuality, Life, and Death* (Chicago: University of Chicago Press, 2006), a major inspiration for the current project.

30. Sorabji, *Emotion*, 45.

31. Sorabji, *Emotion*, 45.

32. Sorabji, *Emotion*, 44–45, 7, 196; Aristotle, *Nicomachean Ethics* 2.6–7.

33. Sorabji, *Emotion*, 194–95, 185, 169–70.

34. Marcus Aurelius, *Meditations*, 4.24, ed. and trans. C. R. Haines, Loeb Classical Library (Cambridge, MA: Harvard University Press, 1916, 1930). Subsequent citations are given parenthetically in the text by the original part divisions, followed by page numbers of this edition's translation or notes.

35. One classicist writing in *The New Republic* says that his Stoicism was "explored privately in the jottings that he kept as philosophical reminders to himself, which we know as the Meditations," but follows this with: "Despite the disjointed feel of the writing, Marcus probably did arrange his work with some kind of publication in mind." Emily Wilson, "Stoicism and Us," *New Republic*, March 17, 2010. Another scholar thinks he definitely wrote for himself; see Birley, *Marcus Aurelius*, 213, 288n5.

36. The quoted words are a maxim of Democrates, a Pythagorean. See Marcus Aurelius, *Meditations* 4.3, trans. Haines, 70n2.

37. Though not completely. See Matthew Arnold, "Emerson," in *Discourses in America* (London: Macmillan, 1885): "Carlyle's perverse attitude towards happiness cuts him off from hope. He fiercely attacks the desire for happiness; his grand point in *Sartor*, his secret in which the soul may find rest, is that one shall cease to desire happiness, that one should learn to say to oneself: 'What if thou wert born and predestined not to be happy, but to be unhappy!' He is wrong; Saint Augustine is the better philosopher, who says: 'Act we *must* in pursuance of what gives us most delight.' Epictetus and Augustine can be severe moralists enough; but both of them know and frankly say that the desire for happiness is the root and ground of man's being. Tell him and show him that he places his happiness wrong, that he seeks for delight where delight will

never be really found; then you illumine and further him. But you only confuse him by telling him to cease to desire happiness; and you will not tell him this unless you are already confused yourself" (49–50).

38. And it is not contradictory for Marcus Aurelius to follow this apparent callousness here with the observation that "one and the same man can be very vehement and yet gentle."

39. See "Stoic Tonics: Philosophy and the Self-Government of the Soul," chap. 9 of Nussbaum's *Therapy of Desire*, 316–58.

40. Here he goes on to urge himself to "let daylight into thy soul" or "never again shall the chance be thine" (2.4, trans. Haines, 29, 31). Instead of enumerating reasons why we should be indifferent to life, he now reminds himself that the proximity of death makes the building of his character urgent. "Wrong thyself, wrong thyself, O my soul! But the time for honouring thyself will have gone by; for a man has but one life, and this for thee is well nigh closed, and yet thou dost not hold thyself in reverence, but settest thy well-being in the souls of others" (2.6, p. 31). Similarly he exhorts himself to "let thine every deed and word and thought be those of a man who can depart from life this moment" (2.2, p. 33).

41. Like a negative infinity.

42. Paul Barolsky, "Poussin's Ovidian Stoicism," *Arion: A Journal of Humanities and the Classics*, 3rd ser., 6, no. 2 (Fall-Winter 1998): 4–10. See also Paul Barolsky, *Ovid and the Metamorphoses of Modern Art from Botticelli to Picasso* (New Haven, CT: Yale University Press, 2014).

43. Barolsky, "Poussin's Ovidian Stoicism," 5.

44. Barolsky, "Poussin's Ovidian Stoicism," 6.

45. Stephens, "Rebirth of Stoicism," 34–39.

46. Stephens, "Rebirth of Stoicism," 34–39.

47. Lawrence C. Becker, *A New Stoicism* (Princeton, NJ: Princeton University Press, 1998), 3–4.

48. L. Becker, *New Stoicism*, 3.

49. L. Becker, *New Stoicism*, 5–7.

50. L. Becker, *New Stoicism*, 13–14.

51. L. Becker, *New Stoicism*, 13–17, 114–18. The phrase is Barbara Herman's, cited by Becker (*New Stoicism*, 13).

52. Epictetus, *Encheiridion* 1, in *Discourses, Books 3–4. Fragments. The Encheiridion*, trans. W. A. Oldfather, Loeb Classical Library (Cambridge, MA: Harvard University Press, 1928), 483. *The Encheiridion* is also called *Handbook*.

53. Epictetus, *Encheiridion* 1, trans. Oldfather, 485.

54. Epictetus, *Encheiridion* 3. And, along these lines comes the following reminder in *Encheiridion* 14, trans. Oldfather: "If you would have your children and your wife and your friends to live forever, you are silly; for you would have the things which are not in your power to be in your power, and the things which belong to others to be yours."

55. Epictetus, *Encheiridion* 5, trans. Oldfather, 487–89.

56. Lucius Annaeus Seneca, *To Polybius on Consolation* 18.8–9, in *Moral Essays*, trans. John W. Basore, vol. 2, Loeb Classical Library (London: W. Heinemann, 1932), 357–89. Other notable reasons include:

- Because you took on a "higher station" as a receiver of petitions, people come to you with their woes, in tears. "You, I say, are not allowed to weep."
- "Think of Caesar." You owe the emperor your position and have made claims that he is most dear to you of anyone. While he is still alive you have no right to complain.
- Are you really grieving for your brother's sake or for yourself? If he is free of feeling, he doesn't suffer, and if he can feel, he would be happy to know he doesn't have all the things in life that seem great but actually bring trouble (wealth, fame, etc.).
- Your brother might actually be better off. "He has not left us, but has gone before."
- We have no right to be surprised by death. It is selfish to see strangers affected by death all the time and then be shocked and surprised when it happens to us: this is just another sign of the human mind's "insatiable greed for all things." . . . Why is it surprising that man should die when his whole life is nothing but a journey toward death?

57. Tom Wolfe, "The Me Decade and the Third Great Awakening," in *Mauve Gloves and Madmen, Clutter and Vine* (New York: Farrar, Straus, and Giroux, 1976), 126–68.

58. Is this just another elaboration of the therapeutic at work, in a possible shift from anticulture to a new culture with its own imperatives? The link between Stoicism and the contemporary approach to emotional difficulty taken in cognitive therapy may be revealing, and there may be an eerie echo of the theory of indifferents in one of the defining texts of our time, the age of the twelve-step program. The Serenity Prayer, originally written by theologian Reinhold Niebuhr, was later adapted to its current version: "God grant me the serenity to accept the things I cannot change; courage to change the things I can; and wisdom to know the difference." However, it is too easy to make the twelve-step program a caricature when, in fact, the practice can often—depending on the particular interpretation, emphasis, and practice—involve a transcendent referent in the form of the nonjudgmentally worded "higher power."

59. John Sellars, *The Art of Living: The Stoics on the Nature and Function of Philosophy*, 2nd ed. (2003; repr., London: Bristol Classical/Press Duckworth, 2009). Subsequent page citations to this work are given parenthetically in the text.

60. The alternative translation provided here is from Epictetus, *Enchiridion* 1.1, trans. Elizabeth Carter (London: Dent, 1966).

61. See Susanne Bobzien, *Determinism and Freedom in Stoic Philosophy*, 330–38, cited in Sellars, *Art of Living*, 134n25. This is usually interpreted to mean things in our control versus those not in our control. But the idea of control may be a modern overlay. The words are actually "all our actions" versus "not all our actions" in the translation by William Abbot Oldfather (Cambridge, MA: Harvard University Press, 1925). This is reminiscent of Hannah Arendt's premium on action in *The Life of the Mind*, vol. 1, *Thinking* (New York: Harcourt Brace Jovanovich, 1978). There is a distinction we should make between something being *our action* and being *in our control*—a world of difference.

62. Sellars makes it clear that "the presence of this structure has been contested," then cites a number of major scholars who do see this structure. See Sellars, *Art of Living*, 134n23.

63. See Diogenes Laertius, *Lives of Eminent Philosophers* 7.108, trans. Hicks, 2:213.

64. Keith J. Bybee, *All Judges Are Political—Except When They Are Not: Acceptable Hypocrisies and the Rule of Law* (Stanford, CA: Stanford University Press, 2010).

65. Scott Soames, *The Dawn of Analysis*, vol. 1 of *Philosophical Analysis in the Twentieth Century* (Princeton, NJ: Princeton University Press, 2003); Simon Blackburn, *Being Good* (Oxford: Oxford University Press, 2001).

66. Richard Sorabji, "Is Stoic Philosophy Helpful as Psychotherapy?," in *Aristotle and After*, ed. Richard Sorabji, BICS Supplement 68 (London: Institute of Classical Studies, 1997), 197–209, quoted in Sellars, *Art of Living*, 170n12.

67. On this, see Wilfred M. McClay, *The Masterless: Self and Society in Modern America* (Chapel Hill: University of North Carolina Press, 1994); and Namhee Lee, "The Spock Paradox: Permissiveness, Control, and Dr. Spock's Advice for a New Psychology of Parenting for Democracy in the Mid-20th Century U.S." (PhD diss., Syracuse University, Syracuse, NY, 2017).

68. See other discussions of the art of living in Sellars, *Art of Living*, 5n27, 55n1.

69. Sorabji, *Emotion*.

70. Massimo Pigliucci, "How to Be a Stoic," *New York Times*, February 2, 2015.

71. Edmund Kern, "Harry Potter, Stoic Boy Wonder," *Chronicle of Higher Education*, November 16, 2001.

72. Kern, "Harry Potter."

73. Nancy Sherman, *Stoic Warriors: The Ancient Philosophy behind the Military Mind* (Oxford: Oxford University Press, 2007).

74. Stockdale, *Thoughts*, 180.

75. McCain and Salter, *Faith of My Fathers*.

76. Sabrina Siddiqui, "Roberta McCain, 106, Cuts Stoic Figure at Son's Memorial Service," *Guardian*, August 31, 2018.

77. Quoted in Ryan Holiday, *The Obstacle Is the Way: Turning Adversity into Advantage* (New York: Penguin Group, 2014), xiv. See Marcus Aurelius, *Meditations* 5.20, trans. Haines, 119.

78. Holiday, *Obstacle Is the Way*, xiv.

79. Holiday, *Obstacle Is the Way*, 2.

80. Holiday, *Obstacle Is the Way*, 3.

81. Greg Bishop, "How a Book on Stoicism Became Wildly Popular at Every Level of the NFL," SI.com, December 7, 2015, https://www.si.com/nfl /2015/12/08/ryan-holiday-nfl-stoicism-book-pete-carroll-bill-belichick.

82. Holiday, *Obstacle Is the Way*, 137.

83. Holiday, *The Obstacle Is the Way*, 139–43.

84. Holiday, *Obstacle Is the Way*, 184.

85. As Martha C. Nussbaum points out on numerous occasions in *Therapy of Desire*, the Stoics are some of the most compelling, absorbed, elaborate, and subtle explorers of the inner world of emotion, even while they argue that it must be overcome.

86. Seneca, *To Polybius on Consolation* 18.8–9.

87. Patricia Cox Miller, *The Corporeal Imagination: Signifying the Holy in Late Ancient Christianity* (Philadelphia: University of Pennsylvania Press, 2009), 27.

88. Sigmund Freud, *Civilization and Its Discontents* (London: Woolf, 1930).

CHAPTER THREE

1. Elizabeth Gilbert, *Eat Pray Love: One Woman's Search for Everything across Italy, India, and Indonesia* (2006; repr., New York: Penguin/Riverhead Books, 2016); *Eat Pray Love*, directed by Ryan Murphy, screenplay by Jennifer Salt (Columbia Pictures 2010).

2. Boris Kachka, "The Power of Positive Publishing," *New York*, January 6, 2013, 5.

3. Elizabeth Gilbert, ed., *Eat Pray Love Made Me Do It: Life Journeys Inspired by the Bestselling Memoir* (New York: Penguin/Riverhead Books, 2016).

4. B. Joseph Pine and James H. Gilmore, "Welcome to the Experience Economy," *Harvard Business Review* 76, no. 4 (1998); B. Joseph Pine and James H. Gilmore, *The Experience Economy* (Boston: Harvard Business Review Press, 1999).

5. For example, Associated Press, "Grand Canyon Tourist Falls 1,000 Feet to His Death While Taking Photos," CBSNews.com, March 29, 2019, https:// www.cbsnews.com/news/grand-canyon-tourist-falls-to-his-death-while -taking-photos-2019-03-29.

6. Elisabeth Lasch-Quinn, "From Inwardness to Intravidualism," *Hedgehog Review* 13, no. 1 (2011); 43–51.

7. Greif, *Against Everything*, 77–78, 85.

8. Greif, *Against Everything,* 82.

9. Francesco Verde, "Epicureanism," in *Oxford Bibliographies* (online), 18, 20, https://www.doi.org/10.1093/obo/9780195389661-0202.

10. Verde, "Epicureanism." In a helpful bibliography of Epicurean writings, Verde conveys several fascinating debates that have arisen in the scholarship that show some of the matters at stake in the different interpretations of Epicureanism. In one of these debates, David Sedley gives an "idealist" account of Epicureans' views of the gods, according to which the gods are "our own idealization of the perfect and happy life to which we aspire." David Konstan instead gives a "realistic account," according to which the gods really exist. In another debate, Cooper thinks Epicureans' view was that all people should pursue pleasure, whereas Wolfe thinks all people by nature seek pleasure. This is a fundamental difference between an ethical and a psychological concept of pleasure (20).

11. Diogenes Laertius, *Lives of Eminent Philosophers* 10.35, trans. R. D. Hicks, vol. 2, Loeb Classical Library (Cambridge, MA: Harvard University Press, 1925, 1931). Subsequent citations of Epicurus's three letters and the maxims are given parenthetically in the text, first by part divisions and then by page numbers of this edition's translation or notes.

12. David N. Sedley, *Creationism and Its Critics in Antiquity* (Berkeley: University of California Press, 2007). See also Sylvia Berryman, "Ancient Atomism," in *Stanford Encyclopedia of Philosophy*, 2005, last revised December 15, 2016, https://plato.stanford.edu/entries/atomism-ancient/#Bib.

13. Sensation should guide everything, teaching us accurately all we know: "Nor is there anything which can refute sensations or convict them of error" (Diogenes Laertius, *Lives* 10.32, trans. Hicks, 2:561). They are inseparable from reason; they can be trusted. Sensations of a different source cannot contradict each other because they are based on different properties, and reason cannot contradict sensation because it depends on sensation.

14. Philosophy ensures happiness. See Diogenes Laertius, *Lives* 10, trans. Hicks, 2:615n-b.

15. We "must hold that nothing suggestive of conflict or disquiet is compatible with an immortal and blessed nature. And the mind can grasp the absolute truth of this" (Diogenes Laertius, *Lives* 10.78, trans. Hicks, 2:609). Epicurus writes of orbits that they must be explained just like other events we experience: "The divine nature must not on any account be adduced to explain this, but must be kept free from the task and in perfect bliss" (10.797, trans. Hicks, 2:625).

16. Titus Lucretius Carus, *De rerum natura* (*On the Nature of Things*), trans. W. H. D. Rouse and Martin Ferguson Smith, Loeb Classical Library

(Cambridge, MA: Harvard University Press, 1924, 1992). Subsequent citations are cited parenthetically in the text by line number followed by page number of this edition's translation or notes.

17. This allusion to Homer's *Odyssey* (Lucretius, *De rerum natura*, p. 190n-a) is, in turn, alluded to by Tennyson in his *Lucretius*: "The Gods, who haunt / The lucid interspace of world and world, / Where never creeps a cloud, or moves a wind, / Nor ever falls the least white star of snow, / Nor ever lowest roll of thunder moans, / Nor sound of human sorrow mounts to mar / Their sacred everlasting calm!"

18. We can read about it in Cicero, Philodemus, Plutarch, and Diogenes of Oenoanda, as well as Lucretius (2.220–25, p. 112) and others.

19. Stephen Greenblatt, *The Swerve: How the World Became Modern* (New York: Norton, 2011). Subsequent page citations to this work are given parenthetically in the text.

20. This blurb's author is Buzzy Jackson of the *Boston Globe*.

21. Thomas Jefferson to William Short, October 31, 1819, quoted in Greenblatt, *Swerve*, 263; Greenblatt also quotes another passage from Thomas Jefferson to John Adams, August 15, 1820, where he expresses an affinity to Epicureanism. Though possibly not the versions used by Greenblatt, the letters can be found in Thomas Jefferson, *Writings*, ed. Merrill D. Peterson (New York: Library of America, 1997).

22. Glenn Altschuler of the *San Francisco Chronicle*.

23. Liana De Girolami Cheney, *Botticelli's Neoplatonic Images* (Potomac, MD: Scripta Humanistica, 1985), 19. See also Christophe Poncet, "Ficino's Little Academy of Careggi," *Bruniana et Campanelliana* 19, no. 1 (2013): 67–76; Maria-Christine (Wien) Leitgeb, "Ficino, Marsilio," in *The Reception of Antiquity in Renaissance Humanism*, ed. Manfred Landfester (Leiden; Boston: Brill, 2017).

24. Cheney, *Botticelli's Neoplatonic Images*, 44. Subsequent page citations to this work are given parenthetically in the text.

25. Poliziano's poem was formally called *La giostra di Giuliano de Medici* or *Stanze* (Cheney, *Botticelli's Neoplatonic Images*, 15).

26. Denis J.-J. Robichaud, *Plato's Persona: Marsilio Ficino, Renaissance Humanism, and Platonic Traditions* (Philadelphia: University of Pennsylvania Press, 2018).

27. See Marsilio Ficino's *Platonic Theology* (1482, 1576).

28. Ficino adds another, *amor ferinus*, "bestial love." No Venus attends this degraded form (Cheney, *Botticelli's Neoplatonic Images*, 35).

29. The concept of *uomo universale* was that the artist should create from this spiritual ascent, cultivating himself "so that he may excel in different humanistic fields and create not only beautiful but contemplative art" (Cheney, *Botticelli's Neoplatonic Images*, 38).

30. "*Virtu* was a positive quality that a leader must have in order to appear as an 'individual' in the eyes of his friends and the people" (Cheney, *Botticelli's Neoplatonic Images*, 37).

31. Martin Jay, *Songs of Experience: Modern American and European Variations on a Universal Theme* (Berkeley: University of California Press, 2005). Subsequent page citations to this work are given parenthetically in the text. There are other such works, such as Jerrold E. Seigel, *The Idea of the Self: Thought and Experience in Western Europe since the Seventeenth Century* (Cambridge: Cambridge University Press, 2004).

32. Stephanie Convery, "Eat, Pray, Love Author Elizabeth Gilbert Says She Is in a Same-Sex Relationship: 'I Love Her, and She Loves Me,'" *Guardian*, September 8, 2016.

33. Elizabeth Gilbert, "Eat, Pray, Crib—Own Author Elizabeth Gilbert's Beautiful Home," YouTube, uploaded April 19, 2014, https://www.youtube.com/watch?v=k8tEOwNTloU.

34. Greif, *Against Everything*, 85–95.

35. Greif, *Against Everything*, 93.

36. Greif, *Against Everything*, 74.

37. Greif, *Against Everything*, 82.

38. Martin Mobberly, "How to Master the Art of Averted Vision," *BBC Sky at Night Magazine*, October 6, 2011, https://www.skyatnightmagazine.com/advice/how-to-master-the-art-of-averted-vision.

39. Greif, *Against Everything*, x.

40. Paul Arras, *The Lonely Nineties: Visions of Community in Contemporary U.S. Television* (Cham, Switzerland: Palgrave Macmillan, 2018), 175–216.

41. Daniel Klein, *Travels with Epicurus: A Journey to a Greek Island in Search of a Fulfilled Life* (New York: Penguin, 2012). Subsequent page citations to this work are given parenthetically in the text.

42. Oscar Wilde, *The Picture of Dorian Gray* (first published in *Lippincott's Monthly Magazine*, July 1890).

43. Daniel Bell argued that the Protestant work ethic supported the imperative of production and the marketplace of advanced industrialism supported the imperative of consumption, installing a basic conflict at the heart of American life in *The Cultural Contradictions of Capitalism*.

44. See their website at https://www.exploretock.com/alinea.

45. "Alinea," Michelin Guide, n.d., accessed 2019, https://guide.michelin.com/us/chicago/alinea/restaurant.

46. Phil Vettel, "Review: Alinea, Now as Much as $385 a Head, Puts on Quite a Show," *Chicago Tribune*, July 15, 2016.

47. See their website at https://www.jacksonandleroy.com/projects/ancient-modern. The builders' full names are Brandon LeRoy and Jeremy Jackson.

48. "Kitchen Gallery: Award Winning Kitchens," n.d., accessed 2019, https://www.subzero-wolf.com/inspiration/kitchens/ancient-modern.

49. https://www.subzero-wolf.com.

50. Rebecca Flint Marx, "Cooking's New Minimalism," *Taste*, November 16, 2017, https://www.tastecooking.com/cookings-new-minimalism.

51. Marx, "Cooking's New Minimalism."

52. See the websites of Slow Food (https://www.slowfood.com) and La Banca del Vino (https://www.bancadelvino.it).

53. *The Lunchbox*, written and directed by Ritesh Batra (DAR Motion Pictures, 2013).

54. Peter Sloterdijk, *You Must Change Your Life*, trans. Wieland Hoban (Cambridge: Polity Press, 2013), 4, 447–52, originally published as *Du musst dein Leben ändern: Über Anthropotechnik* (Frankfurt: Suhrkamp, 2009).

55. Carl Sandburg, "Fog," in *Chicago Poems* (New York: Henry Holt, 1916).

CHAPTER FOUR

1. *300*, directed by Zack Snyder (Warner Bros., 2006).

2. Jeffrey C. Goldfarb, *The Cynical Society: The Culture of Politics and the Politics of Culture in American Life* (Chicago: University of Chicago Press, 1991).

3. Anna-Maija Tolppanen et al., "Late-Life Cynical Distrust, Risk of Incident Dementia, and Mortality in a Population-Based Cohort," *Neurology* 82, no. 24 (May 28, 2014): 2205–12.

4. Louisa Shea, *The Cynic Enlightenment: Diogenes in the Salon* (Baltimore: Johns Hopkins University Press, 2010).

5. Peter Sloterdijk, *Critique of Cynical Reason* (Minneapolis: University of Minnesota Press, 1988), originally published as *Kritik der zynischen Vernunft*, 2 vols. (Frankfurt: Suhrkamp, 1983). His *Spheres* trilogy, television series *Im Glashaus: Das Philosophische Quartett*, and book *You Must Change Your Life* make him an interesting figure here.

6. Klaus (Bamberg) Döring, "Cynicism," in *Brill's New Pauly*, Brill Online Reference Works, 2006, http://dx.doi.org/10.1163/1574-9347_bnp_e1411 040. For instance, he was "seen as an ancient twin brother of Till Eulenspiegel."

7. While the Loeb Classical Library version with Hicks's translation is cited here, a recent version offers a new and accessible translation ideal for reading straight through: Diogenes Laertius, *Lives of the Eminent Philosophers*, ed. James Miller, trans. Pamela Mensch (Oxford: Oxford University Press, 2018). This version also includes essays by prominent scholars, including Anthony Grafton.

8. R. Bracht Branham and Marie-Odile Goulet-Cazé, eds., *The Cynics: The Cynic Movement in Antiquity and Its Legacy* (Oakland: University of

California Press, 2000). In their annotated bibliography, they mention Ragnar Höistad (*Cynic Hero and Cynic King* [Uppsala, Sweden, 1948]) as a scholar who does not accept the anecdotal tradition and is thus an exception to most work on early sources of Cynicism.

9. Döring sees this emerging concept of "cynicalness" as "an offshoot of Cynicism." Döring, "Cynicism." See also Heinrich Niehues-Pröbsting, "The Modern Reception of Cynicism: Diogenes in the Enlightenment," in Branham and Goulet-Cazé, *Cynics*, 329–65.

10. The reception of the term for this movement had perhaps wider flexibility because of the difficulty of resolving conflicting interpretations by appealing to original sources when only such sparse sources were available. So it is difficult to know what to make of Jerome's description of Diogenes as a "victor over human nature" ("naturae victor humanae"), when the very point of Cynicism to so many others was Diogenes's preference for nature over convention. Jerome, *Adversus Jovinianum* 2.14, quoted in Döring, "Cynicism."

11. John Sellars, review of *Cynics*, by W. Desmond, *Classical Review* 60, no. 1 (2010): 56–58.

12. Marie-Odile (Antony) Goulet-Cazé, "Cynicism," in *Brill's New Pauly*, Brill Online Reference Works, 2006, http://dx.doi.org/10.1163/1574-9347_bnp_e626020.

13. Kristen Kennedy, "Hipparchia the Cynic: Feminist Rhetoric and the Ethics of Embodiment," *Hypatia* 14, no. 2 (1999): 48–71.

14. Goulet-Cazé, "Cynicism."

15. Goulet-Cazé, "Cynicism."

16. Diogenes Laertius, *Lives of Eminent Philosophers*, trans. R. D. Hicks, vol. 2, Loeb Classical Library (Cambridge, MA: Harvard University Press, 1925, 1931). Subsequent citations to this minibiography of Diogenes are given parenthetically in the text by part divisions and then by page numbers of this edition's translation or notes.

17. There is numismatic evidence for this. See Branham and Goulet-Cazé, *Cynics*, 90n30.

18. Goulet-Cazé, "Cynicism."

19. This account is from Cercidas of Megalopolis (or of Crete).

20. The inscription continues, "Since thou alone didst point out to mortals the lesson of self-sufficing-ness and the easiest path of life" (quoted from Laertius, *Lives* 2.78, trans. Hicks, 2:81).

21. This is reminiscent of Philip Rieff's permissions and interdictions.

22. Diogenes notoriously contrasted the demands on athletes with the much greater rigors of the philosophical life. For instance, see Philip Bosman, "Selling Cynicism: The Pragmatics of Diogenes' Comic Performances," *Classical Quarterly*, n.s., 56, no. 1 (May 2006): 93–104.

23. Gabriel Herman, *Morality and Behaviour in Democratic Athens* (Cambridge: Cambridge University Press, 2006); Adriaan Lanni, "Social Norms in

the Courts of Ancient Athens," *Journal of Legal Analysis* 1, no. 2 (July 1, 2009): 691–736.

24. For example, Alison Scott-Baumann, *Ricœur and the Hermeneutics of Suspicion* (London: Continuum, 2009).

25. Jay, *Songs of Experience*, 260–61. Subsequent page citations to this work are given parenthetically in the text.

26. This "modalization" entailed the splintering of a unified notion of experience into different practices—"epistemological, religious, aesthetic, political, historical"—with their own institutions, "subcultures of expertise," and premiums on a single aspect of experience seen in isolation, such as cognitive truth or spirituality. Jay, *Songs of Experience*, 260–63.

27. Michel Foucault, "What Is an Author?," lecture, Collège de France, Paris, February 22, 1969, trans. Donald F. Bouchard and Sherry Simon, in *Language, Counter-Memory, Practice*, ed. Donald F. Bouchard (Oxford: Blackwell, 1977), 113–38.

28. Michel Foucault, "How an Experience-Book Is Born," in *Remarks on Marx: Conversations with Duccio Trombadori*, trans. R. James Goldstein and James Cascaito (New York, 1991), 31, quoted in Jay, *Songs of Experience*, 398.

29. Foucault, "How an Experience-Book Is Born," 31–32, quoted in Jay, *Songs of Experience*, 398.

30. Foucault, "How an Experience-Book Is Born," 36, quoted in Jay, *Songs of Experience*, 398.

31. James Miller, *The Passion of Michel Foucault* (New York: Doubleday, 1993).

32. Alasdair MacIntyre, "Miller's Foucault, Foucault's Foucault," *Salmagundi* 97 (Winter 1993): 59–60.

33. Michel de Montaigne, *Essays of Michel de Montaigne*, trans. Charles Cotton (Garden City, NY: Doubleday, 1947).

34. Montaigne, *Essays*, 470.

35. Montaigne, *Essays*, 467.

36. See my coauthored review of *300* for a detailed discussion of this question. Subho Basu, Craige Champion, and Elisabeth Lasch-Quinn, "*300*: The Use and Abuse of History," *Classical Outlook* 85, no. 1 (Fall 2007): 28–32; originally appearing in *SPIKED*, October 3, 2007, http://www.spiked-online.com/index.php?/site/article/3918. Upon its release, the movie was banned in several countries, including Iran.

37. Lionel Trilling, "Hemingway and His Critics" [1939], in *The Moral Obligation to Be Intelligent: Selected Essays/Lionel Trilling*, ed. Leon Wieseltier (Evanston, IL: Northwestern University Press, 2008), 10, 14. Trilling writes, "We had, in other words, quite overlooked the whole process of art, overlooked style and tone, symbol and implication, overlooked the obliqueness and complication with which the artist may criticize life, and assumed that what Hemingway saw or what he put into his stories he wanted to have exist in

the actual world" (17). Yet Trilling thought artists still had moral responsibilities. See, for instance, Trilling, "Manners, Morals, and the Novel" and "The Princess Casamassima," in *Moral Obligation*, 105–19 and 149–177 respectively.

38. Eric McLuhan, *Cynic Satire* (Newcastle-upon-Tyne, UK: Cambridge Scholars, 2015).

39. *The Thin Red Line*, directed by Terrence Malick (Fox 2000 Pictures, 1998). The movie *300* was a remake of *The 300 Spartans*, directed by Rudolph Maté (Twentieth Century Fox, 1962), which had a clear moral, heard in the final voice-over: "'Oh Stranger, tell the Spartans that we lie here obedient to their word.' This last message of the fallen heroes rallied Greece to victory, first at Salamis, as predicted, and then at Plataea. But it was more than a victory for Greece. It was a stirring example to free people throughout the world of what a few brave men can accomplish once they refuse to submit to tyranny."

40. Richard Rorty, *Contingency, Irony, and Solidarity* (Cambridge: Cambridge University Press, 1989).

41. Jonathan Brown, "Back Out of the Vault: Secret Life of the Skull," *Independent*, November 27, 2010.

42. Philip Rieff, *My Life among the Deathworks: Illustrations of the Aesthetics of Authority* (Charlottesville: University of Virginia Press, 2006).

43. Philip Rieff, *Freud: The Mind of the Moralist*, 3rd ed. (Chicago: University of Chicago Press, 1979), 332.

44. P. Rieff, *Freud*, 356.

45. P. Rieff, *Freud*, 356–57.

46. Philip Rieff, *The Crisis of the Officer Class: The Decline of the Tragic Sensibility*, vol. 2 of *Sacred Order/Social Order*, ed. Kenneth S. Piver (Charlottesville: University of Virginia Press, 2007); Philip Rieff, *The Jew of Culture: Freud, Moses, and Modernity*, vol. 3 of *Sacred Order/Social Order*, ed. Kenneth S. Piver (Charlottesville: University of Virginia Press, 2008); P. Rieff, *Charisma*; P. Rieff, *Triumph of the Therapeutic*.

47. P. Rieff, *My Life*, 7. Subsequent page citations to this work are given parenthetically in the text.

48. Ewen, *Captains of Consciousness*.

49. *Killing Us Softly: Advertising's Image of Women*, directed by Margaret Lazarus et al. (Cambridge Documentary Films, 1979). The documentary is based on the research of Jean Kilbourne. See also her book, *Deadly Persuasion: Why Women and Girls Must Fight the Addictive Power of Advertising* (New York: Free Press, 1999).

50. Philip Rieff, *The Feeling Intellect: Selected Writings*, ed. Jonathan B. Imber (Chicago: University of Chicago Press, 1990).

51. Andreas Huyssen, "Foreword: The Return of Diogenes as Postmodern Intellectual," in Sloterdijk, *Critique of Cynical Reason*, ix.

52. Sloterdijk, *Critique of Cynical Reason*, 3. Subsequent citations to this work are given parenthetically in the text.

53. Shea, *Cynic Enlightenment*, 131. Subsequent page citations to this work are given parenthetically in the text.

54. Quoted in Shea, *Cynic Enlightenment*, 158.

55. Thomas McEvilley, *The Shape of Ancient Thought: Comparative Studies in Greek and Indian Philosophies* (New York: Allworth Press, 2002).

56. Sloterdijk, *Critique of Cynical Reason*, 534–47.

57. For example, Richard Dawkins, *The God Delusion* (Boston: Houghton Mifflin, 2006), and Christopher Hitchens, *God Is Not Great: How Religion Poisons Everything* (London: Atlantic, 2007).

58. Karen Salmansohn, *Enough, Dammit: A Cynic's Guide to Finally Getting What You Want Out of Life* (Berkeley, CA: Celestial Arts, 2004).

59. Christopher Lasch, *The True and Only Heaven: Progress and Its Critics* (New York: Norton, 1991), 390–93.

60. Shea, *Cynic Enlightenment*.

61. Paul Fussell, *The Great War and Modern Memory* (Oxford: Oxford University Press, 1975).

62. Vance Packard, *The Hidden Persuaders* (Brooklyn, NY: Ig Pub, 2007).

63. *Mad Men*, created by Matthew Weiner (AMC, 2007–15).

64. Susan Sontag, "Notes on Camp," in *Against Interpretation: And Other Essays* (New York: Farrar, Straus and Giroux, 1966); Dwight Macdonald, "Masscult and Midcult," *Partisan Review*, Spring 1960, 203–33; Theodor W. Adorno, *Negative Dialectics* (London: Routledge, 1966).

65. James Bernauer and David Rasmussen, eds., *The Final Foucault* (Cambridge, MA: MIT Press, 1987).

66. Thomas Flynn, "Foucault as Parrhesiast," in Bernauer and Rasmussen, *Final Foucault*, 102–18. Subsequent page citations to this work are given parenthetically in the text.

67. Sellars, *Art of Living*, 50. Subsequent page citations to this work are given parenthetically in the text.

68. Academic and Pyrrhonian Skepticism extended from the third century BC to the second century AD and included the major figures Pyrrho, Timon, Arcesilaus, Carneades, Aenesidemus, and Sextus Empiricus, among others. The Greek word *skepsis*, investigation, represented their devotion to open-ended inquiry, suspension of judgment, and absence of fixed belief. Katja Vogt, "Ancient Skepticism," in *The Stanford Encyclopedia of Philosophy* (Fall 2018), ed. Edward N. Zalta, https://plato.stanford.edu/archives/fall2018/entries/skepticism-ancient.

69. For Nussbaum's critique of Foucault, see Nussbaum, *Therapy of Desire*, 353–54.

70. Could this not be seen as a later period's interest in memorializing earlier generations? Charles Goldberg writes of a new view of masculinity under the empire in "*Vir Bonus*: Political Masculinity from the Republic to the Principate" (PhD diss., Syracuse University, 2016).

71. Pierre Hadot, *Philosophy as a Way of Life*, trans. Michael Chase (Oxford: Blackwell, 1995).

72. Musonius Rufus, *Reliquae* 36, quoted in Plutarch, *De cohibenda ira* 453d; Michel Foucault, *The Care of the Self*, vol. 3 of *The History of Sexuality* (New York: Pantheon Books, 1978), 46. Subsequent page citations to this work are given parenthetically in the text.

73. Steele Commager, in *The Odes of Horace: A Critical Study* (Bloomington: Indiana University Press, 1962), explains that "pluck the day" is a more apt translation than "seize the day" (273–74). For our purposes this is a crucial difference, as "pluck" has to do with picking (in the sense of selecting *and* harvesting) a ripe piece of fruit or flower in bloom. All this evokes fulfillment, not enjoyment alone. The original line reads: "Carpe diem, quam minimum credula postero" (Pluck the day, trusting as little as possible in tomorrow). Horace, *Odes and Epodes* 1.11, ed. and trans. Niall Rudd, Loeb Classical Library (Cambridge, MA: Harvard University Press, 2004, 2012), 45.

74. Seneca, *On the Shortness of Life* 10.4, 15.5.

75. Epictetus, *Discourses* 1.20, 3.3, in *Discourses, Books 3–4. Fragments. The Encheiridion*, trans. W. A. Oldfather, Loeb Classical Library (Cambridge, MA: Harvard University Press, 1928).

76. Epictetus, *Discourses* 3.22.

77. Matthew B. Crawford, *The World beyond Your Head: On Becoming an Individual in an Age of Distraction* (New York: Farrar Straus and Giroux, 2015).

78. Hadot remarked that André-Jean Voelke was the philosopher he felt closest to in a moving preface to Voelke's *La philosophie comme thérapie de l'âme: Études de philosophie hellénistique* (Paris: Éditions Universitaires Fribourg Suisse, 1993), vii–xiv: "Et pourtant; parmi tous mes amis, parmi tous les philosophes que j'ai connus, c'était lui le plus proche de moi, car nos itinéraires spirituels s'étaient miraculeusement rencontrés" (vii–viii).

79. Hadot, *Philosophy*, 206–7. Subsequent page citations are given parenthetically in the text.

80. For an individualist and aestheticist reading of Foucault that places him in this regard with Nietzsche, Montaigne, and even Socrates, see Alexander Nehamas, *The Art of Living: Socratic Reflections from Plato to Foucault* (Berkeley: University of California Press, 1998).

81. John M. Cooper, *Pursuits of Wisdom: Six Ways of Life in Ancient Philosophy from Socrates to Plotinus* (Princeton, NJ: Princeton University Press, 2012).

82. Cooper, *Pursuits of Wisdom*, 20.

83. In Lucretius's *De rerum natura* the full lines read, "His ibi me rebus quaedam divina voluptas/ percipit atque horror, quod sic natura tua vi/ tam manifesta patens ex omni parte retecta est" (There upon from all these things a sort of divine delight gets hold upon me and a shuddering, because nature thus

by your power has been so manifestly laid open and uncovered in every part). *De rerum natura* 3.28–30, trans. Rouse and Smith, 190–91.

84. M. Crawford, *World beyond Your Head.*

85. Thomas Flynn, "Philosophy as a Way of Life: Foucault and Hadot," *Philosophy and Social Criticism* 31, nos. 5–6 (2005): 609–22.

86. Pierre Hadot, *La philosophie comme manière de vivre* (Paris: Albin Michel, 2001), 214, quoted in Flynn, "Philosophy," 619.

87. Flynn, "Philosophy," 615.

88. Michel Foucault, *Herméneutique du sujet: Cours du Collège de France, 1981–1982* (Paris: Gallimard/Seuil, 2001), 77, quoted in Flynn, "Philosophy," 613.

89. Flynn, "Philosophy," 613.

90. Flynn, "Philosophy," 620. See Jürgen Habermas, "Taking Aim at the Heart of the Present," in *Foucault: A Critical Reader*, ed. David Hoy (Oxford: Basil Blackwell, 1986), 103–8.

91. Montaigne, *Essays*, 870.

CHAPTER FIVE

1. *Interstellar*, directed by Christopher Nolan (Paramount Pictures, 2014).

2. Catherine H. Zuckert, *Postmodern Platos: Nietzsche, Heidegger, Gadamer, Strauss and Derrida* (Chicago: University of Chicago Press, 1996). She offers an original reading of Plato's dialogues in *Plato's Philosophers: The Coherence of the Dialogues* (Chicago: University of Chicago Press, 2009).

3. Paul Allen Miller, *Diotima at the Barricades: French Feminists Read Plato* (Oxford: Oxford University Press, 2016); and his blog post about the importance of ancient ideas in modern thought, "Platonic Reception: That Obscure Object of Desire," *OUPblog*, February 18, 2016, https://blog.oup.com /2016/02/platonic-reception.

4. Sherwin Klein, "Platonic Reflections on Global Business Ethics," *Business and Professional Ethics Journal* 30, nos. 1–2 (2011): 137–73.

5. Thomas A. Szlezák et al., "Plato" in *Brill's New Pauly*, Brill Online Reference Works, 2006, http://dx.doi.org/10.1163/1574-9347_bnp_e927070; Constance C. Meinwald, "Plato," in *Britannica Academic*, s.v. "Plato," accessed February 27, 2020, https://academic-eb-com.libezproxy2.syr.edu/levels/collegiate /article/Plato/108556.

6. Szlezák et al., "Plato"; John M. Cooper, ed., *Plato: Complete Works* (Indianapolis, IN: Hackett, 1997), vii–xxvi; K. Gaiser, *Platons Ungeschriebene Lehre: Studien zur Systematischen und Geschichtlichen Begründung der Wissenschaften in der Platonischen Schule* (Stuttgart: Klett-Cotta, 1962), appendix, *Testimonia Platonica.* These indirect reports should not be discounted, accord-

ing to Szlezák, who belongs to the controversial Tübingen School of Platonist interpretation, which holds that Plato placed a premium on "the oral form."

7. Thomas A. Szlezák et al., "Academy" in *Brill's New Pauly* (Brill Online Reference Works, 2006), http://dx.doi.org/10.1163/1574-9347_bnp_e111350.

8. Szlezák et al., "Academy." For the "divine son of Apollo," Szlezák cites Diogenes Laertius on Plato in *Lives of the Eminent Philosophers* (3.2).

9. Craige B. Champion, "Carneades at Rome: *Philosophos Pragmatikos*," *Mediterranean Antiquity* 19 (2016): 65–85.

10. Szlezák et al., "Academy."

11. Hadot writes that Themistius in Constantinople was also a Neoplatonist as opposed to an Aristotelian, as thought earlier. Pierre Hadot, "Neoplatonism" in *Brill's New Pauly*, Brill Online Reference Works, 2006, http://dx.doi.org/10.1163/1574-9347_bnp_e821260.

12. Hadot, "Neoplatonism."

13. Szlezák et al., "Academy."

14. Pierre Hadot, "Alexandrian School" in *Brill's New Pauly*, Brill Online Reference Works, 2006, http://dx.doi.org/10.1163/1574-9347_bnp_e114130.

15. I. Hadot, in her *Le problème du néoplatonisme alexandrin: Hiéroclès et Simplicius* (Paris: Études augustiniennes, 1978), quoted in Pierre Hadot, "Neoplatonism." Hadot adds that this view goes against that proposed by K. Praechter.

16. Hadot, "Alexandrian School."

17. John Anton, "*Theourgia–Demiourgia*: A Controversial Issue in Hellenistic Thought and Religion," in *Neoplatonism and Gnosticism*, ed. Richard T. Wallis and Jay Bregman (Albany: State University of New York Press, 1992), 9–32. Anton contrasts the inheritance of Plato's philosophical notion in the *Timaeus* of the demiurge or "divine craftsman as creator," the model for artistry of all kinds, with the precepts of theurgy, which taught "magic, evocation, purifications," and "initiation rituals and the dramatic use of symbolism," to which "the Gnostics had openly given primacy." These separate traditions, "the theoretic way and the theurgic way" (13), ranged from Plotinus's view of philosophy as the path to the One to Proclus's integration of theurgy. Anton writes that "Plato bequeathed a view of art that called for the justification of art in a philosophy of life and a theoretical vision of reality" (10).

18. Hadot, "Neoplatonism."

19. Hadot, "Neoplatonism."

20. Michael E. Marmura, "Avicenna," in Popkin, *Columbia History*, 157–63; Michael Flannery, "Avicenna," in *Encyclopedia Britannica Academic*, accessed October 12, 2018, https://academic.eb.com.

21. Alfred L. Ivry, "Averroës," in Popkin, *Columbia History*, 183–87.

22. Hadot, "Neoplatonism."

23. Plato, *Symposium* 178A–B, trans. W. R. M. Lamb, Loeb Classical Library (Cambridge, MA: Harvard University Press, 1925), 101. Subsequent cita-

tions are given parenthetically in the text by part divisions and page numbers of this edition's translation or notes.

24. A stumbling block for many readers of Plato, this is today considered pederasty, both illegal and morally reprehensible, but was accepted in certain circles then. David M. Halperin, John J. Winkler, and Froma I. Zeitlin, *Before Sexuality: The Construction of Erotic Experience in the Ancient Greek World* (Princeton, NJ: Princeton University Press, 1990).

25. The Greek word for body, *soma*, refers to both human physical body and body as object. Henry George Liddell and Robert Scott, comps., *A Greek-English Lexicon* (Oxford: Clarendon Press, 1996), 1749: "any corporeal substance," among its many other meanings.

26. "Beginning from obvious beauties he must for the sake of that highest beauty be ever climbing aloft, as on the rungs of a ladder, from one to two, and from two to all beautiful bodies; from personal beauty he proceeds to beautiful observances, from observance to beautiful learning, and from learning at last to that particular study which is concerned with the beautiful itself and that alone; so that in the end he comes to know the very essence of beauty. In that state of life above all others, my dear Socrates,' said the Mantinean woman, 'a man finds it truly worth while to live, as he contemplates essential beauty'" (211 C–D, trans. Lamb, 207).

27. Ian A. McFarland, "Apophatic Theology," in *Cambridge Dictionary of Christian Theology*, ed. Ian A. McFarland et al. (Cambridge: Cambridge University Press, 2011); John Peter Kenney, *Mystical Monotheism: A Study in Ancient Platonic Theology* (1991; repr., Eugene, OR: Wipf and Stock, 2010); William Franke, "Preface: Apophasis as a Mode of Discourse" and "Introduction: Modern and Contemporary Cycles of Apophasis," both in *On What Cannot Be Said: Apophatic Discourses in Philosophy, Religion, Literature, and the Arts*, vol. 1, *Classic Formulations*, ed. William Franke (Notre Dame, IN: University of Notre Dame Press, 2007), 1–7 and 9–36 respectively. Some postmodernist uses aside, *apophatic theology* was often intricately entwined with rather than in substitution of its counterpoint (*cataphatic* or *kataphatic theology*, a way to approach the divine through affirmative description or statement). This *via negativa* as a way to approach the ineffability of the divine appeared among the early church fathers, Plotinus, and Augustine in late antiquity, Pseudo-Dionysius the Areopagite and Thomas Aquinas in the medieval period, and on up to modern theologians such as Søren Kierkegaard and others not only in the Christian tradition but in Islam, Judaism, Buddhism, Hinduism, and other major religions.

28. Plato, *Symposium* 212A, trans. Alexander Nehamas and Paul Woodruff, in *Complete Works*, ed. Cooper, 494.

29. Origen, *Prologue to the Commentary on the Song of Songs*, in *An Exhortation to Martyrdom, First Principles: Book IV, Prologue to the Commen-*

tary on the Song of Songs, Homily XXVII on Numbers, trans. Rowan A. Greer (Mahwah, NJ: Paulist Press, 1979), 219. Subsequent citations are to this edition's translation and are given parenthetically in the text by page number.

30. John David Dawson, *Christian Figural Reading and the Fashioning of Identity* (Berkeley: University of California Press, 2002), 47.

31. Plotinus, *Enneads* 1.6, trans. A. H. Armstrong, 7 vols., Loeb Classical Library (Cambridge, MA: Harvard University Press, 1966–2006), 1:235. Subsequent citations are to this edition and volume and are given parenthetically in the text by part divisions and page numbers of this edition's translation or notes. The view that beauty involved proportion and symmetry was held by the Pythagoreans of the sixth through the fourth centuries BC, as well as later writers such as the architect Marcus Vitruvius Pollio of the first century BC, author of *De architectura*, discussed in chapter 1. See Sextus Empiricus, *Against the Logicians* 1.108–9, for a discussion of the Pythagoreans' view of beauty.

32. Porphyry, "Life of Plotinus," 25, in Plotinus, *Enneads*, trans. Armstrong, 1:79.

33. We cannot be sure that Porphyry's understanding of the subjects about which Plotinus wrote, as it resulted in his own topical arrangement, mirrored Plotinus's exactly. Lloyd Gerson, in "Plotinus," in *Stanford Encyclopedia of Philosophy*, June 30, 2003; revised June 28, 2018, https://plato.stanford.edu/entries/Plotinus, for the question of Porphyry's organization of Plotinus's works.

34. Rebecca Goldstein, *Plato at the Googleplex: Why Philosophy Won't Go Away* (New York: Vintage, 2015).

35. Nick Romeo, "What Would Plato Think of TV?" *Atlantic*, March 5, 2014.

36. Romeo, "What Would Plato Think."

37. Romeo, "What Would Plato Think."

38. Alan Jacobs, "The Liberal Neoplatonist?" *First Things* 89 (January 1999): 57–61.

39. Patricia Cox Miller, "'Plenty Sleeps There': The Myth of Eros and Psyche in Plotinus and Gnosticism," in *Neoplatonism and Gnosticism*, ed. Richard T. Wallis and Jay Bregman (Stony Brook: State University of New York Press, 1992), 18.

40. Patricia Miller, "'Plenty Sleeps There,'" 19.

41. Porphyry, "Life of Plotinus" 1, ed. Armstrong, 1:1.

42. Pierre Hadot, *Plotinus: Or The Simplicity of Vision* (Chicago: University of Chicago Press, 1993), 23–27.

43. Hadot, *Plotinus*, 19–20.

44. Patricia Miller, "'Plenty Sleeps There,'" 16.

45. Wallis, "NOUS as Experience," in *The Significance of Neoplatonism*, ed. R. Blaine Harris (Norfolk, VA: International Society for Neoplatonic Studies, 1976), 122–24.

46. This particularly speaks to our externally oriented times, when there are astronomic numbers of people with eating disorders and other signs of an absence of self-acceptance.

47. Michael A. Sells, *Mystical Languages of Unsaying* (Chicago: University of Chicago Press, 1994), 17, 22.

48. Sara Rappe, "Metaphor in Plotinus' Enneads v. 8.9," *Ancient Philosophy* 15 (1995): 156–57.

49. Hadot, *Plotinus*, 56.

50. Sorabji, *Emotion*, 196–97, 173.

51. Sorabji, *Emotion*, 203–5; his quote from Plotinus is from *Enneads* 1.2.5.

52. William Ralph Inge, *The Philosophy of Plotinus: The Gifford Lectures at St. Andrews*, vol. 1 (London: Longman's, Green, 1918), 127.

53. Inge, *Philosophy of Plotinus*, 128–31.

54. Digby Anderson, "Spoiled for Choice," in Imber, *Therapeutic Culture*, 180–82.

55. D. Anderson, "Spoiled for Choice," 173.

56. P. Rieff, *Triumph of the Therapeutic*, 5.

57. Augustine, *Confessions* 7.17.23, trans. Henry Chadwick (Oxford: Oxford University Press, 1998), 127. Subsequent citations are given parenthetically in the text by part divisions and page numbers of this edition's translation or notes.

58. Brian Stock, *Augustine the Reader: Meditation, Self-Knowledge, and the Ethics of Interpretation* (Cambridge, MA: Harvard University Press, 2009), 29–30.

59. Eugene Vance, *Mervelous Signals: Poetics and Sign Theory in the Middle Ages* (Lincoln: University of Nebraska Press, 1989), 1–2.

60. Stock, *Augustine the Reader*, 227.

61. Stock, *Augustine the Reader*, 227.

62. Stock, *Augustine the Reader*, 227.

63. For an especially engaging account, see Peter Brown, *Augustine of Hippo: A Biography* (1967; repr., Berkeley: University of California Press, 2000), 91–100.

64. The failure to see poetry as an element of philosophy misses the art of a philosophy of living because if it does not depict our world poetically, its observations are not believable and its feeling states not accurate since we are poetic beings.

65. Augustine, *Confessions*, trans. Chadwick.

66. Albert Camus, *Christian Metaphysics and Neoplatonism*, trans. Ronald D. Srigley (Columbia: University of Missouri Press, 2007), 44. Subsequent page citations to this work are given parenthetically in the text.

67. Phillip Cary, *Augustine's Invention of the Inner Self: The Legacy of a Christian Platonist* (Oxford: Oxford University Press, 2000).

68. P. Rieff, *Triumph of the Therapeutic*, 48.

69. For instance, Justin thought there were actual similarities between Christian doctrine and Greek philosophy, even Christian influences on Greek philosophy, a common notion at that time. See Justin Martyr, *Apologie* 2.13, cited in Camus, *Christian Metaphysics*, 63.

70. G. M. Matthews, *John Keats: The Critical Heritage* (New York: Barnes and Noble, 1971): "Josiah Conder, in a September 1820 *Eclectic Review*, argues that Mr Keats, seemingly, can think or write of scarcely anything else than the 'happy pieties' of Paganism. A Grecian Urn throws him into an ecstasy: its 'silent form,' he says, 'doth tease us out of thought as doth Eternity,'—a very happy description of the bewildering effect which such subjects have at least had upon his own mind; and his fancy having thus got the better of his reason, we are the less surprised at the oracle which the Urn is made to utter:

'Beauty is truth, truth beauty,'—that is all
Ye know on earth, and all ye need to know.

That is, all that Mr Keats knows or cares to know.—But till he knows much more than this, he will never write verses fit to live" (237).

71. Kip Thorne, *The Science of Interstellar* (New York: Norton, 2014), 252–61. This chapter explains some of the science that informs the scene. *Tesseract* is a term from geometry for a shape comparable to a cube but with four dimensions. The word literally means "four-rays," from the Greek τέσσαρα, -ερα, neuter plural and combined form of τέσσαρες, -ερες (four) and ἀκτίς (ray); "tesseract, n," *OED Online* (Oxford University Press, March 2017), www.oed .com/view/Entry/199669?redirectedFrom=tesseract.

72. *Hidden Figures*, directed by Theodore Melfi (20th Century Fox, 2016). The movie was based on a nonfiction book, Margot Lee Shetterly's *Hidden Figures: The American Dream and the Untold Story of the Black Women Who Helped Win the Space Race* (New York: William Morrow, 2016).

73. *A Beautiful Mind*, directed by Ron Howard (Universal Pictures, 2001). Based on the life of John Nash, who won the Nobel Prize for his work in economics, the film depicts Nash's mathematical genius as well as his frequent delusions brought on by paranoid schizophrenia.

74. Hans-Georg Gadamer, "The Relevance of the Beautiful," in *The Relevance of the Beautiful and Other Essays*, ed. Robert Bernasconi, trans. Nicholas Walker (Cambridge: Cambridge University Press, 1986), 43–49. The essay was originally published in German in 1977 in Part I as *Die Aktualität des Schönen*.

75. Gadamer, "Relevance of the Beautiful," 47.

76. Gadamer, "Relevance of the Beautiful," 48.

77. Without such a faculty, we miss the way spiritual time overcomes everyday clock time. When we make everything contingent, we give up on anything with staying power and so only the changeable remains.

78. Robert Reed offers just such a helpful warning in his "Gnosticism 2.0: *Interstellar* and the Religion of Science," *First Things*, December 12, 2014.

79. Albert Einstein, "The Late Emmy Noether," letter to the editor, *New York Times*, May 4, 1935.

80. King's speech (given April 3, 1968, at the Bishop Charles Mason Temple, Memphis, TN) concludes, "Well, I don't know what will happen now. We've got some difficult days ahead. But it really doesn't matter with me now, because I've been to the mountaintop. And I don't mind. Like anybody, I would like to live a long life. Longevity has its place. But I'm not concerned about that now. I just want to do God's will. And He's allowed me to go up to the mountain. And I've looked over. And I've seen the Promised Land. I may not get there with you. But I want you to know tonight, that we, as a people, will get to the promised land. And so I'm happy tonight. I'm not worried about anything. I'm not fearing any man. Mine eyes have seen the glory of the coming of the Lord." Martin Luther King Jr., "Martin Luther King's Final Speech: 'I've Been to the Mountaintop': The Full Text," ABC News, April 3, 2013, https://abcnews.go.com/Politics/martin-luther-kings-final-speech-ive-mountaintop-full/story?id=18872817. See Trudy Becker, "A Source for Ideology: The Classical Education of Martin Luther King, Jr.," *Classical Bulletin* 76, no. 2 (January 1, 2000): 181–89.

81. See, for instance, Aldon D. Morris, *The Origins of the Civil Rights Movement: Black Communities Organizing for Change* (New York: Free Press, 1986), for the role of church congregations, largely female, in bringing about change. In documentary footage from the era, viewers can see the sheer energy and commitment as the camera pans to the audiences of the civil rights speeches delivered in churches throughout the country. See *Eyes on the Prize*, created and executive produced by Henry Hampton (Blackside, 1987–90); and Vicki L. Crawford, Jacqueline Anne Rouse, and Barbara Woods, *Women in the Civil Rights Movement: Trailblazers and Torchbearers, 1941–1965* (Bloomington: Indiana University Press, 1990).

82. Gitlin accounted for the movement as "one of those great uprisings that are the crucibles of America struggling (against much violence and cruelty) to become itself—a commonwealth of free association and mutual aid." The full ensuing line reads: "The New Left wanted to make, out of the lonely crowd, the beloved community—the kernel of a moral awakening that would put intelligence to work in behalf of transcendent values and overcome as much human ugliness as possible." "Todd Gitlin on the Port Huron Statement's 50th Anniversary," *Daily Kos*, April 14, 2012. This article included Todd Gitlin's talk at the event, "On the Port Huron Statement," on April 12, 2012, at the Tamiment Library, New York University.

83. Van Morrison, "I Forgot That Love Existed," *Poetic Champions Compose* (Mercury Records, 1987).

84. Leonard Bernstein, *Serenade (after Plato's Symposium) for Solo Violin, String Orchestra, Harp, and Percussion* (1954), sheet music for violin and piano (Farmingdale, NY: Jalni Publications, 1987), 37. A household name in his time, Bernstein was dedicated not only to writing and performing but to democratizing music, bringing it to the public, and bringing the public to it. Even listening to a few bars would make apparent the exquisiteness of his interpretation of the dialogue.

CONCLUSION

1. Mark Edmundson, *Self and Soul: A Defense of Ideals* (Cambridge, MA: Harvard University Press, 2015).

2. Rita Felski, *The Limits of Critique* (Chicago: Chicago University Press, 2015).

3. Ferdinand Tönnies, *Community and Society*, trans. Charles Loomis (East Lansing: Michigan State University Press, 1957).

4. Sarah Evans wrote of this sphere as crucial for citizenship in her *Free Spaces: The Sources of Democratic Change in America* (New York: Harper and Row, 1986).

5. Friedrich Wilhelm Nietzsche, *Philosophy in the Tragic Age of the Greeks* (Washington, DC: Regnery, 2012), 43. Subsequent page citations to this work are given parenthetically in the text.

6. Marianne Cowan, introduction to Nietzsche, *Philosophy*, 4–5.

7. By *revelatory pedagogy* I mean a way of communicating what we know that allows others to discover the world in a direct way without manipulative intermediaries, preserving the joy of discovery.

8. Mary Ann Glendon, *Rights Talk: The Impoverishment of Political Discourse* (New York: Free Press, 1991).

9. Matthew D. Mendham, "Kant and the 'Distinctively Moral *Ought*': A Platonic-Augustinian Defense against MacIntyre," *Journal of Religion* 87, no. 4 (October 2007): 557.

10. Since then, though, we have debated what that means. Some take it literally to mean that knowledge of virtue makes one virtuous. But that emphasizes unadorned instrumental reason over the divine reason the ancient philosophers had in mind. It begs the question of content.

11. Paul Farwell explains some considerations for determining this in "Aristotle and the Complete Life," *History of Philosophy Quarterly* 12, no. 3 (July 1995): 247–63.

12. Mendham, "Kant," 558.

13. Mendham, "Kant," 559.

14. Mendham, "Kant," 560.

15. According to Mendham, this was adopted by the Stoics and Kant. Mendham, "Kant," 562.

16. Mendham compares Kant and Plato to support a pluralistic view. In Kant's words, the self is not "enrapped in itself as if it were the whole world," but instead "understands and behaves as a mere citizen of the world." Kant quoted in Mendham, "Kant," 563n30.

17. Mendham, "Kant," 563.

18. Mendham, "Kant," 564.

19. John M. Rist, *Real Ethics: Reconsidering the Foundations of Morality* (Cambridge: Cambridge University Press, 2001), 132, quoted in Mendham, "Kant," 564n31.

20. Mendham, "Kant," 564n32, 562n25.

21. Michael J. Sandel, "The Procedural Republic and the Unencumbered Self," *Political Theory* 12, no. 1 (1984): 81–96.

22. National Public Radio journalist David Folkenflik observes that *shamelessness* was the turning point in the gravity of the crisis caused by the lies of the then president, as democracy cannot exist without *shame*, which presumes a vision of the good. "An Evening with NPR's David Folkenflik," presented at Newhouse School of Public Communications, Syracuse University, NY, October 15, 2018.

23. Taneli Kukkonen and Pauliina Remes, "Divine Word and Divine Work: Late Platonism and Religion," *Numen* 63 (2016), 139–46.

24. Joseph Davis, "From the Editors," *Hedgehog Review* 16, no. 2 (Summer 2014): 17.

25. May Sarton, *Journal of a Solitude* (New York: Norton, 1973).

26. Dilman, *Love and Human Separateness*, 2, 27–35. Subsequent page citations to this work are given parenthetically in the text.

EPILOGUE

1. Bob Dylan, "It's Alright, Ma (I'm Only Bleeding)," *Bringing It All Back Home* (Columbia Records, 1964).

2. Milan Kundera, *Immortality* (New York: HarperPerennial, 1990), 4.

3. See Roger Shattuck, *Forbidden Knowledge: From Prometheus to Pornography* (New York: St. Martin's Press, 1996), on the need for a sense of limits in the quest for knowledge.

4. Issa, *Dumpling Field: Haiku of Issa*, trans. Lucien Stryk with the assistance of Noboru Fujiwara (Athens: Swallow Press/Ohio University Press, 1991).

5. *Once*, written and directed by John Carney (Fox Searchlight Pictures, 2007).

6. Glen Hansard and Markéta Irglová, "Falling Slowly," *Once* soundtrack, directed by John Carney (Summit Entertainment, 2007).

7. Pop star Ariana Grande actually wrote a song, upon her breakup with *Saturday Night Live* comedian Pete Davidson, called "Thank U, Next," *Thank U, Next* (Republic, 2019).

BIBLIOGRAPHY

ANCIENT TEXTS

Aristotle. *Nicomachean Ethics*. Translated by H. Rackham. Loeb Classical Library. Reprint, Cambridge, MA: Harvard University Press, 1926, 1934.

———. *Poetics*. Edited and translated by Stephen Halliwell. Loeb Classical Library. Cambridge, MA: Harvard University Press, 1995, 1999.

Augustine. *Confessions*. Translated by Henry Chadwick. Oxford: Oxford University Press, 1998.

Cicero, Marcus Tullius. *De finibus bonorum et malorum* (*On Ends*). Translated by H. Rackham. Loeb Classical Library. Cambridge, MA: Harvard University Press, 1914, 1931.

Epictetus. *Discourses*. In *Discourses, Books 3–4. Fragments. The Encheiridion.* Translated by W. A. Oldfather. Loeb Classical Library. Cambridge, MA: Harvard University Press, 1928.

———. *Encheiridion*. In *Discourses, Books 3–4. Fragments. The Encheiridion.* Translated by W. A. Oldfather. Loeb Classical Library. Cambridge, MA: Harvard University Press, 1928.

———. *Enchiridion*. Translated by Elizabeth Carter. London: Dent, 1966.

Horace. *Odes and Epodes*. Edited and translated by Niall Rudd. Loeb Classical Library. Cambridge, MA: Harvard University Press, 2004, 2012.

Laertius, Diogenes. *Lives of Eminent Philosophers*. Vol. 1. Translated by R. D. Hicks. Loeb Classical Library. Cambridge, MA: Harvard University Press, 1925, 1972.

———. *Lives of Eminent Philosophers*. Vol. 2. Translated by R. D. Hicks. Loeb Classical Library. Cambridge, MA: Harvard University Press, 1925, 1931.

———. *Lives of the Eminent Philosophers*. Edited by James Miller. Translated by Pamela Mensch. Oxford: Oxford University Press, 2018.

Lucretius Carus, Titus. *De rerum natura* (*On the Nature of Things*). Translated by W. H. D. Rouse and Martin Ferguson Smith. Loeb Classical Library. Cambridge, MA: Harvard University Press, 1924, 1992.

Marcus Aurelius. *Meditations*. Edited and translated by C. R. Haines. Loeb Classical Library. Cambridge, MA: Harvard University Press, 1916, 1930.

Origen. *Prologue to the Commentary on the Song of Songs*, in *An Exhortation to Martyrdom, Prayer, and Selected Works*. Translated by Rowan A. Greer. Mahwah, NJ: Paulist Press, 1979.

Plato. *Complete Works*. Edited by John M. Cooper. Indianapolis, IN: Hackett, 1997.

———. *Gorgias*. Translated by Donald J. Zeyl. In *Complete Works*, edited by John M. Cooper. Indianapolis, IN: Hackett, 1997.

———. *Phaedrus*. Translated by H. N. Fowler. 7 vols. Loeb Classical Library. Cambridge, MA: Harvard University Press, 1914, 2006.

———. *Republic*. Translated by G. M. A. Grube. Revised by C. D. C. Reeve. In *Complete Works*, edited by John M. Cooper. Indianapolis, IN: Hackett, 1997.

———. *Symposium*. Translated by W. R. M. Lamb. Loeb Classical Library. Cambridge, MA: Harvard University Press, 1925.

———. *Symposium*. Translated by Alexander Nehamas and Paul Woodruff. In *Complete Works*, edited by John M. Cooper. Indianapolis, IN: Hackett, 1997.

Plotinus. *Enneads*. Translated by A. H. Armstrong. 7 vols. Loeb Classical Library. Cambridge, MA: Harvard University Press, 1966–2006.

Plutarch. *On the Control of Anger*. In *Moralia*, vol 6. Translated by W. C. Hembold. Loeb Classical Library. Cambridge, MA: Harvard University Press, 1939.

Porphyry. "Life of Plotinus." In Plotinus, *Enneads*, vol. 1. Translated by A. H. Armstrong, Loeb Classical Library, 1–90. Cambridge, MA: Harvard University Press, 1966, 1989.

Seneca, Lucius Annaeus. *On Anger*. Translated by James Romm as *How to Keep Your Cool: An Ancient Guide to Anger Management*. Princeton, NJ: Princeton University Press, 2019.

———. *To Polybius on Consolation*. In *Moral Essays*, translated by John W. Basore, vol. 2, Loeb Classical Library. Cambridge, MA: Harvard University Press, 1932.

Valentinus. *The Gospel of Truth*. Translated by Einar Thomassen and Marvin Meyer. In *The Nag Hammadi Scriptures*, edited by Marvin Meyer, 31–47. International ed. San Francisco: HarperCollins, 2007.

OTHER PRINT AND ELECTRONIC SOURCES

Adorno, Theodor W. *Negative Dialektik*. London: Routledge, 1966.

Anderson, Benedict. *Imagined Communities: Reflections on the Origin and Spread of Nationalism*. 1983. Rev. ed. London: Verso, 2006.

Anderson, Digby. "Spoiled for Choice." In *Therapeutic Culture: Triumph and Defeat*, edited by Jonathan B. Imber, 273–88. New Brunswick, NJ: Transaction, 2004.

Anton, John. "*Theourgia–Demiourgia*: A Controversial Issue in Hellenistic Thought and Religion." In *Neoplatonism and Gnosticism*, edited by Richard T. Wallis and Jay Bregman, 9–32. Albany: State University of New York Press, 1992.

Arendt, Hannah. *The Life of the Mind*. 2 vols. New York: Harcourt Brace Jovanovich, 1977–78.

Arnold, Matthew. *Discourses in America*. London: Macmillan, 1885.

Arras, Paul. *The Lonely Nineties: Visions of Community in Contemporary U.S. Television*. Cham, Switzerland: Palgrave Macmillan, 2018.

Associated Press. "Grand Canyon Tourist Falls 1,000 Feet to His Death While Taking Photos." CBSNews.com, March 29, 2019. https://www.cbsnews.com/news/grand-canyon-tourist-falls-to-his-death-while-taking-photos-2019-03-29.

Bakewell, Sarah. *How to Live: Or a Life of Montaigne in One Question and Twenty Attempts at an Answer*. New York: Other Press, 2010.

Barolsky, Paul. *Ovid and the Metamorphoses of Modern Art from Botticelli to Picasso*. New Haven, CT: Yale University Press, 2014.

———. "Poussin's Ovidian Stoicism." *Arion: A Journal of Humanities and the Classics*, 3rd ser., 6, no. 2 (Fall–Winter 1998): 4–10.

Basu, Subho, Craige Champion, and Elisabeth Lasch-Quinn. "*300*: The Use and Abuse of History." *Classical Outlook* 85, no. 1 (Fall 2007): 28–32. Originally published in *SPIKED*, October 3, 2007, www.spiked-online.com/index.php?/site/article/3918.

Beard, Mary. *Confronting the Classics: Traditions, Adventures, and Innovations*. New York: Norton, 2013.

———. *SPQR: A History of Ancient Rome*. New York: Norton, 2015.

———. *Women and Power: A Manifesto*. New York: Norton, 2017.

Becker, Lawrence C. *A New Stoicism*. Princeton, NJ: Princeton University Press, 1998.

Becker, Trudy. "A Source for Ideology: The Classical Education of Martin Luther King, Jr." *Classical Bulletin* 76, no. 2 (2000): 181–89.

Beckerman, Marty. "Millennials Are the Most Cynical Generation Ever, Study Finds." MTV News, September 4, 2014. www.mtv.com/news/1920597/millennials-cynical-study/.

Bell, Daniel. *The Cultural Contradictions of Capitalism*. New York: Basic Books, 1976.

Berlin, Isaiah. *Four Essays on Liberty*. Oxford: Oxford University Press, 1969.

Bernal, Martin. *Black Athena: The Afroasiatic Roots of Classical Civilization*. 3 vols. Piscataway, NJ: Rutgers University Press, 1987–2006.

Bernauer, James, and David Rasmussen, eds. *The Final Foucault*. Cambridge, MA: MIT Press, 1987.

Berryman, Sylvia. "Ancient Atomism." In *Stanford Encyclopedia of Philosophy*. 2005. Last revised December 15, 2016. https://plato.stanford.edu/entries/atomism-ancient/#Bib.

Birley, Anthony. *Marcus Aurelius: A Biography*. 1966. Reprint, New York: Barnes and Noble, 1987.

Bishop, Greg. "How a Book on Stoicism Became Wildly Popular at Every Level of the NFL." SI.com, December 7, 2015. https://www.si.com/nfl /2015/12/08/ryan-holiday-nfl-stoicism-book-pete-carroll-bill-belichick.

Blackburn, Simon. *Being Good*. Oxford: Oxford University Press, 2001.

Bloom, Harold. "Kabbalah." *Commentary*, March 1975.

———. "New Heyday of Gnostic Heresies." *New York Times*, April 26, 1992.

Bobzien, Susanne. *Determinism and Freedom in Stoic Philosophy*. Oxford: Clarendon Press, 2005.

Bosman, Philip. "Selling Cynicism: The Pragmatics of Diogenes' Comic Performances." *Classical Quarterly*, n.s., 56, no. 1 (May 2006): 93–104.

Brakke, David. *The Gnostics: Myth, Ritual, and Divinity in Early Christianity*. Cambridge, MA: Harvard University Press, 2012.

Branham, R. Bracht, and Marie-Odile Goulet-Cazé, eds. *The Cynics: The Cynic Movement in Antiquity and Its Legacy*. Berkeley: University of California Press, 2000.

Brennan, Tad. "Stoic Moral Psychology." In *The Cambridge Companion to the Stoics*, edited by Brian Inwood, 256–94. Cambridge: Cambridge University Press, 2008.

Broderick, Francis L. "The Academic Training of W. E. B. DuBois." *Journal of Negro Education* 27, no. 1 (Winter 1958): 10–16.

Brown, Dan. *The Da Vinci Code*. New York: Doubleday, 2003.

Brown, Jonathan. "Back Out of the Vault: Secret Life of the Skull." *Independent*, November 27, 2010.

Brown, Peter. *Augustine of Hippo: A Biography*. 1967. Reprint, Berkeley: University of California Press, 2000.

Burns, Timothy W., ed. *Brill's Companion to Leo Strauss' Writings on Classical Political Thought*. Boston: Brill, 2015.

Burrus, Virginia. *Saving Shame: Martyrs, Saints, and Other Abject Subjects*. Philadelphia: University of Pennsylvania Press, 2008.

Bybee, Keith J. *All Judges Are Political—Except When They Are Not: Acceptable Hypocrisies and the Rule of Law*. Stanford, CA: Stanford University Press, 2010.

Cahana, Jonathan. "None of Them Knew Me or My Brothers: Gnostic Anti-traditionalism and Gnosticism as a Cultural Phenomenon." *Journal of Religion* 94, no. 1 (January 2014): 49–73.

Cairns, Douglas L. "*Hybris*, Dishonour, and Thinking Big." *Journal of Hellenic Studies* 116 (1996): 1–32.

Camus, Albert. *Christian Metaphysics and Neoplatonism*. 1936. Translated by Ronald D. Srigley. Columbia: University of Missouri Press, 2007.

Carroll, Lewis. *Alice in Wonderland*. 1865. Edited by Donald J. Gray. Norton Critical Edition, 2nd ed. New York: Norton, 1992.

Cary, Phillip. *Augustine's Invention of the Inner Self: The Legacy of a Christian Platonist*. Oxford: Oxford University Press, 2000.

Champion, Craige B. "Carneades at Rome: *Philosophos Pragmatikos.*" *Mediterranean Antiquity* 19 (2016): 65–85.

Chapoutot, Johann. *Greeks, Romans, Germans.* Berkeley: University of California Press, 2016.

Cheney, Liana De Girolami. *Botticelli's Neoplatonic Images.* Potomac, MD: Scripta Humanistica, 1985.

Chiaradonna, Riccardo. "Marsilio Ficino Traduttore della 'Enneadi': Due Esempi." *Bruniana and Campanelliana* 12, no. 2 (2006): 547–52.

Chicago, Judy. *The Dinner Party: A Symbol of Our Heritage.* 1979. Reprint, New York: Penguin, 1996.

Chung, Stephy. "Meet Sophia: The Robot Who Laughs, Smiles, and Frowns Just Like Us." CNN.com, November 2, 2018. https://www.cnn.com/style /article/sophia-robot-artificial-intelligence-smart-creativity/index.html.

Commager, Steele. *The Odes of Horace: A Critical Study.* Bloomington: Indiana University Press, 1962.

Convery, Stephanie. "*Eat, Pray, Love* Author Elizabeth Gilbert Says She Is in a Same-Sex Relationship: 'I Love Her, and She Loves Me.'" *Guardian*, September 7, 2016.

Cook, William, and James Tatum. *African American Writers and Classical Tradition.* Chicago: University of Chicago Press, 2010.

Cooper, John M. *Pursuits of Wisdom: Six Ways of Life in Ancient Philosophy from Socrates to Plotinus.* Princeton, NJ: Princeton University Press, 2012.

Cowan, Marianne. Introduction to *Philosophy in the Tragic Age of the Greeks*, by Friedrich Wilhelm Nietzsche. Washington, DC: Regnery, 2012.

Crawford, Matthew B. *The World beyond Your Head: How to Flourish in an Age of Distraction.* London: Penguin Books, 2016.

Crawford, Vicki L., Jacqueline Anne Rouse, and Barbara Woods. *Women in the Civil Rights Movement: Trailblazers and Torchbearers, 1941–1965.* Bloomington: Indiana University Press, 1990.

Critchley, Simon. *Tragedy, the Greeks, and Us.* New York: Pantheon, 2019.

Cushman, Robert E. *Therapeia: Plato's Conception of Philosophy.* Westport, CT: Greenwood Press, 1976.

Dan, Joseph. "Jewish Gnosticism?" *Jewish Studies Quarterly* 2, no. 4 (1995): 309–28.

Davis, Joseph. "From the Editors." *Hedgehog Review* 16, no. 2 (Summer 2014).

Davis, Nicola. "Ancient Scrolls Charred by Vesuvius Could Be Read Once Again." *Guardian*, October 2, 2019.

Dawkins, Richard. *The God Delusion.* Boston: Houghton Mifflin, 2006.

Dawson, John David. *Christian Figural Reading and the Fashioning of Identity.* Berkeley: University of California Press, 2002.

Deakin, Michael. "Hypatia." In *Encyclopedia Britannica Academic.* Accessed March 1, 2019. https://academic.eb.com.

DeConick, April D. *The Gnostic New Age: How a Countercultural Spirituality Revolutionized Religion from Antiquity to Today*. New York: Columbia University Press, 2016.

De Sio, Henry F. "Stop Blaming Millennials for Being Disillusioned." *Newsweek*, November 1, 2018.

Dilman, Ilham. *Love and Human Separateness*. Oxford: Basil Blackwell, 1987.

Döring, Klaus [Bamberg]. "Cynicism." In *Brill's New Pauly*. Brill Online Reference Works, 2006. http://dx.doi.org/10.1163/1574-9347_bnp_e1411040.

Dreher, Rod. *The Benedict Option: A Strategy for Christians in a Post-Christian Nation*. New York: Sentinel, 2017.

Dworkin, Niquie. "Rieff's Critique of the Therapeutic and Contemporary Developments in Psychodynamic Psychotherapy." *Journal of Theoretical and Philosophical Psychology* 35, no. 4 (November 2015): 230–43.

Edmundson, Mark. *Self and Soul: A Defense of Ideals*. Cambridge, MA: Harvard University Press, 2015.

Einstein, Albert. "The Late Emmy Noether." Letter to the editor. *New York Times*, May 4, 1935.

Evans, Jules. *Philosophy for Life and Other Dangerous Situations: Ancient Philosophy for Modern Problems*. Novato, CA: New World Library, 2012.

———. "The Re-birth of Stoicism." *Philosophy for Life* (blog), November 30, 2012. www.philosophyforlife.org/blog/the-revival-of-stoicism?rq=stoicism.

Evans, Sarah. *Free Spaces: The Sources of Democratic Change in America*. New York: Harper and Row, 1986.

Ewen, Stuart. *Captains of Consciousness: Advertising and Social Roots of the Consumer Culture*. New York: McGraw-Hill, 1976.

Farwell, Paul. "Aristotle and the Complete Life." *History of Philosophy Quarterly* 12, no. 3 (July 1995): 247–63.

Feldblum, Sammy. "Myth Appropriation." *Baffler*, September 21, 2018.

Felski, Rita. *The Limits of Critique*. Chicago: University of Chicago Press, 2015.

Ferrando, Francesca. "Towards a Posthumanist Methodology: A Statement." *Frame: Journal for Literary Studies* 25, no. 1 (2012): 9–18.

Ficino, Marsilio. *Platonic Theology*. 1482, 1576.

Flannery, Michael. "Avicenna." In *Encyclopedia Britannica Academic*. Accessed October 12, 2018. https://academic.eb.com.

Flynn, Thomas. "Foucault as Parrhesiast: His Last Course at the Collège de France (1984)." In *The Final Foucault*, edited by James Bernauer and David M. Rasmussen, 102–18. Cambridge, MA: MIT Press, 1987.

———. "Philosophy as a Way of Life: Foucault and Hadot." *Philosophy and Social Criticism* 31, nos. 5–6 (2005): 609–22.

Foucault, Michel. *The Care of the Self*. Vol. 3 of *The History of Sexuality*. New York: Pantheon Books, 1978.

———. "What Is an Author?" Lecture, Collège de France, Paris, February 22, 1969. Translated by Donald F. Bouchard and Sherry Simon. In *Language,*

Counter-Memory, Practice, edited by Donald F. Bouchard, 113–38. Oxford: Blackwell, 1977.

Fraenkel, Carlos. "Can Stoicism Make Us Happy?" Review of *How to Be a Stoic: Using Ancient Philosophy to Live a Modern Life*, by Massimo Pigliucci. *Nation*, February 5, 2019.

Franke, William. "Introduction: Modern and Contemporary Cycles of Apophasis." In *On What Cannot Be Said: Apophatic Discourses in Philosophy, Religion, Literature, and the Arts*, vol. 1, *Classic Formulations*, edited by William Franke, 9–52. Notre Dame, IN: University of Notre Dame Press, 2007.

———. "Preface: Apophasis as a Mode of Discourse." In *On What Cannot Be Said: Apophatic Discourses in Philosophy, Religion, Literature, and the Arts*, vol. 1, *Classic Formulations*, edited by William Franke, 1–7. Notre Dame, IN: University of Notre Dame Press, 2007.

Freud, Sigmund. *Civilization and Its Discontents*. London: Woolf, 1930.

Furedi, Frank. "The Silent Ascendency of the Therapeutic Culture in Britain." In *Therapeutic Culture: Triumph and Defeat*, edited by Jonathan B. Imber, 19–50. New Brunswick, NJ: Transaction, 2004.

———. *Therapy Culture: Cultivating Vulnerability in an Uncertain Age*. London: Routledge, 2004.

Fussell, Paul. *The Great War and Modern Memory*. Oxford: Oxford University Press, 1975.

Gadamer, Hans-Georg. "The Relevance of the Beautiful." In *The Relevance of the Beautiful and Other Essays*, edited by Robert Bernasconi, translated by Nicholas Walker, 43–49. Cambridge: Cambridge University Press, 1988.

Gaiser, Konrad. *Platons Ungeschriebene Lehre: Studien zur Systematischen und Geschichtlichen Begründung der Wissenschaften in der Platonischen Schule*. Stuttgart: Klett-Cotta, 1962.

Gerson, Lloyd P. *Aristotle and Other Platonists*. Ithaca, NY: Cornell University Press, 2005.

———. "Plotinus." In *Stanford Encyclopedia of Philosophy*, June 30, 2003, revised June 28, 2018, edited by Edward N. Zalta. https://plato.stanford.edu/archives/fall2018/entries/plotinus/.

Gilbert, Elizabeth. "Eat, Pray, Crib—Own Author Elizabeth Gilbert's Beautiful Home." YouTube, uploaded April 19, 2014. https://www.youtube.com/watch?v=k8tEOwNTloU.

———. *Eat Pray Love: One Woman's Search for Everything across Italy, India, and Indonesia*. 2006. Reprint, New York: Penguin/Riverhead Books, 2016.

———, ed. *Eat Pray Love Made Me Do It: Life Journeys Inspired by the Bestselling Memoir*. New York: Penguin/Riverhead Books, 2016.

Gill, Christopher. "The School in the Roman Imperial Period." In *The Cambridge Companion to the Stoics*, edited by Brian Inwood, 33–58. Cambridge: Cambridge University Press, 2008.

Gleiser, Marcelo. "Meaning in a Silent Universe." *New Atlantis*, no. 47 (Fall 2015): 76–86.

Glendon, Mary Ann. *Rights Talk: The Impoverishment of Political Discourse*. New York: Free Press, 1991.

Goldberg, Charles. "*Vir Bonus*: Political Masculinity from the Republic to the Principate." PhD diss., Syracuse University, 2016.

Goldfarb, Jeffrey C. *The Cynical Society: The Culture of Politics and the Politics of Culture in American Life*. Chicago: University of Chicago Press, 1991.

Goldstein, Rebecca. *Plato at the Googleplex: Why Philosophy Won't Go Away*. New York: Vintage, 2015.

Goulet-Cazé, Marie-Odile (Antony). "Cynicism." In *Brill's New Pauly*. Brill Online Reference Works, 2006. http://dx.doi.org/10.1163/1574-9347_bnp_e626020.

———. "Who Was the First Dog?" Appendix B. In *The Cynics: The Cynic Movement in Antiquity and Its Legacy*, edited by R. Bracht Branham and Marie-Odile Goulet-Cazé, 414–16. Berkeley: University of California Press, 2000.

Grafton, Anthony. "The Millennia-Old History of the Apocalypse." *New Republic*, November 8, 1999.

Grafton, Anthony, Glenn W. Most, and Salvatore Settis, eds. *The Classical Tradition*. Cambridge, MA: Belknap Press of Harvard University Press, 2013.

Greenblatt, Stephen. *The Swerve: How the World Became Modern*. New York: Norton, 2011.

Greenwood, Emily. "Re-rooting the Classical Tradition: New Directions in Black Classicism." *Classical Receptions Journal* 1, no. 1 (2009): 87–103.

Greif, Mark. *Against Everything: Essays*. New York: Pantheon, 2016.

Guzman, Zach. "Meet the Company Offering a Chance at Immortality for $200,000." CNBC.com, April 26, 2016. https://www.cnbc.com/2016/04/26/meet-the-company-offering-a-chance-at-immortality-for-200000.html.

Habermas, Jürgen. "Taking Aim at the Heart of the Present." In *Foucault: A Critical Reader*, edited by David Hoy, 103–8. Oxford: Basil Blackwell, 1986.

Hadot, I. *Le problème du néoplatonisme alexandrin: Hiéroclès et Simplicius* (Paris: Études augustiniennes, 1978).

Hadot, Pierre. "Alexandrian School." In *Brill's New Pauly*. Brill Online Reference Works, 2006. http://dx.doi.org/10.1163/1574-9347_bnp_e114130.

———. *The Inner Citadel: The Meditations of Marcus Aurelius*. Translated by Michael Chase. Cambridge, MA: Harvard University Press, 1998.

———. "Neoplatonism." In *Brill's New Pauly*. Brill Online Reference Works, 2006. http://dx.doi.org/10.1163/1574-9347_bnp_e821260.

———. *La philosophie comme manière de vivre*. Paris: Albin Michel, 2001.

———. *Philosophy as a Way of Life: Spiritual Exercises from Socrates to Foucault*. Translated by Michael Chase. Oxford: Blackwell, 1995.

———. *Plotinus: Or The Simplicity of Vision*. Chicago: University of Chicago Press, 1993.

Hall, Edith. *Aristotle's Way: How Ancient Wisdom Can Change Your Life*. New York: Penguin Press, 2018.

Halperin, David M., John J. Winkler, and Froma I. Zeitlin. *Before Sexuality: The Construction of Erotic Experience in the Ancient Greek World*. Princeton, NJ: Princeton University Press, 1990.

Hanegraaff, Wouter J. *New Age Religion and Western Culture: Esotericism in the Mirror of Secular Thought*. Studies in the History of Religions. Leiden: Brill, 1996.

Herman, Arthur. *The Cave and the Light: Plato Versus Aristotle, and the Struggle for the Soul of Western Civilization*. New York: Random House, 2013.

Herman, Ellen. *Romance of American Psychology: Political Culture in the Age of Experts*. Berkeley: University of California Press, 1996.

Herman, Gabriel. *Morality and Behaviour in Democratic Athens*. Cambridge: Cambridge University Press, 2006.

Higgins, Charlotte. "The Cult of Mary Beard." *Guardian*, January 30, 2018.

Hitchens, Christopher. *God Is Not Great: How Religion Poisons Everything*. London: Atlantic, 2007.

Holiday, Ryan. *The Obstacle Is the Way: Turning Adversity into Advantage*. New York: Penguin Group, 2014.

Hornblower, Simon, and Antony Spawforth, eds. *The Oxford Classical Dictionary*. Oxford: Oxford University Press, 1999.

Howard, Gerald. "Reasons to Believe." *Bookforum*, February/March 2007.

Huizinga, Johan. *The Waning of the Middle Ages*. Translated by Frederik Jan Hopman. New York: Doubleday, 1954. Originally published as *Herfsttij der Middeleeuwen* (Haarlem: Haarlem Tjeenk Willink, 1919).

Hunter, James Davison. *Culture Wars: The Struggle to Define America*. New York: Basic Books, 1991.

———. *Death of Character: Moral Education in an Age without Good or Evil*. New York: Basic Books, 2001.

Huyssen, Andreas. "Foreword: The Return of Diogenes as Postmodern Intellectual." In *Critique of Cynical Reason*, by Peter Sloterdijk, translated by Michael Eldred. Minneapolis: University of Minnesota Press, 1987.

"Hypatia at *The Dinner Party*." Brooklyn Museum, n.d. Accessed January 13, 2020. https://www.brooklynmuseum.org/eascfa/dinner_party/place_settings/hypatia.

Imber, Jonathan B. *The Anthem Companion to Philip Rieff*. London: Anthem Press, 2017.

———, ed. *Therapeutic Culture: Triumph and Defeat*. New Brunswick, NJ: Transaction, 2004.

Inge, William Ralph. *The Philosophy of Plotinus: The Gifford Lectures at St. Andrews*. Vol. 1. London: Longman's, Green, 1918.

Inwood, Brian, ed. *The Cambridge Companion to the Stoics*. Cambridge: Cambridge University Press, 2008.

———. "Stoicism." In *Brill's New Pauly*. Brill Online Reference Works, 2006. http://dx.doi.org/10.1163/1574-9347_bnp_e1123400.

Irvine, William B. *A Guide to the Good Life: The Ancient Art of Stoic Joy*. Oxford: Oxford University Press, 2009.

Issa. *Dumpling Field: Haiku of Issa*. Translated by Lucien Stryk with Noboru Fujiwara. Athens: Swallow Press/Ohio University Press, 1991.

Ivry, Alfred L. "Averroës." In Popkin, *Columbia History*, 183–87.

Jacobs, Alan. "The Liberal Neoplatonist?" *First Things* 89 (January 1999): 57–61.

James, William. "Will to Believe." *New World* 5 (1896): 327–47.

Jay, Martin. *Songs of Experience: Modern American and European Variations on a Universal Theme*. Berkeley: University of California Press, 2005.

Jefferson, Thomas. *Writings*. Edited by Merrill D. Peterson. New York: Library of America, 1997.

Jonas, Hans. *The Gnostic Religion: The Message of the Alien God and the Beginnings of Christianity*. 2nd enl. ed. London: Routledge, 1963.

Kaag, John. "Need a New Self-Help Guru? Try Aristotle." *New York Times*, January 23, 2019.

Kachka, Boris. "The Power of Positive Publishing." *New York*, January 6, 2013.

Kant, Immanuel. *Observations on the Feeling of the Beautiful and Sublime*. 1764. Translated by John T. Goldthwait. Berkeley: Univerity of California Press, 1960.

Kennedy, Kristen. "Hipparchia the Cynic: Feminist Rhetoric and the Ethics of Embodiment." *Hypatia* 14, no. 2 (1999): 48–71.

Kenney, John Peter. *Mystical Monotheism: A Study in Ancient Platonic Theology*. 1991. Reprint, Eugene, OR: Wipf and Stock, 2010.

Kern, Edmund. "Harry Potter, Stoic Boy Wonder." *Chronicle of Higher Education*, November 16, 2001.

Kilbourne, Jean. *Deadly Persuasion: Why Women and Girls Must Fight the Addictive Power of Advertising*. New York: Free Press, 1999.

King, Karen L. *Images of the Feminine in Gnosticism*. Harrisburg, PA: Trinity Press International, 2000.

———. *What Is Gnosticism?* Cambridge, MA: Belknap Press of Harvard University Press, 2005.

King, Martin Luther, Jr. "Martin Luther King's Final Speech: 'I've Been to the Mountaintop': The Full Text." ABC News, April 3, 2013. https://abcnews .go.com/Politics/martin-luther-kings-final-speech-ive-mountaintop -full/story?id=18872817.

Klein, Daniel. *Travels with Epicurus: A Journey to a Greek Island in Search of a Fulfilled Life*. New York: Penguin, 2012.

Klein, Sherwin. "Platonic Reflections on Global Business Ethics." *Business and Professional Ethics Journal* 30, nos. 1–2 (2011): 137–73.

Korab-Karpowicz, W. Julian. "Political Realism in International Relations." In *Stanford Encyclopedia of Philosophy*, summer 2018 ed., edited by Edward N. Zalta. https://plato.stanford.edu/archives/sum2018/entries/realism-intl -relations/.

Kralik, Brandon. "Contemporary Classical Painting Is Still Growing." *Huffpost*, June 4, 2013. https://www.huffpost.com/entry/contemporary-classical -painting-is-still-growing_b_3370484.

Kuczynski, Alex. "Groundhog Almighty." *New York Times*, December 7, 2003.

Kukkonen, Taneli, and Pauliina Remes. "Divine Word and Divine Work: Late Platonism and Religion." *Numen* 63 (2016): 139–46.

Kundera, Milan. *Immortality*. New York: HarperPerennial, 1990.

Kurzweil, Raymond. *The Singularity Is Near*. New York: Viking, 2015.

Ladner, Gerhart B. "The Philosophical Anthropology of Saint Gregory of Nyssa." *Dumbarton Oaks Papers* 29, no. 12 (1967): 59–94.

Lanni, Adriaan. "Social Norms in the Courts of Ancient Athens." *Journal of Legal Analysis* 1, no. 2 (July 1, 2009): 691–736.

LaPorte, Nicole. "Furor Feeds 'Da Vinci': Pic Bucks Controversy to Attract Huge Public Interest." *Variety*, May 15, 2006.

Lasch, Christopher. *The Culture of Narcissism: American Life in an Age of Diminishing Expectations*. New York: Norton, 1978.

———. "Gnosticism, Ancient and Modern: The Religion of the Future." *Salmagundi* 96 (Fall 1992): 27–42.

———. *The True and Only Heaven: Progress and Its Critics*. New York: Norton, 1991.

Lasch-Quinn, Elisabeth. *Black Neighbors: Race and the Limits of Reform in the American Settlement House Movement, 1890–1945*. Chapel Hill: University of North Carolina Press, 1993.

———. "From Inwardness to Intravidualism." *Hedgehog Review* 13, no. 1 (2011): 43–51.

———. "Our Cultural Divides." *Washington Times*, June 19, 2004. https:// www.washingtontimes.com/news/2004/jun/19/20040619-104223-7375r/.

Lasch-Quinn, Elisabeth, and Matthew D. Stewart. "Philip Rieff as Social/Cultural Theorist." In *The Anthem Companion to Philip Rieff*, edited by Jonathan B. Imber, 117–29. London: Anthem Press, 2018.

Lears, T. J. Jackson. *No Place of Grace: Antimodernism and the Transformation of American Culture, 1880–1920*. New York: Pantheon Books, 1981.

Lee, Namhee. "The Spock Paradox: Permissiveness, Control, and Dr. Spock's Advice for a New Psychology of Parenting for Democracy in the Mid-20th Century U.S." PhD diss., Syracuse University, 2017.

Lee, Philip J. *Against the Protestant Gnostics*. New York: Oxford University Press, 1993.

Leitgeb, Maria-Christine (Wien). "Ficino, Marsilio." In *The Reception of Antiquity in Renaissance Humanism*, edited by Manfred Landfester. Leiden; Boston: Brill, 2017.

Letendre, Denise R. "Divine Feminine Spirituality." In *Encyclopedia of Gender and Society*, edited by Jodi O'Brien, 206–7. London: Sage Publications, 2009.

Levine, Joseph M. "Ancients, Moderns, and History." In *Humanism and History: Origins of Modern Historiography*. Ithaca: Cornell University Press, 1987.

Liddell, Henry George, and Robert Scott, comps. *A Greek-English Lexicon*. Oxford: Clarendon Press, 1996.

Lyotard, Jean-François. *The Postmodern Condition: A Report on Knowledge*. Manchester, UK: Manchester University Press, 1984.

Macdonald, Dwight. "Masscult and Midcult." *Partisan Review*, Spring 1960, 203–33.

MacIntyre, Alasdair. *After Virtue: A Study in Moral Theory*. 1981. 3rd ed. Notre Dame, IN: University of Notre Dame Press, 2007.

———. "Miller's Foucault, Foucault's Foucault." *Salmagundi* 97 (Winter 1993): 54–60.

Malafronte, Allison. "Patricia Watwood: 'Venus Apocalypse.'" *Fine Art Today* (weekly newsletter from *Fine Art Connoisseur Magazine*), May 23, 2013.

March, Jennifer R. "Gaia or Ge." In *Dictionary of Classical Mythology*, 2nd ed., 200–201. Oxford: Oxbow Books, 2014.

Markschies, Christoph. "Does It Make Sense to Speak about a 'Hellenization of Christianity' in Antiquity?" *Church History and Religious Culture* 92, no. 1 (2012): 5–34.

———. *Gnosis: An Introduction*. Translated by John Bowden. New York: Continuum Books, 2003. Originally published as *Die Gnosis* (Munich: C. H. Beck, 2001).

Marmura, Michael E. "Avicenna." In Popkin, *Columbia History*, 157–63.

Marx, Rebecca Flint. "Cooking's New Minimalism." *Taste*, November 16, 2017. https://www.tastecooking.com/cookings-new-minimalism.

Matthews, G. M. *John Keats: The Critical Heritage*. New York: Barnes and Noble, 1971.

McCain, John, and Mark Salter. *Faith of My Fathers*. New York: Harper, 2008.

McClay, Wilfred M. *The Masterless: Self and Society in Modern America*. Chapel Hill: University of North Carolina Press, 1994.

———. "The Strange Persistence of Guilt." *Hedgehog Review* 19, no. 1 (Spring 2017): 40–55.

McEvilley, Thomas. *The Shape of Ancient Thought: Comparative Studies in Greek and Indian Philosophies*. New York: Allworth Press, 2002.

McFarland, Ian A. "Apophatic Theology." In *Cambridge Dictionary of Christian Theology*, edited by Ian A. McFarland, David A. S. Fergusson, Karen Kilby, and Iain R. Torrance. Cambridge: Cambridge University Press, 2011.

McKie, Robin. "No Death and an Enhanced Life: Is the Future Transhuman?" *Guardian*, May 6, 2018.

McLuhan, Eric. *Cynic Satire*. Newcastle-upon-Tyne, UK: Cambridge Scholars, 2015.

Meinwald, Constance C. "Plato." In *Britannica Academic*, s.v. "Plato." Accessed February 27, 2020. https://academic-eb-com.libezproxy2.syr.edu /levels/collegiate/article/Plato/108556.

Mendham, Matthew D. "Kant and the 'Distinctively Moral *Ought*': A Platonic-Augustinian Defense against MacIntyre." *Journal of Religion* 87, no. 4 (October 2007): 556–91.

Meyer, Marvin, and Elaine H. Pagels. Introduction to *The Nag Hammadi Scriptures*, edited by Marvin Meyer, International ed., 1–13. San Francisco: HarperCollins, 2007.

Miller, James. *The Passion of Michel Foucault*. New York: Doubleday, 1993.

Miller, Patricia Cox. *The Corporeal Imagination: Signifying the Holy in Late Ancient Christianity*. Philadelphia: University of Pennsylvania Press, 2009.

———. "'Plenty Sleeps There': The Myth of Eros and Psyche in Plotinus and Gnosticism." In *Neoplatonism and Gnosticism*, edited by Richard T. Wallis and Jay Bregman, 223–38. Stony Brook: State University of New York Press, 1992.

Miller, Paul Allen. *Diotima at the Barricades: French Feminists Read Plato*. Oxford: Oxford University Press, 2016.

———. "Platonic Reception: That Obscure Object of Desire." *OUPblog*, February 18, 2016. https://blog.oup.com/2016/02/platonic-reception.

Mobberly, Martin. "How to Master the Art of Averted Vision." *BBC Sky and Night Magazine*, October 6, 2011. https://www.skyatnightmagazine.com /advice/how-to-master-the-art-of-averted-vision.

Montaigne, Michel de. *Essays of Michel de Montaigne*. 1580–95. Translated by Charles Cotton. Garden City, NY: Doubleday, 1947.

Morris, Aldon D. *The Origins of the Civil Rights Movement: Black Communities Organizing for Change*. New York: Free Press, 1986.

Morris, Thomas V. *The Stoic Art of Living: Inner Resilience and Outer Results*. Chicago: Open Court, 2004.

Moss, Eric Owen, and Brad Collins. *Gnostic Architecture*. New York: Monacelli Press, 1999.

Murdoch, Iris. *The Sovereignty of Good*. London: Cambridge University Press, 1967.

Myers, Ken. "An Ancient Modern Confusion." *Mars Hill Audio*, February 13, 2006. http://marshillaudio.org/addenda/ancient-modern-confusion.

Nehamas, Alexander. *The Art of Living: Socratic Reflections from Plato to Foucault*. Berkeley: University of California Press, 1998.

Niehues-Pröbsting, Heinrich. "The Modern Reception of Cynicism: Diogenes in the Enlightenment." In *The Cynics: The Cynic Movement in Antiquity and Its Legacy*, edited by R. Bracht Branham and Marie-Odile Goulet-Cazé, 329–65. Berkeley: University of California Press, 2000.

Nielsen, Christina. "The Da Vinci Code and Modern Therapy." *Good Therapy Australia*, March 2, 2005. https://www.goodtherapy.com.au/flex/the-da-vinci-code-and-modern-therapy/447/1.

Nietzsche, Friedrich Wilhelm. *Philosophy in the Tragic Age of the Greeks*. 1873. Translated by Marianne Cowan. Washington, DC: Regnery, 2012.

Noack, Rick. "Panoramic Views of the Ancient World—in Modern Day Germany." CNN.com, January 13, 2012.

Nolan, James L., Jr. *The Therapeutic State: Justifying Government at Century's End*. New York: New York University Press, 1998.

Nolan, James L., Jr., and Sandra Davis Westervelt. "Justifying Justice: Therapeutic Law and the Victimization Defense Strategy." *Sociological Forum* 15, no. 4 (December 2000): 617–46.

Nussbaum, Martha C. *The Fragility of Goodness: Luck and Ethics in Greek Tragedy and Philosophy*. 1986. Reprint, Cambridge: Cambridge University Press, 2001.

———. *The Therapy of Desire: Theory and Practice in Hellenistic Ethics*. Princeton, NJ: Princeton University Press, 1994.

O'Meally, Robert G. *Romare Bearden: A Black Odyssey*. New York: DC Moore Gallery, 2007.

O'Regan, Cyril. *Gnostic Return in Modernity*. Albany: State University of New York Press, 2001.

Owens, Mitchell. "How James Ivory's Love of Architecture Impacts Cinema History." *Architectural Digest*, August 9, 2019.

Packard, Vance. *The Hidden Persuaders*. 1957. Brooklyn, NY: Ig Pub, 2007.

Pagels, Elaine H. *The Gnostic Gospels*. 1979. London: Phoenix, 2006.

Perrottet, Tony. "The Man Who Saved Havana." With photography by Néstor Martí. *Smithsonian Magazine*, May 2018.

Petrzela, Natalia Mehlman, and Christine B. Whelan. "Self-Help Gurus Like Tony Robbins Have Often Stood in the Way of Social Change." *Washington Post*, April 13, 2018.

Pfau, Thomas. "The Philosophy of Shipwreck: Gnosticism, Skepticism, and Coleridge's Catastrophic Modernity." *MLN* 122, no. 5 (December 2007): 949–1004.

Pies, Ronald W. *Everything Has Two Handles: The Stoic's Guide to the Art of Living*. Lanham, MD: Hamilton Books, 2008.

Pigliucci, Massimo. "How to Be a Stoic." *New York Times*, February 2, 2015.

Pine, B. Joseph, and James H. Gilmore. *The Experience Economy*. Boston: Harvard Business Review Press, 1999.

———. "Welcome to the Experience Economy." *Harvard Business Review* 76, no. 4 (1998): 97–105.

Poncet, Christophe. "Ficino's Little Academy of Careggi." *Bruniana et Campanelliana* 19, no. 1 (2013): 67–76.

Popkin, Richard H., ed. *The Columbia History of Western Philosophy*. New York: MJF Books, 1999.

———. Introduction to part 1, "Origins of Western Philosophic Thinking." In *The Columbia History of Western Philosophy*, edited by Richard H. Popkin, 1–5. New York: MJF Books, 1999.

Quigley, Kathleen. "Inside Architecture's New Classicism Boom." *Architectural Digest*, August 7, 2018.

Rankine, Patrice. *Ulysses in Black: Ralph Ellison, Classicism, and African American Literature*. Madison: University of Wisconsin Press, 2006.

Rappe, Sara. "Metaphor in Plotinus' Enneads v. 8.9." *Ancient Philosophy* 15, no. 1 (Spring 1995): 155–72.

Red Pill Junkie. "Take the Red Popcorn: Gnosticism in Cinema." *Mysterious Universe*, October 27, 2014. https://mysteriousuniverse.org/2014/10/take-the-red-popcorn-gnosticism-in-cinema/.

Reed, Robert. "Gnosticism 2.0: *Interstellar* and the Religion of Science." *First Things*, December 12, 2014.

Review of *Pompeii: The Life of a Roman Town*, by Mary Beard. *Current World Archaeology* 32 (November 4, 2008).

Rieff, David. "Victims, All? Recovery, Co-dependency, and the Art of Blaming Somebody Else." *Harper's Magazine*, October 1991.

Rieff, Philip. *Charisma: The Gift of Grace, and How It Has Been Taken Away from Us*. New York: Pantheon Books, 2007.

———. *The Crisis of the Officer Class: The Decline of the Tragic Sensibility*. Vol. 2 of *Sacred Order/Social Order*. Edited by Kenneth S. Piver. Charlottesville: University of Virginia Press, 2007.

———. *The Feeling Intellect: Selected Writings*. Edited by Jonathan B. Imber. Chicago: University of Chicago Press, 1990.

———. *Freud: The Mind of the Moralist*. 1954. 3rd ed. Chicago: University of Chicago Press, 1979.

———. *The Jew of Culture: Freud, Moses, and Modernity*. Vol. 3 of *Sacred Order/Social Order*. Edited by Kenneth S. Piver. Charlottesville: University of Virginia Press, 2008.

———. *My Life among the Deathworks: Illustrations of the Aesthetics of Authority*. Charlottesville: University of Virginia Press, 2006.

———. *The Triumph of the Therapeutic: Uses of Faith after Freud*. 1966. 40th Anniversary ed. Edited by Elisabeth Lasch-Quinn. Wilmington, DE: ISI Books, 2006.

Riesman, David. *The Lonely Crowd: A Study of the Changing American Character*. New Haven, CT: Yale University Press, 1950.

Rist, John M. *Real Ethics: Reconsidering the Foundations of Morality*. Cambridge: Cambridge University Press, 2001.

Robertson, Donald. *The Philosophy of Cognitive-Behavioural Therapy (CBT): Stoic Philosophy as Rational and Cognitive Psychotherapy*. London: Karnac, 2010.

Robichaud, Denis J.-J. *Plato's Persona: Marsilio Ficino, Renaissance Humanism, and Platonic Traditions*. Philadelphia: University of Pennsylvania Press, 2018.

Roche, Helen, and Kyriakos N. Demetriou, eds. *Brill's Companion to the Classics, Fascist Italy and Nazi Germany*. Brill's Companions to Classical Reception Series, vol. 12. Leiden: Brill, 2017.

Rodgers, Daniel T. *Age of Fracture*. Cambridge, MA: Harvard University Press, 2011.

Romeo, Nick. "What Would Plato Think of TV?" *Atlantic*, March 5, 2014. https://www.theatlantic.com/entertainment/archive/2014/03/what-would -plato-think-of-tv/284222/.

Ronnick, Michele Valerie. "Twelve Black Classicists." *Arion: A Journal of Humanities and the Classics*, 3rd ser., 11, no. 3 (Winter 2004): 85–102.

Rorty, Richard. *Achieving Our Country: Leftist Thought in Twentieth-Century America*. Cambridge, MA: Harvard University Press, 1998.

———. *Contingency, Irony, and Solidarity*. Cambridge: Cambridge University Press, 1989.

Ruether, Rosemary R. *Gaia and God: An Ecofeminist Theology of Earth Healing*. San Francisco: Harper San Francisco, 1992.

Said, Edward W. *Orientalism*. New York: Vintage Books, 1978.

Sandburg, Carl. "Fog." In *Chicago Poems*. New York: Henry Holt, 1916.

Sandel, Michael J. "The Procedural Republic and the Unencumbered Self." *Political Theory* 12, no. 1 (1984): 81–96.

Sandoz, Ellis. Introduction to *Science, Politics, and Gnosticism*, by Eric Voegelin. 1968. Reprint, Wilmington, DE: ISI Books, 2004.

———. *The Voegelinian Revolution: A Biographical Introduction*. Baton Rouge: Louisiana State University Press, 1981.

Sanghani, Radhika. "How It Feels to Have 'Millennial Burnout.'" BBC 3, February 27, 2019.

Sarton, May. *Journal of a Solitude*. New York: Norton, 1973.

Schofield, Malcolm. "Stoic Ethics." In *The Cambridge Companion to the Stoics*, edited by Brian Inwood, 233–56. Cambridge: Cambridge University Press, 2008.

Schulz, Kathryn. "The Self in Self-Help." *New York*, January 6, 2013.

Scott-Baumann, Alison. *Ricœur and the Hermeneutics of Suspicion*. London: Continuum, 2009.

Seddon, Keith. *Stoic Serenity: A Practical Course on Finding Inner Peace*. Barking, UK: Lulu, 2006.

Sedley, David N. *Creationism and Its Critics in Antiquity*. Berkeley: University of California Press, 2007.

———. "The School, from Zeno to Arius Didymus." In *The Cambridge Companion to the Stoics*, edited by Brian Inwood, 7–32. Cambridge: Cambridge University Press, 2008.

Seigel, Jerrold E. *The Idea of the Self: Thought and Experience in Western Europe since the Seventeenth Century*. Cambridge: Cambridge University Press, 2004.

Sellars, John. *The Art of Living: The Stoics on the Nature and Function of Philosophy*. 2003. 2nd ed. London: Bristol Classical Press (Duckworth), 2009.

———. Review of *Cynics*, by W. Desmond. *Classical Review* 60, no. 1 (2010): 56–58.

Sells, Michael A. *Mystical Languages of Unsaying*. Chicago: University of Chicago Press, 1994.

Shapiro, Fred R. "Who Wrote the Serenity Prayer?" *Chronicle of Higher Education*, April 28, 2014. https://www.chronicle.com/article/Who-Wrote-the-Serenity-Prayer-/146159.

Shattuck, Roger. *Forbidden Knowledge: From Prometheus to Pornography*. New York: St. Martin's Press, 1996.

Shea, Louisa. *The Cynic Enlightenment: Diogenes in the Salon*. Baltimore: Johns Hopkins University Press, 2010.

Shelley, Percy Bysshe. *The Complete Poetical Works*. Edited by Thomas Hutchinson. Oxford: Oxford University Press, 1925.

Sherman, Nancy. *Stoic Warriors: The Ancient Philosophy behind the Military Mind*. Oxford: Oxford University Press, 2007.

Shetterly, Margot Lee. *Hidden Figures: The American Dream and the Untold Story of the Black Women Who Helped Win the Space Race*. New York: William Morrow, 2016.

Siddiqui, Sabrina. "Roberta McCain, 106, Cuts Stoic Figure at Son's Memorial Service." *Guardian*, August 31, 2018.

Sloterdijk, Peter. *Critique of Cynical Reason*. Translated by Michael Eldred. Minneapolis: University of Minnesota Press, 1987. Originally published as *Kritik der zynischen Vernunft*, 2 vols. (Frankfurt: Suhrkamp, 1983).

———. *You Must Change Your Life*. Translated by Wieland Hoban. Cambridge: Polity Press, 2013. Originally published as *Du musst dein Leben ändern: Über Anthropotechnik* (Frankfurt: Suhrkamp, 2009).

Sneyd, Rose. "Reflections from a Visiting Scholar: Arnold at the Armstrong Browning Library." *Armstrong Browning Library and Museum Blog*, June 19, 2017. https://blogs.baylor.edu/armstrongbrowning/2017/06/19/reflections-from-a-visiting-scholar-arnold-at-the-armstrong-browning-library/.

Soames, Scott. *The Dawn of Analysis*. Vol. 1 of *Philosophical Analysis in the Twentieth Century*. Princeton, NJ: Princeton University Press, 2003.

Sontag, Susan. "Notes on Camp." In *Against Interpretation: And Other Essays*. New York: Farrar, Straus and Giroux, 1966.

Sorabji, Richard. *Emotion and Peace of Mind: From Stoic Agitation to Christian Temptation*. Oxford: Oxford University Press, 2000.

———. *Self: Ancient and Modern Insights about Individuality, Life, and Death*. Chicago: University of Chicago Press, 2006.

Stamp, Elizabeth. "Billionaire Bunkers: How the 1% are Preparing for the Apocalypse." CNN Style, August 7, 2019. https://www.cnn.com/style /article/doomsday-luxury-bunkers/index.html.

Stead, G. C. "The Valentinian Myth of Sophia." *Journal of Theological Studies* 20 (1969): 75–104.

Stein, Janice Gross. *The Cult of Efficiency*. Toronto: House of Anansi Press, 2011.

Stephens, William O. "The Rebirth of Stoicism." *Creighton Magazine*, Winter 2000.

Stock, Brian. *Augustine the Reader: Meditation, Self-Knowledge, and the Ethics of Interpretation*. Cambridge, MA: Harvard University Press, 2009.

Stockdale, James B. *Thoughts of a Philosophical Fighter Pilot*. Stanford, CA: Hoover Institution, 1995.

Szlezák, Thomas A., et al. "Academy." In *Brill's New Pauly*. Brill Online Reference Works, 2006. http://dx.doi.org/10.1163/1574-9347_bnp_e111350.

———. "Plato." In *Brill's New Pauly*. Brill Online Reference Works, 2006. http://dx.doi.org/10.1163/1574-9347_bnp_e927070.

Talbot, Margaret. "Whiteness in Classical Sculpture." *New Yorker*, October 22, 2018.

Taylor, Charles. *Sources of the Self: The Making of the Modern Identity*. Cambridge, MA: Harvard University Press, 1989.

Thorne, Kip. *The Science of Interstellar*. New York: Norton, 2014.

Thurman, Howard. *Jesus and the Disinherited*. New York: Abingdon-Cokesbury Press, 1949.

"Todd Gitlin on the Port Huron Statement's 50th Anniversary." *Daily Kos*, April 14, 2012. https://www.dailykos.com/stories/2012/4/14/1083452 /-Todd-Gitlin-on-the-Port-Huron-Statement-s-50th-Anniversary.

Tolppanen, Anna-Maija, et al. "Late-Life Cynical Distrust, Risk of Incident Dementia, and Mortality in a Population-Based Cohort." *Neurology* 82, no. 24 (2014): 2205–12.

Tönnies, Ferdinand. *Community and Society*. 1887. Translated by Charles Loomis. East Lansing: Michigan State University Press, 1957.

Trigg, Joseph W. *Origen*. London: Routledge, 1998.

Trilling, Lionel. "Hemingway and His Critics." 1939. In *The Moral Obligation to Be Intelligent: Selected Essays/Lionel Trilling*, edited by Leon Wieseltier, 11–20. Evanston, IL: Northwestern University Press, 2008.

———. "Manners, Morals, and the Novel." 1948. In *The Moral Obligation to Be Intelligent: Selected Essays/Lionel Trilling*, edited by Leon Wieseltier, 105–19. Evanston, IL: Northwestern University Press, 2008.

———. "The Princess Casamassima." 1948. In *The Moral Obligation to Be Intelligent: Selected Essays/Lionel Trilling*, edited by Leon Wieseltier, 149–77. Evanston, IL: Northwestern University Press, 2008.

Tumber, Catherine. *American Feminism and New Age Spirituality: Searching for the Higher Self, 1875–1915*. Lanham, MD: Rowman and Littlefield, 2002.

Vance, Eugene. *Mervelous Signals: Poetics and Sign Theory in the Middle Ages*. Lincoln: University of Nebraska Press, 1989.

Van Den Broek, R. "The Present State of Gnostic Studies." *Vigilae Christianae* 37, no. 1 (March 1983): 41–71.

Van Hoof, Lieve. "Greek Rhetoric and the Later Roman Empire: The 'Bubble' of the 'Third Sophistic.'" *L'antiquité Tardive* 18 (2010): 211–24.

Verde, Francesco. "Epicureanism." In *Oxford Bibliographies* (online), August 31, 2015. https://www.doi.org/10.1093/obo/9780195389661-0202.

Vernezze, Peter. *Don't Worry, Be Stoic: Ancient Wisdom for Troubled Times*. Lanham, MD: University Press of America, 2005.

Vettel, Phil. "Review: Alinea, Now as Much as $385 a Head, Puts on Quite a Show." *Chicago Tribune*, July 15, 2016.

Voegelin, Eric. *Science, Politics, and Gnosticism*. 1968. Reprint, Wilmington, DE: ISI Books, 2004.

Voelke, André-Jean. *La philosophie comme thérapie de l'âme: Études de philosophie hellénistique*. Paris: Editions Universitaires Fribourg Suisse, 1993.

Vogt, Katja. "Ancient Skepticism." In *The Stanford Encyclopedia of Philosophy*, Fall 2018 ed., edited by Edward N. Zalta. https://plato.stanford.edu/archives/fall2018/entries/skepticism-ancient.

Wallis, Richard T. "NOUS as Experience." In *The Significance of Neoplatonism*, edited by R. Blaine Harris, 121–54. Norfolk, VA: International Society for Neoplatonic Studies, 1976.

Walter, Jess. *Beautiful Ruins: A Novel*. New York: Harper, 2012.

Wendling, Lauren A. "Higher Education as a Means of Communal Uplift: The Educational Philosophy of W. E. B. Du Bois." *Journal of Negro Education* 87, no. 3 (Summer 2018): 285–93.

Wickberg, Daniel. "What Is the History of Sensibilities? On Cultural Histories, Old and New." *American Historical Review* 112, no. 3 (June 2007): 661–84.

Wilde, Oscar. *The Picture of Dorian Gray*. First published in *Lippincott's Monthly Magazine*, July 1890.

Williams, Michael A. *Rethinking "Gnosticism": An Argument for Dismantling a Dubious Category*. Princeton, NJ: Princeton University Press, 1996.

———. Review of *The Gnostic New Age: How a Countercultural Spirituality Revolutionized Religion from Antiquity to Today*, by April D. DeConick. *Catholic Historical Review* 103, no. 2 (2017): 321–23.

Wilson, Catherine. *How to Be an Epicurean: The Ancient Art of Living Well.* New York: Basic Books, 2019.

Wilson, Emily. "Stoicism and Us." *New Republic*, March 17, 2010.

Winterer, Caroline. *The Culture of Classicism: Ancient Greece and Rome in American Intellectual Life, 1780–1910.* Baltimore: Johns Hopkins University Press, 2001.

———. *The Mirror of Antiquity: American Women and the Classical Tradition, 1750–1900.* Ithaca, NY: Cornell University Press, 2007.

Wolfe, Tom. *A Man in Full: A Novel.* New York: Farrar, Straus and Giroux, 1998.

———. "The Me Decade and the Third Great Awakening." In *Mauve Gloves and Madmen, Clutter and Vine*, 126–68. New York: Farrar, Straus, and Giroux, 1976.

Woodruff, Paul. "Sophists." In *Encyclopedia of Classical Philosophy*, edited by Donald J. Zeyl, Daniel Devereux, and Phillip Mitsis. Westport, CT: Greenwood, 1997.

Yeomans, Emma. "The Far Right Is Using Antiquity to Rebrand Itself—but Classicists Are Fighting Back." *New Statesman America*, July 4, 2018.

Zarmakoupi, Mantha. *The Villa of the Papyri at Herculaneum: Archaeology, Reception, and Digital Reconstruction.* Berlin: Walter de Gruyter, 2010.

Zeyl, Donald J., Daniel Devereux, and Phillip Mitsis, eds. *Encyclopedia of Classical Philosophy.* Westport, CT: Greenwood, 1997.

Zuckert, Catherine H. *Plato's Philosophers: The Coherence of the Dialogues.* Chicago: University of Chicago Press, 2009.

———. *Postmodern Platos: Nietzsche, Heidegger, Gadamer, Strauss and Derrida.* Chicago: University of Chicago Press, 1996.

FILMS

300. Directed by Zack Snyder. Warner Bros., 2006.

The 300 Spartans. Directed by Rudolph Maté. Twentieth Century Fox, 1962.

Agora. Directed by Alejandro Amenábar. Focus Features, 2009.

A Beautiful Mind. Directed by Ron Howard. Universal Pictures, 2001.

The Da Vinci Code. Directed by Ron Howard. Columbia Pictures, 2006.

Eat Pray Love. Directed by Ryan Murphy. Screenplay by Jennifer Salt. Columbia Pictures, 2010.

Eternal Sunshine of the Spotless Mind. Directed by Michel Gondry. Focus Features, 2004.

Eyes on the Prize. Created and executive produced by Henry Hampton. Blackside, 1987–90.

Gladiator. Directed by Ridley Scott. Universal Pictures, 2000.

Groundhog Day. Directed by Harold Ramis. Columbia Pictures, 1993.

Hidden Figures. Directed by Theodore Melfi. 20th Century Fox, 2016.

Interstellar. Directed by Christopher Nolan. Paramount Pictures, 2014.

Into the Wild. Directed by Sean Penn. Paramount Vantage, 2007.

Jefferson in Paris. Directed by James Ivory. Touchstone Pictures/Merchant Ivory Productions, 1995.

Julie and Julia. Directed by Nora Ephron. Columbia Pictures, 2009.

Killing Us Softly: Advertising's Image of Women. Directed by Margaret Lazarus et al. Cambridge Documentary Films, 1979.

The Lunchbox. Written and directed by Ritesh Batra. DAR Motion Pictures, 2013.

Mamma Mia! Directed by Phyllida Lloyd. Relativity Media/Playtone/Littlestar, 2008.

The Matrix. Written and directed by Lana Wachowski and Lilly Wachowski (as the Wachowski Brothers). Warner Bros., 1999.

Once. Written and directed by John Carney. Fox Searchlight Pictures, 2007.

On Location with James Ivory. Directed by James Ivory. Design in Mind film series. Institute of Classical Architecture and Art, 2019.

Robert A. M. Stern: Always a Student. Directed by Robert A. M. Stern. Design in Mind film series. Institute of Classical Architecture and Art, 2018.

A Room with a View. Directed by James Ivory. Merchant Ivory Productions/ Goldcrest Films/Film Four International, 1985.

Sideways. Directed by Alexander Payne. Michael London Productions, 2004.

The Thin Red Line. Directed by Terrence Malick. Fox 2000 Pictures, 1998.

The Truman Show. Directed by Peter Weir. Paramount Pictures, 1998.

Under the Tuscan Sun. Directed by Audrey Wells. Touchstone Productions, 2003.

Winter Light (Nattvardsgästerna). Directed by Ingmar Bergman. Svensk Film-industri, 1963.

I N D E X

Aristotle, 6, 27, 29, 42–43, 105, 127, 131, 133, 176, 270–73, 275, 324, 337–40, 342, 360n22, 395n11
Arrival (movie), 319
ars vitae, 246, 347
art of living, 1, 2, 8, 9, 18, 28, 40, 42, 43, 74, 90, 128, 129, 133, 205, 217, 246–47, 253–57, 260, 329–30, 350, 357
arts and crafts, 40, 81, 127, 130–32, 214, 389n17
Asisi, Yadegar, 37
askesis, 128, 132
astrology, 42
atheism, 59, 87, 167, 240
Athens, 4, 33, 99, 100, 149, 209, 211, 214, 270, 272–74
Athos, 112
Augustine, Saint, 28, 85, 210, 296, 303, 307–9, 312, 314, 342, 368n25, 374n37, 390n27
  Confessions, 85, 304–7
Averroës (Ibn Rushd), 275
Avicenna (Ibn Sina), 275

Badiou, Alain, 269
baptism, 64–65
Barolsky, Paul, 114–16
Basil of Caesarea, 274
Beard, Mary, 39
Bearden, Romare, 35, 325
beautiful life, the, 340–43
Beautiful Ruins (Walter), 45
beauty, 104, 214, 219, 303, 326
  as moral category, 172–74, 277–79, 281–82, 285–88, 291–96, 300, 302–3, 313, 318, 320–23, 342–43, 348
Becker, Lawrence, 8, 117–20
beloved community, 323–25, 394n82
Bergman, Ingmar, 206
Bernstein, Leonard, 326, 395n84
Berry, Wendell, 262

Black Athena, 34, 362n54
black hole, 265, 313
Bloom, Harold, 71–72
Botticelli, Sandro, 169–75, 323
Bourdain, Anthony, 8
brevity of life, 106, 109, 112–14

Caesar, Julius, 1–2
Cambridge Platonism, 275
Cambridge University, 297
Camus, 307–12
Cappadocia, 272
careerism, 336
Carneades, 272, 386n68
carpe diem, 249, 387n73
Carroll, Lewis, 51
Cartesian self, 23–24, 58, 260. *See also* Descartes, René
catharsis, 11, 29, 345
Catholicism, 49, 85, 169
Cato the Younger, 100
celebrity culture, 45, 147, 283, 287, 334, 341
Champaigne, Philippe de, 314
chaos, 16, 28, 31–32, 59, 80–81, 125, 187, 276, 336–38
character education, 38, 135
chariot allegory, 28, 116
Cheney, Liana De Girolami, 171–75, 381n30
Chicago, Judy, 40
Child, Julia, 8, 149
Christianity, 30, 40, 59–60, 62–66, 71, 78, 80, 86, 102, 104, 118, 142, 168–69, 172, 207, 210, 221, 233, 260, 269, 273–74, 280, 300, 307–12, 342, 368n28, 390n27, 393n69
Chrysippus, 99, 102, 104, 272
Cicero, 1–2, 100, 129, 246
Classica Africana, 35, 363n57
classical education, lack of, 34, 38, 363n58
classical liberalism, 336

discipline, 185, 242, 252, 332, 340
  Augustine and, 306
  Cynic, 213–15, 217
  Epicurean, 194
  Platonic, 174–75, 314, 320
  Stoic, 105, 108, 120, 122–24, 137,
    252
discoveries of ancient texts, 44–45,
  57
disillusionment, 237–38
divine feminine, 49, 88, 166, 365n4,
  372n75
divine reason, 28, 111, 116, 135,
  395n10
divine spark (*pneuma*), 66, 374n23
Dostoevsky, Fyodor, 346
doxa, 58
Dreher, Rod, 31
dualism, 293
  Gnostic, 70–72, 80, 85, 88–89
  mind/body, 24, 178, 280, 289, 329
  Plotinus and, 291–95, 297
Dublin, 353–55
DuBois, W. E. B., 35
duty, 129, 338–42
Dylan, Bob, 350

early Christian church, 30, 65, 310
early church fathers, 274, 280, 310,
  390n27
Early Modern period, 4, 176, 234,
  275
Eat Pray Love (movie), 145, 178–82,
  191, 199–200
Edmundson, Mark, 331
education, and classicism, 38
  in Britain, 39–40
Einstein, Albert, 43, 318, 322–23
elitism, 23, 86
Elshtain, Jean Bethke, 262, 341
embodiment, 64, 80, 155, 322, 345
  crisis, 23–25, 52, 89, 342
  Gnosticism and, 83, 89

revisionist views of Platonism and,
  289
Emerson, Ralph Waldo, 262, 374n37
emotion, 5, 104, 329, 342
  Aristotle on, 105, 296
  Augustine on, 306
  crisis, 95–96, 183, 227, 321
  Cynics on, 217
  depth of, 125–26, 286, 326
  emotional-moral economy, 42
  emotivism versus, 19
  Epicureans on, 159
  instrumentalization of, 261, 331–32
  inwardness and, 355–58
  judgment, 104–8, 124
  palette of, 356
  passions, 28, 62, 104, 116, 183, 185,
    245, 256, 286, 356
  Platonists on, 174, 285
  Plotinus on, 290–300, 302–3, 296,
    307
  reason versus, 5, 24, 299, 261,
    284–85, 331, 361n31
  restraint, 97, 113, 120–24
  robot Sophia and, 80
  role in the therapeutic, 17–19
  self-formation and, 142–44, 331
  soul and, 28, 300
  spiritual longing replaced by, 180
  Stoics on, 26–28, 99, 117, 134–35,
    139, 192, 293, 341, 376n58,
    378n85
  tragic proportions of, 186
  transcendence and, 143, 257, 302–3
  unleashing, 15, 126, 140
  See also specific emotions
emotivism, 15–16, 19, 223, 286,
  360n22
Emperor Julian, 273
Emperor Justinian, 273
enlightened self-interest, 339
Enlightenment, 23–24, 59, 178, 206,
  208, 218, 237–38, 240, 242, 261

Greece, 3, 29, 30, 100, 188–91, 324, 385n39
greed, 19, 212, 260, 376
    corporate, 341
Greenblatt, Stephen, 8, 165–69, 175, 353
Gregory of Nyssa, 274
Greif, Mark, 22, 148, 183–84, 186, 199
grief. *See* loss
Groundhog Day (movie), 78

Habermas, Jürgen, 261
Hadot, Ilsetraut, 273–74
Hadot, Pierre, 273–74, 291, 294
    versus Michel Foucault, 248, 253–61
Hamer, Fanny Lou, 324
happiness, 4–6, 9–10, 16, 26, 101–2, 104, 119, 148, 149, 156, 159, 161, 176, 179–80, 188, 206, 255, 258, 325, 336–39, 345, 374n37, 379n14
Harnack, Adolf von, 56, 312
Harry Potter, 136–37
health, 18, 27–28, 70, 80, 85, 101, 105, 134, 160, 345, 373n18
    love and, 277
    paradigm, 88
hedonism, 147, 183, 185, 192, 341
Hegel, 60–61, 238, 368n24
Hellenization of Christianity, 56, 312, 367n16
helping professions, 8, 19
Herculaneum, 150, 351
heresiology, 56
Herman, Arthur, 42–43
Herman, Ellen, 17
Hidden Figures (movie), 315–20, 343
Hipparchia, 210
Hobbes, Thomas, 25, 61–62, 368n27
Holiday, Ryan, 138–39
holism, 69–71, 74, 80, 201, 223–24

Holy Grail, 49, 73, 85, 166
Homer, 27, 380n17
how to live, 1, 3, 4, 7–8, 11–12, 87, 89, 97, 131, 133, 149, 152, 180, 183, 191, 201, 211, 213, 217, 245, 247–48, 299, 300, 303, 335, 340, 342
hubris, 76–78, 82–83, 90, 268
human connection, 184, 262, 315, 319, 327, 331, 346–48, 351
human flourishing, 2, 103–4, 119, 320, 330, 334–35
human limits, 14, 61, 79, 82, 87, 130, 143, 161, 184, 306, 322, 327, 349–53, 357, 369n31
human nature, 64, 103, 117, 134, 140, 205, 369n31, 383n10
humanist sublime, 318
humanities, 329
humility, 28, 87, 184, 198, 224, 233, 259, 277, 302, 335–36
Hunter, James Davison, 17, 50
Hypatia, 40, 274
hypocrisy, 41, 129, 187, 214, 216, 259
hypomnemata, 258

"I Forgot That Love Existed" (Van Morrison), 325
Iamblichus, 272–74
ideals, 10, 25, 59, 89, 185, 287, 319, 331, 343
ill-health, 28, 73, 96, 103, 298
illumination, 77, 292–94, 314, 321, 325
illusion, reality as, 89
illusion versus reality, 51–55, 75–77, 89–90, 279–80
illusion versus truth, 279–80, 286, 322
Imber, Jonathan, 17
immanence, 59, 103, 143, 289, 311, 320, 368n25
"immanentization," 60–61

Latrobe, Benjamin Henry, 36
Lawrence, D. H., 11
Leal, Eusebio, 84
Leonardo da Vinci, 48–49, 365n2
liberalism, 8, 336
liberationism, 65–67, 70, 235, 248
libido dominandi, 62
lifestyle, 133, 197, 232, 247, 253, 255, 343
lifework, 356
living from within, 305, 321–23
living philosophy, 334–35
logic, 26–27, 62, 77, 83–84, 102–3, 106, 118–19, 128, 130, 152, 158, 162, 271, 322, 333, 338, 353
logos, 27, 61, 128, 135, 244
loneliness, 10, 199, 265, 345, 351
loss, 5, 9, 10, 106–8, 120–21, 124–26, 141–42, 227, 266, 291, 296, 304, 307, 315, 321, 342
Louvre Museum, 47
love, 10, 14, 28–29, 41, 60, 62, 125, 140, 164, 171–75, 179, 180–83, 199, 229, 235, 257, 261–3, 266, 268, 276–83, 285–96, 302–3, 305, 307, 311–12, 315, 320–26, 329, 331, 335, 339, 345–48, 351, 354–57, 394n82
loving ought, the, 339–40
Lucretius, 150, 163–69, 175, 257, 353, 380n17, 387n83
Lunchbox, The (movie), 147, 198–99
lust, 31, 61, 107, 183
Lyotard, Jean-François, 31, 287

MacIntyre, Alasdair, 15, 31, 222–23, 289, 336, 337–38, 340, 341, 360n22
MacLaine, Shirley, 68–69
Malreaux, André, 319–20
Mamma Mia! (movie), 147
Manicheanism, 31, 70, 85, 305

manipulation, 15–16, 230, 241, 319, 331–32, 342–43
manipulation, philosophy as bulwark against, 343
Marcion, 311
Marcus Aurelius, 3, 94, 100, 117, 120, 142, 149, 249
    chairs of philosophy, 3, 149, 272
    character in *Gladiator* (movie), 120
    Meditations, 105–14, 116, 138, 249, 374n35, 375n38
market, 11, 20, 24, 31, 33, 81, 138, 196, 212, 236, 335, 336
marketing, 2, 24, 148, 236
Marx, Karl, 59
Mary Magdalen, 72, 372n75
materialism, Stoic, 103
math, 29, 270–71, 275, 315, 317–18, 322, 343
Matrix, The (movie), 50–52, 75–76, 118, 206, 284
McCain, John, 98, 137, 372n8
Me Decade, 341
Me Too movement, 341
meaning, search for, 2, 6, 9–12, 14, 31, 50, 58, 87–88, 188–90, 262, 291
means and ends, 335, 340–42
medical analogy for philosophy, 26, 159, 161, 333–34
medieval Islam, 275
meditation, 13, 31, 135, 183, 239, 256, 278, 306, 311, 330
memory paradox, 306
Mendham, Matthew, 336–40, 396n15
meritocracy, 317–18
metriopatheia, 105, 296
Michelangelo, 48–49, 234–35
Middle Ages, 60, 118, 169, 207, 274
Middlemarch (George Eliot), 346
Milbank, John, 269
military, 19, 105, 137, 270
"Millennial Cynicism," 35–36
Miller, Patricia Cox, 142, 290–91

personality types, 42–43
Pharos (website), 38–39
Philo, 272
philosopher as exile, 333–34
philosophia, 1, 60, 329, 334–35, 368n24
philosophical exercises, 128, 255–60
philosophos versus *sophos*, 60
philosophy as life, 343–45
philosophy as practical, 26–27, 102, 116, 119, 129–32, 140, 255, 257, 260, 268, 308, 320, 330–35, 340, 343–44
phronesis, 131–32
physics, 2, 73, 102–3, 128, 149–51, 154–59, 257–59, 297, 318
physics, and moral living, 257, 259
Pickstock, Catherine, 269
Pigliucci, Massimo, 6, 135, 137
Plato, 28–30, 32, 41, 43, 60, 69, 149, 192, 244, 269–74, 276, 279–81, 283–87, 289, 337–40, 388n6, 389n17, 390n24, 396n16
  Apology of Socrates, 270
  Camus on, 310
  cave allegory, 77, 284–85
  Diogenes and, 211–12, 217, 261
  forms (*see* Plato: intelligible world)
  healing arts, 29
  influence on Augustine, 307–8
  intelligible world, 172–73, 279, 291–94, 301–3, 370n51
  Marsilio Ficino and, 171–73
  Martin Luther King Jr., influence on, 323–24
  modern thinkers influenced by, 269
  Nietzsche on, 334
  noninstrumentalism, 344
  Phaedrus, 28, 60, 284, 368n24
  Republic, 370n51
  Serenade (Leonard Berstein), 326
  Sophist, 29

Symposium, 40, 276–80, 286, 326, 395n84
  —apophatic (negative) theology in, 279
  —Diotima of Mantinea in, 277–79
  —health, 277
  —honor, 276
  —ladder of love and, 278–79
  —Socrates's speech in, 277–80
  —soul, immortality of, 278
  —soul mates, 277
  —view from top of ladder of love, 278–79
Timaeus, 80, 103
in Van Morrison lyrics, 325
Platonic love, 174–75, 268, 276–83, 285, 302, 314, 320, 323, 339
Platonic wonder, 78, 302, 320
Platonism, 2, 9, 32, 43, 85, 100, 172, 193, 245, 261, 296–308, 340
  ancient, 269–83, 286–95, 308–12, 393n69
  New, 265–69, 283–86, 213–27, 343–47, 396n16
Plaza Vieja (Havana, Cuba), 84
pleasure, 104, 105, 161, 177, 180, 184
  of criticizing pleasure, 212, 215
  Diogenes on, 215
  in Epicureanism, 149, 159–62, 164, 166, 190
  Foucault on, 250
  gastronomic, 194–98
  versus joy in Seneca, 254–55, 257
  versus licentiousness, 160
  Montaigne on, 224–25
  pain and, 159–61
  Pierre Hadot's critique of Foucault on, 254–55
  as virtue, 192–93
Plotinus, 142, 268, 272–74, 281–83, 287–300, 314, 322–23, 343–44, 389n17, 390n27
  Augustine and, 307–8

Plotinus (*cont.*)
  Camus on, 308–12
  criticism of Gnosticism by, 71,
    300–303
  Enneads, 289
  on inner beauty, 281, 320
  love and universe in, 282–83
  love in, 320
  Marsilio Ficino and, 171–72
  Martin Luther King Jr. and, 323
Plutarch, 247, 249, 272
Plutarch the Athenian, 273
Polemo, 101
Polemon the Athenian, 271
polis, Greek, 102, 216, 256
political philosophy, 271, 308, 340
Pollio, Marcus Vitruvius, 48, 391n31
Pompeii, 39, 351
popular culture as popular education,
    13
Porphyry, 247, 272–74, 282
Port Huron Statement, 324, 394n82
positive psychology, 16, 240
positivism, 57–8
posthumanism, 79, 86
postmodernism, 31–32, 81, 176,
    218–19, 287
Poussin, Nicolas, 114–16
practical philosophy, 26–27, 102, 116,
    119, 129–32, 140, 255, 257, 260,
    268, 320, 330–32, 335, 340, 344
practicality of idealism, 43, 295, 320,
    343–44
prayer, 107, 139, 306, 376n58
pre-Socratic philosophers, 151, 333
Primavera (Botticelli), 169–75, 323
princess pink, 91
private acts in public space, 22
Proclus, 273–74, 389n17
projects, human, 119–20
Protestantism, 56, 71, 381n43
Proust, Marcel, 346

Pseudo-Dionysius the Areopagite,
    274, 390n27
psyche, 10, 64, 172, 229, 247, 314,
    352
psychologization, 7, 11, 17
psychotherapy, 64–65, 298
public good, 22–23, 32, 336, 370n51
public philosophy, 21, 43, 268, 308,
    320, 335–36, 340–43, 395n84
public/academic divide, 38, 232, 256,
    335–36
public/private dichotomy, 216
Pythagoras, 69, 274
Pythagoreanism, 269, 271, 391n31

quality, 12–13, 105, 155, 198, 224,
    289, 311, 320, 331–32, 347, 353
Quine, W. V. O., 275

racial discrimination, 34, 141, 315–18,
    362n54
Radical Orthodoxy, 269
Raphael
  The School of Athens, 33, 168
Rappe, Sara, 291, 294
Rashomon (movie), 83
ratio, 57–58
realism, 130, 178, 228, 299, 368n27
Realm of Flora (Poussin), 115–16
recognition, 271, 319–21
Reformation, 60
Reich, Wilhelm, 11
relation to physical world, human,
    268
relativism, 25, 29–30, 32, 286
  as modern sophistry, 29, 32, 286
  moral, 162, 217, 341
religious belief, 10, 50, 85, 175,
    368n23
Renaissance humanism, 275
reputation, 101, 105, 109, 114, 117,
    123, 215

vanity, 83, 109–10, 125, 141, 286
vastness of universe, 106, 113
vengeance, 122, 126
veritas, 314
victimization, 8, 17, 22–23, 87–88,
   95–96, 299, 329
Villa dei Papiri, 45, 50
violence, 3, 10, 28, 40, 82, 124–26,
   140, 183, 187, 226, 231, 236,
   243, 262, 341, 371–72n74,
   394n82
virtue as knowledge, 103, 120, 131,
   253, 286, 310, 337–39, 395n10
virtue ethics, 336–41
Vitruvian Man, The (da Vinci), 48,
   365n2
Voegelin, Eric, 57–63, 90, 367n22,
   368n24
voluptas, 250, 254, 257, 387n83

Wallis, Richard, 292
Ward, Graham, 269
Watwood, Patricia, 37–38
Weil, Simone, 269
welfare state, 8, 87–88
well-being, 4, 14, 67, 70, 96, 147, 162,
   191, 269, 336–38
West, Cornel, 341
Winter Light (movie), 206
Wittgenstein, Ludwig, 345
Wolfe, Tom, 98, 126, 360n20
women's liberation movement, 64
world of others, 41, 141, 201, 331,
   335, 357

Xenocrates, 271

Zeno of Citium, 99–102, 209–10, 248,
   271, 373n18

ELISABETH LASCH-QUINN

is professor of history at Syracuse University.

She is the author of numerous essays and books, including *Black Neighbors* (winner of the Berkshire prize) and *Race Experts*.

Lightning Source UK Ltd.
Milton Keynes UK
UKHW050403060223
416497UK00009B/160

9 780268 108908